KNOWING THE DIFFERENCE

Despite a widespread interest in epistemological questions – an interest which feminism shares with other contestatory groups – feminist contributions to this controversial field are relatively scarce. Even within feminist thinking, there are divergent and often contradictory views.

At the centre of this volume is the question of difference: both the difference which the adoption of a feminist perspective produces in relation to traditional knowledge and the difference that differences between women make to feminist perspectives. This awareness of difference requires a re-evaluation of issues of objectivity and the justification of knowledge-claims in ways that focus attention on the subjects who constitute the knowledge-producers.

Knowing the Difference features an international list of contributors coming from social science as well as philosophy backgrounds; it includes essays by Rosi Braidotti, Gemma Corradi Fiumara, Sabina Lovibond, Liz Stanley and Anna Yeatman as well as by a range of other new and innovative thinkers. Using approaches and methods from both analytic and Continental philosophy, the contributors address both issues of traditional epistemology and questions raised by postmodernist critiques.

This collection includes some of the most recent thinking in epistemology and will introduce both philosophers and feminists to the wide range of feminist perspectives in current epistemological debates.

Kathleen Lennon teaches Philosophy at the University of Hull and is the author of *Explaining Human Action* (1990). **Margaret Whitford** is Reader in Modern French Thought at Queen Mary and Westfield College, University of London. She is the author of *Luce Irigaray: Philosophy in the Feminine* (1991). Both editors are founding members of the Society for Women in Philosophy and have been working in the field of feminist philosophy for many years.

KNOWING THE DIFFERENCE

Feminist perspectives
in epistemology

Edited by
Kathleen Lennon and
Margaret Whitford

London and New York

First published 1994
by Routledge
11 New Fetter Lane, London EC4P 4EE

Simultaneously published in the USA and Canada
by Routledge
29 West 35th Street, New York NY 10001

Phototypeset in Garamond by Intype, London
Printed and bound in Great Britain by
Clays Ltd, St Ives plc

Printed on acid free paper

British Library Cataloguing in Publication Data
A catalogue record for this book is available from the British Library.

Library of Congress Cataloging in Publication Data
Knowing the difference: feminist perspectives in epistemology/
edited by Kathleen Lennon and Margaret Whitford.
p. cm.
Includes bibliographical references and index.
1. Objectivity. 2. Feminist theory. 3. Knowledge, Theory of.
I. Whitford, Margaret. II. Lennon, Kathleen.
BD220.K76 1994
121'.082–dc20 93–37965
CIP
ISBN 0–415–08988–3 (hbk)
ISBN 0–415–08989–1 (pbk)

In the consciousness of our failures, we risk lapsing into boundless difference and giving up on the confusing task of making a partial, real connection. Some differences are playful; some are poles of world historical systems of domination. Epistemology is about knowing the difference.

Donna Haraway, 'A manifesto for cyborgs'

CONTENTS

CONTENTS

CONTRIBUTORS

Ismay Barwell teaches in the Philosophy Department at Victoria University, Wellington, New Zealand. She has recently published articles in *Hypatia, Journal of Aesthetics and Art Criticism* and *Philosophy and Literature* in the area of feminist epistemology and feminist aesthetics. She is currently writing a book on feminist aesthetics.

Rosi Braidotti has been full professor and Chair of Women's Studies in the Humanities at the University of Utrecht since 1988. She was awarded a Ph.D. in philosophy from the Sorbonne in 1981 with a dissertation on Foucault and feminism. She is the author of *Patterns of Dissonance: A Study of Women in Contemporary Philosophy*. She has also published extensively on feminist theory, psychoanalysis, Continental philosophy and the history of ideas. A collection of her essays, called *Nomadic Subjects*, is forthcoming from Columbia University Press.

Gemma Corradi Fiumara took her BA degree at Barnard College, Columbia University where she studied as a Fulbright scholar. She has a doctorate of the University of Rome, where she now teaches as an associate professor. She is the author of *Philosophy and Coexistence, The Other Side of Language: A Philosophy of Listening* and *The Symbolic Function: Psychoanalysis and the Philosophy of Language*.

Meena Dhanda first studied philosophy at Panjab University, Chandigarh. She is currently completing her doctorate in philosophy at the University of Oxford on questions of personal identity and acknowledgement of persons. Her publications include 'L'Eveil des intouchables en Inde' in *Le Respect* (ed. Catherine Audard, Paris: Editions Autrement, 1993). Since September 1992, she has been lecturing in philosophy at the University of Wolverhampton.

Annette Fitzsimons is an Irish woman, presently Senior Lecturer in Sociology at the University of Humberside. She is a member of the Hull

Centre for Gender Studies and reviews editor of the *Journal of Gender Studies*. Her main research interests are gender and work and gender and technology.

Miranda Fricker studied philosophy and French at Oxford, followed by an MA in women's studies at the University of Kent. She is currently a doctoral student at Wolfson College, Oxford, working on the question of whether postmodernist epistemology is appropriate to feminism. She has published an article on 'Reason and emotion', in *Radical Philosophy* and three of her MA essays were published in the University of Kent Women's Studies Occasional Papers Series. She teaches a course on feminist philosophy at Birkbeck College, University of London.

Kimberly Hutchings lectures in philosophy in the School of Humanities and Social Sciences at the University of Wolverhampton. She is writing a book on Kant's political philosophy and its influence on contemporary political thought. Her current research is in the areas of the philosophy of international relations, feminist theory, the philosophies of Kant and Hegel and applied ethics.

Marnia Lazreg is an Algerian sociologist interested in feminist theory and epistemology, development and cultural studies. She is Associate Professor of Sociology and Women's Studies at Hunter College, City University of New York. Her most recent publications include an essay on 'Feminism and difference: the perils of writing as a woman on women in Algeria', which appeared in *Conflicts in Feminism* (ed. Marianne Hirsch and Evelyn Fox Keller), and an article, 'Gender and politics in Algeria: unravelling the religious paradigm', which appeared in *Signs* in 1990. She is at present completing a book on women in Algeria to be published by Routledge in 1994.

Kathleen Lennon is a lecturer in the Department of Philosophy at the University of Hull. She is also a member of the Hull Centre for Gender Studies, and on the editorial board of the *Journal of Gender Studies*. She works and publishes primarily in philosophy of mind and feminist theory. Her publications include *Explaining Human Action* (1991) and the co-edited collection *Reduction, Explanation and Realism* (1992, with David Charles).

Sabina Lovibond is a Fellow of Worcester College, Oxford, where she teaches philosophy. Her publications include *Realism and Imagination in Ethics* (1983) and *Ethics: A Feminist Reader* (edited with Elizabeth Frazer and Jennifer Hornsby, 1992).

Oshadi Mangena is an Azanian woman currently lecturing in the Department of International Relations and Public International Law at the University of Amsterdam. She has a BA in political science and public administration from the University of South Africa and a Master's degree in development studies from the Institute of Social Studies, The Hague. She is also a qualified nurse and midwife. She is particularly interested in African perspectives on women and development.

Diana Sartori is preparing a Ph.D. in philosophy at Padua University and participates in the activities of the women's philosophical community Diotima; she has contributed articles on Teresa d'Avila and Hannah Arendt to the collaborative publications *Mettere al mondo il mondo* (Giving birth to the world) and *Il Cielo stellato dentro di noi* (The starry sky within us). Her other research interest is the philosophy of science and the feminist debates in this field; she is attached to the women's scientific community Ipazia (Hypatia) in Milan, and has contributed articles to the collective works *Autorità scientifica, autorità femminile* (Scientific authority, women's authority) and *Insegnare scienza* (Teaching science).

Anne Seller teaches philosophy and women's studies at the University of Kent, and has been a frequent visiting lecturer at the University of Colorado, USA. The essay in this collection is a direct response to the experience of visiting Mother Teresa Women's University in India as part of the LINK programme organized by the British Council.

Liz Stanley is a senior lecturer in sociology at the University of Manchester. Formerly British and Irish editor of *Women's Studies International Forum* she is currently co-editor of *Sociology*. Her main recent publications include *Feminist Praxis: Research, Theory and Epistemology in Feminist Sociology* (edited, 1990), *The Auto/Biographical I: Theory and Practice of Feminist Auto/Biography* (1992), *Debates in Sociology: Challenge and Change in a Discipline* (edited with David Morgan, 1993) and *Breaking Out Again: Feminist Ontology and Epistemology* (with Sue Wise, 1993).

Susan Strickland is currently completing her Ph.D. in feminist epistemology at the University of Hull. She is particularly interested in the role of experience in theories of knowledge, and issues of objectivity and perspectivity. Previous papers on difference, Gadamer and Winch have been published in the University of Hull Occasional Papers in Philosophy series.

Alessandra Tanesini is a lecturer in philosophy at the University of Wales College of Cardiff. She has done work in philosophy of language and feminist philosophy, and completed her Ph.D. at the University of Hull.

She is currently researching in feminist epistemology and post-analytic philosophy.

Janna Thompson is a senior lecturer in philosophy at La Trobe University, Melbourne. She specializes in social philosophy and has taught courses on feminism for many years. She has recently published *Justice and World Order: A Philosophical Inquiry* (1992).

Margaret Whitford teaches French at Queen Mary and Westfield College, University of London. She has recently published *Luce Irigaray: Philosophy in the Feminine* (1991) and *The Irigaray Reader* (1991), and is co-editor (with Carolyn Burke and Naomi Schor) of a forthcoming collection of essays on Irigaray, *Engaging with Irigaray*.

Caroline Williams lectures in the Department of Politics at Southampton University. She is completing a doctoral thesis in political theory at University College, Swansea, focusing on the problematic of the subject in contemporary social and political theory.

Anna Yeatman currently holds the Chair of Sociology at Macquarie University in Sydney. An Australian, she has an honours degree in politics and graduate degrees in sociology. From mid-1991 to mid-1993, she was the Foundation Professor in Women's Studies at the University of Waikato in New Zealand. Apart from her work in social and political theory, she has been engaged in a number of Australian-based public management and public policy consultancies. Both aspects of her work are expressed in her book *Bureaucrats, Technocrats, Femocrats: Essays on the Contemporary Australian State* (1990). Her most recent book is *Postmodern Revisionings of the Political* (1994). She is currently planning a research project on knowledge and the restructuring of the professions.

ACKNOWLEDGEMENTS

The idea for this collection was conceived in conjunction with the conference on 'Women, power and knowledge', organized by the Society for Women in Philosophy, and held at the Beechwood Conference Centre in Leeds in September 1991. The editors are indebted to SWIP for opportunities to discuss issues in feminist philosophy provided over many years. Kathleen would also like to thank Hull Centre for Gender Studies and her graduate and undergraduate students for longstanding stimulus, support and critique.

The editors are particularly grateful for the extensive secretarial support they have received from Celia Williams at Queen Mary and Westfield College, University of London.

Rosi Braidotti's paper 'Body-images and the pornography of representation' originally appeared in the *Journal of Gender Studies*, vol. 1, no. 2 (November 1991); we would like to thank the *Journal of Gender Studies* for permission to reprint it in this collection.

INTRODUCTION

Kathleen Lennon and Margaret Whitford

PRELIMINARY REFLECTIONS

Feminism's most compelling epistemological insight lies in the connections it has made between knowledge and power. This, not simply in the obvious sense that access to knowledge enables empowerment; but more controversially through the recognition that legitimation of knowledge-claims is intimately tied to networks of domination and exclusion. This recognition has moved issues of epistemology from the world of somewhat esoteric philosophy to the centre-stage of contemporary culture. Not only philosophers, but also social scientists, political theorists, historians and literary theorists are now urgently addressing epistemological questions. Work within feminist epistemology therefore shares preoccupations and critical moments with other important strands of recent thought: the writings of Marxists and critical theorists, who for decades have argued that much of contemporary culture reflects bourgeois interests; southern scholars who have pointed to the Eurocentrism of contemporary knowledge-production; radical philosophers of science, who have highlighted the role of value judgements in scientific practice; and, importantly for this volume, the theorists of what is now called postmodernism.

Feminist work in epistemology also shares with at least some of these intellectual movements a commitment to social change and links with other emancipatory struggles against oppression (not only the traditional left, but also black, gay, ecological, peace and other movements). This generates a tension that is apparent in current feminist theorizing. Feminism is a movement rooted in Enlightenment ideals of justice and freedom. It tries to understand the social order, so as to devise effective strategies for change. None the less it shares, with the other directions of thought referred to above, a critique of these ideals and an awareness of the power/knowledge nexus which they so effectively disguise.

A résumé of the recent history of work in feminist epistemology clearly reveals this tension. A few years ago feminist writing on epistemology was concerned to expose the masculinity of different areas of knowledge. Social

1

and natural science attracted a good deal of attention, but also literature, history and philosophy, among others. The claims that what passed for knowledge was 'masculine' came in several forms: that the problems to be investigated/discussed reflected only male experience of the world; that the theoretical frameworks adopted reflected the structure of masculine gender-identity in contemporary culture; that the narratives constructed served the interests of men as a group, promoting their position and legitimating the subordination of women; that the whole symbolic order by means of which knowledge-claims were articulated privileged the male and conceptualized the female only as that which lacked masculinity. (This strand in the argument was particularly associated with writings from the European continent influenced by Lacanian psychoanalytic perspectives.)

Underlying these critiques was a recognition of *difference*. Men and women occupied different situations within society and had characteristically different experiences. Moreover these differences were exemplified in the products of the predominantly male knowledge-producers. These criticisms therefore had repercussions for the *objectivity* which much knowledge, for example that of science, claimed for itself. The objectivist paradigm which these criticisms appeared to undermine was that frequently identified in critical writing as associated with Enlightenment thinking. Within that framework knowledge is referential – it is about something (the object) situated outside the knower. Knowledge is said to mirror an independently existing world, as that world really is. Putative knowledge reaches these goals by conforming to a set of criteria for testing and validation. These criteria are universal. These criteria can also in principle be applied by anyone, with the same results. Genuine knowledge does not reflect the subject who produced it.

Feminist work both challenged the objectivity, as thus defined, of many contemporary areas of knowledge, and claimed that such a goal of objectivity was itself masculine in one or all of the senses outlined above. In mounting such a critique, feminism was joining its voice to those voices coming from the other quarters already mentioned. In each of these critiques both the possibility and desirability of objectivity as characterized in the Enlightenment paradigm is being challenged. In different ways all of these strands of thought implicate *the subject* in the production of knowledge. It is argued that it is not simply due to bad practice that masculine subjects have allowed their subjectivity to imprint on their product. Such imprinting of subjectivity is inevitable. Knowledge bears the marks of its producer. Given this, feminists were concerned to ensure that female subjectivity should also be allowed to make its mark on knowledge-production. For some feminist writers, there was an emphasis on the experiences of women, or attention to women's perspectives or to the problematics generated by women's position in society. This led to the development of feminist standpoint theory. Within social science, feminists,

2

along with other critics, insisted that the subjectivity of the researched be reflected in the project design and find articulation in the end result (see Mangena, this volume). For feminist writers influenced by the Lacanian account of the symbolic order, it seemed necessary to break open or disrupt that order in order to make possible the articulation of female subjectivity (see Williams, this volume).

To recognize the implicatedness of the subject in the knowledge produced is to make the context of discovery relevant to the context of justification. Gone is the Enlightenment idea of an Archimedean point where a universal knower can stand and see the world without perspective. All knowers are situated (spatio/temporally, historically/culturally/socially), and these dimensions of situation all become part of the epistemological context. In rejecting the Archimedean point, however, feminist standpoint epistemologies (along with their Marxist counterparts) retained certain elements of Enlightenment thinking. The referential function of knowledge was maintained, while at the same time it was assumed that knowledge anchored in the 'subjectivity of the oppressed' (see Hutchings, this volume) would be less distorted than that deriving from the dominant group. This privileging of 'the subjectivity of the oppressed' gained most plausibility within the critical moment of theorizing. Attention to women's experiences/position/perspective was able to throw into relief both the gaps in accepted theory and the masculinity of their narratives. When feminists face the reconstructive moment in knowledge-production, it is less clear why the narratives which are produced from their standpoint should be considered as less distorted/more adequate than the masculine one. This is particularly the case once the possibility of a universalizing overview has been abandoned and it is recognized that the subjectivity implicated in the knowledge is necessarily a partial one.

This difficulty is compounded by another which has come to occupy the centre-stage. The second problem comes from a recognition not only of difference between men and women, but of differences within the category 'woman'. The initially most visible forms of feminist writing came from a restricted group of women, predominantly white, middle-class, living in colonizing or ex-colonizing countries. These writers were producing a new narrative which, from the perspective of other women, suffered from the same falsely universalizing pretensions as the masculine knowledge originally critiqued. Feminists committed to the articulation of what was 'other' in relation to masculine thought had to confront the challenge of other 'others' for whom they constituted a new hegemony and in relation to whom they themselves stood in positions of power and domination. Women as a group are not homogeneous. They have very different experiences, perspectives and problematics, depending on variables such as class, country, age, colour or sexuality. Their positions in power relationships also vary considerably. In addition to this lack of unity within the

3

category of the female subject, there is, it is argued, a lack of unity *within* each individual female subject. Psychoanalytic work in particular emphasizes a fragmentation and lack of coherence within the consciousness and life-histories of individual subjects. The knower, or knowing subject, is now defined by opacity rather than transparency. It is gendered, historically situated, with an unconscious mind, subject to linguistic and social determinants. This subject is more like a railway junction where signifiers, discourses and messages meet or flash past, than a source, origin or mirror. Any epistemological project whose aim is the articulation of female subjectivity seems therefore inevitably conflictual and contradictory.

In the context of these difficulties, many feminists felt the attraction of strands of thought associated with postmodernism. The element of postmodernist thought particularly apposite here was the recognition that all our interactions with reality are mediated by conceptual frameworks or discourses, which themselves are historically and socially situated. There is no way of stepping outside of these to check them against an independent reality, or to legitimate them by means of universal and discourse-transcendent criteria of rational assessment. We have to give up the project of providing a totalizing theory of the nature of reality and recognize that we cannot unify into a coherent whole the multiple and diverse experiences which derive from the multiple situations in which knowledge-producers are placed. Fragmentation and contradictions are inevitable and we will not necessarily be able to overcome them. Within this context there is not only a displacement of the purely mirroring goal of the objectivist paradigm of knowledge, together with its insistence on context-independent criteria of legitimation; for many theorists, the referential function of knowledge also becomes redundant. For it is the latter which required coherence and unity between our narratives.

However, feminism as a political project requires that the feminist claims of distorting and subordinating trends within masculine knowledge be regarded as legitimate, and legitimate generally, not only for feminists. This makes it difficult to simply abandon objectivity and the referential claims of knowledge. At the same time, the problem of legitimation remains, so long as the *only* alternative to a discredited value-free objectivity appears to be a postmodern pluralist free-for-all.

It is against the background of these debates that the essays in the present volume have been written. Most of the contributors are engaged in a reassessment both of an Enlightenment package, which seems to allow no role for subjectivity in the formation of knowledge, and of a postmodernism in which the referential and legitimating function of knowledge seems lost. In the essays we are presenting it is the tension between these views which has proved intellectually fruitful, indicating that a more complex thinking about epistemology cuts across any straightforward classification.

OBJECTIVITY AND THE KNOWING SUBJECT

Although we have divided the chapters into two sections, 'Objectivity and the knowing subject' and 'Knowledge, difference and power', it will be clear to the reader that we could have found numerous other ways of organizing them to bring out their convergences and divergences. Here we would just like to indicate briefly some of the themes which seem to us to be particularly salient.

The main issue in the first section 'Objectivity and the knowing subject' is how to talk about objectivity in the light of our understanding that all knowledge is socially situated and representation a political act. The section opens with two contributions which in different ways problematize the notion of objectivity. First is an essay by Rosi Braidotti on 'Body-images and the pornography of representation'. The tendency of modern science and technology is to assume a link between visibility and truth. However, in Braidotti's view, the authority of such technology is as perverse as it is pervasive. She argues that the idea that visibility equals truth is a deep-rooted fantasy. Seeing the world, bodies, etc., is not a mechanical operation, simply registering what is objectively out there. What one sees is a product of positioning, and different accounts of the world involve political struggles over *how* to see and *how* to interpret. Braidotti argues that a politics of visual culture is required; vision implies responsibility, it is not a neutral activity, and women need to challenge the ways in which bio-medical science presents its 'advances', looking for built-in power structures. (Braidotti's paper could be read in conjunction with Annette Fitz-simon's contribution later in this section, which offers a more positive account of women's possible relation to technology, and with Anna Yeatman's essay in Part II, on the politics of representation.)

Gemma Corradi Fiumara, in her chapter 'The metaphoric function and the question of objectivity', resists the dichotomy between subject and object, emphasizing the embodiment of subjects and their positioning in, and interrelatedness with, the world which is their object: an 'organismic' relation in her terms. Such a relation means that subjects and objects are mutually constituting. The project of knowledge-creation must be seen as involving a 'dialogical' interaction between them which moves away from privileging or yielding epistemological priority to either side (see also Hutchings, later in this section). For Fiumara this dialogical interaction finds its linguistic expression in metaphor. The danger with a model of objectivism which finds expression in literal language is that it immobilizes something that should be a continually evolving process, and thus threatens with atrophy our mental and rational capacities.

These chapters are followed by four contributions which argue for the need to defend some form of objectivity, on the grounds that the outright rejection of it leads to serious difficulty. Marnia Lazreg's paper 'Women's

experience and feminist epistemology: a critical neo-rationalist approach'
offers a critique of the grounding of knowledge in experience which is
associated with the privileging of female subjectivity found in much standpoint theory. Lazreg argues that exclusive emphasis on subjectivity precludes engagement with the different subjectivities of others and the wider
social structures within which they are situated. Lazreg argues that there
needs to be some independent criterion against which feminist (and particularly western feminist) accounts can be measured, one that transcends the
partiality of views, whether 'feminist' or 'masculinist'. Lazreg concludes
that objectivity is not the opposite of subjectivity; it is not a fixed point
but a process towards an ever-receding goal. Her chapter should be read
in conjunction with several of the chapters in Parts I and II, notably
those by Anne Seller, Liz Stanley and Oshadi Mangena. Lazreg's chapter
challenges both Seller and Stanley, who argue for the epistemological value
of the first-person account, and converges with Mangena, who argues,
like Lazreg, that the privileging of women's or feminist standpoints in
epistemological theory is a theoretical mistake. Both Lazreg and Mangena
situate themselves as non-western critics of western theory. Lazreg's argument also signals a warning. Feminism is not served if it tries to be
foundationalist in its turn. The aim is not to replace one inadequate foundation with another.

Sabina Lovibond in her chapter 'The end of morality?' accepts, along
with Lazreg and other defenders of objectivity, the need for some objectivity in our methods of knowledge-collection, at least in the sense of non-
arbitrary and non-individualistic criteria for the assessment of knowledge-
claims, and some answerability to a community of knowers. While feminists may have good reason to endorse the postmodernist critique of regulatory ideals, none the less the wholesale rejection of them leads to a position
where political action would become impossible, making the radical democratic impulses of feminism untenable. We need to reject the tendency in
postmodernism to equate rationality with coercion, and instead make a
distinction between ratiofascism and rationality. In relation to the knowing
subject, Lovibond argues that the centred subject might equally be seen as
a regulatory ideal. Integration is not a given, it is rather something we
aspire to as a condition of intelligibility. (There are close links here with
Liz Stanley's description of the subject later in this section.)

Lovibond's chapter raises the question of legitimation and the role of
the community in legitimating epistemic or moral claims. These issues are
further pursued by Ismay Barwell in 'Towards a defence of objectivity'.
Although she argues for the need for objectivist criteria to justify our
feminist demands and assess our strategies for change, Barwell, together
with other contributors to this section, rejects the objectivist orthodoxy
that knowledge should be value-free, refusing the dichotomy whereby
inquiry is *either* guided by values and interests *or* by 'the facts'.

6

The main part of the chapter discusses two recent studies by Helen Longino and Sandra Harding, whose work has perhaps been the most crucial in determining the shape of feminist debates around epistemology. (Further discussion of Longino can be found in the chapters by Fricker and Sartori, later in this section.) Comparing Longino's 'minimalist' objectivity requirement and Harding's 'strong objectivity', Barwell concludes that it is possible to be too 'minimalist' and goes on to use Harding's account to contest Longino. Longino's point was that the non-epistemic values operative in epistemic practices do not necessarily prevent those practices from being objective. But she does not show how to mediate between conflicting points of view within a given practice. Harding's 'strong objectivity' offers a way of countering these difficulties with Longino's account by including conflicting points of view as part of the evidential grounds for assessing beliefs (see also Strickland in Part II). Objectivity requires a challenge from marginal others who – for particular subject-matters and limited periods – may constitute privileged perspectives for critique. Barwell concludes that Harding's 'strong objectivity' seems to offer a regulatory ideal in which there is the possibility of a transcendent point of view, but one which does not assume an Archimedean point of view that is not subject to reassessment.

Like Barwell, Miranda Fricker in 'Knowledge as construct: theorizing the role of gender in knowledge' draws on Longino; but while accepting that values inform epistemological enquiry she is concerned to allow space for 'the world' to constrain what can be said. She addresses directly the problems raised for epistemology by feminist postmodernism, rejecting what she sees as its inherent anti-realism. Fricker argues that we need an ideal of truth, transcending situated perspectives, as a regulatory ideal, without which consensus can only be an act of coercion performed by one group against other groups. She ties in her realism, however, with a holistic epistemology (in Quine's sense) which rejects foundational beliefs. Our beliefs confront reality as a *whole system* and adjustments are made by means of coherentist criteria.

These contributors are arguing for some new form of rationalism to inform our epistemic practices. What distinguishes each of these defences of objectivity from the treatment of the notion within the Enlightenment paradigm, however, is the insistence on the *accountability* of our knowledge production (see also Yeatman, in Part II), not only to the community of scientists but also to the community of feminists. What is at issue is the possibility of constructing a 'feminist science' or 'feminist knowledge'. This is the central theme of the following chapter by Diana Sartori: 'Women's authority in science'. For Sartori our goal is *trustworthy* knowledge, whose authenticity requires overcoming science's self-enclosure and developing constitutive criteria which are answerable to our feminist practice. Sartori's chapter introduces the terms of a quite different debate, that of a certain strand of Italian feminism associated with the feminist philosophical community Diotima and the Milan Women's Bookstore Collective. For Sartori, conflicts or disagreements in the gender and science debates involve the whole contentious issue of women's authority – their authority as knowers and legitimators. The argument of this particular strand of feminism is that authority in our society is determined by a paternal symbolic order in which the figure of a symbolic female authority, or symbolic mother, is absent. The problem is the contradiction between being a woman and having authority. Sartori argues that, despite the image of itself which it often presents, science is not in fact a self-enclosed and self-referring domain, distinct from politics and the organization of the wider society; there is an integral link between truth and its social origins. For Sartori we need to establish social and symbolic links between women that can be carried into science and transform it.

Many of the writers in this section, including Sartori, have moved away from a stance which views science as irremediably male, towards the project of transforming science so that it can work for women. Annette Fitzsimons, in her chapter 'Women, power and technology', sees this process as one in which feminists might reconceive science and technology, so that they are no longer exclusively seen in terms of domination and control, where power is understood as 'power over'. She suggests instead a framework in which both science and technology could be conceived of as routes to empowerment. Drawing on Foucault's account of the knowledge/power regime, Fitzsimons points out (cf. Hutchings, below) that power does not only prevent, it also enables. She argues for a feminist engagement with the issues of technology with the aim of making the latter more available to women.

In Liz Stanley's chapter, 'The knowing because experiencing subject: narratives, lives and autobiography', we return to the question of postmodernism and its political implications. Stanley shows that the dichotomies presented by a staged confrontation between Enlightenment and postmodernist accounts of the self are resistible. Recognition of a fractured or multiple self is compatible with a focus on narrative in providing an analysis of such a self. Attention to the central role played by narrative in the accounts we provide of ourselves also makes clear that the implicatedness of subjectivity in the construction of knowledge (we construct the narrative) does not preclude its referentiality. Drawing on autobiographical fragments of her own life at the time of her mother's illness and death, Stanley argues that autobiography is an activity that itself centres the subject (cf. Lovibond, above) and focuses the attempts of that subject to make sense of its fractures, its existence in time and its experiences. Stanley also argues (contra Lazreg, above) that experiential claims are no more problematic than other kinds of knowledge claims and are equally available for analytical and theoretical investigation.

The issue of the role of subjectivity in knowledge-production is taken up by Kimberly Hutchings in 'The personal is international: feminist epistemology and the case of international relations'. Hutchings takes international relations as an example of the problems of an inadequate account of the relation between object and subject. She rejects an account of the subject/object relationship in which subject and object are held to be self-identical, and knowledge dependent on the erasure of the difference between them. She argues that this leads to an impasse in theory, since the aim of knowledge can then easily be shown to be an impossible ideal: we are left with the alternative of false knowledge or no knowledge at all. To a certain extent, feminist theory shares this dilemma. But Hutchings argues that feminist standpoint theory in international relations offers an alternative which could help us to rethink the traditional concepts of knowledge. She suggests a more dialectical account of knowledge which allows for the possibility of meaningful knowledge without implying a transcendent standard, for the knower is already implicated in the known. The subject and its experiences are partially constitutive of the reality to be known, while reality is also constitutive of the identity and experiences of its subjects. Hutchings also insists on the tentativeness of all knowledge-claims. Our own situatedness is dependent on a network of interrelations, a grasp of which leads us outwards, even if never to a grasp of the whole (cf. Strickland, in Part II).

Finally, Caroline Williams's chapter on 'Feminism, subjectivity and psychoanalysis' presents a poststructuralist reading of Lacan which critiques the notion of objectivity. In Williams's argument, psychoanalysis has shown the impossibility of any correspondence theory of truth. If we take seriously the Lacanian version of psychoanalysis, we have to see the symbolic order – where the knowing subject of philosophy situates itself – as no more than a provisional fixation or stabilization which enables the construction of knowledge. However, behind and beyond the symbolic order lies the Real (not to be confused with more phenomenological conceptions of reality), that which remains unsymbolized and inaccessible, but whose effects continue to exercise their disruption of any attempts at complete closure, permanent stability, complete knowledge or rationality. Williams argues that we can find in Lacan an implicit alliance between the real and the feminine, which offers some promise to feminist attempts to change the world. Williams interprets the work of Irigaray as an exposure of the unconscious infrastructure of epistemology which can usefully inform feminist attempts to revise and construct epistemologies which recognize their own impermanence, so that they do not simply fall into endless oscillating repetitions of the epistemologies under critique.

KNOWLEDGE, DIFFERENCE AND POWER

The chapters of Lazreg, Barwell and Hutchings in Part I introduce the theme of difference which is the critical focus of chapters in the second part of this volume. For many of the writers, there is 'no vantage point outside the domain of contested knowledge' (Yeatman, this volume) and the issue of how difference is to be negotiated becomes a major concern in Part II. The debate with postmodernism is central for many of the contributors, who question whether the postmodernist insistence on diversity is an adequate response to the challenge difference presents to any dominant epistemological regime. One proposal could be that different subjectivities enter into dialogue with each other. Such an idea is at the basis of the consensual route to moral knowledge espoused in Thompson's paper and the 'dialogue within a community' explored in Seller's. But, as Thompson points out, it matters how consensus is reached, so that agreements reached when there are inequalities of power don't count. Moreover, Seller's chapter shows the difficulty of finding conditions that would allow a dialogue, based on equality. The notion of dialogue can have problematic echoes of Rorty's 'conversation', in which we share with each other our viewpoints, but there is no imperative that judgements be made. Theorists concerned to maintain the referentiality of our knowledge-claims, however, require a basis for judgement. Indeed Seller concludes that genuine engagement with others is not possible without the making of judgements. Several theorists, therefore, move from a dialogical model of dealing with difference to a more dialectical one. For Dhanda, what is required is the acknowledgement of others as persons, the recognition that there may be points of view other than one's own and a preparedness to re-evaluate our own position. Strickland makes a connected point. Differences are a challenge to our own position and require re-evaluation based on a recognition of our interrelations with others. For Mangena we are required to evaluate and accommodate different experiences to reach a characterization of situations as a whole.

The opening chapter by Anna Yeatman, on 'Postmodern epistemological politics and social science' discusses the tension-ridden situation of oppositional intellectuals (e.g. feminists in the academy) who find themselves in conflict between two constituencies, the academic intellectual one, often with a foundationalist view of knowledge, and the group constituted as 'others' by the academic elite, which contests the legitimacy of the elite's claims to knowledge. For Yeatman, following Foucault, any epistemology constitutes a regime of power, and oppositional intellectuals find themselves pulled between the power invested in the reigning epistemology – in which they are inevitably complicit to some extent – and the demand for accountability coming from the oppositional and contestatory constituency with which they identify. The paper raises the crucial and central question of feminist knowledge and its relation to power, and the problematic of the knowing subject who is also a member of the class of objects of knowledge.

Alessandra Tanesini's chapter, 'Whose language?', takes issue with the postmodern rejection of gender and explores the epistemological implications of the concept of 'woman', attempting to steer a course between its unacceptable pretensions to totality and the destabilizing effects of fragmenting the category. Her argument is that language provides concepts which are normative rather than simply descriptive. Drawing on Wittgenstein's claim that meaning is *correct* use she goes on to present claims about meanings as claims about how concepts *ought* to be used: 'Meaning-claims are proposals about emendation or preservation. . . . These claims become prescriptive if one is entitled to make them.' This account both avoids a transcendental view of normativity and equally refuses to accept relativism. Similarly, epistemic norms are seen to arise out of justificatory practices. 'Knowledge', 'justification' and 'reason' are not norms to be abandoned but like 'woman', concepts to be fought over, a locus of struggle. Epistemology is not a matter of simply describing social practices but an arena where negotiation takes place. Thus Tanesini firmly rejects Rorty's account, which would tie meaning and epistemology to current practice and leave no space for feminists to differ from their 'communities'. (This chapter connects with points made in the chapters by Barwell and Fricker in Part I.)

Janna Thompson's chapter on 'Moral difference and moral epistemology' also raises the crucial question of who or what counts as the relevant community when we are legitimating knowledge-claims, and the problem of the plurality of communities. Thompson is concerned with a democratic politics: how to deal with conflicts that arise between groups of people with fundamentally different moral perspectives and specifically in cases where women and men come to different conclusions in their ethical decisions. She argues for the inherently collective nature of ethical decision-making. Her community is defined by all those who share the basic moral premise of communicative ethics. Her solution allows for the possibility that men and women might converge or diverge; that they do not necessarily form separate constituencies, though on some issues they might. In this view, rationality does not imply universal assent (which would return us to coercion) but rather a commitment to seeking a resolution that everyone can live with. A decision reached by such a community, Thompson argues, is what *defines* moral knowledge (cf. Seller and Dhanda, below).

Anne Seller's chapter, 'Should the feminist philosopher stay at home?' illustrates the acute difficulty of establishing the community which Thompson's paper requires to ground moral knowledge. Through an analysis of her experience in an Indian university, Seller shows what happens when the dialogic attempt to understand 'others' takes place in a context which – whatever the intentions of the interlocutors – is defined by historical circumstances and power relationships that pre-exist it. Seller shows in the most concrete way how the ideal of a democratic epistemology has to confront real issues of *power* and accountability. She concludes that dialogues do occur intermittently on the basis of common concerns. Moreover there are other ways of being with people, apart from having dialogues, ways which can force us to rethink our own positions within a context which includes others.

These alternatives to dialogue are explored by Meena Dhanda in her chapter on 'Openness, identity and acknowledgement of persons'. This chapter charts a course between an unsatisfactory liberal tolerance (relativism) and an equally unsatisfactory postmodern pluralism. The question of multiple differences and plural identities is one that has been foregrounded particularly by feminist postmodernism, and is one that can lead to a kind of moral and epistemological dead-end in which any action or decision becomes coercive with respect to a different group (see the chapters by Fricker and Lovibond in Part I), so that the only solution appears to be complete inaction or inertia. This appears to be one of the contradictory consequences of a thoroughgoing feminist postmodernism. For Dhanda, disagreements about identities are in part ethical disagreements and she is concerned with the process whereby we set about resolving such disagreements. Difference is not something we just recognize (agreeing to differ, live and let live, as in the liberal framework). It may require some change from us; not necessarily that of adopting the other's point of view, which is usually not possible, but certainly *changing* in order even to acknowledge its legitimacy.

The change in us which acknowledgement of difference requires is also at the forefront of Susan Strickland's chapter 'Feminism, postmodernism and difference'. Strickland rejects as 'consumerist' the postmodernist treatment of difference; she sees it as a device whereby dominant groups can appear to acknowledge alternatives without engaging with the challenge which they present. It is not acceptable to feminists insisting on the difference of male and female experience, or to other marginalized groups contesting the hegemony of certain forms of feminism. Genuine engagement with difference requires a reassessment of one's own situation and its relations (including power relations) to that of others. This process is a dialectical one, and is open-ended. It requires a refusal to accept that perspectives are closed; but rather sees them as 'open processes' which evolve by dialectical interactions with the positions of others. (There are some similarities here with the position of Sandra Harding, discussed by Barwell in Part I, as well as with those of Dhanda and Mangena in Part II.)

Finally, Oshadi Mangena's chapter 'Against fragmentation: the need for holism' takes up some of the issues raised in Yeatman's paper, specifically the problem involved in the epistemological requirement of objectivity and what this means for the groups who have traditionally been the 'objects' of knowledge and research. However, unlike Yeatman but in common with Strickland, she rejects postmodernism and its fragmentation. She also has reservations about feminist social science, despite its attempts to introduce a subject/subject relation between researcher and researched. In her view, restricting feminist social science to the experiences and domain of women introduces a new fragmentation into the research process by excluding men. Mangena sketches out a holistic approach which would aim at an over-all coherent narrative of *concrete* situations, incorporating the experiences of male and female, colonizers and colonized. The aim of such an approach is to characterize a concrete whole in a way that articulates the interrelatedness of its parts and respects the specificity of different experiences (cf. also Lazreg in Part I).

FURTHER REFLECTIONS

What these essays make clear is that in the present context, feminist epistemology is neither the specification of a female way of knowing (there is no such thing) nor simply the articulation of female subjectivity which reveals itself to be diverse, contradictory and at least partially discursively constructed through patriarchal oppositions. Feminist epistemology consists rather in attention to epistemological concerns arising out of feminist projects, which prompt reflection on the nature of knowledge and our methods for attaining it.

The essays suggest that, in the face of the epistemological challenge presented by difference, there are two directions which seem unworkable. To seek for a minimal consensus with which all parties could feel happy seems like an untenable and receding hope; to settle for a relativistic pluralism which does no more than agree to differ sidesteps the seriousness of the challenge and leaves out of account inequalities of power. For many, a dialectical solution is required, which takes into account the power and conflict, and the competing interests, at the heart of the epistemological enterprise, and which accepts the necessity for the self to change in the pursuit and acquisition of knowledge. This is a process for which our diverse female experiences provide the tensions and problematics that are our point of entry into the epistemological debate.

There is another reason for taking a dialectical approach, which lies in the history of our present categories. The insistence on the difference between male and female experiences or differences between colonizing and colonized viewpoints was not something which simply originated in critiques of falsely universalizing perspectives. It was already implicit within the dominant discourses. Their presentation of the 'feminine' or 'the African' as an 'Other' to the norms of the 'human' or the 'rational' played a central legitimating function for structures of domination and colonization. This means that there is a difficult path to tread. On the one hand we must be wary of making a fetish of 'otherness', simply reversing the hierarchy of the original categories. The danger here is that the binary structure remains intact, dividing the world along pre-determined fault-lines, attributing a spurious homogeneity to the categories and suggesting their radical incommensurability or impermeability to change. On the other hand, we have to keep clearly in mind that from the perspective of the powerless, the encounter with dominant frameworks can be literally over-powering, and that the only possibility of resistance may be to insist on the specificity of difference. We have to negotiate between the repetition and stasis implicit in the first position and the possibilities of resistance inherent in the second, while recognizing that there are sometimes situations in which, because of the limitations of our perspective, we cannot distinguish clearly between them.

The feminist challenge showed the political dimension of acts of representation and made it impossible to ignore the power relations at the heart of knowledge-production. In its insistence that we attend to the social origins of knowledge-production, such a challenge was not simply a contribution to the sociology of knowledge. By showing that the situations of knowing subjects, their positions within technologies of power, were central to the critical and justificatory goals of the epistemological enterprise, it engaged directly with epistemology itself. However, to the extent to which feminism has moved from its moment of critique to that of construction, it has become implicated within the power network. It is feminists' difficult confrontation with this position which has generated the critique from other 'others' which many of our contributors have been grappling with. This is all to the good. For otherwise, feminism is in danger of producing its own 'grand narrative', the contingent locatedness of which becomes disguised from its participants.

Part I

OBJECTIVITY
AND THE KNOWING
SUBJECT

1

BODY-IMAGES AND THE PORNOGRAPHY OF REPRESENTATION

Rosi Braidotti

An image is a stop the mind makes between uncertainties.
(Djuna Barnes)

INTRODUCTION

In this paper, I would like to (try and) take some of the issues involved in the medicalization of the female reproductive body and situate them within the area of contemporary feminist theories of subjectivity. This problem-area refers to the project of enacting and theorizing an alternative female subjectivity and of finding adequate forms of representation for it.

To situate this issue within the debate on the structures of the contemporary philosophical 'subject', I will be using Michel Foucault's idea of embodiment, or of bodily materiality: the materialism of the flesh. This notion defines the embodied subject as a material, concrete effect, that is, as one of the terms in a process of which knowledge and power are the main poles. The idea of a constant, continuous all-pervading normativity is alternatively defined as the microphysics of power, bio-power or as the technology of the self.

In trying to evaluate the position of the body in such a framework, Foucault (1963, 1966) distinguished between two lines of discourse: one is the anatomo-metaphysical one (which has to do with explanation), and the other is the techno-political one, which has to do with control and manipulation. The two intersect constantly, but Foucault argues that they acquire different prominence at different times.

In the first volume of his *Histoire de la Sexualité* (1976), Foucault analyses the organization of sexuality in our post-metaphysical or post-modern world according to this double axis. On the one hand, we can make a distinction or a category relating to the techniques of medicalization of the reproductive body (*scientia sexualis*), and on the other, the arts of existence or practices of the self (*ars erotica*). Modernity as a whole, argues Foucault, marks the triumph of the medicalization process, or rather of

17

the simultaneous sexualization and medicalization of the body, in a new configuration of power which he describes as 'bio-power' – the power of normativity over the living organism.

It can be argued, of course, that the management of living matter has always been a priority for our culture, and that what is new now is the degree of mastery that bio-technology has acquired over life. Foucault emphasizes the fact that since the Enlightenment the embodied subject has been located at the centre of the techniques of rational control and productive domination which mark the order of discourse in modernity. As a consequence of the crisis of metaphysics, and the related decline in the Enlightenment, understood as the belief in reason as the motor of historical progress, however, a set of interrelated questions about the embodiment of the subject has become not only possible but also necessary. The body as mark of the embodied nature of the subject thus becomes the site of proliferating discourses, forms of knowledge and of normativity: economy, biology, demography, family sociology, psychoanalysis, anthropology, etc. can all be seen as discourses about the body.

Following the Foucauldian reading, a new division of labour seems to have emerged between the sciences of life – the bio-discourses – and the human or social sciences. The former concentrate on the anatomo-metaphysical analysis of how the embodied subject functions; their aim is to explain and analyse. The latter pertain to the technico-political in that they elaborate a discourse about the nature of the human. In other words, the human sciences are intrinsically connected to normativity and control, in so far as they take into account, by definition, the question of the structure of the subject. In this respect, they are necessarily connected to the question of an ethics or a politics; which is not necessarily the case for the hard or for the bio-medical sciences.

This division of labour corresponds to the splitting of the bodily entity according to the twofold schema Foucault proposes: on the one hand the body is simply another object of knowledge, an empirical object among others: an organ-ism, the sum of its organic parts, an assembly of detachable organs. This is the body which clinical anatomy studies, measures and describes. On the other hand, no body can be reduced to the sum of its organic components: the body still remains the site of transcendence of the subject, and as such it is the condition of possibility for all knowledge. Foucault concludes that the body is an empirical-transcendental double.

A major role is played by the discourse of psychoanalysis which is one of the major retheorizations of the body. Far from being a mere therapy, psychoanalysis has developed into a philosophy of desire and a theory of the body as libidinal surface, a site of multiple coding, of inscription – a living text. Although Foucault's theoretical relationship to psychoanalysis, and especially to Lacan, is far from simple, I take it as a fact that Foucauldian epistemology acknowledges the corporeal roots of subjectivity.

There is, however, a paradox in this analysis of the embodied nature of the modern subject, which is rich in implications for feminists. The body emerges at the centre of the theoretical and political debate at exactly the time in history when there is no more unitary certainty or uncontested consensus about what the body actually is. Given the loss of Cartesian certainty about the dichotomy mind/body, one can no longer take for granted what the body is. The absence of certainty generates a multiplicity of different discourses about the body. Modernity is therefore the age of the inflationary overexposure and yet absence of consensus as to the embodied, material nature of the subject. The body has turned into many, multiple bodies.

In this framework of simultaneous overexposure and disappearance of the body, the case of reproductive technologies is a very significant one, in that it both highlights and exacerbates the paradoxes of the modern condition. With the reproductive technologies, the split between reproduction, or *scientia sexualis* and sexuality, or *ars erotica* becomes institutionalized and officially enacted.

Obviously, the present situation does not arise out of the blue: the split between sexuality and reproduction, *as far as women are concerned*, has quite a history. I would sum it up by saying that, with chemical contraceptive techniques (the pill) we could have sexuality without reproduction – sex without babies. With the latest reproductive techniques, especially *in vitro* fertilization, we can have reproduction without sexuality – babies without sex. This paradox conceals, in my opinion, many theoretical and political challenges.

BIO-POWER AND WOMEN

Organs without bodies

Of great significance for feminism is the way in which the new reproductive technologies, by normalizing the dismemberment of the body, transform the body into a mosaic of detachable pieces. The phenomenon of 'organs without bodies' is, of course, a respectably ancient one: in the eighteenth century, with the transformations in the status of the embodied subject that I briefly sketched above, the study of the body through the practice of anatomy was momentous enough as a bio-technological innovation to require the construction of special institutions devoted to this task. The clinic and the hospital are the new monuments of the new scientific spirit; they transform the body into an organ-ism, or mass of detachable parts. They also suitably transform the relationship between the doctor and the patients, in a mirror relationship that Foucault describes admirably at the end of *Histoire de la folie*, as well as in *Naissance de la clinique*. As usual, however, Foucault devotes little or no attention and insufficient emphasis to the specific case of women's bodies. That the body that is so often studied, comprehended and intellectually possessed is the woman's, and especially the mother's body, is a point that seems to escape Foucault's attention.

Nevertheless, the point remains: genealogically speaking, the invention of a clinical structure is linked to the medical practice of anatomy. This is the practice that grants to the medical sciences the right to go and see what goes on inside the human organism. The actual elaboration of the discourse of clinical anatomy can be considered as quite a scientific progress, when compared to the centuries-old taboos that had forbidden the access to the 'secrets of the organism'. We must remember that our culture had traditionally held the body in awe, severely regulating knowledge relating to it. Not only was it forbidden to open up the body in order to disclose its mechanisms, but also it was absolutely sacrilegious to use the bodily parts for the purpose of scientific investigation. The dissection of corpses was forbidden till the fifteenth century and after that it was subject to very strict regulation. Even nowadays, the field of organ transplant is ruled by a web of laws and regulations that restrict the gift of organs and their usage for scientific experiments.

Clearly enough, clinical anatomy is a death-technique, it has to do with corpses and fresh supplies of organs. As such it marks an epistemological shift in the status of the body; the living body becomes, in the process of clinical anatomy, a living text, that is to say material to be read and interpreted by a medical gaze that can decipher its diseases and its functions. Anatomy results in a representation of the body as clear and distinct – *visible*, and therefore intelligible.

As the French psychoanalyst Pierre Fedida has suggested (1971), the opening of corpses in the practice of anatomy marks an epistemological break *vis-à-vis* the scientific order of the previous centuries. The rational, visible organism of modern science marks the end of the fantastic, imaginary representations of the alchemists, and consequently empties out the body of all its opacity and mystery. The paradox is that this new process of decoding and classifying the bodily functions – which opens up new, unexplored spaces to the medical gaze – also closes the body off in a new concept: that of the appropriate shape, form and function of the organs. The different organs, in other words, only make sense and become decodable, readable and analysable because they all belong to the same assembled unity, the same organ-ism: like the letters of a corporeal alphabet.

Organized in this manner, the knowledge that the bio-medical sciences get from the organism is, as Foucault put it: 'epistemologically related to death' (Foucault 1963: 200), in that the dead body alone can disclose its mysteries about life. In turn this changes the position of the doctor: whereas in the pre-scientific period the idea of illness was associated with a metaphysics of evil, in which the visible organ was a sign of disease or malfunction, in modern times it comes closer to a hermeneutics in which the organ produces a symptom. It is because humans are mortal that they can fall ill: the notion of death becomes the horizon to which the idea of illness is attached. The visibility and intelligibility of the living organism are very closely related to the notion of death. 'Des cadavres ouverts de Bichat à l'homme freudien, un rapport obstiné à la mort prescrit à l'univer- sel son visage singulier et prête à la parole de chacun le pouvoir d'être indéfiniment entendue' (200).

What is so striking about the discourse and the practice of clinical anatomy, with its closeness to death, is that it marks an experience of loss of illusions. The fantastic, imaginary dimension that was so strong in the discourse of the alchemists, the simple curiosity before the living organism's complexity, is replaced by the detached power of observation of the clinical standpoint. The body that is open to scrutiny, to observation by the bio- medical gaze, is a body that can be manipulated; it is a useful, purposeful body, that can produce knowledge, thus legitimating the power of the bio- medical profession.

The bio-technological universe clarifies and makes manifest the tend- encies that had been operative since the beginning of what we call modern technology and science. Modern science is the triumph of the scopic drive as a gesture of epistemological domination and control: to make visible the invisible, to visualize the secrets of nature. Bio-sciences achieve their aims by making the embodied subject visible and intelligible according to the principles of scientific representation. In turn this implies that the bodily unity can be split into a variety of organs, each of which can in turn be analysed and represented.

In modern bio-chemical research, thanks to the advances of molecular biology, we have gone well beyond the organs, reducing the field of study to tissues, cells and micro-organisms. The phenomenon that I called 'organs without bodies' has concentrated on smaller and smaller entities. The change in size also marks a shift in the scale of the exchanges. The commer- cialization of living matter has grown larger and more effective than ever. Traffic in organs, but also in tissues and cells – in other words, the commercialization of living material for the purpose of medical research or treatment is a world-wide phenomenon, with the Third World providing most of the spare parts: foetuses from Korea, kidneys from Brazil, eyeballs from Colombia.

The idea of traffic in organs, or the exchange of living material rests on a number of theoretical hypotheses that I find questionable: it confuses the parts with the whole and it encourages what I consider to be the perverse notion of the interchangeability of organs. That is to say that all organs, or living material are *the same*, and thus one kidney is as good as any other, one uterus will do as well as any other. An ovary is an ovary is an ovary. All organs are equal, but some are more equal than others; consequently, all organs are equally exchangeable and the laws trying to regulate this market are notoriously ineffective.

What worries me about the theoretical underpinnings of this practice is the falsely reassuring notion of the *sameness* of the bodily material involved. In my opinion it conceals the importance of *differences* in determining what I would call the singularity of each subject.

Killing time

Let me make the same point from another angle, directly related to the new reproductive technologies: what is at stake in all this dismemberment and free circulation of organs or living cells is the disruption of time, or temporality. I stated before that clinical anatomical observations required a corpse, dead material, as the basic matter or text to be decoded. It thus bore a direct relationship to death. The phenomenon of 'body-snatching' in the nineteenth century proved a very fertile ground not only for a macabre trade, but also for the popular imagination to speculate about the horrors of modern science.

In modern bio-technologies, time is arrested in a much more subtle manner; just think of what happens to the reproductive process in the artificial insemination cases: the freezing of the sperm, the ova and the embryo suspends the process indefinitely (one can fertilize one's egg now and bring it to completion in twenty years' time).

In vitro fertilization has another kind of discontinuity in terms of reproduction: there is first the hormonal pre-treatment of the patient; then the farming of the ripe eggs; the actual artificial insemination; the division of the cells *in vitro*; the transferral of the embryo into the uterus. At the same time, the new social forms of procreation, such as surrogate motherhood, divide the reproductive continuum into different levels of mothering, corresponding to different moments in the time-sequence: there is the ovular mother, the uterine mother, the social mother.

This dislocation of temporality has paved the way for another phenomenon that I would describe as perverse; it can best be illustrated by an extreme example: inter-generational procreation by transplant. This is not only the stuff that Fay Weldon's novels are made of (for instance, *The Cloning of Joanna May*), there has already been a case of a mother carrying her daughter's babies to birth, and the issue has attracted the attention of various bio-ethics committees that are supposed to legislate on this matter.

Inter-generational procreation seems to me to crystallize the dangers of the idea of *sameness*: if all uteruses are equal and interchangeable, all women are the same on the scale of their function as baby-carriers. That this alleged sameness should abolish all other axes of differentiation, be it race, or age, is a matter of great concern. What this means, in fact, is an illusion of commonness among women, which conceals the very pernicious forms of social control and therefore of hierarchical powers, that are being set up in the field of reproduction. It is a sort of 'equality' of all female bodies, which paves the way for deeper and more profitable forms of exploitation.

The phenomenon of organs without bodies, with the institutionalization of the dismembered condition, is, moreover, also the pre-text to the deployment of one of the oldest, not to say the most primordial of all fantasies: that of being in total control of one's origins, that is of being the father/mother of one's self. I think contemporary culture is fascinated by the myth of parthenogenesis. This implies the denial or the blurring of generational time, of one's position in time, in relation to others. This is also a way of avoiding or short-circuiting the acknowledgement of one's origins in a woman's body. The merry-go-round of bodily parts, or cells, or tissues, that do not belong anywhere lays the preconditions for the fantasy that one does not really come from anywhere specific, from any one bodily point. When the parental body is bracketed off, the mother as site of origin is dislocated. The maternal thus abstracted, the very notion of origin becomes suspended. This seems to me one of the side-effects of the interchangeability of organs that I described as 'organs without bodies'. The time-factor no longer allows us to symbolize fundamental differences, as if we were living in a continuous present.

The social and cultural repercussions of this bio-scientific imaginary seem to me just as perverse: the fantasy of being at the origin of oneself, that is of not having to recognize one's beginning as originating in others – one's parents – is manifested very strongly in popular culture, especially in cinema. Of late there have been many movies where the fantasy of being self-generated is very powerfully marketed. The denial of intergenerational time and space used to be the stuff neuroses were made of; today it is a fashionable event. The best representative of this trend is Steven Spielberg, whose characters sum up the main features of our contemporary scientific culture: one of them – Indiana Jones – has no mother, just a father who is an archaeologist, like himself, with a strong interest in the secret. In almost every Indiana Jones film there is an encounter with God the Father. Spielberg's films, like *ET* and *Gremlins*, flirt with an infantile fantasy about procreation; the films offer many fantastic answers to the question, 'where do babies come from?'; in the case of the *Gremlins* parthenogenesis is explicitly represented, in other films it is more subtly hinted at. Very significant in this respect is the series *Back to the Future*, which features a young boy who travels back in time to make sure that his parents meet, fall in love and actually conceive him.

Another striking example of the same tendency is James Cameron's *Terminator*, a very violent film which functions as one retrospective contraception technique in that the cyborg-killer (Schwarzenegger!) has to eliminate the mother of his future enemy, thus preventing his conception. No time left for the present, life is lived as a death-bound flashback.

From the visible to the visual

I mention the cinema and popular culture also because more than anything else, the dismemberment of the body and the suspension of the time-structure have to do with the idea of visibility, with looking, and consequently with the gaze. We saw earlier how Foucault analyses the importance of visibility as a leading principle in the scientific representation of the human body.

According to psychoanalytic interpretation, the scopic drive is linked to both knowledge and control or domination. In other words, it is the practice of opening something up to see how it functions; the impulse to go and see, to 'look in' is the most fundamental and child-like form of control over the other's body. In this sense, the curiosity that pushes the child to break his/her toy to see how it is made inside can be seen as the most primitive form of sadism. Applied to the scientific practice, this analysis is quite devastating: it makes clinical anatomy into an adult version of infantile sadism. It is the expression of curiosity linked to the most archaic sadistic impulses. It can be argued that the mother's body is the privileged target of this violence, in that it represents the origins of life, and one's own origins. Evelyn Fox Keller (1989), stresses the violent and sadistic implications of what we could call the contemporary bio-medical perversion.

Paradoxically enough, clinical anatomy, with its sadistic subtext, is an exercise in mastery that aims at denying death. By trying to reduce the body to an organism, a sum of detachable parts, it implies that the body is but that: what you see is what you get. There is an inevitable slippage from the visible to the mirage of absolute transparency, as if the light of reason could extend into the deepest murkiest depths of the human organism, as if the truth consisted simply in making something visible.

The modern techniques of visual reproduction, especially echograms and echography, mark a powerful intensification of this trend. Earlier, I argued that by comparison with traditional clinical anatomy, the bio-sciences of today have acquired the means of intervening in the very structure of the living organism, right into the genetic programme, changing the bodily structure from within. On the technological front, molecular biology has increased the bio-medical gaze to infinite proportions, allowing for an unprecedented investigation of the most intimate and infinitesimal fibres of nature. The unity of the organism is thus dissolved into smaller and smaller living parts; this shift corresponds to a much greater power of vision.

We are moving beyond the idea of visibility, into a new culture of visualization; thanks to ultra-sound techniques the invisible itself today can be visualized; that which the naked eye does not even begin to grasp can be the object of imaged representation. The bio-scientist is, quite literally, the great spectator of life; he can at long last represent the unrepresentable: the bottom of the ocean, outer space, but also the inside of the womb, the depths of the uterine chamber, that great mystery that has always held mankind in suspense.

The fixing into images is a spatio-temporal system related to the stopping or arresting of time. Roland Barthes's book on photography is neither the first nor the last analysis of the image as being linked to death and immobility. In this respect, the sadistic impulse of the bio-medical gaze becomes even more of a death-drive with these new visualization techniques.

Offering everything for display or show, representing the unrepresentable (like the origins of life), means producing images that displace the boundaries of space (inside/outside the mother's body) and of time (before/after birth). It amounts to suspending time in the illusion of total vision, of the absolute transparency of living matter.

Furthermore, the visualization techniques give a great autonomy or independence to the object they represent. The image acquires a life of its own, distinct from anything else. It is quite clear that echograms of the foetus confer upon it an identity, a visual shape, a visible and intelligible existence that the foetus would not usually have. The act of visualization emancipates the object that it represents; it makes it into an object of consumption, it allows it to circulate, it detaches it from the mother's body where it is located.

Apart from the fantasy of absolute domination that is expressed in this process, I want to stress also that this visualization produces an attitude that I would describe as medical pornography. I am using the term pornography in the sense suggested by Susanne Kappeler (1986) as being a system of representation that reinforces the commercial logic of the market economy. The whole body becomes a visual surface of changeable parts, offered as exchange-objects.

In pornography, sex is represented through the spectacle of organs interpenetrating each other, but that proves a very unsatisfactory image for the act itself. There is always something more to experience than the image can show. And yet the triumph of the image is precisely what marks scientific culture. Like the visual nature of pornographic culture, it cheats; it shows you a bloody mess of red flesh and it tells you: this is the origin of life. Pornography shows you organs getting in and out of each other, and tells you: this is sexual pleasure. Both rest on the fantasy that visibility and truth work together. I want to argue that they do not and that there is always more to things than meets the eye. There is no adequate *simulacrum*: no image is a representation of the truth.

This new medical pornography, resting as it does on the detachment of the foetus from the mother's body, on the dismemberment of bodily unity and the traffic of the parts for the whole, has enormous social and political consequences. A film made by the anti-abortion lobbies, *The Silent Scream*, proves this point. This is allegedly the film of an abortion, through echography, with a powerful reactionary sound-track that gives a voice to the foetus's alleged 'feelings' about being 'murdered'. It is interspersed with images of concentration camps. There is no question as to the effect that this piece of right-wing propaganda has had on the American audience, nor can we underestimate the role it played in making abortion legislation recede in many states of the union. As Rosalind P. Petchesky (1987) pointed out, the theoretical point is that, detached from the mother's body, the foetus has an identity of its own, but it is also reduced to the level of a detachable organ; unrelated to the site of its growth, it is subject to disembodiment.

FEMINIST INSIGHTS

The pessimistic side to my position is that the bio-medical technology which is manipulating women by promising them a baby at all costs also fits into the logic of a system where sexuality is power. This comes as no surprise. That bio-medical technologies should encourage the masculine fantasy of self-generation, reversing the Oedipal chain so as to feed the infantile fantasies of all-powerfulness through self-generation, at a time when the parental roles are being mechanized, is also a matter of great concern. That the emancipation of the foetus in our ever-so-patriarchal culture should happen at the expense of the mother is terrifying, but not surprising. Although I do not mean to strike a note of total opposition to science and technology, I would like to repeat the warning against some of their perverse effects.

There is also, however, an optimistic side to my conclusion: feminists have been fast and effective in their critiques and actions against the perverse effects induced by the new technologies. Thus, over the last ten years many women and feminist theorists have done a great deal of work on the question of the visible and of visibility. Their analysis is now being applied to the problem of reproductive technologies so as to try and elaborate effective policies. The starting point is the recognition that the visual metaphor is a constant in western culture. The act of seeing or the gaze as synonym for mental representation and for understanding has been an important image ever since Plato. The idea as double, or mental image of the real thing is part of everything our culture has constructed in the way of knowledge. Descartes's notion of 'clear and distinct ideas' is only the modern rendition of an old-standing habit that Gayatri Spivak describes as 'clarity fetishism'.[1]

Psychoanalytic theory, which in many respects criticizes classical theories of representation, confirms the primacy of sight as a site of legitimation of knowledge: Lacan's mirror stage perpetuates the tyranny of the logocentric gaze.

This is what the feminist critics like Luce Irigaray have been arguing; Irigaray focuses precisely on the issue of identification and on the overwhelming importance granted to the gaze. In many respects, Irigaray's project can be seen as an attempt to replace the visual with the tactile, seeing with touching. In her analysis of Irigaray's work, Margaret Whitford (1986) draws our attention to the importance of the notion of the imaginary in her work. She plays Irigaray's imaginary against Lacan's mirror and reads it as a critique of the primacy granted to the gaze as the dominant model of representation in our culture. Not only does Irigaray criticize the flat surface of Lacan's mirror as a reductive model of the human psyche – to which she opposes the concave surface, the speculum – but also she suggests that the mirror-function is the specific role that women are expected to play. Women are the flat surface that is supposed to reflect the male subject; her bodily surface, deprived of any visible organs, without anything to see is the mirror. Let me just remind you here of Freud's essay on the Medusa's head as the expression of the horror of the feminine. Her flat bodily surface shows her lack and also the importance of the phallus as signifier of desire.

Evelyn Fox Keller (1983) takes up in a very critical manner the French critiques of the visual metaphor. She singles out the importance of sight – the most noble of the senses – as the qualifier for western knowledge, stressing the ways in which it allows for the separation from subject to object. Keller stresses the way in which the scientific position is one of detached observation, identifying the objects of knowledge at a distance. This kind of position produces the idea of neutrality and objectivity in the sense of allowing for no particularity about the site of observation.

Keller points out the paradox, however, that this neutral and objective stance is available only to individuals who are socially and culturally constructed as norm-al, in the sense of corresponding to the standards of normality as associated with masculinity. As a consequence, women are disqualified from the capacity to achieve adequate neutrality and therefore they lose the site/sight of the subject.

Keller, along with Genevieve Lloyd (1984) and Susan Bordo (1986), develop the argument about masculinization and rationality; they emphasize that the opposition of knower and known, subject and object is the same qualitative distinction as mind and body, *res extensa* and *res cogitans*. The masculine element of this consists precisely in the detachment, the perception of clear and distinct determination of boundaries between self and world. Separation and autonomy are indeed the central features of the masculine standpoint.

In the feminist analysis, this detachment and objectivity are connected to the fantasy of self-generation, of being father/mother of oneself, thus denying the specific debt to the maternal. Adrienne Rich and Luce Irigaray have also related the notion of scientific detachment and objectivity to the unwillingness or the downright denial of the fact that one is of woman born. It is a form of flight from the feminine.

Another school of thought develops the point suggested by Irigaray, in terms of stressing the tactile, or the importance of touching, as a counter-model for knowledge. Jessica Benjamin (1986) turns to Winnicott's object-relations theory as a model to argue that self and other are inextricably linked. Arguing that what allows for the creation of subjective space is the idea of receptivity and mutuality, she develops a theory of transitional space as the connecting space, an interface which allows for contact and not only for separation.

According to de Lauretis the feminist theories of subjectivity today are moving in the direction of the subject as a process of interconnected relations. Central to this project, according to de Lauretis (1986), is the need to detach the female feminist subject, that is to say real-life women as agents and empirical subjects, from the representation of Woman as the fantasy of a male imagination. The struggle is therefore over imaging and naming: it is about whose representations will prevail.

In a similar vein the postmodernist feminist philosopher Donna Haraway (1991a) also starts from the recognition that there is a structurally necessary connection between seeing and the mind, which she translates into the idea of disembodiment. Thus, Descartes sees only clear and distinct ideas because he has no body, and he denies his embodied nature. By the same token, androids, cyborgs, scanners, satellites, electronic microscopes and telescopes see the most clearly of all.

Haraway tries to rescue the faculty of seeing, of vision, and to repossess it for feminist discourse, redefining objectivity along the way. She calls this new epistemological project 'situated knowledges' (1991b: 183–202), as opposed to the 'cannibal eye' of unlimited disembodied vision. Objectivity, in her terms, is not about the transcendence of limits but rather about partial perspectives, which make us accountable for what we learn how to see. Arguing that modern visualization techniques shatter the very idea of one-dimensional seeing or the passive mirror function, Haraway suggests that we learn to see in compound, multiple ways, in 'partial perspectives'; she calls it 'passionate detachment' – like the eye of a travelling lens.

Vision requires a politics of positioning; positioning implies responsibility. Vision is the power to see, thus 'struggles over what counts as rational accounts of the world are struggles over how to see'.

Feminist embodiment implies 'significant prosthesis', relating to the world as a material semiotic field of forces at play. The world is no mere passive matter awaiting interpretation, or decoding by a scanning eye.

It is no mere screen ground or surface, but actor and agent, requiring interaction.

Haraway concludes that feminism is about 'a critical vision consequent upon a critical positioning in unhomogeneous, gendered social space'.

According to Haraway, in the present struggle over visual politics and the naming of new bio-technological realities, feminists must reject the knowledge ruled by phallo-logocentric premises and disembodied vision, for the sake of the connections which situated knowledge make possible.

Faced with the wealth of feminist reflection on the power of vision, the visible and the visual, I prefer to end on a rather optimistic note. It seems to me that effective feminist interventions in the field of bio-medical power will require strong attention being paid to the politics of visual culture and the pervasiveness of pornography as the dominant structure of representation in scientific as well as in popular discourse. The naked eye may have been replaced by electronic lens, but the objectification and commercialization of what it beholds have grown bigger than ever. It is in those factors that I would locate the pornographic mode, as a form of discursive and material domination. In this respect, it would be a great pity if the whole feminist debate in reproductive technologies failed to use the instruments and the insight of disciplines other than the social sciences.

NOTE

1 Spivak's remark was made at the congress 'Double trouble' held at the University of Utrecht in May 1990.

REFERENCES

Benjamin, Jessica (1986), 'A desire of one's own: psychoanalytic feminism and intersubjective space' in *Feminist Studies/Critical Studies*, ed. Teresa de Lauretis, Bloomington: Indiana University Press, pp. 78–101.

Benjamin, Jessica (1988), *The Bonds of Love: Psychoanalysis, Feminism and the Problem of Domination*, New York: Pantheon.

Bordo, Susan (1986), 'The Cartesian masculinization of thought' in *Signs*, vol. 11, no. 3, pp. 439–56.

De Lauretis, Teresa (ed.) (1986), *Feminist Studies/Critical Studies*, Bloomington: Indiana University Press.

Fedida, Pierre (1971), 'L'Anatomie dans la psychanalyse' in *Nouvelle Revue de Psychanalyse* 3, pp. 109–26.

Foucault, Michel (1963), *Naissance de la clinique*, Paris: Presses Universitaires de France. Trans. as *The Birth of the Clinic*, trans. Alan Sheridan, London: Tavistock and New York: Pantheon, 1973.

Foucault, Michel (1966), *Les Mots et les choses*, Paris: Gallimard. Trans. as *The Order of Things*, trans. Alan Sheridan, London: Tavistock and New York: Pantheon, 1970.

Foucault, Michel (1972) *Histoire de la folie à l'âge classique*, Paris: Gallimard, 2nd edition. Trans. as *Madness and Civilization*, trans. Richard Howard, New York: Pantheon, 1965 and London: Tavistock, 1967.

Foucault, Michel (1976), *Histoire de la sexualité vol. I: La Volonté de savoir*, Paris: Gallimard. Trans. as *The History of Sexuality*, vol I, trans. Robert Hurley, New York: Pantheon, 1978 and London: Allen Lane, 1979.

Foucault, Michel (1984a), *Histoire de la sexualité vol. II: L'Usage des plaisirs*, Paris: Gallimard. Trans. as *The Use of Pleasure*, trans. Robert Hurley, Harmondsworth: Penguin, 1985.

Foucault, Michel (1984b), *Histoire de la sexualité vol. III: Le Souci de soi*, Paris: Gallimard. Trans. as *The Care of the Self*, trans. Robert Hurley, Harmondsworth: Penguin, 1986.

Haraway, Donna J. (1991a), 'A cyborg manifesto: science, technology and socialist-feminism in the late twentieth century' in Donna J. Haraway, *Simians, Cyborgs and Women: The Reinvention of Nature*, London: Free Association Books, pp. 149–81.

Haraway, Donna J. (1991b), 'Situated knowledges: the science question in feminism and the privilege of partial perspective' in Donna J. Haraway, *Simians, Cyborgs and Women: The Reinvention of Nature*, London: Free Association Books, pp. 183–201.

Irigaray, Luce (1974), *Speculum de l'autre femme*, Paris: Minuit. Trans. as *Speculum of the Other Woman*, trans. Gillian C. Gill, Ithaca: Cornell University Press.

Kappeler, Susanne (1986), *The Pornography of Representation*, Cambridge: Polity Press.

Keller, Evelyn Fox (1983), *A Feeling for the Organism: The Life and Work of Barbara McClintock*, New York: Freeman.

Keller, Evelyn Fox (1989), 'Van de Geheimen van het leven tot de geheimen van de Dood', *Tijdschrift voor Vrouwenstudies* 38, pp. 253–70.

Keller, Evelyn Fox and Grontkowski, Christine R. (1983), 'The mind's eye' in *Discovering Reality: Feminist Perspectives on Epistemology, Metaphysics, Methodology, and Philosophy of Science*, ed. Sandra Harding and Merrill B. Hintikka, Dordrecht: Reidel, pp. 207–24.

Lloyd, Genevieve (1984), *The Man of Reason: 'Male' and 'Female' in Western Philosophy*, London: Methuen.

Petchesky, Rosalind Pollack (1987), 'Foetal images: the power of visual culture in the politics of reproduction' in *Reproductive Technologies: Gender, Motherhood and Medicine*, ed. Michelle Stanworth, Cambridge: Polity Press, pp. 57–80.

Whitford, Margaret (1986), 'Speaking as a woman: Luce Irigaray and the female imaginary', *Radical Philosophy* 43, pp. 3–8.

Whitford, Margaret (1989), 'Rereading Irigaray' in *Between Feminism and Psychoanalysis*, ed. Teresa Brennan, New York and London: Routledge, pp. 106–26.

THE METAPHORIC FUNCTION AND THE QUESTION OF OBJECTIVITY

Gemma Corradi Fiumara

THE LIFE OF LANGUAGE

The relation with a world outside discourse – somehow constraining what can be said – could be better developed in conjunction with a scrutiny of the sort of language which contributes to shaping such reality.[1] This language in fact may tend towards a construction of the world – nature, persons, culture – prevalently suited to controlling it rather than towards a view of things allowing for dialogic exchange and mutual enrichment.

Even though generally acclaimed, dialogue turns out to be rather problematic in a philosophical culture which may be unsuited for authentic listening.[2] Mutual enrichment is equally a problem. As we persist in breaking reality down into a multiplicity of objects (of study), we are induced to automatically adapt any alien structure to our own in the process of trying to appreciate, 'receive', just *that* structure (Quine 1969: 1).

And although in contemporary philosophy we have gradually substituted language for the notion of a knowing mind and words for concepts, a subject-object cognitive model still seems to prevail. This does not ultimately allow for the mutual enrichment we seek: not through philosophical work that derives from an abstract rationality intent upon controlling the world,[3] but rather through work that potentially emanates from our incarnate condition.

I should thus like to turn to an investigation of the metaphoric potential of human linguisticity in order to explore ways of interaction which might allow for reciprocal enrichment. It is perhaps appropriate to point out that dialogic exchange and mutual development in no way constitute either alternatives to objectivity or compromises with it. I hope that the work I am pursuing will tend towards 'increasing' objectivity by creating ever-new opportunities for greater precision, in such a way that objective knowledge is not attained at the cost of reducing the complexity of 'objects' nor of prohibiting the recontextualization of concepts.

Objective knowledge may be regarded as directly dependent upon a sufficiently shared epistemology, that is upon a commensurable cluster of hypotheses and terms through which the attributions of meaning could be adjudicated; as is known, a complex of basic rules which indicate how rational agreement can be achieved constitutes the basis of epistemologies (Rorty 1980: 316, 318, 333). Such rational agreement, however, is in turn strictly dependent upon a sufficiently endorsed literal language. Within such conceptual areas we conveniently operate by means of a calculus of propositions or appropriate algorithms. But if we try to think of language as part of life and thus subject to evolution, and degradation, we can begin to see that the relative stability of objectivity could not possibly be equated with permanence.

Even though a comprehensive 'logic' capable of accounting for both affects and deductions, for life and abstraction, has not yet been expressed in human culture, it is possible that the mode of being which may generate this new rationality is already at work. It is not impossible that in Neanderthal times some members of the human community may have thought 'Greek', that some of our contemporaries may think 'Neanderthal', and others still think 'future'. Pristine originality may be an illusion, since germinal ideas may be at work well before a conventional founder proclaims them with sufficient persuasiveness to elicit recontextualizations. Official founders may utilize the full implications of ideas that precursors lived by, albeit with a scarce grasp of their 'revolutionary'[4] force. And once language has become excessively disembodied in the history of hominization, it may well become indifferent to life and death, destruction and construction, inasmuch as the representationalist preoccupations associated with objectivity of meaning absorb most of our 'philosophical' concerns.

The sort of approach I am putting forward may ultimately challenge the map of an internalized culture whose order relies upon unbreakable distinctions between domains which are classified as either experiential or formal, synthetic or *a priori*, bodily or mental, instinctual or rational, in an endless sequence of comparable and irreducible dichotomies.

Although a thorough description of the syntactic and logical structure of metaphor would surely prove enlightening, its omission need not be fatal for our present purposes. The enforcement of such a prerequisite would probably imply a dependence upon whatever form of literalness may prevail at a given moment and consequently a refusal to explore anything for which we do not have a sufficiently shared philosophical vocabulary.

For instance, we still do not know what has led metaphoricity to become a 'metaphor' for all the non-literal dynamics of language which develop outside of the homogeneous vocabularies of any normal discipline (in the Kuhnian sense of 'normal science'). Etymologically, the meaning of 'metaphor' is perhaps quite close to the metabolic aspects of our organismic life. To 'metaphorize' means to carry a term beyond the place where it belongs and thus link it with a context otherwise alien to it.[5]

In the way of a first approximation one could suggest that literal language can be referred to any intra-epistemic vocabulary while non-literal uses of language refer to inter-epistemic hermeneutical efforts.

There seems to be a change of punctuation in our philosophical discourse inasmuch as we no longer start from 'philosophical language' as if antecedent life conditions were irrelevant to the development of such language. Else Barth critically points out that much of our philosophy cognitively operates in a *social-solipsistic* style 'in which physical objects may be of importance as such but where *no* verbal contact or other sign contact between humans occur, *or are taken into consideration*' (Barth 1991: 71–104, my emphasis). Conversely, the present inquiry is inspired by an outlook on life and language which assumes their reciprocal interaction. Any concept of either life or language that does not account for their interconnectedness will probably fail to yield more than superfluous artefacts; these have little to offer an inchoate philosophical culture pursuing the quest for a language capable of inter-epistemic communication. In fact, if we can no longer count on the location of an Archimedean point of departure, then we can more humbly opt for a logic of interdependencies.

The perplexity induced by most forms of shifts in the way we do philosophy is not so much due to a recognition that cultural life cannot be conceived of as stationary, but rather to the frustration of the philosophically induced desire for an ultimate point of departure, whether in language or in facts, that we could use as a starting-point for giving order to our view of the world.

While exploring the metaphoricity of humans it is therefore essential to point out that reality is not just shaped according to the metaphors that we generate;[6] this would imply that we have assumed as a cognitive basis, or specific starting-point, the modern version of the mind – language. And, similarly, we cannot posit any ultimate datum which we should simply receive into our minds, for this would also imply that we have chosen a privileged basis external to us.

A metaphoric approach which regards language as an expression of life may disclose that our experience has no such foundations (contrary to what some philosophers would like), but only manages a fairly stable vocabulary deriving from consensual conglomerations in our biological and cultural history. In the mainstreams of our history we ultimately confront a slow metamorphosis of interpretative assumptions through which we organize experience.

The generally shared notion of an immaterial mind and language is made possible for us by a philosophical neglect of our organismic life; and our incarnate languages, moreover, are made objects of inquiry only with regard to critical or pathological circumstances. That the notion of an embodied language becomes linked with defectiveness and illness is not a purely contingent matter. There is also a suspicion that language as a lived experience seems to be retrieved for discussion only as a reaction to antecedent valuational exclusions.

Even though the body is no longer viewed as the locus of passions and errors,[7] in contemporary culture concern for our condition of living creatures is confined within the neutral discourse of objective science. And yet, our life-dependent language remains latently conceived of by philosophy as that which naturally inclines us to error and clouds the potential lucidity of discourse. It is no mere coincidence that our philosophy systematically ignores the languages of infancy, senescence and madness – even though these are essential aspects of human linguisticity, continuously worthy of hermeneutic attention. But what is the difference between hermeneutics and confusion, pragmatism and anomie, tolerance and chaos, metaphor and madness? This is the challenging question. We can no longer sacrifice areas of our linguisticity in favour of the lucidity of regulated literalness, any more than we can renounce areas of univocity, correspondence and coherence just because it is becoming possible to inquire into novel aspects of experience which exceed those areas. Here too we have a problem of onto-valuational dualism which may well vanish to the extent that it becomes clear to us that coping with philosophical problems can no longer be a simple question of either/or stances but rather a demanding process of both/and dynamics.

OBJECTIVE KNOWLEDGE AND
CREATIVE THOUGHT

As soon as we invoke our Greek origins we see that our linguistic tradition is not so distant from the Platonic legacy of Cartesian rationalism, positing a coextensiveness of mind and 'philosophically purified' intellect. Plato 'demonstrates' that one cannot grasp the truth via any corporeal senses, but must apply 'pure and unadulterated thought to the pure and unadulterated object'.[8] Descartes similarly argues that the mind cannot achieve clear and distinct knowledge through a reason which is not liberated from reliance upon the senses.[9]

In our Cartesian heritage, understanding is nothing less than the rational mind operating independently of all corporeal influences. This tremendously constraining assumption, which detaches us from life, would compel us to think of our rationality not only in terms of relative stability but indeed of a lifeless permanence or delusional eternity.

As Leder suggests, in any such perspective the human body would come to be identified with 'mindless passions or passive automaticities' (Leder 1990: 126). Relegated to but one term of a duality, the 'life' that remains is somewhat curtailed and only approachable in terms of a restricted range of abilities.

More physiologically inclined than his predecessor – and thus not entirely preoccupied with the purity of thinking – Aristotle proclaims that

> the greatest thing, by far, is to be a master of metaphor. It is the one thing that cannot be learnt; and it is also a sign of genius since a good metaphor implies an intuitive perception of similarity of dissimilars.[10]

Whether or not the primary function of a good metaphor is the appreciation of the similarity of dissimilars, the naturalist philosopher, reacting to Platonic transcendence, insists that our metaphoric potential is, by far, 'the greatest thing' in language – indeed a 'sign' of our 'genius' for creativity and survival.

It is perplexing that in spite of such a clear indication by the celebrated thinker of what is the salient function of language ('by far the greatest thing and a sign of genius'), the topic of metaphor has been systematically ignored through the centuries. Perhaps in the early stages of our western culture, priority has been wisely accorded to the sort of rationality which could generate a productive tradition of objectivity. But our philosophy might now appear sufficiently consolidated to allow itself a fuller reflection on the nature of our specific human 'genius' and a more daring approach to the question of objectivity.[11]

The expanding interest in metaphor may indicate a prolonged repression of a latent awareness of the life of language and of its specific 'genius'. Having had to recognize literalness as a sedimentation of extinct metaphors, philosophers have become attracted by metaphoric processes as a way to regain the life-dependent quality of our culture. Through such a reconnection of life and thought we also derive a philosophical appreciation of the imaginative and intuitive 'genius' of human linguisticity.

Quine significantly argues that

> the ... absence of an adequate study of imagination in our ... theories of meaning and rationality is symptomatic of a deep problem in our current views of ... cognition. The difficulty ... is not a matter of mere oversight. ... The problem is far more distressing, for it concerns our entire orientation toward these issues, based as it is upon a widely shared set of presuppositions that deny imagination a central role in the constitution of reality.[12]

The paradigms of rationality are in fact still regarded as organizing forms which transcend the structures of affective experience. And although it is usually granted that metaphorical projections may be part of our mental processes in creating novel connections, such attempts are typically regarded as mere 'psychological' antecedents, irrelevant to the construction of our ways of reasoning.

The multiplicity of features contained within imaginative, metaphoric language includes the dynamics of transference, transport, transgression, alienation, impropriety, identity, linkage, mediation, exile, evasion, transformation, deviation, conjunction. A notably diversified array of synergic intellectual activities. When all this is connected with the shared recognition that metaphors also die out in the literalness of normal and accredited discourses (and thus must also be born and develop), we can see that language itself ceases to be an aseptic, abstract field and becomes as challenging as life itself. Metaphoric projection is thus one of the principal means whereby our life-experience gains access to our mental operations. As our human condition of living creatures is coessential to the way we reason,[13] the exploration of transitional links between our biological experiences and dialogic exchanges can ultimately afford an enriched account of human rationality.

THE EVOLUTION OF KNOWLEDGE

It is interesting that Aristotle's treatment of metaphor is significantly open to its social implications. He seems to suggest in a variety of ways that 'slaves' must speak plainly before their masters and thus abstain from the 'genius' of metaphor. For instance: 'it is not quite appropriate that fine language should be used by a slave or a very young man'.[14] Imaginative linguistic efforts may serve in fact to try to transform the worldview of interlocutors and, obviously, slaves are not supposed to compete with their masters – not even in 'metaphoric' terms.

If we regard the 'slave' as an emblematic figure standing for whoever has insufficient contractual power in whatever situation, the injunction to avoid 'fine language'[15] and not to engage in metaphor can be equated with the prohibition that forbids even envisaging changes in a conceptual structure. To ensure that slaves remain constrained in such a stable way that the burden of their own submission does not weigh on the master but is conveniently placed upon the slaves themselves, it is an essential pre-emptive condition that they be persuaded to speak plainly, avoid fine language and keep their minds confined within one vocabulary. Granting permission to address their superiors metaphorically would be comparable to a recognition of the slave's capacity to travel from one epistemic context to another, while their 'own' (imposed) language is confined to producing self-confirming prophecies supporting the epistemology from which it emanates.[16]

The central assumption of any epistemology is that, to be rational, we need to develop a common ground of agreement where all disputes are ultimately susceptible of resolution. In Rorty's version: 'To construct an epistemology is to find the maximum amount of common ground with others. The assumption that an epistemology can be constructed is the assumption that such common ground exists' (1980: 316). In this perspective all 'metaphorical' expressions highlighting the existence of such common ground of rationality will be welcome in any sufficiently normalized culture (in the Kuhnian sense). Such 'metaphors' indeed will be at a premium inasmuch as they strengthen the vocabulary, mentality and ideology which a given epistemic framework encompasses.[17]

On the other hand, should metaphors be created which endanger such alleged common ground, these would be likely to be either ignored or regarded as purely 'metaphorical'. In fact, non-literal expressions indirectly suggesting that there is insufficient common ground in the literalness of our more comprehensive epistemic assumptions seem a provocation against rationality. If certain non-literal expressions are *perceived* as contrary to any normal vocabulary serving to adjudicate knowledge-claims, they may be erroneously or inadvertently construed as daring to insinuate that there are no ways 'at all' for negotiating rational agreement. Even in the lucidity of philosophical debates we easily conclude with the fallacy that moving *away* from something is equivalent to arguing against it. The sort of commensurability advocated within certain epistemic traditions may actually be revealed as the sort of closeness which, while giving the impression of allowing for internal translatability, is actually sustained by one of its frequent by-products – a latent animosity towards foreign epistemologies.

A live language which shares in the organismic domain as well as in the conscious and willed levels of the mind is as problematic for the philosopher as it is for the individual. In order to regulate the varied richness of language, the prevalent human tendency is to acquire idealized standards of normative linguistic behaviour. Reliance on the literalness of cultural concepts may, however, conceal the danger of devaluing all those inner experiences that could perhaps be expressed metaphorically but certainly not in the literal terms of the commensurable standards. On the other hand, reaching for, or prefiguring, a future stage of philosophical maturity, we could appreciate that creative processes may have their own as yet unknown lawfulness which is often obscured and even distorted by our current stringent requirements for intellectual formalizations; at this prefigurative stage we may reacknowledge and explore the profound inner world of beliefs and desires.[18] I am arguing in favour of a transition from the cultural narcissism of isolated intra-commensurable epistemologies pursuing 'objective' knowledge, to a hermeneutic weaving of inter-epistemic circuits.

Along with the exacerbated and dominant forms of literalness, a devaluation of the metaphorically oriented aspects of knowledge is tacitly enforced. Inconspicuous forms of rationality, operating outside of a dominant epistemology, may reveal characteristics such as force, strength, vitality or virtue, even though they exhibit little contractual power. On the other hand, forms of rationality, or persons, who have power, may be lacking in force to such an extent that they conveniently ignore inconspicuous forms of rationality or individuals upon whose force they depend. Although the notions of force and power may be regarded as the basic axes of any cultural coexistence, their logical confusion appears necessary for the safeguard of whatever power is at work. An outlook of static literalness deriving from the excessive valuation of any epistemology may, for instance, conceal the distinction between the power of discourse on the one hand, and the developmental, sustaining force of listening, on the other.[19]

Linguistic philosophy has perhaps supported the custom of formulating problems in such a way that language remains detached from life and from the revolutionary characteristics revealed by the exploration of 'unconscious' processes, as if language could function in a framework of lifelessness. As a result, it remains difficult to understand what the disturbing consequences of profound beliefs and desires might be for our thinking processes. Inevitably, then, we tend to gravitate towards the area of conventional, regulated, literal language with only a formal interest in beliefs and desires.

What is remarkable in philosophical writing is that, usually, in order to typify areas in which regular and predictable descriptive behaviour is *not* at work, authors tend to conjure up examples regarding absolute strangers such as extra-galactics, 'savages' or slaves[20] – in earlier centuries. The hypothesis of such interlocutors is probably more comfortable than the idea of segregated parts of the mind; ultimate strangers, moreover, may be less disquieting than fellow speakers in our own language 'uttering sentences' from too-distant points in the life-cycle, or from unacceptable styles of life operating at the periphery of the regular and hence regulative (language) games.

As the increasingly cosmopolitan condition and growing demands of our global-village world inevitably reverberate in philosophy, special difficulties are created for our rationality to cope with; at the same time, previously unacknowledged resources may be activated for the construal of such a puzzling merging of worldviews.

A clearly codified area of thought, whether among persons or within the same individual, could almost be regarded as a vast tautology within which we can conveniently operate. Thus, the development of some reasonable interaction between different epistemic languages, or between differently 'speaking' aspects of the same mind, stands out as one of the main challenges that the human sciences must face.[21] In this perspective, then, language poses its major problems at the level of inter-linguistic construal, and the recognition of these difficulties will continue as long as the desire for personal or cultural survival is strong enough to make us persist in the metaphoric attempts necessary to reconnect different languages or different domains of literalness.

In fact, the notion of 'polylogism' may not only apply to the diversity of cultures but to the individual as well, where it indicates the coexistence and interaction of several discourses – which might even be expressed in different languages in the case of a multilingual person. The general notion of polylogism thus indicates the diverse strata of our mental organization, the difficulty of complete translations from one internal language to another and the modes of their interaction within the individual. And if we regard polylogism as the general human condition, then polylingualism would appear to be a particularly rich case of polylogism on account of the fact that plurality of discourses is further organized by language differences (Amati Mehler *et al.* 1990).

As other living creatures may be credited with some capacity to think, even though they are not properly verbal, we cannot equate our thinking with language; similarly we cannot equate mastery of a standard language with a sufficient guarantee for comparable experiences and representations. Such uncritical assumptions entail the risk of relapsing into a sort of narcissistic, pre-Babelic illusion of total communication.

Like most myths, perhaps the story of Babel (Genesis 11, 1–9) is also two-sided. On the one side, it tries to indicate the impossibility of attempting bold constructions and maintaining the comfort of a universal communication. On the other side, the myth evokes the nostalgia for an ideal, original condition which once existed and which has had to be relinquished in the process of developing more complex and diversified constructions. Such an ideal antecedent state may be thought of in terms of total 'objective' communication. Like other myths pertaining to the story of human linguisticity, it proclaims the need for an emancipatory separation as a condition for the development of what might be regarded as more powerful forms of world-control. And yet the suspicion remains that the reason why the quest for objective knowledge is at the core of philosophical games may be because it would ultimately 're-establish' an ideal condition of communication in our technological era; such an 'ideal' might explain our inexhaustible search for truth-conditions and standards of meaning.

Our longing for a 'previous' condition of unequivocal language may be what supports our persistent search for standards of accurate representation and objectivity. Should the flourishing research on truth-conditions reach a cluster of conclusive convergences the end result might be sufficient to reproduce a pre-Babelic structure of successful communication.

THE RISKS OF LITERALNESS

Offering advantages such as sparing the individual the tensions of inner life, the adherence and tributes to literalness may ultimately induce us to identify with external situations and objects to the point of actually refusing all forms of inner dynamics. There are persons, remarks Bion, 'whose contact with reality presents most difficulties when that reality is their own mental state' (1978: 9). In this perspective we are quite distant from a view of metaphoric language as an intriguing topic of scholarly concern: the development of metaphoric language appears instead as cogently related to the actual development of our philosophical life. Evolving individuals confined within the unidentifiable constraints of a prevalently literal linguisticity may laboriously seek construals of their metaphoric attempts in interactive conditions different from their own, that is, in other cultural groups which are hospitable to their metaphors and capable of utilizing them; or, conversely, they may creatively develop the art of a secret intra-psychic dialogue as an alternative to impossible interpersonal exchanges.

As the quality of life operating through unequivocal, objective language is oriented towards facts and action, vicissitudes involving beliefs, desires and conflicts come to be regarded as perplexingly non-mental, and simply appear as natural pauses in the regular course of successfully manipulating the world by means of objective knowledge. In such a context, even recreational activities may be lacking in playfulness and may be performed with the same systematic attitude as any other productive activity. And literalist styles tend to shape the quality of life in ways which are difficult to monitor because the standard ways of observation largely depend upon the regular vocabulary underlying our epistemologies.

The literalist inclination could ultimately be viewed as a life-damaging compulsion to be 'normal'. We can identify this propensity whenever a tendency prevails to paraphrase or translate our spontaneous metaphoric attempts into objective literal expressions even at the cost of annulling original meanings and de-symbolizing our own linguisticity. Wittgenstein remarks that

> you can only succeed in extricating people who live in an instinctive rebellion against language; you cannot help those whose entire instinct is to live in the herd which has created this language as its own proper mode of expression.[22]

Should this tendency become systematic to the point where we discard our nascent thoughts, we would then become permanently confined within the boundaries of literalness. And whenever forced to confront complex life situations or 'foreign' areas of literalness, the atrophy of our capacities would be inevitably revealed.

The sort of literal language which is appropriate within certain areas of human culture may be easily amenable to territorial extensions inasmuch as it has come to be hierarchically regarded as the most valuable language – the only one linked with objectivity and thus rightfully entitled to be exported or expand. Such a hierarchization could be fatal to the inner lives of humans and might result in a form of control so severe that it could ultimately damage the joint evolution of affects and cognition.

Ontogenetically, stereotyped ways of literal discourse may be used to keep under control vicissitudes of hope and despair, and such a standardized vocabulary may become ossified into categories which define life itself even though they are remote caricatures of it. The end result is a 'mental' apparatus which only serves the purpose of excluding the individual from life.[23]

Attempts at introspective life are blocked inasmuch as the metaphoric creativity of the subject has been corrected and reduced to a literal language which denies the innumerable vicissitudes of inner life. The persistent prevalence of literal language may stabilize in a sort of behaviour more suited to the discharge of affects than to the communication and use of internal dynamics. In this sort of linguistic life, action is preferable to any sort of elaboration and creativity; substitution of situations, persons and things becomes preferable to any form of repair and transformation. Broken objects are replaced with new objects in a general style emanating from the consumption of standard goods and worldviews rather than from the laborious generation of culture.

And indeed, which literal language would allow for fathoming our own depths in a way that would enable us to gain some familiarity with our profound resources for coping with the world? Once such language is discredited in favour of the literal language whose power is guaranteed by the commensurability of a standard epistemology, no instruments are left for dealing with our own selves.

It is possible that new forms of pathology are now emerging or else that we are now gaining an awareness of painful styles of life which have always existed. These life-damaging inclinations may be conceived of as a tendency to gravitate towards literalness in such a way that more personal and creative expressions are progressively atrophied. What is left is a mute pain due to the curtailment of inner life, while it becomes difficult or impossible to make any sense of one's irrepressible metaphoric efforts. In some cases it is almost as if a literalist vicarious personality were produced, capable only of objective transactions and virtually incapable of authentic interpersonal relations. Almost an inclination to be an object among objects.

What we may ultimately gain from this approach to objectivity is a measure of greater freedom in playing with figures and backgrounds in the exploration of the philosophical language through which we evolve.

NOTES

1 See on this topic Arbib and Hesse (1986). In this integrated account of how humans construct reality through interaction with their social and physical

world, see especially ch. 8: 'Language, metaphor and a new epistemology', pp. 147–61.

2 For a discussion of this problem, see Corradi Fiumara (1990).

3 It is perhaps appropriate to quote a sample piece of testimony from Aristotle:

> For where there is nothing in common to ruler and ruled, there is not friendship either, since there is no justice; e.g. between craftsman and tool, soul and body, master and slave; the latter in each case is benefited by that which uses it, but there is no friendship or justice towards lifeless things.
> Aristotle, *Nicomachean Ethics*, bk viii, 1161a31–1161b2 in Aristotle (1985)

4 The term 'revolutionary' is used in a general Kuhnian sense. See Kuhn (1970).

5 'Metaphor consists in giving a thing a name that belongs to something else' (Aristotle, *Poetics*, 1457f. 8–9 in Aristotle 1985).

6 See on this topic Lakoff and Johnson (1980).

7 Aristotle, *Politics*, bk i, 1252a31–1252b1 in Aristotle (1985).

8 Plato, *Phaedo* 66a in Plato (1960).

9 'The body has an obstructive effect on the soul' (Cottingham 1976: 8). As is known, this same thesis is maintained by Descartes in many of his writings. See Descartes (1985).

10 Aristotle, *The Poetics*, para. 22, 1459a5–8 in Aristotle (1985).

11 'Our skill with metaphor, with thought, is one thing – prodigious and inexplicable; our reflective awareness of that skill is quite another thing – very incomplete, distorted, fallacious, over-simplifying' (Richards 1936: 116).

12 W. V. O. Quine, 'Two dogmas of empiricism' (Quine 1961: 41).

13 Else Barth cogently argues that the distinction between the *social-solipsistic* and *communicative* approaches is of high explanatory value: 'In the philosophy of science, in fact, distinctions between different sorts of human activity are sometimes recognized, but not as so fundamentally different that names have been given to them.' She demonstrates that in logic the situation is even worse since most logicians are very far from recognizing the theoretical interest of the *communicative phase* and the logical dimensions of it (Barth 1991: 87–8).

14 Aristotle, *Rhetoric*, bk iii, 10–15 in Aristotle (1985).

15 Ibid.

16 Significantly, Aristotle remarks: 'I will hereafter explain what is the proper treatment of slaves, and why it is expedient that liberty should always be held out to them as the reward of their services' (Aristotle, *Politics*, bk vii, 1330a30 in Aristotle 1985).

17 In a densely metaphoric style, Aristotle remarks:

> For that which can foresee by the exercise of the mind is by nature lord and master, and that which can with its body give effect to such foresight is a subject and by nature a slave; hence master and slave have the same interest.
>
> (Aristotle, *Politics*, bk i, 1252b1 in Aristotle 1985)

18

> Beliefs, desires and intentions are a condition of language, but language is also a condition for them. On the one hand, being able to attribute beliefs and desires to a creature is certainly a condition of sharing a convention with that creature.
>
> (Davidson 1985: 280)

19 See G. Corradi Fiumara, 'The power of discourse and the strength of listening' (Corradi Fiumara 1990: 52–72).
20 'Now it is clear . . . that the citizens of a state have not found out the secret of managing their subject population' (Aristotle, *Politics*, bk ii, 1269b5–12 in Aristotle 1985).
21 On this problem, see Corradi Fiumara (1992).
22 Ludwig Wittgenstein, Big Typescript MS 213, 423 in Wright (1969: 483–503). Also quoted in A. Kenny, 'Wittgenstein on the nature of philosophy' (McGuinness, 1982: 16).
23 Referring to Wittgenstein's notebooks of the war period, McGuinness remarks that 'It is as if he had bridged – or was about to bridge – some gap between his philosophy and his inner life' (McGuinness 1988: 243).

REFERENCES

Amati Mehler, Jacqueline, Argentieri, S. and Canestri, J. (1990), 'The Babel of the unconscious', *International Journal of Psycho-Analysis*, no. 71, pp. 569–83.

Arbib, Michael and Hesse, Mary B. (1986), *The Construction of Reality*, Cambridge: Cambridge University Press.

Aristotle (1985) *The Complete Works of Aristotle*, the Revised Oxford Translation, 2 vols, edited by Jonathan Barnes, Bollingen Series LXXX 1.2, Princeton: Princeton University Press.

Barth, Else M. (1991), 'Waiting for Godot: on attitudes towards artefacts vs. entities, as related to different phases of operation in cognition', *Epistemologia*, vol. 14, pp. 77–104.

Bion, Wilfred (1978), *Attention and Interpretation: A Scientific Approach to Insight in Psycho-Analysis and Groups*, London: Tavistock.

Corradi Fiumara, Gemma (1990), *The Other Side of Language: A Philosophy of Listening*, London and New York: Routledge.

Corradi Fiumara, Gemma (1992), *The Symbolic Function: Psychoanalysis and the Philosophy of Language*, Oxford: Blackwell.

Cottingham, John (ed.) (1976), *Descartes' Conversation with Burman*, Oxford: Clarendon Press.

Davidson, Donald (1985), *Inquiries into Truth and Interpretation*, Oxford: Clarendon Press.

Descartes René (1985), *The Philosophical Writings of Descartes*, ed. J. Cottingham, R. Stoothoff and D. Murdoch, Cambridge: Cambridge University Press.

Kuhn, Thomas S. (1970), *The Structure of Scientific Revolutions*, Chicago and London: Chicago University Press (first published 1962).

Lakoff, George and Johnson, Mark (1980), *Metaphors We Live By*, Chicago and London: Chicago University Press.

Leder, Drew (1990), *The Absent Body*, Chicago and London: Chicago University Press.

McGuinness, Brian (1988), *Wittgenstein: A life. Young Ludwig 1889–1921*, London: Duckworth.

McGuinness, Brian (ed.) (1982), *Wittgenstein and His Times*, Oxford: Blackwell.

Plato (1960), *Collected Dialogues*, ed. Edith Hamilton and Huntington Cairns, Princeton: Princeton University Press.

Quine, Willard Van Orman (1961), *From a Logical Point of View*, New York: Harper Torchbooks (first published 1953).

Quine, Willard Van Orman (1969), *Ontological Relativity and Other Essays*, New York: Columbia University Press.

Richards, I. A. (1936), *The Philosophy of Rhetoric*, Oxford: Oxford University Press.
Rorty, Richard (1980), *Philosophy and the Mirror of Nature*, Oxford: Blackwell.
Wright, G. H. von (1969), 'The Wittgenstein papers', *Philosophical Review*, vol. 79, pp. 483–503.

3

WOMEN'S EXPERIENCE AND FEMINIST EPISTEMOLOGY

A critical neo-rationalist approach

Marnia Lazreg

> Feminists have this nasty habit of counting bodies and refusing not
> to notice their gender.
>
> (Catharine MacKinnon 1987: 35)

A characteristic feature of 'second wave' feminism is not only its radical critique of extant theories and methodologies both in the social and natural sciences, but also a search for a feminist theory and even epistemology. Indeed all theoretical frameworks were found inadequate and feminists seemed poised to effectuate a new Copernican revolution. Yet, close examination of academic feminism shows a loss of momentum and theoretical stagnation in spite of increased intellectual production. Women have never been written about by so many women, yet the riddle 'woman' has never loomed so large.

There is a sense among some feminists that the task undertaken may be too grand. For example, scientist Elizabeth Fee (1983: 22) noted that 'at this historical moment, what we are developing is not a feminist science, but a feminist critique of existing science'.

Along with this realization of slowed progress, there is an awareness that the feminist intellectual enterprise may not be what it affirms to be: an alternative to traditional ways of knowing. Indeed, it may even unwittingly concur in and reinforce what it has set out to combat. As a result, feminists are now doing a critique of critical feminism. Joan Smith (1983: 89–109), for example, eloquently argues that feminist scholarship, in trying to avoid biological determinism and economic reductionism, 'has come close to achieving the opposite result'.

This chapter contributes to this process of self-examination by questioning the premise on which the present search for a feminist epistemology is grounded. I argue that the existing theoretical stagnation and uncertainty finds its root in feminists' reliance (no matter the conjunctural justification) on the concept of women's experience as the foundation of theory con-

45

struction. Although feminists have denounced positivism for its gender bias, they also base their criticism of conventional knowledge on the concept of experience which, I shall argue, belongs to a classical empiricist tradition, the very source of positivist science. This conception of subjective experience cuts across feminist works of all political persuasions. In this sense, contemporary feminist thinking is marked by some degree of essentialist thinking. Essentialism is understood here as the tendency to conceive of women's experience as providing women, because they are women, with a privileged position in their pursuit of truth. I further argue that reliance on a subjective conception of women's experience leads to a number of methodological paradoxes which jeopardize the project of elaborating a feminist epistemology.

Using major feminist works in the social and natural sciences, I will briefly analyse the ways in which women's experience is invoked and the paradoxes it creates. I am treading a delicate line by recognizing that women's experience is a valuable resource and at the same time arguing that reliance on it implicitly or explicitly bogs the search for a new epistemology in the same quagmire as traditional gender-unaware epistemologies. I will also suggest a possible alternative to the present theoretical impasse.

EXPERIENCE: A CRITICAL TOOL OF THE SOCIAL AND NATURAL SCIENCES

The emergence of women's studies in academic institutions was predicated upon the assertion of the common and universal characteristics of women as encapsulated in the concept of experience. ' "Experience" was seized upon by academic feminists to define a field of study' (Eisenstein and Jardine 1980). Women could be studied separately from other subject-matters; their assumed common experience of womanhood constituted an autonomous area of inquiry. Above and beyond its strategic use in defining women's studies as a new field of knowledge, the concept of experience was also used as a critical tool for analysing the prevailing methods and theories of the social and natural sciences. Feminists drew attention to the invisibility of women in traditional academic disciplines and/or to the 'distortions and misinterpretations of women's experience' (Westcott 1979: 423).

Thus, Elise Boulding was able to point out that historian McNeill's *The Rise Of The West* contained two references to women in 1,000 pages (1976: 4)! Another feminist critic remarked that when woman does figure in men's texts she is 'measured in masculine terms' and 'considered an abstract deviation of the essential humanity, she is a partial man or a negative image of man, or the convenient object of man's needs' (Westcott 1979: 423). The record had therefore to be corrected by either revealing women's experience wherever it was absent (as in history) or introducing it in the social sciences as a 'source of a general expression of the world' so that women could be 'represented equally with men' (Smith 1979: 137, 147).

A critical tool of analysis of the shortcomings of the social and natural sciences, the concept of experience had also become a vantage point from which to elaborate an alternative theory, and for some feminists, an epistemology. It is at the point where the concept of experience is transformed into a multiple-purpose concept that it becomes problematical.

A perusal of feminist sociologists' critiques of sociological theory and methodology reveals a consensus on what is wrong with the discipline and an equally general consensus on what should be done about it. Thus, sociology is seen as typically neglecting the study of feelings and emotions. Arlie Russell Hochschild argues that sociology ought to include the 'feminine eye' and provide a third image of the social actor that is neither only cognitive nor driven by the unconscious. Rather, sociology ought to focus on the 'sentient actor who is both conscious and feeling'. The sociological project consists of determining the relationship between the 'innerworld of feeling' and 'the cultural world of labels' as it takes place within institutional settings such as the family or 'the secretarial pool' (1975: 280, 283, 287–8).

In a similar vein, Anna Yeatman (1986: 160) points out that sociology should include the 'domestic domain' (the domain of women's experiences) as part of the public domain and in this process de-gender the sexual division of labour which accounts for the identification of each domain with one gender.

Dorothy Smith (1979) cogently argues that the methodological requirements of sociological practice 'suspend' the social character of knowledge. In her view scientific objectivity with its 'anonymity, impersonality, detachment and impartiality' has led to the constitution of women as mere 'objects' of knowledge rather than as subjects acting within a historically changing environment and reflecting back on the knower (158). Thus,

> we have learned to discard our experienced worlds as a source of concerns, information and understandings of the actualities of the social world and to confine and focus on 'insights' within the conceptual frameworks and relevances given in the discipline.
>
> (1979: 159)

According to Smith, there is a

> disjuncture . . . between the forms of thought . . . and a world experienced at a level prior to knowledge or expression, prior to that moment at which experience can become 'experience' in achieving social expression or knowledge, or can become 'knowledge' by

achieving that social form, in being named, being made social, becoming actionable.

(1979: 135)

Smith locates this 'rupture in experience' in power relations between men and women, in which 'men dominated over women' (137).

Like Smith, Meredith Gould (1979–80) advocates 'a radical break with prior forms of conceptualization' and proposes to expand the existing sociology of knowledge to incorporate 'women's experiential base' into an autonomous phenomenon. Jessie Bernard (1981: 31) suggests the study of the 'female world' whose existence she legitimates in psychological and political terms. She argues that there is more to the female world than 'oppression'. Excessive emphasis on the latter has 'deleterious effects on female self-image and self-esteem as well as on knowledge'. Studying the female world 'may raise consciousness about the strength of the female world available for dealing with male misogyny and oppression'.

In sum, the critiques of the social sciences as represented by sociologists centres on the poverty of the methodological requirement of *objectivity*, the dualistic nature of sociological concepts, 'the absence of concepts that tap women's experience, the viewing of women as an unchanging essence independent of time and place, and the narrowness of the concept of human being reflected in limited ways of understanding human behaviour' (Westcott 1979: 424–5).

The alternative methodology suggested is exactly the reverse of the one under attack. Thus, Shulamit Reinharz (1983: 171–2) set up a list of the principles and rules of current scientific research and counterposed to them her own. One column shows characteristics of rationality in its instrumental conception; the other subjectivity in its expressive meaning. One would be hard put to disagree with an 'experiential method that would, among other things, emphasize a close relationship between researcher and subject of research, an awareness of one's values that might affect the research process and a greater sensitivity to change'. It is, however, a method that appears to be tailored to narrowly defined feminist needs and goals as far as problem formulation and selection are concerned. In addition, the new method is associated with the political project of 'raising the consciousness of the subjects studied' (e.g. women). It requires a 'feminine cognitive style – in the positive sense of artistic, sensitive, integrated, deep, intersubjective, empathic, associative, affective, open, personalized, aesthetic and receptive' (1983: 183). In fact, as Maria Mies (1983: 122) points out, men may not have the experiential knowledge necessary to study 'exploited groups'. They lack most of all a 'sociological imagination'. This shows the extent to which objectivism in the social sciences is perceived as unmitigated 'masculinism'. Yet it was a male, C. W. Mills, who first attacked the same kind of methodology feminists are opposed to in a book precisely entitled 'the sociological imagination'.

Dorothy Smith (1979: 174) recommends that conceptual frameworks be dropped as the starting-points of social research and the latter begin instead with experience as it unfolds in everyday life. A 'sociology for women' is thus identified with the study of the 'everyday world'. While an adequate knowledge of what women do on a daily basis is welcome, it is essential to bear in mind that women's lives are also affected by what they do not do in the 'everyday world'.

The new methodology sometimes takes the form of a return to the 'personal', which finds its expression in the ethnomethodology of gender. This approach has attracted feminists interested in uncovering the ground rules of gender attribution in the course of everyday social interaction (Kessler and McKenna 1978). Harold Garfinkel's study of transvestite 'Agnes' (1967) is taken as a model for this kind of analysis. Yet ethnomethodology has positivist underpinnings, and may not have the liberating potential it is perceived to have. It aims at uncovering the ground rules that individuals follow consciously or unconsciously in order to carry out their interactions in a seemingly orderly manner. Uncovering rules is different from understanding them or changing them (Bourdieu 1977: 21-32). In this sense, Garfinkel is an heir to Emile Durkheim. His neglect of issues of power may very well go counter to feminists' stated project of change.

The feminist critique of the natural sciences similarly denounces objectivity as a form of male bias (Keller 1982: 590-1). Such bias is manifested in the selection of problems to investigate as well as in the design and interpretation of experiments.

Feminist criticism of the natural sciences, however, is often more tempered and less ready to offer specific alternatives. Thus Margrit Eichler (1980: 129) modestly states that 'most precepts of feminist science still take the form of "don'ts" rather than "do's"'. Going one step further, Elizabeth Fee (1983: 15-16) questions the 'monolithic' view of science as reducible to objectivity.

Similarly, Helen Longino and Ruth Doell (1983: 206-7) denounce feminists' failure to provide a systematic and 'adequate methodological analysis' of science which would focus on a 'more comprehensive understanding of the operation of male bias in science, as distinct from its existence'.

Evelyn Fox Keller (1985) attempted to do just this by criticizing the 'neutrality' and 'objectivity' of natural science.[1] Although she provided insight into the gendered nature of the scientific enterprise, she fell prey to a subjectivist interpretation. She reduced male scientists' propensity to map stereotypical conceptions of gender-relations onto the natural world to the dynamics of their own psychosexual development. A heavy reliance on a psychoanalytic perspective on sexist science can be misleading. Indeed, Keller's view leaves open equally plausible alternative explanations. For example, it may be argued that male scientists' bias is the reflection of unrepressed 'subjectivity' rather than, as Keller points out, impersonal objectivity (117). Paradoxically, Keller also finds herself approving of an eroticized conception of matter which she opposes to an 'adversarial' view. In other words, her 'psychosociology of scientific knowledge' has not transcended the woman's body (126).

Perhaps the most comprehensive analysis of the 'science question in feminism' is Sandra Harding (1986). Her work is crucial because it presents a critique of feminists' 'undertheorization of the whole field [of science]' (20). Going one step further than Keller, she attempts 'to identify the causal tendencies in social life that leave traces of gender projects on all aspects of the scientific enterprise' (35). In spite of her keen awareness of the 'paradoxes' of feminist criticism of the sciences, Harding subscribes to the notion that a woman-centred science is a better science than existing science, at least temporarily. This is so because, according to Harding, a feminist science is based on the woman's experience as it is expressed in menstruation, abortion and self-health care (142–5). Like Keller, she is unable to escape the 'problématique' of the body.

Harding's critique of objectivity rests on her understanding, if not discovery, that science is a social activity. As such it cannot lay claim to value-neutrality. Sociologists have long recognized and studied the social foundations of scientific activity and debated the merits of its value-neutrality. The point is to determine in what ways science could become gender-free once it has become gender-conscious.

In sum, feminist critiques of the social sciences and the natural sciences are based on the concept of experience understood as a configuration of subjective characteristics deemed absent in the sciences questioned, and which only women can provide. Critiques do not sufficiently examine the relationship between objectivity and subjectivity. By opposing one to the other, they implicitly reinforce the very dichotomy they aim at overcoming.

Academic feminists' objections to the methodology of the social and natural sciences are essentially objections to positivism. At stake is an insufficiently articulated rejection of the positivist *philosophy* which holds that science (seen as the search for laws) is the only valid way of knowing, as well as a rejection of the positivist practice of objectivity equated with the erasure of women.

Although experience provides the vantage point from which to criticize the social and natural sciences, it is seldom defined in any systematic way. It is generally taken as a given, a self-explanatory concept that each feminist specifies in her own way. Thus, it is used to refer alternately to feelings, emotions, the personal, personality, 'line of fault', etc. . . . (Smith 1979: 135). The conflation of the various meanings (social, psychological and physiological) attributed to the concept of experience is a source of distortion. Indeed, my social position may explain my actions in the world. However, my biological characteristics may be incidental to them. This conflation of meaning reflects an essentialist assertion of womanhood. In this sense the feminist movement since its inception in the 1960s, may be analysed as an act of public assertion of the female constitutive self (see Firestone 1970; Atkinson 1974; Rich 1976; Daly 1978; Hartsock 1983; Gilligan 1980). This is fine, but can we build a new epistemology on a conception of experience as elusive as it is diverse and multiple, as we begin to think of the concrete cultural, national, economic and political contexts that shape the world's women's lives?

This approach is by necessity a-historical. It is unable to answer a number of crucial questions. For example, can experience and experience alone constitute a valid basis for knowledge? Should knowledge about women dispense with scientific criteria? In other words, what is the relationship between science and experience? Can we know women scientifically?

EMPIRICISM, FEMINISM AND EXPERIENCE

In so far as experience is central to the empiricist philosophy and theory of knowledge, one might think that feminists' use of this concept is grounded in a discernible intellectual tradition. Yet feminists generally do not explicitly seek any grounding for experience and often act as if they had just discovered its import. It seems as though any relationship between feminists' use of experience and that of acknowledged empiricists is either fortuitous or the result of the unexamined (and therefore unsuspected) effect of an intellectual tradition steeped in pragmatism and positivism.

It is worth recalling that pragmatism, which has suffused American schools and universities since the nineteenth century, has received little attention from feminists. Yet, as John Dewey put it, pragmatism 'is merely empiricism pushed to its legitimate conclusions' (Novack 1973: 29). In this sense, empiricism appears in the feminist theoretical discourse as its 'diurnal philosophy', existing but unstated (Bhaskar 1978: 255). This has had fateful consequences as will be shown below.

The most significant characteristic of empiricist philosophy is that it neglects a number of crucial issues: (1) it does not address the contradiction between the individual character of experience and the social character of knowledge. As a social product, knowledge constitutes a 'material cause' of cognitive acts. Knowledge at any given time includes 'antecedent knowledge, facts and theories' (Bhaskar 1978: 187). While knowledge may not be analysed in terms of individual experiences, it is however analysable in terms of the *social* category of experience. This means that 'my experience includes *the experience of others*' (187). As far as feminist theorizing is concerned, this means that the concept of experience as it is currently used is insufficient since it includes men as a referent rather than as a constitutive component. Men are usually seen as having constructed women's reality instead of being engaged in a continuous process of interaction with women that is equally constructive of *their* reality. (2) Empiricist philosophy does not investigate the conditions under which experience becomes 'epistemically significant in science' (Bhaskar 1978: 30). Is all experience relevant, for example, to a theory of knowledge?

THE PARADOXES OF FEMINIST EMPIRICISM

The preceding discussion makes it clear that I am not using the phrase 'feminist empiricism' in the way that Sandra Harding did (1991: 111–18). She defines it as feminists' desire to cleanse research of its anti-women biases through stricter adherence to scientific methodology and a greater involvement of women in research activities. Indeed, to overcome gender-bias, feminist empiricism could not simply adhere to the canons of existing scientific practice as Harding suggests. It still has to rely on an 'extra' corrective criterion. In other words, what is the 'feminist' component of 'feminist empiricism' based upon if not some conception of experience? Harding leaves untouched the question as to whether the feminization of the scientific practice can affect the 'norms of science' (1991: 113).

A number of paradoxes implicit in feminist scholarship become evident when the relationship between feminism as a theoretical practice and empiricism is examined.

(1) In their attempts to oppose the scientistic bias inherent in positivist social and natural science, feminists have appealed to experience in an ontologized form – the very foundation of the view they struggle against. To claim that women's experience is a source of true knowledge as well as the substance of the world to be known (the 'female world') constitutes the same 'epistemic fallacy' as the one encountered by classical empiricists. In other words, identifying the characteristics of women living in a male-dominated society does not necessarily mean that these characteristics constitute knowledge of women.

The feminist position is doubly jeopardized in that it does not recognize that an epistemology based in experience may not yield access to knowledge of the social structures within which experience takes place or to the social antecedents of that same experience. Furthermore, it does not recognize that the 'female world' so constituted is the creation of neither females nor males alone and requires for its elucidation a genuinely integrated theoretical effort, one that frees itself of the body, be it men's or women's. We need to know how men envision their own reality, how women interpret men's reality, as well as the reality men interpret for them.

(2) The masked ontology inherent in the epistemic concept of experience is antithetical to feminists' desire to be free from the constraints of estab-

lished systems of knowledge. It is equally at odds with the feminist project to make visible women's contribution to human history. Indeed, as pointed out earlier, the feminist/empiricist conception of experience as the only source of valid knowledge confines women to the realm of the experience-able. That which is not experienced is (implicitly) not knowable or worthy of being known. That which exists but is not experienced is either neglected or deemed beyond the pale.

Thus, the experience of 'other' women (from different cultures or races) is either denied (and subsumed under one's own) or deemed incomprehensible except to those women. Yet the study of these women is the testing-ground of the validity of feminist knowledge. Feminist scholarship about these women is by and large based on the construction of an abstract anthropological subject deemed 'oppressed' and the documentation of such 'oppression'. Studies of women in the Middle East, especially Algeria (Lazreg 1990) constitute the most telling examples of this research practice. When some women strive to look into 'other' women's experiences without neutralizing them they still end up providing distorted accounts of them. Indeed, in wanting to document the various ways in which different women construct their worlds and manage their lives, researchers lose sight of their involvement in a double problem of crucial epistemological significance.

First, *they* have objectified 'other' women by turning them into objects of their study. This may very well be an inescapable fact of doing research. However, as feminists we must confront its ethical consequences, for example, the appropriation of 'other' women's voices. Second, the process of studying 'other' women results in constructing for them a new subjectivity. This new subjectivity may intersect with the one experienced by the women in question. However, there is no guarantee that it does, and it often does not. I have yet to understand myself, to find myself, in the studies done by feminists about Middle Eastern women. This means that there is no mechanism (epistemological or otherwise) whereby women can move from one type of experience to another. Hence the fact that as scholarship about women in western societies has increased there has not been a parallel increase in feminists' ability to understand women whose experiences (as culturally framed) are different from theirs. The individualistic character of experience so conceived does not allow for intersubjectivity, a necessary requirement for the understanding of difference within and between gender.

I find Harding's formulation of the questions she raises about what it would mean for western feminists to 'learn from the standpoint of women of Third World descent' (1991: 245) in their musings over science and technology interesting but troubling. First, I have yet to know what it means to be of 'Third World descent'. These women's counterparts are defined as 'First World', 'North Atlantic', of 'European descent'. Although these labels are an improvement over the generic 'women of colour', they are still inadequate and beg the issue. Non-Third World women (why not?) are said to 'learn to ask different questions by starting their thought from accounts that begin in Third World women's lives'. This solution is mechanistic. Is it a matter of asking the right questions? Or is it a matter of coming to grips with the fact that 'First World' women's lives are another modality of 'Third World' women's lives? It is symptomatic of Harding's ambivalence that she uses the terms (borrowed from A. Rich) of 'disloyalty to civilization' to refer to what 'First World' women ought to do to broaden their horizons.[2] Implied here, although with a dash of irony, is the notion that de-centring one's self may be perceived as a loss of 'civilization' But is it? What is civilization?

This experiential ontology further prevents feminists from dealing with the woman question in their work as a historically evolving phenomenon. Indeed, if women's experience defines the world, *there is no independent criterion against which to test feminist constructions of that world*. The a-historical bias in feminist theorizing affects even those among feminists who claim to be dealing with historical phenomena. For example, the work of Zillah Eisenstein (1979: 5–55) and Heidi Hartmann (1979: 206–47) on patriarchy is in fact a-historical in the sense that patriarchy (conceived as 'male supremacy') is analysed as constant (therefore unchanging) and can only be understood in terms of itself. Patriarchy is portrayed as the expression of maleness, and therefore biology. Although feminist historians have generally been less reductive in their approach to women than sociologists and psychologists, they have not always been able to escape the temptation to essentialize women's 'historical experience'.[3]

(3) The constructionist trend in feminist theorizing seems to be a consequence of the paradoxical empiricist conflation of experience with the world. The individual, the knower, stands in a privileged relation to reality, whose structures are ultimately in herself. Yet, this feminist knower does not have the status of a subject endowed with consciousness which might escape men's reification, manipulation or construction of it, assertions to the contrary notwithstanding.

The poverty of experience as theorized may very well account for a number of feminists' attraction to the discursive/deconstructionist approach to social reality. 'Discourse' dispenses with the crucial issue of consciousness as an identifiable historical component of the relationship between self and society.

(4) The discontinuous nature of experience, the world and knowledge is left unexamined by feminists. They often assume an unwarranted correspondence between the three orders of reality. Individual experiences may be 'out of phase' with the knowledge they make possible or with the nature of the world they inform us about. In other words, a woman's experiences as a woman may not determine her behaviour. Feminist historians and anthropologists have increasingly uncovered the existence of a

feminist practice (in the sense of a gender-conscious activity) at times and in societies where feminism would have been 'objectively' deemed impossible. Yet their findings have not been used to theorize experience.

(5) Last but not least, the ontological use of experience relies on the very foundation that the feminist theoretical project seeks to dispel. Assumed is a female 'nature' that women's experience reveals. How else can one understand the argument that 'woman' is a social construction, while experience (defined in feminist terms) is called upon to explain what in fact she *is* after she has dismantled men's 'construction' of her?

Alison Jaggar's discussion of the role played by the 'woman's standpoint' in developing a feminist epistemology underscores this paradox (1983: chs 6, 11). Implicitly, the woman's standpoint is seen as neutral in the sense of not being interest-bound. It is also claimed to demystify a male-constructed reality. This may be so, except that the new standpoint itself reflects the 'interests' or needs of *one* human group only. There is still a need for a standpoint that transcends feminist and 'masculinist' views, each being a partial view of reality.

In sum, contemporary feminists' use of experience as the foundation of a theory of knowledge fits into the tradition of the empiricist school of philosophy and encounters many of the same epistemological problems.

IS A FEMINIST EPISTEMOLOGY POSSIBLE?

The search for a woman-centred epistemology has resulted in a disappointing eclecticism, primarily due to the feminist quandary about what to do with existing epistemologies. For example, Louise Levesque-Lopman's laudable attempt at using existing phenomenological tools of analysis to do feminist research is nevertheless also confined to 'the world as women actually experience it' (1988: xiii). Jane Duran's search for a 'gynocentric model' for a feminist epistemology rests on a combination of cognitive psychology and feminist insights provided by Carol Gilligan. Duran's proposal is as disembodied as the one she rejects. To wit: 'The fleshed-out version of the model with which we are already working, CCP [Contextualist and Communicative Principles], is inherently related to the computational model of the mind' (1991: 124).

A search for a valid epistemology must confront three main problems: first, knowledge of women must be scientific without necessarily being positivistic. Although it is important to point out the gendered character of science, it is no less important to investigate existing alternative models of scientific inquiry. For example, the feminist view of science overlaps with *Naturphilosophie* of the nineteenth century. This romantic philosophy of science was daring and ambitious in its scope. As Gusdorf (1985: 327) put it, it was 'able to take on the universe and elaborate adequate concepts, in contrast with positivistic agnosticism with its intellectual and moral restrictions that deny human consciousness the right to a vision of totality'. In the absence of a shared and generalized capacity for ESP, it does not seem possible to dispense with science.

Second, knowledge of women must confront the ontological issue implicit in grounding itself in the female subject. One implication of this fact is the assumption that there is a female nature that has a privileged access to truth. A second and opposite implication is that there is no truth, and that knowledge based on the female subject is as valid as knowledge based on an androcentric subject. Either way, feminist epistemology is doomed to intellectual ghettoization. Only power can determine which epistemology will predominate. Postmodernist feminism (Rabine 1988; Poovey 1988; Diamond and Quinby 1988), often seen as a tool of epistemic liberation of women, is unable to provide an alternative way of theorizing gender other than in terms of discursive resistance. Indeed, postmodernist feminism is predicated upon the death of the subject which is replaced by the 'grammatical subject, a fictitious support of discourse' (Poovey 1988: 333).

Third, the radical relativism inherent in feminists' theorizing must be examined. If the present state of the social and natural sciences bespeaks more error than truth, then an idea of truth must be upheld that has an independent existence from individual experience yet is acceptable to collectivities. The idea of truth cannot simply be jettisoned. The constructionist stance at the core of feminist enquiry has addressed the causes of the social constructions of women primarily as the product of men's will and domination as expressed in the concept of 'patriarchy', a transhistorical system that can only be explained by reference to itself. Reconstructing women differently cannot dispense with some idea of truth without running the risk of theorizing 'as if' men did not exist. The fact that some men did the same to women is no excuse.

Fourth, perhaps it is time to clearly distinguish the notion of the 'subject' from the notion of the 'body'. The philosophical category for the 'subject' is analytically separate from the biological and sociological categories of the 'body'. The 'body' has itself been the subject of a categorical split between 'sex' (biology/nature) and gender (sociology/culture). The insistence upon the dichotomy sex/gender has escaped feminist criticism of binary oppositions. It has also led to a politics of gender-identity whereby one identifies one's self as a woman, and looks at the world 'as a woman' (Spelman 1988: 160–87). This is responsible for what Donna Haraway (1991: 134–5) has termed an inability to see 'how bodies including sexualized and racialized bodies appear as objects of knowledge and sites of intervention in "biology" '. In addition, she points out that 'gender identity discourse is also intrinsic to feminist racism, which insists on the non-reducibility and antagonistic relation of coherent women and men'.

The ways in which experience has been used show that the concept has turned into what Bachelard (1974: 163) called in another context an 'epistemological obstacle'. It has been 'placed before and above criticism, a necessary and integral element of the scientific mind'. In other words, experience itself must be subjected to criticism. This critical practice gives to objectivity its meaning, understood as a process rather than the opposite of subjectivity. The scientific mind, according to Bachelard, 'must criticize everything: sensation, common sense, even the most constant practice, even etymology, for, the word which is made to sing and seduce rarely encounters thought' (123).[4]

This exercise is all the more important in that science (again!) is now providing evidence that men, just like women, experience bodily changes assumed to be associated with women only. This has epistemological implications in the sense that the present feminist focus on incontrovertible *differences* between women and men must be rethought. The very notion of a gendered subject serving as a centre of knowledge must be re-examined.

The kind of rationalism suggested here is different from the one that feminists have rejected. It is true that classical philosophical thought was marked by a 'fixed rationalism' based on the Aristotelian formalistic principle of identity (A=A). It maintained a sort of imperial affirmation of a consensus of all human beings before the occurrence of any experience (Bachelard 1974: 108). In so doing it also excluded some people (men and women) from the realm of reason.

A modified conception of rationalism as advocated by Bachelard is a useful point of departure for feminists in their attempt to explain gender relations. If feminism is to take part in a scientific culture, it must begin with an 'affective *and* intellectual catharsis... in order to finally give reason reasons to evolve' (162). Bachelard proposes a rationalism that allows for the diversity and multiplicity of experiences. It is a dialectical rationalism that acknowledges the structured nature of culture-bound rationalisms or 'regional rationalisms' and attempts to go beyond immediate experience to achieve 'scientific experience' (109, 160).

Within this perspective, 'reason does not have the right to give a privileged status to immediate experience'. The scientific experience is seen as 'essentially a rectification of knowledge, a broadening of the frameworks of knowledge.... Its structure forms the consciousness of its historical mistakes.'

The assumed collective character of women's experience may be necessary to engage in the act of negating antecedent knowledge but it is not sufficient to rectify that knowledge and transform it. A new object of knowledge must be constituted which *includes* what is negated. In the absence of a constituted feminist 'problématique' – the site of interaction between experience and constituted knowledge – there logically seems to be little validity to our claim that the extant knowledge about women is biased (Bachelard 1974: 128). Indeed, feminists are currently faced with the task of having to confront inadequate conceptions of women on grounds other than that such conceptions do not allow for subjectivity.

CONCLUSION

This chapter has shown how the concept of experience has often been reduced to refer to the body in its natural or social functions. It pointed out that the feminist claim that experience constitutes a tool of critical analysis, a worldview and a ground for a new epistemology is problematical.

The current use of experience by feminist social scientists is an unexamined outgrowth of the classical empiricists' conception of knowledge. As such it suffers from the same shortcomings, namely: an 'epistemic fallacy' whereby experience is given ontological status, and a form of methodological individualism whereby reality is seen as analysable in terms of individual experiences. These shortcomings are at the core of the paradoxes of empiricist thought as practiced by contemporary academic feminists.

Should experience then be rejected as the foundation of a valid feminist epistemology? The answer to this question revolves around the aims that feminism as an intellectual movement is expected to accomplish. Knowledge of women does not require any specific feminist epistemology. A feminist epistemology might be an answer to a 'masculinist epistemology'. But it does not seem to be an answer to the current crisis of 'western' knowledge. Knowledge conceived of as a corrective to a one-sided knowledge of women (or, for that matter, of men of different classes, races or cultures) cannot be gender- (or class- or race-) based without defeating its purpose.

Women's experience writ large may and should be used as a way of defining a 'problématique' requiring the application of self-critical rational thought to immediate experience as it encounters constituted knowledge. Experience may and can provide insights into the relationship between gender and social structure. However, the establishment of a subjectivist epistemology based on the body may only end where it began: in the body.

It is time to bring experience down from the pedestal it has been placed on and examine it critically. The essentialist element in feminist thought of all intellectual persuasions must be seen as a moment in its development. It bears similarities with the 'Black is beautiful' movement and 'négritude' movement in their celebration of a unique selfhood. Unlike these movements, feminism also makes a claim to political power which transcends the boundaries of a gendered special group. The present crisis requires a search for an approach that places experience in its proper perspective; a search for a science that is empirical without being empiricist (Bernstein 1983), 'an alternative to the positivism that has usurped the title of science'

(Bhaskar 1978: 8). The choice is not between science and experience, objectivity and subjectivity. The point is to realize that objectivity is an ever-receding goal and to strive to reach it is an unending historical process.

The suggested neo-rationalist approach combines features of Bachelard's 'supra-rationalist' conception of science and Bhaskar's materialistic realism. This view proposes to recognize the existence of reason alongside sense-perception. It also emphasizes the reality of antecedent knowledge within which and against which feminist thought must define itself.

There are already trends among feminists that are favourable to redirecting feminist academic practice towards a neo-rationalist goal. Sandra Harding (1984: 50) advocates a 'more modern conception of rationality'. Similarly Isaac Balbus suggests a 'new form of non-instrumental, empathic reason' (1982: 286).

Finally, women's experience has no privileged or immutable nature. It is part of social activity, historically specific and susceptible to change. The task before feminists is to determine the conditions under which such activity becomes genderized. It is also to capture what is *human* in women and men.

Underlying this perspective is a notion of freedom. Women cannot be reduced to their experiences without denying them the will and ability to change. They cannot be perceived as mere shells filled with the sum of their sense-perceptions. A sociology of freedom in spite of social determinations is perhaps more difficult to achieve than a sociology of victimization. But it is worth a try!

NOTES

NB This chapter deals primarily with academic feminists, often referred to in the text as 'feminists'. Although I take a hard critical look at a number of feminists, it goes without saying that I do not think or believe that feminist scholarship is wrong. I merely seek to challenge feminists to question the premises on which their work rests.

1 What is problematic about Keller's conception of a feminist science is her ambiguity. For example, it is not clear whether Barbara McClintock's achievement is due to her being a female (having a 'feeling for the organism'), a marginal scientist or both. The danger of biological reductionism is too great to ignore. Indeed, women's assumed connectedness to nature appears to account for their insights into the object of the sciences. This begs the question that Longino and Doell rightly raise in relation to scientific discovery and gender. They argue that Galileo, a man, dared question the notion that 'man' was at the centre of the universe. He threatened 'the medieval idea that human uniqueness was signified by the earth's location at the centre of the universe created by God' (1983: 207). The authors call for a distinction to be made between psychological, cultural and logical issues in criticizing sexism in the sciences.
2 I find it interesting that Sandra Harding (1986) would point out that feminism draws on movements of political liberation taking place in the Third World.

She further argues that there are similarities between the 'African worldview' (suppressed by colonial domination) and the feminist standpoint. While she develops this line of inquiry with a great deal of caution, she falls short of drawing any conclusion from it. As a non-western woman, I interpret the rise of the 'feminine worldview' as part of the logical development of 'western' social, economic and political thought. The 'African worldview' (if indeed there is one defined as categorically as Harding does using Vernon Dixon's formulation) stems from a different historical context. As a formerly colonized woman, I find it difficult to equate colonialism in the Third World with gender inequality in Europe or North America. This is a case where thinking by analogy muddies issues instead of clarifying them. It is instructive to note that Harding raised the question as to whether African women, who partake in the 'African worldview', are not in fact in a better position than European/American women to develop a feminist epistemology, but avoided giving an answer to it (Harding 1986: 195).

3 Gerda Lerner (1979: 145–59, 168–80) has discussed from a critical perspective the various approaches adopted by feminist historians.

4 It must be noted that one of the few discussions of reason was made by Carol McMillan (1982). She argued that by ignoring an investigation of the role played by reason in the dialectical relationship between 'man' and 'nature', feminists 'encourage a new sexism which makes it impossible to see the motivation for adopting a sexist position as anything other than a sort of will-to-power' (57).

REFERENCES

Atkinson, Ti-Grace (1974), *Amazon Odyssey*, New York: Links Books.

Bachelard, Gaston (1974), *Textes choisis*, ed. Dominique Lecourt, Paris: Presses Universitaires de France.

Balbus, Isaac (1982), *Marxism and Domination*, Princeton: Princeton University Press.

Bartky, Sandra Lee (1977), 'Toward a phenomenology of feminist consciousness' in *Feminism and Philosophy*, ed. Mary Vetterling-Braggin, Frederick A. Elliston and Jane English, Totowa, NJ: Littlefield, Adams and Co., pp. 22–34.

Bernard, Jessie (1981), *The Female World*, New York: The Free Press.

Bernstein, Richard (1983), *Beyond Objectivism and Relativism*, Philadelphia: University of Pennsylvania Press.

Bhaskar, Roy (1978), *A Realist Theory of Science*, Atlantic Highlands, NJ: Humanities Press.

Bhaskar, Roy (1979), 'On the possibility of social scientific knowledge and the limits of naturalism' in *Epistemology, Science, Ideology*, ed. John Mepham and David-Hillel Ruben, Atlantic Highlands, NJ: Humanities Press, pp. 107–40.

Boulding, Elise (1976), *The Underside of History*, Boulder, CO: Westview Press.

Bourdieu, Pierre (1977), *Outline of a Theory of Practice*, Cambridge: Cambridge University Press.

Daly, Mary (1978), *Gyn/Ecology: The Metaethics of Radical Feminism*, Boston: Beacon Press.

Diamond, Irene and Quinby, Lee (eds) (1988), *Feminism and Foucault*, Boston: Northeastern University Press.

Duran, Jane (1991), *Toward a Feminist Epistemology*, Savage, MD: Rowman and Littlefield.

Eichler, Margrit (1980), *The Double Standard*, New York: St Martin's Press.

Eisenstein, Hester and Jardine, Alice (1980), *The Future of Difference*, Boston: G. K. Hall and Co.

Eisenstein, Zillah (1979), 'Developing a theory of capitalist patriarchy' in *Capitalist Patriarchy and the Case for Socialist Feminism*, ed. Zillah R. Eisenstein, New York: Monthly Review Press, pp. 5–40.

Fee, Elizabeth (1983), 'Women's nature and scientific objectivity' in *Women's Nature*, ed. Marian Lowe and Ruth Hubbard, New York: Pergamon Press, pp. 9–27.

Firestone, Shulamith (1970), *The Dialectic of Sex*, New York: Bantam Books.

Garfinkel, Harold (1967), *Studies in Ethnomethodology*, Englewood Cliffs, NJ: Prentice Hall.

Gilligan, Carol (1980), 'In a different voice: women's conception of self and of morality' in *The Future of Difference*, ed. Hester Eisenstein and Alice Jardine, Boston: G. K. Hall and Co., pp. 247–317.

Gould, Meredith (1979–80), 'The new sociology', *Signs*, vol. 5, no. 3, pp. 459–67.

Gusdorf, Gustave (1985), *Le Savoir romantique de la nature*, vol. 12, Paris: Payot.

Haraway, Donna J. (1991), *Simians, Cyborgs and Women*, New York: Routledge and London: Free Association Books.

Harding, Sandra (1984), 'Is gender a variable in conceptions of rationality – a survey of issues' in *Beyond Domination*, ed. Carol C. Gould, Totowa, NJ: Rowman and Allanheld, pp. 43–63.

Harding, Sandra (1986), *The Science Question in Feminism*, Ithaca: Cornell University Press.

Harding, Sandra (1991), *Whose Science? Whose Knowledge? Thinking from Women's Lives*, Ithaca: Cornell University Press.

Hartmann, Heidi (1979), 'Capitalism, patriarchy and job segregation by sex' in *Capitalist Patriarchy and the Case for Socialist Feminism*, ed. Zillah R. Eisenstein, New York: Monthly Review Press, pp. 206–47.

Hartsock, Nancy (1983), *Money, Sex and Power*, New York: Longman.

Hochschild, Arlie R. (1975), 'The sociology of feeling and emotion: selected possibilities' in *Another Voice*, ed. Marcia Millman and Rosabeth Moss Kanter, New York: Anchor Doubleday, pp. 280–307.

Jaggar, Alison M. (1983), *Feminist Politics and Human Nature*, Brighton: Harvester.

Keller, Evelyn Fox (1982), 'Feminism and science', *Signs*, vol. 7, no. 3, pp. 589–602.

Keller, Evelyn Fox (1985), *Reflections on Gender and Science*, New Haven: Yale University Press.

Kessler, Suzanne J. and Wendy McKenna (1978), *Gender – An Ethnomethodological Approach*, New York: John Wiley and Sons.

Kimball, Gayle (ed.) (1981), *Women's Culture – The Women's Renaissance in the Seventies*, Metuchen, NJ: The Scarecrow Press.

Lazreg, Marnia (1990), 'Feminism and difference: the perils of writing as a woman on women in Algeria' in *Conflicts in Feminism*, ed. Marianne Hirsch and Evelyn Fox Keller, New York: Routledge, pp. 326–48.

Lerner, Gerda (1979), *The Majority Finds Its Past*, New York: Oxford University Press.

Levesque-Lopman, Louise (1988), *Claiming Reality: Phenomenology and Women's Experience*, Savage, MD: Rowman and Littlefield.

Longino, Helen and Doell, Ruth (1983), 'Body bias and behavior: a comparative analysis of reasoning in two areas of biological science', *Signs*, vol. 9, no. 2, pp. 206–27.

MacKinnon, Catharine A. (1987), *Feminism Unmodified: Discourses on Life and Law*, Cambridge, MA and London: Harvard University Press.

McMillan, Carol (1982), *Women, Reason and Nature*, Princeton: Princeton University Press and Oxford: Blackwell.

Mies, Maria (1983), 'Toward a methodology for feminist research' in *Theories of Women's Studies*, ed. Gloria Bowles and Renate Duelli Klein, Boston: Routledge and Kegan Paul, pp. 117–39.

Mills, C. Wright (1966), *Sociology and Pragmatism*, New York: Oxford University Press.

Novack, George (1973), *Empiricism and Its Evolution*, New York: Pathfinder Press.

Poovey, Mary (1988), 'Feminism and deconstruction', *Feminist Studies*, vol. 14, no. 1, pp. 51–65.

Rabine, Leslie W. (1988), 'A feminist politics of non-identity', *Feminist Studies*, vol. 14, no. 1, pp. 11–31.

Reinharz, Shulamit (1983), 'Experiential analysis: a contribution to feminist research' in *Theories of Women's Studies*, ed. Gloria Bowles and Renate Duelli Klein, Boston: Routledge and Kegan Paul, pp. 162–91.

Rich, Adrienne (1976), *Of Woman Born*, New York: W. W. Norton and Co.

Smith, Dorothy E. (1979), 'A sociology for women' in *The Prism of Sex*, ed. Julia A. Sherman and Evelyn Thornton Beck, Madison, WI: University of Wisconsin Press, pp. 135–88.

Smith, Joan (1983), 'A feminist analysis of gender: a mystique' in *Women's Nature*, ed. Marian Lowe and Ruth Hubbard, New York: Pergamon Press, pp. 89–109.

Spelman, Elizabeth V. (1988), *Inessential Woman*, Boston: Beacon Press.

Westcott, Marcia (1979), 'Feminist criticism of the social sciences', *Harvard Educational Review*, vol. 49, no. 4 (November), pp. 422–30.

Yeatman, Anna (1986), 'Women, domestic life and sociology' in *Feminist Challenges*, ed. Carole Pateman and Elizabeth Gross, Sydney: Allen and Unwin, pp. 157–72.

4

THE END OF MORALITY?

Sabina Lovibond

Feminist theory and postmodernist theory have a common stake in the project which defines 'worldly philosophy' (see Habermas 1987: 52) – that of contributing to the historical self-awareness of their own age. They thus have a common interest in the status of that cluster of ideas which has been constitutive of the western humanist tradition, and which is receiving correspondingly intense scrutiny from the growing band of commentators who believe we are living through the demise of that tradition.[1] Feminism, as Seyla Benhabib has noted (1991: 137–9), has played an active part in the elaboration of such characteristically anti-humanist themes as the 'death of man', the 'death of history' and the 'death of metaphysics'. Yet these discussions are inherently destabilizing in that they leave us wondering how, if at all, the normative commitments of a movement of resistance to sexual domination can be made intelligible against the background of a philosophy which forswears Enlightenment categories such as 'emancipation', 'progress' and 'critique'.

Although 'endism'[2] made dramatic advances during the 1980s both in academic and in more topical writing, it has in fact a much longer history, beginning (arguably) with Hegel's portrayal of his own system as a culmination of past speculative efforts. The idea that philosophy itself may be coming to an end has subsequently been nurtured by thinkers as diverse as Marx and Heidegger, and qualifies today as virtually mainstream (see Baynes, Bohman and McCarthy 1987). My starting-point in this chapter will likewise be a classic text: Nietzsche's announcement of the *end of morality* in the closing pages of his *Genealogy of Morals* (1887).

> As the will to truth gains self-consciousness . . . morality will gradually *perish* now: this is the great spectacle in a hundred acts reserved for the next two centuries in Europe – the most terrible, most questionable, and perhaps also the most hopeful of all spectacles.
>
> (Nietzsche 1969: Essay III, §27)

This particular 'endist' thesis appears at first sight to relate to a clearly delimited region of our experience. But the appearance is potentially misleading, for Nietzsche's 'morality' comprises not just the sphere of values and conduct, but the whole restless compulsion to measure *reality* against our ideals and to labour over the defects which this comparison brings to light. And since one of the realities that we treat in this way is the *cognitive state* in which we may find ourselves at any given moment, 'morality' in this inclusive sense is as much an epistemological as a practical category: it consists in an orientation not only towards goodness, but also towards truth.[3]

For Nietzsche, what makes the will to truth especially piquant and 'questionable' is the element of cruelty expressed in rationalist, or truth-orientated, habits of thought. The advent of 'morality' in the narrow sense acquaints humanity with a kind of self-directed violence, the object of which is to bring our actions (and eventually our thoughts) into line with moral imperatives; 'morality' in the extended sense enriches the idea of purposive suffering by making us responsible also to the imperatives of science (*Wissenschaft*). In the case of positivism (the method of the natural sciences as standardly conceived), these imperatives centre on a demand for the expulsion of sensuous elements from the life of enquiry (Nietzsche 1969: Essay III, §24); while in the case of more sophisticated accounts of the truth-seeking process – accounts which owe more to the dialectical tradition and which represent truth as 'idealized rational acceptability'[4] – violence is present in the guise of *critique*. The critical impulse manifests itself in the will to 'burn a contradiction, a contempt, a "No" ' (Nietzsche 1969: Essay II, §18) into the body of our existing belief-system, to purge it of its faults (for example, of any peculiarities of cognitive viewpoint (see Williams 1978: 240 ff.), and make it *worthy* of acceptance.

As an alternative to this epistemology of displaced aggression, Nietzsche permits himself the dream of a post-moral condition of 'second innocence'. This would consist not in a renunciation of violence, injury and exploitation, but in *forgetfulness* of the guilt imputed to us by the moral interpretation of existence; not in the disappearance of 'evil' from the world, but in the supersession of the perspective from which 'evil', and consequently guilt, are visible at all. On the side of cognition, accordingly, it would mean an end to the conviction that one is *responsible* to all the relevant evidence or arguments; that one cannot possibly have a *right* to one's present intellectual position; that it is bound to be untenable by universal or absolute standards. The alternative attitude would be that of the one who speaks without first asking himself whether his utterance will be acceptable to others – to the 'community of enquirers', the bearers of that shared, stable body of opinion in which realist epistemology invites us to take refuge. Speech as the manifestation of an *active* (as opposed to 'reactive') force would disdain to make itself answerable to the judgement of the 'herd'. For 'there is *only* a perspective seeing, *only* a perspective "knowing" '; judgement cannot be purged of all wilfulness or affect, and if it could, 'what would that mean but to *castrate* the intellect?'[5]

It is this distinctive, and more abstract, 'morality' – the kind that informs the entire truth-orientated habit of thought – which seems to provide an implicit point of reference for much postmodernist theory, and to be conceptually connected with the Enlightenment values exposed to sceptical attention there. And it is 'morality' in this sense whose prospects will occupy the rest of my discussion. My argument will be that although there may be abundant justification, from the perspective of any given historically situated subject, for an ironic or suspicious attitude to the regulative ideals of rational discourse, still the attempt to reject all subjective identification with these ideals leads to positions from which it is unclear that any normative judgement can issue at all – and in particular, to positions strangely at variance with the radical political impulses that make 'postmodernism' attractive to many people. In this sense my agenda will be drawn up in the same spirit as Kant's in his Preface to the first Critique (Kant 1933: Avii-xii, Bxxiv-xxxvii), where he sets out to chart a course for human thinking between scepticism or anarchism (on one side) and dogmatism or authoritarianism (on the other). Oppositional movements such as feminism find their natural expression, or so I shall suggest, in the kind of thinking which has a permanent *disposition* to challenge authority, but without embracing the ('totalizing') view that it is impossible *in principle* to speak ingenuously of a 'true' assertion or of a 'legitimate' authority without succumbing to metaphysical delusion.

I want to begin by pursuing the idea that to be *within morality*, in the extended sense of 'morality' which encompasses the 'will to truth', is simply to adopt the attitude of responsibility indicated (though not, of course, advocated) in Nietzsche's text – that is, to acknowledge an obligation to answer for yourself before a community of fellow-subjects with whom you stand on a footing of equality. The community in question would be, not an empirically existing one, but a notional one defined in terms of the project common to its members: that of constructing a certain kind of *order* out of the plurality of thoughts and purposes represented within it.

This way of formulating the project of 'morality' is suggested by Nietzsche's sense of his own role in the history of philosophy: specifically, his self-imposed mission to subvert Kantianism. For Kant's philosophy undoubtedly prefigures Nietzsche's in point of the abstraction with which it pictures 'moral' requirements. His 'categorical imperative' is the supreme principle, not of conduct alone – the context in which it is familiar as the 'moral law' – but of all reasoning (properly so called). For it is this principle which supplies the constraints on what we can think, not just about practical questions but about *any* kind of question, if our thought is to win acceptance within the community of those for whom the questions arise. Just as the moral law owes its authority to the fact that we *make it for ourselves* (that it is not imposed by any alien authority), so the principles governing rational enquiry more generally owe *their* authority to the fact that they issue from within the community of enquirers – that they too form part of an attempt to solve from the inside, or 'immanently' (rather than by appeal to tradition or religious dogma), the 'problems that arise when an unco-ordinated plurality of agents is to share a possible world' (O'Neill 1989: 16). To conceive of yourself as a member of the Kantian 'kingdom of ends' is to associate yourself with the common task cut out for all those who are minded to proceed co-operatively in a world without God: the task of resolving conflict in a way that will command the assent of all individuals who have so associated themselves.

Kantian 'morality' consists then, as is well known, in submission to the categorical imperative as a constraint on possible courses of *action*. But it consists also in submission to another requirement, namely that our *thinking* too (in so far as it is of more than merely personal interest, and therefore in so far as it matters, what or how we think) should be of a kind in which all can share.

By invoking the *Genealogy of Morals* I have deliberately created an atmosphere in which the language of 'submission' is likely to cause a particular set of bells to ring. For 'submission' is a political term, a term belonging to the vocabulary of power-relations; and although (after Nietzsche) we may no longer be scandalized by the idea of a connection between *power* and *knowledge*, we are all the more likely to feel some curiosity about the political commitments of any given rationalist programme.

Kant himself would have had a clear conscience in this respect, at any rate in regard to the philosophical constituency existing in his own day. For his assumptions are, subject to that historical limitation, *democratic*. *Anyone* who is capable of thinking in an independent yet disciplined way is entitled to recognition, without fear or favour, as a fellow-participant in the collective human effort of 'Enlightenment'. And with the passage of time (and the emergence of new political movements) the idea of democracy has been interpreted with ever-increasing rigour, so that the 'kingdom of ends' has experienced, as it were, a population explosion: from its modest origins as the preserve of a few million educated European bourgeois, it has grown to take in people who would once have stood to those few in the relation of wives, servants and even colonial subjects.

However, certain recent developments in philosophy reveal disaffection with the modernist project of construction; in particular, with its inbuilt yearning towards 'closure' – towards a practical realization of the human potential for stable, because rational, order. Jean-François Lyotard, the writer who has carved out an unquestioned place for the word 'postmodernism' in the language of philosophy, has sought to discredit this project by way of his concept of 'meta-narratives' (Lyotard 1984: Introduction and 31–41). For him personally, as a disenchanted Marxist, the most significant 'meta-narrative' is perhaps that of *emancipation*, the story in terms of which particular political tendencies can be assessed as 'progressive' or 'reactionary' (that is, as agreeing with or running counter to the course of history, viewed as a purposive and meaningful totality). But if the meta-narrative of emancipation has become incredible, so too, for Lyotard, has (what we might call) the meta-narrative of *enquiry*. For among the foremost objects of philosophical suspicion in recent years have been the two ideas which regulate the modernist constructive project, as much on its purely cognitive as on its practical side. These are, first, that of a 'regime of truth' – Michel Foucault's (ironically distanced) term for the humanly created rational order which Kant pictured as a 'kingdom of ends';[6] and, second, the counterpart of this 'regime' or 'kingdom' in the individual mind, namely the 'integrated' or 'centred' condition in which the mind contains nothing experienced as *alien to itself* (the condition of 'organic unity' or wholeness).

Both these ideas (to repeat) have recently been the target of 'debunking' analysis. On the side of the objective world, the idea of a *regime*, whether as political or epistemological ideal, has come under pressure from the anti-authoritarian considerations of writers such as Paul Feyerabend and Gilles Deleuze (as well as those of Lyotard and Foucault). On the side of the subject, the (ultimately Platonic) ideal of *integration* has been challenged not only on theoretical grounds issuing from Lacanian psychoanalysis, but also on grounds suggested by the political concerns of new movements such as feminism. For example, as Toril Moi has written in relation to critical theory:

> An aesthetics recommending organic unity and the harmonic interaction of all parts of the poetic structure . . . is not politically innocent. A feminist might wonder why anyone would want to place such an emphasis on order and integration in the first place.[7]

And as Chris Weedon has noted in connection with Julia Kristeva's account of the 'inherent instability of the unitary subject of rational discourse', the contrary emphasis is valuable in its own right since it is *only* a 'conscious awareness of the contradictory nature of subjectivity' that can 'introduce the possibility of political choice between modes of femininity in different situations and between the discourses in which they have their meaning' (Weedon 1987: 88, 87).

It's important to notice that what we are dealing with here is a debunking conception of truth (or reason) *as such* – not a critique of some historically specific cognitive 'regime' (as, for example, with the Marxist notion of 'bourgeois ideology'), but a challenge to *any* habit of thought regulated by the idea of a (universal) 'truth'. In this superficial sense, then, the debt of postmodernism to the thought of Nietzsche is obvious enough. Yet when we scratch the surface we seem to encounter a political paradox. For Nietzsche's complaint against truth-orientated thinking laid claim to an *aristocratic* motive: a disgust with the democratic principle (transferred, as it were, to the sphere of epistemology) that even the powerful can properly be summoned before the 'tribunal of reason' and required to account for themselves. By contrast, the recent 'rage against Enlightenment' (Bernstein 1985: 25) (the rejection of 'truth', 'reason' and the like in so far as these are supposed to transcend existing discursive practice) looks more like a variant on the theme that 'all power corrupts'. The very idea of a *legitimate* 'regime of truth', even when projected into an ideal future, is now seen as a kind of bureaucratic ruse; hence there can no longer be any hope of replacing (false) 'ideology' with (genuine) 'knowledge' by means of a politically motivated remaking of cognitive institutions. Isn't this the typical attitude of what Nietzsche saw fit to call the 'rabble' – of those whose rallying-cry is 'Away with all masters' (Nietzsche 1973: §204)?

The answer comes back that this reproach is misplaced. For it involves a misinterpretation of the gesture with which we are concerned – the refusal to be party to the construction of a rationalist 'regime'. That refusal claims kinship not with the resentful or 'reactive' tendencies of mass politics, but rather with the conception of oneself as an *author*, a point of origin, of evaluations. The idea of an integrated moral or cognitive order is psychologically self-discrediting for the very reason that it betrays a desire for the approval of an external authority. And the Kantian device of representing the authority in question as *not* really external (because it is allegedly the outward expression of our rational, or 'real', selves) – this device is simply a more subtle manifestation of the forces that subjected us to morality in the first place. The Kantian critique, according to Deleuze, even turns these forces into 'something a little more "our own"'. . . . When we stop obeying God, the state, our parents, reason appears and persuades us to continue being docile because it says to us: it is you who are giving the orders'.[8]

Other critics of the Kantian vision – the vision of a universal rational community – speak in a less overtly Nietzschean vein, but share some of the same concerns. In particular, there is a perception of something menacing in the urge to establish communication among the multiplicity of 'language games' that confront us when we look at human thought and practice naturalistically. Thus for Lyotard, any systematic pursuit of intellectual *rapprochement* smacks of 'terror' (1984: 82); while for Feyerabend it is indicative of what he memorably calls 'ratiofascistic dreams', drawing from him the observation that

> Helping people does not mean kicking them around until they end up in someone else's paradise . . . *an abstract discussion of the lives of*

people I do not know and with whose situation I am not familiar is
not only a waste of time, it is also inhumane and impertinent.[9]

These thinkers, then, recoil from the idea that one might hope to arrive,
through free, disinterested dialogue, at a result (whether practical or
theoretical) which any rational being could be expected to endorse.

The furthest point to which one might be carried by this movement of
recoil from universalism would be the point of inability to accept *anything*
public as capturing the content of one's thoughts or feelings. How (one
might ask) could I allow my unique subjectivity to be made to submit to
some *abstraction*, some *general idea*, which would mediate between me
and other subjects by furnishing us with a common thought – and so with
a point of intellectual identity? Isn't this process of mediation, as Nietzsche
maintained, necessarily one of *vulgarization* – a systematic infliction of
violence on the inexpressible in order to make it fit the expressive forms
available within some arbitrary language (Nietzsche 1973: §268)?

The political implications of this particularist impulse are boldly
developed in a dialogue between Foucault and Deleuze dating from the
1970s,[10] where the question at issue is the kind of strategy appropriate to
a revolutionary politics. One thought which emerges from the discussion,
and which goes against the whole way of thinking of the traditional
(Marxist) left, is that it is no longer acceptable for anyone to *represent*
anyone else – the reason being that this would involve subordinating the
individual experience of the one represented to some abstract idea which
is supposed to generate a common identity embracing both him/her and
the representative (for example, 'trade unionist' or 'communist').[11] The
moral of this thought is: away with the mass organization, and let every
oppressed person give free rein to his or her own specific powers of
disobedience!

The same movement of recoil is observable in connection with the
second of our two problematic ideas – that of *integrated subjectivity*. The
'integrated' mental condition, as mentioned earlier, was one of freedom
from any alien presence (such as an unruly 'appetite') of which one might
be inclined to say, 'That is not the *real me*'. (This form of words is meant
to recall various well-known rationalist manoeuvres in moral psychology,
notably in relation to 'weakness of will'.) Here too, one factor contributing
to disenchantment with the rationalist tradition has been a politically motivated resistance to the demand for hierarchy. The question has been raised:
doesn't this demand stem from a kind of totalitarianism of the psyche,
answering to the 'totalitarian' epistemology which envisaged all parties
converging on a single, stable representation of reality? And the suspicion
exists that the very idea of a unitary personality – the idea of a voice
which has *authority* to speak on behalf of the whole person (see Plato,
Republic, 442c) – has its home within an ascetic or 'slave' morality of self-

formation: one that works by relaying the voice of God, the state or our parents inside our own heads and claiming for it the status of a 'real' or 'better' self over against the 'false, private self' of our desires! Emancipation from morality on this (subjective) side would mean being able to say unapologetically that the subject of speech and action is 'always a multiplicity, even within the person who speaks and acts' (Deleuze in Foucault 1977: 206); or that the name of each one of us is 'Legion, for we are many' (Anscombe 1981: vol. II, 31). It would mean renouncing, or at any rate tempering, the rationalist ambition to make ourselves answerable for every one of our actions – the ambition to be 'an animal with the right to make promises' (Nietzsche 1969: II, §1).

In this connection too, of course, there is something paradoxical in the attempt to enlist Nietzsche as a precursor. After all, Nietzsche's own ethical taste – his standard of value in human character – derives from a classical tradition which concurs with Platonism in regarding the fragmented or 'hysterical' condition as one to be *overcome* in the process of ethical formation. He believes, in keeping with the standard pagan conception of ethics as 'moral grooming' (Brown 1989: ch. 1), that in order to arrive at our own identity – to 'become what we are' (Nietzsche 1974: §270) – it is necessary to free ourselves from excessive emotional suggestibility and to gain a proper measure of intentional control over our own actions.[12] So, just as the impulse to reject 'regimes of truth' seemed at first to be tarred with the brush of anarchism, the impulse to reject centred subjectivity may also wear the look of something 'ignoble' (as Nietzsche might put it) – a gesture of hatred addressed by disorderly spirits to the bearers of an order they themselves will never achieve.

But here again paradox can be dispelled, and a kind of consistency regained, if we remember that the pursuit of centred subjectivity will vary in meaning according to the context in which it is set. Removed from its familiar (Platonist) surroundings, where the centred condition is pictured as being one of responsiveness to the claims of the *universal*, this pursuit will no longer be an expression of the 'will to truth'. Instead, we begin to glimpse a different, 'post-moral' motive for seeking psychic integration and for trying to make ourselves answerable for our future actions. This would be the quasi-aesthetic motive of 'giving style to one's character' (Nietzsche 1974: §290) – true 'style' in this sense consisting simply in the ability to express the quantum of active force that one is, one's own measure of value-creating energy, without falling into disorientation or incoherence. Not, that is to say, in the successful channelling of that energy into expressive forms which will stand up to the critical scrutiny of some herd-like '*community* of rational beings'.

It would be misleading, then, to represent Nietzsche's anti-moralism as a matter of hostility to 'regimes' as such, whether in a political or in a psychological context. His vision of life after morality is, rather, one of *irresponsibility* – of a dispensation under which those who have it in them to construct something, to leave a mark or build a monument, do so cheerfully and without compunction. And that means: without giving way to democratic scruples or to a wish for peaceful coexistence with the human race at large.

On this point, however, there is some distance between pure Nietzscheanism and the position of most contemporary critics of Enlightenment. Even the most celebrated members of this group can sometimes be observed trying to find their way between (on one side) the resolute refusal of any common moral or conceptual scheme, and (on the other) the kind of terrorism in the pursuit of theoretically determined goals which Feyerabend calls 'ratiofascism'. Foucault, for instance, can conclude his essay 'What is Enlightenment?' by speaking of 'our impatience for liberty' (Rabinow 1986: 50); while Lyotard insists – however obscurely, given his overall philosophical position – that *justice* is 'not outmoded' as a political value (Lyotard 1984: 66). These certainly look like signs of a residual desire for connectedness or solidarity – for identification with a political subject larger than the individual, which could be the bearer of whatever values may be thought to have withstood the impact of postmodernity. But if that is so, it seems to follow that philosophy is, after all, not yet in a position to tear up the Kantian agenda which I mentioned at the outset – the project of thinking in a way that would be adequately defended against both 'scepticism' and 'dogmatism'. And in the space remaining to me I want to explore the possibility that, even when we have taken on board all that is intellectually and morally compelling in the postmodernist assault on 'universal reason', we may still find ourselves within a 'problematic', or framework of enquiry, which is essentially that of Kant. For the contemporary counterpart of the Kantian project is, I think, that of distinguishing – though not necessarily in an abstract, criteriological way – between *rationality* and '*ratiofascism*': between that measure of integration which is a precondition of our being able to speak to each other and inhabit a common emotional world, and on the other hand the attempt to suppress differences coercively out of a sheer inability to live with them. This task, I suggest, is analogous to that of distinguishing between *morality* and *moralism*, where 'moralism' means the attempt to force a moral interpretation on phenomena which are best seen from some other perspective. I suspect in fact that much of the glamour surrounding the vision of an end to morality, whether in the familiar or in the abstract, post-Nietzschean sense of the word, is due to a failure to keep these distinctions before the mind; and if I can bring them more clearly into view this chapter will have served its purpose.

Recall the idea of a 'regime of truth' which we borrowed from Foucault. This idea belongs within the setting of a 'naturalized epistemology', in the sense introduced by Quine and now indispensable to the theory of knowledge. Indispensable, because twentieth-century epistemology works with a conception of reason that has been 'irrevocably desublimated'[13] – revealed, that is, in all its historical and cultural particularity. Human reason is now understood not as the sign of our participation in something that goes *beyond* our merely natural existence,[14] but as one expression of our identity as a natural species whose members are exposed to an enormous variety of environmental and social conditions. Against this background, the various branches of knowledge which have been of interest to epistemological theory (including, centrally, natural science) can be demystified and understood critically as 'institutions or processes in the world' (Quine 1969: 84). And this is tantamount to saying that they can be understood as 'regimes of truth'. For a 'regime' in general is simply an ordered state of some complex whole (where this state is maintained by the behaviour of rational agents) – in conjunction, if you like, with the process by which such a state is maintained.

To develop our sympathies with this naturalistic outlook, we can review the following points, which I hope are uncontroversial. Take any knowledge-gathering episode: it might be the formation of an opinion about an everyday matter of fact, or (more experimentally) by a learner in the course of an organized learning process, or it might be the *hazarding* of a judgement by an academic or professional 'expert' about a contested specialist question. Any such act is subject to appraisal by a community of those qualified for the task: at one extreme the specialist peer-group, at the other, nothing less than the totality of those competent in the relevant natural language. Truth, as J. L. Austin has reminded us (1970: 129–30), is a *value* – one of 'various degrees and dimensions of success in making statements'. To earn the accolade of being called 'true', a judgement must pass the test of public appraisal; and the labelling of an assertion as 'true' records that it has done so. (That is, it *shows*, as opposed to *saying*, this.) To have our judgements rejected by the relevant appraising community is a kind of discipline or admonition to do better – differently, more acceptably – in future. In fact, if we pursue this line of reflection, we arrive at one of the central thoughts in the later philosophy of Wittgenstein, namely that the experience of being *guided* or *directed* in our judgement is at the root of our identity as judging subjects.[15] And we shall find it natural to picture a 'regime of truth' as a system of linguistic rules or methodological principles in which individuals have to become competent in so far as they aspire to think at all. The desire to share in meaningful activity is, in other words, logically bound up with the desire for incorporation into a 'community of rational beings', or – to adopt a more modest, 'desublimated' idiom – into a community of thinkers in whom we could have moral and epistemic confidence.

But then this same desire will necessarily direct us towards that other object of scepticism, the ideal of psychic integration. Why 'necessarily'?

Well, the connection as I see it is as follows. If there is nothing that we regard as a *legitimate* regime of truth, then there will equally be nothing that we accept as a paradigm of *sound* judgement, and hence nothing that counts for us as correctness or incorrectness in characterizing reality – except of course in an attenuated, reductive sense: correctness as that which is *called* 'correct' within a certain 'language game'. But if there is nothing that we recognize, in all sincerity, as incorrectness, then there will be no need for the kind of internal differentiation of the self by which we identify ourselves with one practical or judgemental tendency (in ourselves) as against another – that is, by which we order our thought and behaviour in relation to norms. So there will be nothing to motivate the construction of an ordered, *organized*, self – a self exhibiting the properties of 'organic unity' and internal hierarchy. Conversely, if we do acknowledge the claim exerted by communal norms of any kind, we are to that extent obliged to distinguish between the acceptable and the unacceptable within the realm of thought (or conjecture) and of feeling. And with this pattern of discrimination there emerges, as a matter of conceptual necessity, the outline of a 'real' or 'rational' self – the self with which the individual identifies for the purposes of utterances and actions for which he or she can expect to be held to account.

Now I must stress that this line of thought, if there is anything in it at all, falls into the category of transcendental arguments – arguments relating to the very conditions of possibility of a certain kind of mental operation (or indeed, as in the present case, to the possibility of cognitive activity quite generally). Because it has this transcendental status, the line of thought I have been pursuing does not lead to any conclusion about the *extent* to which we have reason to commit ourselves to ideals of psychic integration or of incorporation into a cognitive 'regime'. And I want to make it clear that it is no part of my purpose to advocate this non-sceptical attitude (to 'regimes of truth') as preferable to the sceptical or suspicious one. As it happens, I regard the 'decentring of the epistemological and moral subject' (or rather the recognition that centred subjectivity can be at most a 'regulative idea' for us) as one of the most liberating developments in twentieth-century thought, and the breakdown of cultural homogeneity in 'developed' societies as one of the most important historical processes occurring in our life time. But then, nothing I have said so far debars me from taking these views. For I have not yet addressed myself in any direct way to the work of *evaluating* the order-imposing drives considered in this chapter – those that maintain 'regimes of truth' and those that construct the 'centred' subject. My immediate concern is simply to point out that, at the limit, the rejection of centred subjectivity is inconsistent with any ambition to express ourselves in a public language; it is something that could be proposed only in anticipation of a non-discursive or 'silent' future.[16] For it is impossible to *talk* (as opposed to 'emitting inarticulate sounds' (Wittgenstein 1967: part I, §261) without admitting into one's inner life whatever internal organization is needed for the purpose of *following a rule* – acknowledging a contrast between right and wrong ways of proceeding, and regulating one's own behaviour in the light of this contrast. And it is worth remembering that without the common system of meanings which a (public) language supplies, we should be unable to attribute any meaning or value to the 'difference' of other subjects: however brilliantly plural our human surroundings, that plurality is wasted on us in so far as we lack the capacity for an imaginative response to others, and this is a capacity which comes to us as part of the process of socialization (including linguistic socialization).

Short of the limit, though – and more hopefully from the standpoint of democratic political movements – criticism of the ideal of integration may issue not in a *totalizing* but, instead, in a *fallibilist* move: a gesture of dissociation from Feyerabend's 'ratiofascism' on its psychological side. The thought here would be that however persuasive the foregoing transcendental argument, no actual 'regime' exhibits anything like the degree of perfection that would warrant an attempt to remake ourselves down to the last detail in accordance with its demands (see Lovibond 1989–90, esp. at §VII); and it might also be that no politics (and in particular, no politics of change) can be adequate to our needs if it neglects the workings of the unconscious (and thereby the precarious and provisional nature of human identity in general).[17] If we make this kind of move we place the idea of the fragmented subject at the service of a demystified ('desublimated') rationalism: one which would recognize that autonomy, like truth, is 'of this world', or in other words that it is an ideal invented by finite (and thus never wholly 'autonomous') creatures. To take this view of the regulative ideas of cognitive 'morality' would not be to jettison them but to rethink them in terms of a more fully naturalist understanding of our cognitive powers.

It would be consistent with this policy to admit that perhaps there is some truth in the mocking suggestion that critical thinking contains an inbuilt 'work ethic' – a capacity to suffer, to do violence to one's inclinations and in general to submit to the kind of treatment that Nietzschean thinking brings together under the heading of 'cruelty'. That suggestion, however, should not necessarily be a source of embarrassment. For it might be that the 'cruelty' which goes into the self-maintenance of the truth-orientated subject – the subject who is actually fragmented, but in search of internal unity – is something neither good nor bad in itself, but merely potentially one or the other. True, there is a risk that we may overestimate the value of order and so establish within ourselves the psychological equivalent of a dictatorship; but then there is a countervailing risk that we may romanticize the fragmented, decentred condition by representing it as a force for social change when, really, it would be more accurately regarded as a manifestation of post-political apathy – and the alternative, the (severe, 'puritanical') attempt to form a fixed purpose and act on it, as the real threat to existing power structures.

In that case, our fallibilist revision of the truth-orientated habit of thought might issue in an attitude to its regulative ideas which would be compounded of respect or 'reverence' (on one hand) and suspicion or irony (on the other). Reverence in this sense (and again, it is pretty well the Kantian sense: 'not a feeling *received* through outside influence, but one *self-produced* by a rational concept' (Kant 1948: 66n.)) because of the logical connection I have noted between *rule-following* and the capacity for internal differentiation and self-criticism; irony or suspicion because of the ideological character of the values of organic unity, and because of the difficulty of treading the line between rationalism and 'ratiofascism'. But I am not suggesting that we ought to start casting about for some *a priori* formula which would tell us once and for all how to hold 'reverence' and suspicion in due balance. Rather, the appropriate relation between these two attitudes will be a mutually correcting or 'dialectical' one, and the balance between them at any given moment will be the outcome of this continual process of mutual correction: not too much nostalgia for unity or stability, on pain of enclosing ourselves within an arbitrarily 'normal' mode of cognition; not too much centrifugal frenzy, on pain of ceasing to be able to speak effectively to one another when our lives may depend on the ability to do so. We might think of the attempt to operate simultaneously within the field of force of both these demands as one aspect of our participation in the 'unsocial sociability' of modernity.

Or we might conclude with the following thought, which seems to me to express a rationalism free from delusions of grandeur: the thought that order (be it moral, political, cognitive or what have you) is *potentially*, though perhaps never *actually*, satisfactory; that it makes a claim on us which we can neither ignore nor (really) fulfil. And we might be able to get some intuitive sense of this point by considering the intrinsic difficulty of the subject position – for example, to begin as close to home as possible, that of the subject of speech. When I try to talk sense, I try to project a (however provisionally) unified personality: I intend my audience to perceive me as exercising a quasi-artistic control over my own communicative action. Yet whatever I say, my speech is liable the very next moment to leave me feeling dissatisfied – feeling that I have not expressed myself definitively or even adequately. But *what* was I trying to express, then? (Who am 'I'?) From one point of view the task seems hopeless ('It is always a multiplicity that speaks and acts'); the speaking subject (that is, the actively, creatively, speaking subject) is engaged in a constant struggle to transcend itself, it 'supersedes and jettisons [its own external records] as soon as they are formed' (Collingwood 1938: 275). But from another point of view it seems enormously easy: witness our readiness to credit *others* with unified subjectivity on the strength of their speech, their *performance* as speakers. It is the formal authority of the speaker's position that induces us to suspend disbelief in his or her inward ambiguity, to credit him or her with the unity of an autonomous, diachronically consistent thinker. And when *I* speak – I have to suspend disbelief in the same way in relation to myself.[18]

NOTES

1 See Flax (1990: 39):

> It seems increasingly probable that Western culture is in the middle of a fundamental transformation: A 'shape of life' is growing old. In retrospect, this transformation may be as radical (but as gradual) as the shift from a medieval to a modern society.

2 I borrow this term from the title of an article by Paul Hirst in *The London Review of Books*, 23 November 1989.

3 Nietzsche (1969: Essay III, §27):

> Christianity *as a dogma* was destroyed by its own morality; in the same way Christianity *as morality* must now perish, too; we stand on the threshold of *this* event.... Christian truthfulness ... must end by drawing its *most striking* inference, its inference *against* itself; this will happen ... when it poses the question *'what is the meaning of all will to truth?'*

4 Baynes, Bohman and McCarthy (1987: 7); see also Hilary Putnam in the same collection (224).

5 Nietzsche (1969: Essay III, §12). I discuss this passage in greater detail in Lovibond (1989).

6 Cf. Foucault, 'Truth and power' in Rabinow (1986: 72ff).

7 Moi (1985: 85); see also Michael Payne, Introduction to Moi (1990: 10).

8 Deleuze (1983: 89, 92). Any uncertainty about the significance of the word 'docile' is laid to rest a few pages later (106), when we are told that the usefulness of philosophy consists in 'turning thought into something aggressive, active and affirmative. Creating free men ... [*sic*]'.

9 Feyerabend (1987: 305) (emphasis in original). For a feminist analogue see Iris Marion Young (1987: 62), who condemns as covertly authoritarian the ideal of an impartial moral reason judging 'from a point of view outside of the particular perspectives of persons involved in interaction [and] able to totalize these perspectives into a whole, or general will'.

10 'Intellectuals and power' in Foucault (1977).

11 Cf. Stanley and Wise (1983: 83, 84):

> there is no 'going beyond' the personal, that chimera of contemporary feminist theory.... Feminism's alternative to conventional theorizing must reject collecting experiences merely in order to generalize them out of all recognition. Instead it should be concerned with going back into 'the subjective' in order to explicate, in order to examine in detail what this experience is.

12 See Nietzsche (1968: 65): 'All unspirituality, all vulgarity, is due to the incapacity to resist a stimulus – one *has* to react, one obeys every impulse.'

13 See Baynes, Bohman and McCarthy (1987:4): 'the epistemological and moral

subject has been definitively decentred and the conception of reason linked to it irrevocably desublimated.'

14 Cf. the Platonic view of human beings as 'creatures not of earth but of heaven' (*Timaeus*, 90a).

15 See Wittgenstein (1969: §493): 'So is this it: I must recognize certain authorities in order to make judgements at all?'; and the rule-following considerations more generally.

16 This is a possibility which sometimes appears to strike a chord with Nietzsche, who is capable of seeing consciousness itself as a 'defect of the organism' (Nietzsche 1968: 125).

17 Cf. Jacqueline Rose's insistence at once on 'the fully social constitution of identity and norms' and on 'that point of tension between ego and unconscious where they [sc. identity and norms] are endlessly remodelled and endlessly break' (Rose 1986: 7).

18 An earlier version of this chapter was presented as a lecture in the Department of Philosophy at the University of Richmond, Virginia in April 1991 in a series on 'Rationality, ideology and difference'. The series was convened by Lorenzo Simpson, whom I would like to thank for the stimulus provided by his invitation.

REFERENCES

Anscombe, G. E. M. (1981), *Collected Philosophical Papers*, Oxford: Blackwell.

Austin, J. L. (1970), *Philosophical Papers*, ed. G. J. Warnock, Oxford: Oxford University Press.

Baynes, Kenneth, Bohman, James and McCarthy, Thomas (eds) (1987), *After Philosophy: End or Transformation?*, Cambridge, MA and London: MIT Press.

Benhabib, Seyla (1991), 'Feminism and postmodernism: an uneasy alliance', *Praxis International*, vol. 11, no. 2 (July), pp. 137–49.

Bernstein, Richard J. (ed.) (1985), *Habermas and Modernity*, Oxford: Polity Press.

Brown, Peter (1989), *The Body and Society: Men, Women and Sexual Renunciation in Early Christianity*, London: Faber and Faber.

Collingwood, R. G. (1938), *The Principles of Art*, Oxford: Oxford University Press.

Deleuze, Gilles (1983), *Nietzsche and Philosophy*, trans. Hugh Tomlinson, London: Athlone Press.

Feyerabend, Paul (1987), *Farewell to Reason*, London: Verso.

Flax, Jane (1990), 'Postmodernism and gender relations in feminist theory' in *Feminism/Postmodernism*, ed. Linda J. Nicholson, London: Routledge, pp. 39–62.

Foucault, Michel (1977), *Language, Counter-Memory, Practice*, ed. Donald F. Bouchard, trans. Donald F. Bouchard and Sherry Simon, Oxford: Blackwell.

Habermas, Jürgen (1987), *The Philosophical Discourse of Modernity*, trans. Frederick Lawrence, Cambridge, MA: MIT Press.

Kant, Immanuel (1933), *Critique of Pure Reason*, trans. Norman Kemp Smith, London: Macmillan.

Kant, Immanuel (1948), *Groundwork of the Metaphysic of Morals*, trans. H. J. Paton as *The Moral Law*, London: Hutchinson.

Lovibond, Sabina (1989), 'Feminism and postmodernism', *New Left Review*, no. 178, pp. 5–28.

Lovibond, Sabina (1989–90), 'True and false pleasures', *Proceedings of the Aristotelian Society*, vol. 90, part 3, pp. 213–30.

Lyotard, Jean-François (1984), *The Postmodern Condition: A Report on Knowledge*, trans. Geoff Bennington and Brian Massumi, Manchester: Manchester University Press.

Moi, Toril (1985), *Sexual/Textual Politics*, London: Methuen.

Moi, Toril (1990), *Feminist Theory and Simone de Beauvoir*, Oxford: Blackwell.

Nietzsche, Friedrich (1968), *Twilight of the Idols* and *The Antichrist*, trans. R. J. Hollingdale, Harmondsworth: Penguin.

Nietzsche, Friedrich (1969), *The Genealogy of Morals*, trans. Walter Kaufmann, New York: Random House.

Nietzsche, Friedrich (1973), *Beyond Good and Evil*, trans. R. J. Hollingdale, Harmondsworth: Penguin.

Nietzsche, Friedrich (1974), *The Gay Science*, trans. Walter Kaufmann, New York: Random House.

O'Neill, Onora (1989), 'Reason and politics in the Kantian enterprise' in Onora O'Neill, *Constructions of Reason: Explorations of Kant's Practical Philosophy*, Cambridge: Cambridge University Press, pp. 3–27.

Quine, W. V. O. (1969), *Ontological Relativity and Other Essays*, New York and London: Columbia University Press.

Rabinow, Paul (ed.) (1986), *The Foucault Reader*, Harmondsworth: Penguin.

Rose, Jacqueline (1986), *Sexuality in the Field of Vision*, London: Verso.

Stanley, Liz and Wise, Sue (1983), *Breaking Out: Feminist Consciousness and Feminist Research*, London: Routledge and Kegan Paul.

Weedon, Chris (1987), *Feminist Practice and Poststructuralist Theory*, Oxford: Blackwell.

Williams, Bernard (1978), *Descartes: The Project of Pure Enquiry*, Harmondsworth: Penguin.

Wittgenstein, Ludwig (1967), *Philosophical Investigations*, trans. G. E. M. Anscombe, Oxford: Blackwell.

Wittgenstein, Ludwig (1969), *On Certainty*, ed. G. E. M. Anscombe and G. H. von Wright, trans. Denis Paul and G. E. M. Anscombe, Oxford: Blackwell.

Young, Iris Marion (1987), 'Impartiality and the civil public: some implications of feminist critiques of moral and political theory' in *Feminism as Critique*, ed. Seyla Benhabib and Drucilla Cornell, Oxford: Polity Press, pp. 56–76.

5

TOWARDS A DEFENCE OF OBJECTIVITY

Ismay Barwell

Within recent years there has been a widely expressed feeling that feminist theory has reached some sort of impasse. It is diagnosed by Linda Nicholson and others as part of a more general crisis in theory but it comes with an additional difficulty for feminists since the charge is laid that some styles of theorizing which were treated with respect in the past are profoundly and inescapably implicated in the dominant western point of view which is that of white males. It is argued that these theoretical approaches depend on attitudes and assumptions which are central to the way in which the dominant version of masculinity has been constructed in that culture. The concept of objectivity is one upon which much of this critical discussion has focused. The charge is serious because it is accompanied by the claim that there is no way to unpick parts of the tradition and turn them to feminist use. It is supposed that the tradition has to be accepted or rejected as a whole. This is not an issue I will pursue in this chapter because it raises very complicated considerations about holism but it does seem to me to be the case that the history of thought is better understood as a continuum rather than a series of sudden moves from points of view which are incommensurable with each other.

Science and philosophy have been two practices within which a dominant tradition has seen objectivity tied up in both the methodology and the goals of the practice. Within feminist theory the movement has been from accepting the traditional goals of theory while denying that they are realized by actual practices to a wholesale rejection of the goals.

The grounds for this rejection have been various. The process of reasoning which is described by Sandra Harding (1986) is that which has already been described above. From the complaint that practices which purport to be objective don't live up to their own standards the move is to reject those standards as irredeemably androcentric. By this is meant that they are bound up with masculinity or one dominant version of it in a way which means that they are not usable by feminists. Another direction of criticism derives from the argument that objectivity can only be a feature of anything if there are epistemological foundations, and there are no such foundations. An epistemological foundation was anything which was thought to be a privileged basis for cognitive certainty. Such a basis was supposed to have been provided by 'I think, therefore I am' in the Cartesian system, sense-data statements in that of the logical empiricists and universal cognitive capacities together with their structuring concepts in a Kantian system. This criticism assumes that objectivity requires 'complete justifications' and that 'complete justifications' require foundations.

Yet another objection arises from ontological and semantic considerations. One such consideration turns on the nature of the concepts which are used in the social sciences and in related disciplines such as aesthetics, art criticism and literary theory. It might be plausible to suppose that the natural sciences aim to arrive at concepts which single out natural kinds, but it is not plausible to suppose that this is the aim of the social sciences or aesthetics. The concepts which are used in these practices are of kinds which are at least partially constituted by the thoughts and the actions of people. Natural kinds are not constituted by how people think and talk about them.

It seems to me that there are two themes in these criticisms which are relevant to feminist theory. The first is that objectivity of method or theory is not possible. The second is that even if it were possible it is not desirable, or at least not desirable for feminists. I will discuss the desirability of objectivity for feminism, but before I do so, I think it is necessary to consider what objectivity or, at least, what the 'received' notion which is being denied, actually involves.

So, what is objectivity?

> Objectivity is a characteristic which has been applied to beliefs, individuals, theories, observations, and methods of inquiry. It is generally thought to involve the willingness to let our beliefs be determined by 'the facts' or by some impartial and nonarbitrary criteria rather than by our wishes as to how things ought to be.
>
> (Longino 1990: 62)

Objectivity has both metaphysical and epistemological aspects. Objectivity in its metaphysical aspect is a feature of theories, descriptions or the perspectives to which they give rise. It is this aspect at which the third sort of criticism is directed. As I have already indicated, the metaphysical aspect might be construed semantically in terms of truth and the referential commitments of a particular discourse or it might be construed in terms of the independent existence of the subject-matter of the discourse from that (or any) discourse.

Realism and realist assumptions involve a commitment to a world which exists independently of thought, action and language. Whether this independence is an independence of particular thoughts and actions or of particular areas of thought and action (discourses) or of thought and action in general and just what this independence amounts to, is one of those theoretical swamps which I will avoid in this paper as far as I can. I accept that a minimal notion of the independently existing as that which is intersubjectively accessible is required and moreover this minimal notion will be required, not just for the possibility of objective theories, but also for the possibility of objective ways of knowing.

An objective method or way of knowing the world is one which is directed by non-arbitrary and non-subjective criteria for generating and for accepting or rejecting the beliefs, hypotheses and theories which make up a body of knowledge. Sometimes the standards for the non-arbitrary are set so high that the only criteria which could meet them would be those provided by rules which are universally applicable.

The contemporary denial of objectivity is a denial of the attainability and desirability of both its aspects. In a context where the metaphysical is salient, then the focus of critical attention will be directed upon notions of objective truth and objective reality. If a theory or perspective is objective, then it is about an independently existing reality (in some sense of independently existing) and it claims that it is giving an accurate or true account of that reality. The theory purports to accurately represent the world 'as it really is'. The world is presented 'in its true colours'. In addition, objective theories are supposed to involve a 'God's-eye view' which transcends any particularity of situation or perspective (Fraser and Nicholson 1990). The rejection of objectivity involves the assertion that there is no world with 'true colours' for a theory to accurately represent and no 'God's-eye view' from which anything can be viewed. These two claims are not always distinguished but they should be. An accurate account need not be a view from nowhere.

When the focus is on epistemological questions, the sceptical argument is directed towards the possibility of objective enquirers who adopt objective methods which lead to true theories. The most common reason given for a sceptical conclusion is that there can be no value-free enquiry. Clearly the assumption behind this reason is that whenever values or interests are shown to be influencing an enquiry or informing a method then the enquiry and the method are not objective because the facts are not directing. Either values and interests are guiding the enquiry or the facts are. It was assumed that at most one of these can be at work.

This is an issue that I will pursue further but before I do so I want to pause to consider why the received notion was supposed to confer a positive value on that to which it applied. When objectivity was a characteristic of a theory, the theory was supposed to provide accurate explanations of how and why things happened as they did. Accuracy or truth were valuable either because they 'could be relied upon' or because they had intrinsic value. It is this connection with truth which is crucial. The ultimate value of objectivity lies in its connection with truth and truth must be preserved as a regulatory principle in at least some theoretical enterprises.

This explains why some ideal of objectivity is desirable for feminist theoretical practice. If an argument is needed for this I think that it is to be found in the fact that feminism in all its various varieties does understand itself to be a radical movement for social change. It aims at producing societies which are more just than those it finds already in existence. Surely the theoretical wing of feminism will require descriptions and analyses of the social arrangements about which the judgements about justice and injustice are being made, as well as explanations of how they come about and are sustained in existence. These theories aim at revealing not just 'how things are', but also the possibilities which are present for bringing about change.

Moreover, feminist theoretical practice has among its responsibilities that of giving reasons why change is required and of making the demand for change accountable by demonstrating that it conforms to some standard for judging social arrangements. This job is made possible only if it has both reliable theories of how things are and how they might be and a critical understanding of the criteria it uses for accepting some theories and rejecting others. If it accepts this accountability then it will require robust facts about the social world which can be used as evidence for the claim that the current social arrangements are oppressive to women and which act as premises for recommendations for change. These robust facts will be located in theories which are called upon when feminists give reasons for their claims that the changes they envisage are possible and that they are desirable. This point about feminism is a claim made for all radical political movements by Stephen Crook in 'Radicalism, modernism and postmodernism'(1990). It is a point about the responsibility that such movements must take to give reasons for their analyses and for their recommendations for change. This responsibility extends to their being self-conscious about the standards of justification which they are employing. They must have reflective views about what counts as a justification. I think that this accountability requires that some of its practices aspire to an ideal of objectivity.

When objectivity was a characteristic of a method, then its value lay in the connection between it and objective theories. Although few advocates of objectivity of method believed that adopting such a method was a guarantee of the production of objective theories, they did think that it made the production of such theories more likely. Some may even have thought that it was necessary. Objectivity of method is a good because it leads to the good of accuracy or truth.

Along with other contemporary feminists who see a point in having a usable notion of objectivity, I think that much of the received notion of objectivity should be thrown out. The point of this process of spring-cleaning is to produce an ideal of objectivity which will be adequate for our theoretical needs. It should be clear that I am accepting that a practice which aims at objectivity does so because of the connection between objectivity and truth. Objectivity is a characteristic which enhances the probability that true theories will be the outcome. When the subject-matter of a practice is genuinely indeterminate, so that there are no 'facts of the matter', then truth will not be an appropriate goal for theorizing nor objectivity a regulatory ideal. Having said this, there are three cobwebs which can obviously be swept away. The first is the notion that an objective theory or understanding yields a perspective which is a 'God's-eye view' or a 'view from nowhere'. The second is that objectivity of a practice requires 'complete justifications' where this entails that there are epistemological foundations about which there can be Cartesian certainty. The third is the nonsensical idea that there could be a theoretical practice which was not governed by some values as a consequence of its self-understanding of its constitutive goals. This is going to be one of the central themes of this paper, so I will spend a little time explaining it further.

Constitutive goals are those which are taken to be essential to the practice. Constitutive values and norms will be those which flow from an understanding of those goals and which regulate the practice. For example, if a constitutive goal of the natural sciences is the production of explanations of the natural world, then the governing values and constraints follow from what counts as a good explanation. Acceptable scientific practice will be that which generates good explanations. If the production of true theories is adopted as one of the goals, then similarly truth will operate as a regulatory principle.[1]

Contextual values are those values and norms which derive from goals which are not essential to the practice. To continue with the example of natural science, political goals such as the achievement of social justice and aesthetic goals such as the production of elegant and harmonious structures are usually considered inessential to it. Thus, any values and standards which flow from an understanding of these goals would be contextual.

Examples of epistemic values are truth or accuracy, explanatory power, evidential fit and comprehensiveness, simplicity and consistency with other theories. It may be the case that these values are in tension with each other. For example, many people have thought that as values of whole theories the goals of accuracy or truth and that of explanatory power may conflict. For this reason, some philosophers of science have thought that either truth is not a value appropriate to whole theories or it is one which might be passed over in favour of other values. One might properly prefer a theory which is only an approximation or an idealization but which has the virtues of using concepts which pick out natural kinds and explanatory schemata which correctly capture 'objective dependencies'.[2] It is clear that theoretical practices differ with respect to which epistemic goals they adopt and how they interpret them. This will mean that they will differ in the values which govern their activities.

Therefore, objectivity of method cannot be understood as a characteristic which only applies to practices which operate independently of all value. Perhaps the criticism should be rephrased as a charge that it is not possible to have a method for generating beliefs (for accepting and rejecting hypotheses) which filters out all other values, thus permitting only episte-mic ones to direct. I accept this criticism. However, I will not accept that whenever values other than epistemic can be seen to be influencing an inquiry it follows that the inquiry is not objective.

In this next section I want to discuss two very recent books in feminist epistemology. These are *Science as Social Knowledge* by Helen Longino (1990) and *Whose Science? Whose Knowledge?* by Sandra Harding (1991) in which ideals of objectivity are discussed and recommended to feminists. These books represent the latest stages of the first two moments of Hard-ing's own account of the progress of feminist epistemology and they share many of the salient similarities which these two moments share. Amongst these are their insistence that relativism must be avoided (at least to the extent that some positions can be assessed as less false than others) and a view that scientific knowledge is cumulative and progressive. Another significant similarity is their insistence that a desirable notion of objectivity does not, and cannot, require freedom from non-epistemic values. How-ever, there is a difference in emphasis between the two and a disagreement concerning the degree to which current practice in the sciences realizes an adequate notion of objectivity.

The first moment, to which Longino belongs, is that of feminist empiri-cism. From this approach, the constitutive goals and values of science are more or less all right. If there is a problem, then it lies with the application of the ideals in contemporary social and political arrangements. Earlier feminist empiricists thought that the problem with scientific practice was that it did not live up to its own ideal of 'value-free' research and their recommended solution was to include more women as practitioners. Hard-ing believes that this kind of feminist empiricism must be doomed to inconsistency on the relation of politics to enquiry. They are at the same time upholding the view that the ideal of objectivity to which they aspire is one which takes no account of social position and saying that, if people who occupy a certain social position (women) are included, then the practice will become more objective. This criticism of the first moment was correct, but it assumes that feminist empiricism must continue to maintain both an ideal of objectivity which permits no values other than epistemic ones to be operative and the epistemic irrelevance of social position and experience.

Longino reinterprets traditional scientific practice for feminists. One of the chief virtues of her book is the way in which the scientific enterprise, and in particular, empiricism, is not taken to begin and end with logical empiricism. For Longino the salient feature of objectivity for a practice is that the tastes and preferences of individual practitioners be subordinated to standards which are derived from the constitutive goals of the practice and that there be widespread agreement about the interpretation and realization of these standards. For Longino, the constitutive goals of science are purely epistemic and will involve some notion of truth or accuracy, of 'getting it right' or, at least, of 'not getting it wrong'. The values which flow from these goals must include some notion of evidential support. In addition, and crucially, there must be a process which she calls 'transformative criticism' which is accepted as a normal part of the practice. Having their research results subjected to the process of transformative criticism is a central part of what is involved in the subordination of individual practitioners to the standards of the practice.

It is clear that both the natural and the social sciences are practices which are committed to seriously considering evidence in the procedures they adopt before research results can be accepted as justified and received into the body of knowledge. In my earlier quotation from Longino she characterized a practice as objective if it allowed 'the facts' to guide the enquiry. I take it that evidence is what constitutes 'the facts'.

She calls her account of evidence 'contextual' because of the crucial role that is played by background beliefs and assumptions. She claims that the evidential relation must be seen as a three-place relation. It holds between a state of affairs, event or situation which is the evidence, another state of affairs, event or situation which is the hypothesis and a set of background beliefs. Evidence is only evidence for a hypothesis in the light of background beliefs asserting a connection between them (Longino 1990: 44).

On Longino's account there need not be any theory-neutral language or any possibility of theory-unmediated observation. All that is required is that there be an intersubjectively accessible way of identifying the state of affairs which is given in evidence and that there should be agreement about this description in any theoretical dispute. Obviously, some disputes will founder at this point, but it is important to recognize that this is what they will do without agreement. The agreed description of the evidence need not be (and may never be) theory-free. All that is needed is that the theory with which it is laden should be one shared by both parties. It is also possible that the theory with which it is laden is not any of those which are being disputed.

At one point (1991: 149), Harding talks about 'theory-unmediated' experience. However, it is clear from what she goes on to say about it that this is not 'theory-free' experience or observation in Longino's sense. Harding means experiences or observations which involve cultural beliefs and attitudes which are so taken for granted as to be invisible. Her way of dealing with these is to require that 'all cultural agendas and assumptions' should be treated as evidence and available for critical scrutiny.

Longino wants to preserve the distinction between evidence and background assumptions, though as we will see later these background assumptions will need to be treated as seriously as 'the facts'. To preserve the distinction enables one to see how contextual values cannot be eliminated from justificatory processes which involve evidence. The background beliefs are an intrinsic feature of the evidential relation so they will always be present to influence research and enquiry. Typically these background beliefs contain some values which are not epistemic, but rather political, moral, aesthetic or economic.

Longino's views are one version of the underdetermination of hypotheses by evidence. In her story the methods generated by the epistemic constitutive values cannot guarantee the practice's independence from contextual values. It will be normal for a decision about whether or not an hypothesis should be adopted to be underdetermined by all relevant epistemic considerations, so it will be normal for some decisions to be influenced by political and other values. Moreover, once a model or hypothesis has been adopted then this will influence how further evidence is to be interpreted and will yield conclusions which are compatible with it. What this means for the practising scientist is that she should not allow any belief which fails her epistemic standards to guide her adoption of hypotheses, though it may be the case that for many of them no such scrutiny is appropriate. This will exhaust the scientist's accountability to her scientific community. Often this accountability will leave her with a choice of models which come out in a tie as far as epistemic criteria are concerned. At this point the scientist can adopt one in terms of her political or religious or moral allegiances.

No scientist will be just a scientist. Longino identifies herself as a feminist scientist, which seems to mean that wherever in the normal carrying out of her scientific practice, contextual values have a role to play, she can allow her commitment to her feminist community to guide her enquiry. It is up to an individual scientist to work out her responsibilities to her political as well as to her scientific community. However, it is clear that she must be responsive to the ideals of her political community as well as to some sub-set of the standards endorsed in her scientific community. 'These allegiances are themselves interactive as the political ideals may indicate a priority ordering for the scientific standards and vice versa' (Longino 1990: 192).

Longino gives as an example her reasons for the choice of a selectionist model of the mind rather than a linear-hormonal approach. The latter is crudely the view that foetal gonadal hormones organize the brain at critical stages of development, thus disposing the organism as an adult to respond in set ways to a range of environmental stimuli. This model denies that any role is played by intentional states of the organism in the determination of its behaviour. Intentional states are those states which have representational content of both the organism and the world in which it acts. A selectionist theory will be more complex than a linear-hormonal theory since it will allow not just the interaction of physiological and environmental factors but also the interaction of these and the representational content of some of the organism's brain states or processes.

The assumption that intentional states can be effective in the determination of some behaviour is not itself a value-laden assumption, but Longino thinks that the decision to adopt it is motivated by value-laden considerations. The selectionist model allows for the possibility of human agency and she thinks that the decision to adopt a model which allows a place for agency is motivated by a desire to see ourselves and others as sometimes capable of acting on the basis of perceptions of self and society in order to bring about changes in self and society. Longino locates this desire as arising out of a value which is held by her feminist community. In this situation she can allow her commitment to her feminist community to guide her choice of hypothesis and do this self-consciously.

The last element in Longino's account of objectivity is that provided by her notion of 'transformative criticism'. Even if background assumptions cannot be eliminated from the enquiry, they can all be revealed and subjected to critical scrutiny by the community of practitioners, though not, perhaps, all at once. The scientific community is a community in so far as its members see themselves as practitioners in a common practice and this will involve some measure of agreement about epistemic goals and values. The community will also share some (but no specific) cultural values and assumptions.

The critical scrutiny which the scientific community brings to bear on hypotheses and theories offered to it, will be in terms of the epistemic values which follow from its epistemic goals. The criticism can be at many different levels. Criticism can be directed at the description and adequacy of the evidence; it can take the form of locating suspect assumptions which reflect gender and cultural bias and which are required for the evidential connections to be made. Or, more importantly for feminism, it can challenge deeply-held cultural beliefs which are implicated in many chains of reasoning and which have remained invisible because unchallenged.

For Longino, the objectivity of a practice can be measured by how well it realizes four criteria of transformative criticism. These are:

1 There should be recognized avenues for the criticism. Such avenues are conferences, journals and seminars.
2 The critics and the criticized must share standards. These standards will derive from the values which are shared. These values must include some

epistemic values, since these are the constitutive values of the practice, but it will also involve some of the contextual values as well.

3 Differences in authority between practitioners should be dependent solely on their performances in the practice. This means that no point of view should be more authoritative than another because of political power or racial superiority or any other sort of social dominance.

4 The community should be responsive to the criticism which is produced. When this is of contextual values then this means that it should be prepared to change any community values which are directing the enquiry and, in particular, the acceptance of hypotheses as knowledge. I suppose that sexist and racist assumptions will be prime examples of these.

I call this a minimalist account of objectivity, but maybe it is too minimalist. Is this a sufficient condition for objectivity in a practice? In the first place, if there is too much consensus among the practitioners about contextual values and beliefs which are based on them, then there will be no challenges issued to those values. Their existence and their operation will be invisible. This would seem to be what feminists were saying in the first place about the scientific and philosophical practice. If this point is taken, then before a practice can be objective there will have to be a range of points of view within the ranks of the practitioners from which challenges can, and do, come. This account does not guarantee that there will be critical points of view from within the community.

My second worry is that it is not clear when widely held community values and beliefs will need to be changed in response to a criticism of them. It is very seldom the case that a challenge will prove beyond any doubt that a certain belief should be abandoned. If a belief is deeply entrenched so it is 'common sense', then a challenge to it may be accommodated in a number of other ways. There are well-known strategies for doing this. For example, the criticism is accommodated by being regarded as mad or deviant or 'merely' the expression of emotion, and if this is accompanied by an explanation of why the person should come to hold such a belief there may be no compulsion to change. This I think is the hardest question for anyone who wishes to hold that there is a possibility that theoretical practices can be objective. The same problem arises for those who want to maintain that there can be an objective moral point of view from which a social theory of justice can be constructed.

Since this is the most worrying point I will make it again in a slightly different way. Objectivity is said to require the inclusion of other points of view and in particular, points of view which are critical. On the other hand it is not clear how a point of view should be included if one is practising objectively. This account of objectivity makes an objective point of view or practice a matter of procedure. If the right procedures are being followed then the practice is objective. This approach will not answer the hard question of how a particular point of view should be included on a particular occasion. It is clear that it must be recognized and listened to seriously and attentively. But then some will be passed over as false, confused, unsubstantiated, etc. Women know only too well how this may have more to do with how it is presented and by whom than anything about its content.

Sandra Harding has been consistently advocating the need in the construction of knowledge for decision procedures which both valorize the social context of enquiry and avoid relativism. The fact that she has now returned to argue for a sophisticated standpoint theory is one way in which the Marxian strain which is evident in the first of these two requirements makes itself felt. Her latest book contains a sustained argument that the Hegelian/Marxian tradition to which she belongs has the resources to avoid relativism and meet what she considered to be the most damning criticism of previous standpoint positions. This is that they are unable to provide linkages with the standpoints of other oppressed groups. In this chapter, my interest in her project is limited to considering whether the ideal of objectivity which she advocates is one which would offer a way of resolving the shortcomings of the minimalist empirical ideal.

My first worry about the Longino account of objectivity was that it did not guarantee that there would be critical points of view in the practice. It seemed that a practice could be objective without any range of critical points of view being offered and particularly without any criticisms which challenged fundamental cultural assumptions and values. This would be likely to happen if the practitioners were of the same social group or gender and had roughly the same interests. Harding's notion of 'strong objectivity' seems designed to meet this problem. 'Strong objectivity' involves the notion of 'strong reflexivity' (Harding 1991: 163) which requires that all background assumptions, cultural agendas and influences must be rendered visible and their power recognized. They will then be open to critical examination *within* scientific research processes. I take it that they will then be open to the scrutiny which is involved in 'transformative criticism'.

This must mean that she thinks decisions about what hypotheses are to be accepted are *never* determined entirely by epistemic values. The background beliefs will always involve contextual values which have a part to play in every decision. These are at the moment hidden and their role is unacknowledged.

The revolution which strong reflexivity would entail requires two other things – the first is a change in the way in which the subject-matter is regarded. Strong reflexivity

would require that the objects of inquiry be conceptualised as gazing back in all their cultural particularity and that the researcher, through theory and methods, stand behind gazing back at his own socially situated research project in all its cultural particularity and its relationships to other projects of his culture – many of which (policy development in international relations, for example, or industrial expansion) can be seen only from locations far away from the scientist's actual daily work.

(Harding 1991: 163)

For this conceptualization to be possible, critical oppositional theories from the perspective of the lives of 'Others' must have been developed. It is this requirement which may offer a solution to the first difficulty. The achievement of strong reflexivity will ensure that there is not too much consensus, since a practice can be strongly reflexive only as a result of the critical presence of members of groups which are marginalized and oppressed.

What about the second worry? This was the concern that transformative criticism according to epistemic values alone does not provide strong enough criteria for the assessment of competing claims. Again strong objectivity seems designed to deal with this. Any scientist who is committed to a notion of strong objectivity will be obliged to conceptualize her research project according to the requirements of strong reflexivity and this will have involved taking account of theories which are being produced from the perspectives of 'Others'. To take account of these critical perspectives confers the ability to see some aspects of the world more clearly. For this claim to be plausible one must understand what is supposed to be involved in the achievement of such a critical perspective. The claim is not that an oppressed group has such a perspective automatically as a result of their oppression. A critical perspective is achieved only after a group works out an 'immanent critique' of an existing set of beliefs and the social arrangements which they justify. This 'immanent critique' reveals inconsistencies in the package of theory and world which is on offer. The critique will show not just that the package is inconsistent on its own terms but also how it is inconsistent and thus open up the way to an alternative amended version. In its turn this version will be subjected to a critique, which is why any privilege can only be for a time and in relation to a specific set of arrangements.

If these claims about the authority of critical perspectives are accepted then they will obviously possess the tools for the assessment of other perspectives and the basis for decision procedures for dealing with conflict.

I offer the following as my understanding of how a strongly reflexive practice might operate. Such a practice will be composed of groups which are identified as epistemologically privileged with respect to certain areas but not the whole world. These groups will make decisions within their own areas of expertise but some of these decisions will have consequences for the practice as a whole. Among these are decisions made about the relative worth of competing theories or hypotheses. These impact on wider practice because from the reasons which are operative in the process of making these comparative judgements, principles can be derived and made explicit. These principles will be among those which the practice as a whole will use to regulate its comparative decisions.[3] They must be justified by being shown to further the epistemic goals which are constitutive of the practice.

At this point two possibilities present themselves. The first is that the principles which are used by the various groups are not just different but incompatible. In this case the practice will not have consensus about how conflicts should be resolved and will not be able to regulate itself successfully enough to count as objective. The second possibility is that the principles will provide the basis for a point of view which is transcendent in the only way that 'transcendence' can be understood on this account of objectivity. If the principles are sufficiently compatible then the ideal will require reflective equilibrium between the decisions they would determine and those that are made by the various groups which constitute the practitioners. This means that some of the decisions within the groups will be affected by these principles and these in their turn will be altered in the light of actual decisions made. In this way the practice will be self-regulating according to standards which are not in danger of being arbitrarily interpreted by individuals or groups.

If this interpretation is right then it appears that Harding's notion of strong objectivity does offer an ideal in which there are decision procedures for resolving conflicts and principles which can be appealed to in giving justifications of these. However, it is a departure from the traditional notion where a practice was objective if its operative principles were such that they in some sense belonged to 'men everywhere'[4] and could provide a 'complete justification' of decisions taken. These principles are not based on some supposedly universal characteristic nor do they promise complete justifications. Nevertheless they are non-arbitrary to the extent that they apply to every practitioner because they are based upon an understanding of the constitutive goals of the practice. The transcendent point of view to which they give rise will be achievable only if there is sufficient compatibility among the principles which are used by groups which are often critical of each other but which have epistemological privilege in their own areas.

Some hybrid account of objectivity based upon the views of the two theorists whom I have discussed is the most attractive that feminism has been offered so far. Longino's contribution is an account which shows that non-epistemic values can be operative in decision procedures within theoretical practices without one having to give up the notion that these practices are objective. However, she does not offer a strong enough account of objectivity for feminist purposes because she rules out only the personal and the idiosyncratic and does not show how to establish decision procedures by which conflicting points of view within the practice can be assessed and the conflicts resolved. Harding's strong objectivity addresses both these inadequacies. Although she does not discuss this possibility it seems that a practice might be able to achieve a point of view from which it could regulate itself and that this point of view could be called 'transcendent' without that description being too misleading.

Such an account emphasizes plurality of viewpoints together with the beginning of a notion about how these viewpoints might interact and the possibility of decision procedures by which cases of conflict can be resolved. As I have already said, a practice which conformed to this ideal would be self-regulating according to standards which were not in danger of being arbitrarily co-opted by either individuals or groups. However, there are some problems and lacunae which remain. The authority which is given to critical perspectives will need to be demonstrated. Just what their competence amounts to, over what subject-matters it can be exercised and the extent to which it can be relied upon are all matters which remain to be established. The big advance on this account from all previous feminist standpoint accounts is that it does not suppose that the privilege must extend to the whole world, nor that social characteristics and experience will be equally relevant for all subject-matters. Another advantage is that the privilege is only for a time and, as the practice changes, a point of view which is privileged must expect to give way to others. There is no temptation to suppose that a position might be reached which yields something like the Archimedean point for which both Descartes and Kant strived.

NOTES

1 A useful way to understand the controversy with which I opened the paper is in terms of a lack of consensus within contemporary feminism. There are some who think that the goal is the production of theories of social justice as well as theories about natural and social reality. They think that these theories will require truth or some substitute epistemic value which operates as a regulatory principle. There are others who are suspicious about the notion of theories and think that feminist practice should aim only at the notion of 'insights'.

2 Philip Kitcher (unpublished manuscript) is an example of someone who thinks that 'significant truth' is the aim of theory-building in the natural sciences. 'Significant truth' is explanatory significance first and truth after.

3 The competence these practitioners exhibit must be such that they do, most of the time, 'get it right'. The situation cannot be parallel to that which appears to hold in the case of inductive inferences where it seems that people of more than average intelligence are prone to perform bits of reasoning, the principles of

which could not be used as a basis for a theory of inference. The gambler's fallacy is a popular example in the literature.

4 This phrase is used by Rawls (1951: 181). He is describing the cognitive character-istics which are possessed by his competent judges and says that these must not be characteristics which are possessed by them as a race or a class or a group since none of these are characteristics which are relevant for coming to know.

REFERENCES

Boyne, Roy and Rattansi, Ali (eds) (1990), *Postmodernism and Society*, London: Macmillan.

Crook, Stephen (1990), 'Radicalism, modernism and postmodernism' in *Postmodernism and Society*, ed. Roy Boyne and Ali Rattansi, London: Macmillan, pp. 46–75.

Duran, Jane (1991), *Toward a Feminist Epistemology*, Savage, MD: Rowman and Littlefield.

Fraser, Nancy and Nicholson, Linda J. (1990), 'Social criticism without philosophy: an encounter between feminism and postmodernism' in *Feminism/Postmodernism*, ed. Linda J. Nicholson, New York and London: Routledge, pp. 19–38.

Gross, Elizabeth (1986), 'Conclusion: what is feminist theory?' in *Feminist Challenges*, ed. Carole Pateman and Elizabeth Gross, Sydney: Allen and Unwin, pp. 190–204.

Haraway, Donna J. (1985), 'A manifesto for cyborgs: science, technology and socialist feminism in the 1980s', *Socialist Review*, no. 80, pp. 65–107 (reprinted in *Feminism/Postmodernism*, ed. Linda J. Nicholson, New York and London: Routledge, pp. 190–233).

Harding, Sandra (1977), 'Does objectivity in the social sciences require value-neutrality?', *Soundings*, 60, pp. 351–66.

Harding, Sandra (1986a), 'The instability of the analytic categories of feminist theory', *Signs*, vol. 11 no. 4, pp. 645–64.

Harding, Sandra (1986b), *The Science Question in Feminism*, Milton Keynes: Open University Press.

Harding, Sandra (1991), *Whose Science? Whose Knowledge? Thinking from Women's Lives*, Milton Keynes: Open University Press.

Harding, Sandra and Hintikka, Merrill B. (eds) (1983), *Discovering Reality: Feminist Perspectives on Epistemology, Metaphysics, Methodology, and Philosophy of Science*, Dordrecht: Reidel.

Hartsock, Nancy (1983), 'The feminist standpoint: developing the ground for a specifically feminist historical materialism' in *Discovering Reality: Feminist Perspectives on Epistemology, Metaphysics, Methodology, and Philosophy of Science*, ed. Sandra Harding and Merrill B. Hintikka, Dordrecht: Reidel, pp. 283–310.

Hekman, Susan (1990), *Gender and Knowledge: Elements of a Postmodern Feminism*, Cambridge: Polity Press.

Longino, Helen (1987), 'Can there be a feminist science?', *Hypatia*, vol. 2, no. 3, pp. 51–64.

Longino, Helen (1990) *Science as Social Knowledge: Values and Objectivity in Scientific Inquiry*, Princeton: Princeton University Press.

Nicholson, Linda J. (ed.) (1990), *Feminism/Postmodernism*, New York and London: Routledge.

Putnam, Hilary (1990), 'The idea of science', *Midwest Studies in Philosophy*, vol. 15, pp. 57–64.

Rawls, John (1951), 'Outline of a decision procedure for ethics', *The Philosophical Review*, vol. 60, pp. 177–97.

Rawls, John (1972), *A Theory of Justice*, Oxford: Clarendon Press and Cambridge, MA: Harvard University Press.

Smith, Dorothy E. (1974), 'Women's perspective as a radical critique of sociology', *Sociological Inquiry*, vol. 44, no. 1, pp. 7–13, reprinted in *Feminism and Methodology*, ed. Sandra Harding, Milton Keynes: Open University Press, 1987, pp. 84–96.

6

KNOWLEDGE AS CONSTRUCT
Theorizing the role of gender in knowledge
Miranda Fricker

VALUES AND PHILOSOPHY

What does feminism require of an epistemology? With this question the apparent novelty in *feminist* philosophy immediately declares itself, since the question seems to imply that feminist values are theoretically prior to strictly philosophical requirements in epistemology. Yet there are arguments to suggest that it is in fact the unacknowledged norm for socio-political concerns to permeate, if not precede, philosophical ones. We do not need postmodernism to tell us that philosophy cannot take place in a social vacuum, and there has been important feminist research devoted to revealing the dubious values at work in traditional metaphysical agendas – the way, for example, that in the western tradition the concept 'woman' has been systematically aligned with other concepts specifically associated with irrationality.[1] Feminist philosophy, then, forms a vital part of a dissident tradition whose principal novelty *vis-à-vis* its commitment to a set of values is not so much to *have* such a commitment, but rather to make this commitment *explicit*. However, the precise nature and degree of the influence which socio-political factors exercise on belief and enquiry need to be properly theorized, and we should think of this project as involving both deconstructive and reconstructive phases – we cannot tear down the house and build nothing in its place.

With this dual project in mind I will discuss two closely related lines of argument, given respectively by Helen Longino and Sandra Harding, from which we may infer the need for an epistemology which gives a strong role to socio-political values. I will then argue, however, that this movement in the direction of a sociological account of knowledge must be restricted by a further consideration: if political convictions are to be more than a historical accident, more than the meanderings of a free-floating political vocabulary, then a (non-naive) realist account of empirical[2] belief must be sustained. This is because, it will be argued, if empirical beliefs are not seen to pick out real states of affairs in the world, then we forgo the right to present empirical claims as *reasons* for or against political views. And if under these circumstances we continue regardless to use empirical claims for political argument, then we are merely acting out a charade of rational political discourse. This argument for the normative dependence of political beliefs upon empirical ones underlies the case which will then be brought against postmodernism with reference to a feminist postmodernist position presented by Donna Haraway. Finally I will suggest that a certain kind of coherentism is more promising for feminism (though its feminist adaptation will inevitably require further development), in so far as it succeeds in giving a strong role to values in the determination of belief, *without* sacrificing the empirical anchorage required by our politics. But first, we may specify two general theoretical restrictions.

TWO EPISTEMOLOGICAL RESTRICTIONS

There are two specifications for any adequate epistemology which provide the ground-rules for the line of argument in this paper. They are: first, that it must posit norms for belief; and second, that it must distinguish between a first and second-order perspective on belief in a way which sustains the capacity for self-criticism. Without these two requirements, we would be burdened with an epistemology forbidding us to think of ourselves as *believers* in any but the most impoverished sense. To take the first requirement, if there is nothing that we *ought* to believe, but merely a range of possible beliefs to choose from at will, then this renders belief a largely arbitrary business. How can I genuinely *believe* it is raining if I simultaneously hold that I might equally well believe it is dry and sunny? Where belief does not suggest itself to the subject with normative force, it is not genuine belief at all.

Turning to the second requirement – that a theory of knowledge must distinguish between a first and second-order perspective to enable self-criticism – we can see that it is in fact implied by the first requirement, since any postulated norms would be worthless without some means of supervising our loyalty to their standards. Regardless of this implication from the first to the second requirement, however, it is also *empirically* imperative that an epistemology can account for how it is indeed possible to criticize our own practices at least up to a point, since human beings plainly have some limited self-critical faculty. That is what feminist critique is; that is what epistemology is. Its practice marks the shift from a first to a second-order register, or, if you like, from language to meta-language. With these minimal ground-rules in place, we may now move on to consider a feminist case for giving a strong role to values in epistemology.

TWO VIEWS OF VALUE-NEUTRALITY:
FALSE IDEAL AND MYTH

Helen Longino has argued that the ideal of a value-neutral science is misconceived (Longino 1989). In essence her argument has four main steps.

1 First, she makes use of 'the underdetermination thesis', that theory is underdetermined by data,[3] in order to argue that values of some kind are always involved in the formation and evaluation of hypotheses.

2 Second, it follows from this that there is no way of eliminating *a priori* the invocation of values in hypothesis formation and evaluation.

3 Third, she sets up a possible distinction between 'constitutive' values internal to the sciences, which determine rules of method, etc., and 'contextual' values external to proper scientific practice, which are culturally or socially contingent. But it follows, once again, from the underdetermination thesis, that there are no formal grounds to differentiate between these two types of values.

4 Fourth, this means that science which explicitly invokes 'contextual' (e.g. feminist) values is not necessarily 'bad' science.

The overall aim of the argument, then, is to show that there can, at least sometimes, be 'good' science which invokes socio-politically relevant ('contextual') values:

> This is not to say that all scientific reasoning involves value-related assumptions. Sometimes auxiliary assumptions will be supported by mundane inductive reasoning. . . . If, however, there is no a priori way to eliminate such assumptions from evidential reasoning generally, and, hence, no way to rule out value-laden assumptions, then there is no formal basis for arguing that an inference mediated by contextual values is thereby bad science.
>
> (Longino 1989: 207)

One of the corollaries of this position, as Longino points out, is that science which invokes androcentric values is not necessarily bad science either. We may therefore infer that any qualitative difference between androcentric science and feminist science has to be argued for on other grounds – presumably moral and political.

While I have greatly compressed the argument here, I hope this is sufficient to convey what I see as the main achievement of Longino's position. It sets out the theoretical grounds on which we may appeal to feminist values in enquiry by showing that values, some of which will inevitably be socio-politically relevant, lie at the heart not just of explicitly politically motivated research programmes, but rather at the heart of 'science-as-usual'. Notably it also illustrates the usefulness of the underdetermination thesis for feminist epistemology – a thesis which is central to the coherentist approach I will be recommending.

Longino's argument, then, stops short of claiming that social values are *necessarily* invoked in scientific enquiry. Sandra Harding, however, does embrace that stronger thesis. She argues that value-neutrality in science and research practice more generally is an impossibility, a myth. Once again, this is not just because the description and interpretation of data require a metaphysics, but rather because these processes also inevitably invoke socially relevant values. In both her most recent books (1986 and 1991) Sandra Harding explores the relative merits of different feminist epistemological stances, and a consistent salient feature of her discussions is a sense of the inevitability that any epistemic perspective, mainstream or otherwise, will 'bear the fingerprints' of its patron social group. Accordingly, therefore, feminist oppositions to mainstream thought must themselves continually seek a more acute critical self-awareness regarding the influence of their own particular gender, class and race perspectives. If one is in a position to voice opposition at all, then one is in a position of some power. Hence:

> Will not the selection and definition of problems always bear the social fingerprints of the dominant groups in a culture? With these questions we glimpse the fundamental value-ladenness of knowledge-seeking and thus the impossibility of distinguishing between bad science and science-as-usual.
>
> (Harding 1986: 22)

This political and epistemological insight leads her into a measured sympathy with feminist postmodernism,[4] in the characterization of which she draws substantially on the work of Donna Haraway (particularly 'A manifesto for cyborgs' (1990); first published in 1985). Both Harding's and Longino's views of value-neutrality, then, independently suggest that we can no longer think of socio-political values as necessarily distorting factors in belief-justification, with the result that an adequate epistemology must take this into account. It is in this sense that feminism demands an epistemology with a strong role for values, although so far it remains open quite how strong a role they should be given. In my discussion of Donna Haraway I will argue that the postmodernism she recommends in 'A manifesto for cyborgs' contains a dangerous ambiguity over this issue which urgently needs spelling out. But first, an argument for a realist account of empirical belief.

THE POLITICAL AND THE EMPIRICAL: A DIALECTICAL RELATION

There can be more or less realist accounts of empirical belief. The crucial distinction is whether we consider there to be a mind-independent reality placing normative constraints upon what we may correctly believe about the world. I will use the word 'realist' to describe any theory which incorporates this view (though in itself it is not necessarily a very strong realism). We may note that both Longino and Harding make certain realist assumptions in their arguments. Unsurprisingly, as a scientist, Longino holds that empirical data constrain what we may believe about the world: 'Obviously model choice is also constrained by (what we know of) reality, that is, by the data' (Longino 1989: 213). Harding, too, tends to talk of 'less distorted' belief, or the increased 'plausibility' of a certain theory, in similarly realist terms: 'many claims, clearly motivated by feminist concerns ... appear more plausible – *more likely to be confirmed by evidence* – than the beliefs they would replace' (Harding 1986: 24; my emphasis).

We can see, then, that a realist reliance on the empirical underwrites both Longino's and Harding's positions. But I would suggest an argument specifically to justify such realist assumptions. It takes the form of a generalization about political belief, to which there may be some exceptions but without detriment to the argument. It is this: *political beliefs are unintelligible in isolation from relevant empirical claims about real states of affairs in the world.* What would it mean, for example, to be committed to the eradication of poverty, or of violence against women, without a realist commitment to the empirical proposition that, say, whole communities are periodically wiped out by famine, or that many women suffer domestic violence and other forms of attack by men? Similarly, part of the motive for feminist epistemology is obviously political, but the backbone of this politics is a set of beliefs about real states of affairs and, in particular, real experiences had by women (and it makes no difference that these experiences are essentially mediated by culture, language and history).

The view that empirical claims underwrite political ones in this way is borne out if we think of the form political arguments usually take. Arguments for a given political action, say, writing off Third World debt, or increasing funding for women's refuges, inevitably turn on empirical claims respectively about the economies of developing countries, or the numbers of women who are battered. (This, of course, does not entail that empirical propositions are sufficient to determine political ones – empirical agreement is clearly no guarantee of political agreement.) Yet without a realist account of these empirical claims, we cannot invoke them as reasons for or against different political views or actions. Without an account of empirical beliefs which says that, if true, they pick out real states of affairs in the world, why should anyone's political opinions be influenced by them? In the absence of such an account, these kinds of political arguments are not *arguments* at all, but rather the mere taking of turns to profess commitment to an empirically free-floating proposition. This is a travesty of political consciousness. That we should seek an epistemology which allows us in principle to appeal to states of affairs as rational constraints upon political thought is therefore of vital importance to feminism.

This line of thought provides a counterweight to Longino's and Harding's discussions of how the empirical is permeated by the political or, put more generally, how fact is permeated by value. My argument suggests that the converse is also true, and the combined result is a picture of facts and values standing in dialectical relation. Earlier I made the general claim that it is an essential feature of belief that it should suggest itself to the subject with normative force. We have now come to the more specific claim that if political belief is to be answerable to empirical matters in the way that much of our political discourse presupposes, then we must have a realist account of empirical belief, for in such discourse the political presupposes the empirical as a normative constraint. Moreover, I have made the stronger claim that if we were to absolve ourselves of the need for realism by dropping this normative constraint, we would not be able to make adequate sense of our political commitments. To drop the constraint would be to sever our most deeply felt political convictions from the very states of affairs which inspire them, and to reduce them to epistemologically arbitrary by-products of history. It is sometimes argued that belief is best understood as a function of politics, and that we should therefore renounce any metaphysical claims about how reality constrains thought.[5] If what I am suggesting is right, then political consideration can be no *substitute* for normative constraints imposed by reality, since the former presuppose the latter. I hope by now to have established a realist restriction on how strong a role we should attribute to socio-political values in a feminist epistemology, and in the light of this we are now better equipped to discuss Donna Haraway's postmodernism.

A DANGEROUS AMBIGUITY

Weak and strong interpretations

The epistemological stance in Donna Haraway's article, 'A manifesto for cyborgs' (1990) grows out of its politics, and it is deliberately not set out in the form of an analytical argument. My representation of Haraway's epistemological position, then, is very much an extrapolation. This may partly explain the crucial ambiguity I find in her position, which is generated by the contrast between her bold expression of key postmodernist themes, such as the 'fracture' of social identity, and various isolated remarks of a somewhat modernist flavour about the general role of epistemology. I will therefore identify a weak and a strong interpretation of Haraway's position and, while agreeing whole-heartedly with the position emerging from the weak reading, I will argue that the problems associated with the strong show what can go wrong if we give socio-political values *carte blanche* to determine belief.

Haraway's central idea is the 'permanent partiality' of social and political identity. She argues that we must cease to base feminist politics on any supposedly universal common identity as women, and substitute some other form of solidarity or 'affinity' which would not rely upon the false and oppressive naturalization which, she argues, identity-politics necessarily invoked: '*The permanent partiality of feminist points of view* has consequences for our expectations of forms of political organization and participation' (1990: 215; my emphasis). It also has consequences for epistemology, however, since the dynamic of fracture affects not only our social and political identities, but thereby our epistemic perspectives too. Haraway pictures a world where the inhabitants (the part-machine, part-organism 'cyborgs'), are 'not afraid of permanently partial identities and contradictory standpoints' (1990: 196). The relation for Haraway between the 'permanent partiality' of social identity and that of epistemic perspective is compellingly expressed by Sandra Harding:

> Why not seek a political and epistemological solidarity in our oppositions to the fiction of the naturalized, essentialized, uniquely 'human' and to the distortions, perversions, exploitations, and subjugations perpetrated on behalf of this fiction? Why not explore the new possibilities opened up by recognition of the permanent partiality of the feminist point of view?
>
> (Harding 1986: 193)

Why not, indeed! *If*, that is, we give this rhetorical question a certain (weak) interpretation. A weak reading would interpret the commitment to 'permanent partiality' as an acknowledgement that *impartiality* is neither possible nor intelligible, and therefore as an affirmation of the view (a version of which was attributed earlier to Sandra Harding) that value-neutrality is a myth. On the weak reading, then, 'permanent partiality' may be understood as an expression of the essentially 'situated'[6] nature of knowledge. This acknowledgement obliges the subject to place herself within the critical field, opening her mind to how her own 'situation' may influence her beliefs. It therefore expresses the political and methodological imperative not to eclipse the perspectives of others.

Certain comments by Haraway lead one to suppose that she would support this weak reading of her position. There is apparently no obituary intended for epistemology in this postmodernism, since she warns us that 'in the consciousness of our failures, we risk lapsing into boundless difference and giving up on the confusing task of making partial, real connection. Some differences are playful; some are poles of world historical systems of domination. *Epistemology is about knowing the difference*' (1990: 202–3; my emphasis). In contrast to the general tenor of this comment, however, we must now consider a strong reading of Haraway's position, especially since there is an anti-'totality' argument elsewhere in her paper which seems to impose this stronger interpretation.

On the strong reading it is not just an overdeveloped sense of failure which would lead us into a chaos of 'boundless difference' with nothing to systematize our beliefs, but rather it is Haraway's unqualified recommendation of 'permanent partiality' itself. Since no restrictions upon the splintering dynamic of partiality are specified, the strong interpretation would feature 'permanent partiality' not merely as the acknowledgement of the situatedness of knowledge, not merely as a political and methodological imperative, but as an epistemological ideal in itself: crudely put, the more partial the perspective, the more reliable the beliefs which issue from it. On this reading, Haraway's warning against the collapse into 'boundless difference' is in vain, for her proposal provides no basis on which to have the recommended splintering stop short of this collapse. As long as the partiality of perspective is presented as desirable in itself, then what justification could one give for halting its progress? Merely affirming the desirability of making 'partial and real connection' is insufficient to neutralize the acid of this deconstructive principle, and this has the devastating consequence that there is no way of justifying the maintenance of any shared belief-system without committing a pernicious act of coercion: the eclipsing of the perspective or potential perspective of some person or group. Without a shared belief-system we clearly cannot sustain the minimal realism which I have argued is necessary to feminist politics (and which Haraway, at times, seems to recommend); nor can we maintain norms for belief; nor sustain any systematic self-critical practice. The strong reading of Haraway's position, then, would not meet any of the three epistemological conditions I have argued for as desirable for feminism.

The war on 'totality'

So far the discussion has been ambivalent as to whether Haraway's arguments commit her to the weak or the strong reading of her position. But, as mentioned above, she presents an argument against 'totality' which rules out the weak interpretation: 'The feminist dream of a common language, like all dreams for a perfectly true language ... is a totalizing and imperialist one. In that sense, dialectics too is a dream language, longing to resolve contradiction' (1990: 215). However, the weak reading of Haraway, which emphasizes the situatedness of knowledge, does not demand the rejection of 'totality'; on the contrary, I would suggest it specifically requires some form of 'totality' *as a regulatory ideal*. While all belief is inevitably permeated by social, historical and linguistic influences, our practices of belief-justification must nevertheless be orientated to an ideal of truth. If belief is non-arbitrary – that is, normatively constrained – then it follows that it is indeed orientated to such an ideal, for norms cannot be operative in a directionless discourse. Yet this, I take it, would be ruled out by Haraway's argument against 'totality'. Moreover, such an ideal of truth must be that of a *unitary* – i.e. self-consistent – truth, for if it were not internally coherent then it would not be placing any constraints upon the direction of discourse, since any new proposition would be equally (in)compatible with the existing body of belief. If this is right, then there is no middle ground here for Haraway: either we retain the 'totality' of a unitary truth as a regulatory ideal, or we suffer the dire consequences of the strong postmodernist position. Her unqualified attack on 'totality', then, burdens her with that disastrously and unnecessarily strong position.[7]

The suggestion that we should retain the 'totalizing' ideal of a unitary truth just to orientate our epistemic practice is quite compatible with the political and methodological imperative not to eclipse others' perspectives. This imperative obliges us to remain sceptical about any given claim to truth, as does the thought that unitary truth is only an ideal, and thus in practice unattainable. This thought generates a keen sense of our fallibility, and so of the need to keep our belief-system as loose and open as possible, entertaining contradictory beliefs not because contradiction is *in principle* epistemologically tolerable, let alone desirable, but because to do so is a rational response to the awareness of our situatedness and our resulting epistemic limitations. I would agree with Haraway, then, that entertaining contradictory beliefs and viewpoints must comprise part of our methodology, and furthermore that doing so can be a positive epistemic resource in a desperately complex world. But the crucial disagreement with Haraway here is that this methodology of openness does not entail *believing contradictions*, for the entertainment of contradictory beliefs is strictly provisional: contradiction remains intolerable at the level of epistemology. On this view, we also retain a second form of 'totality' in the sense that epistemology remains a single integrated project (as it appears Haraway, in her less postmodernist moments, might wish). It is just that this integrated epistemology is more complex and politically sophisticated than during the reign of value-neutrality. The need for a regulatory ideal of self-consistent truth combined with a methodology of openness recommends a fallibilistic, coherentist epistemology. As long as this can be made compatible with a realist account of the empirical, perhaps that is where we should be headed.

A FEMINIST COHERENTISM

To summarize: we started with two closely related feminist arguments undermining the ideal of value-neutrality in knowledge, from which we inferred the need for an epistemology which gives a strong role to values (at least some of which will be socio-politically relevant). We then considered a particular feminist postmodernist position as a candidate for such an epistemology, endorsing the weak reading which affirms the essential situatedness of all belief, but rejecting the strong reading for the reason that it goes too far, resulting in epistemological chaos. I then suggested that we must supplement the weak reading with the regulatory ideal of a unitary truth, and that, provided we retain a methodology of openness, we could do so without detriment to the political imperative not to eclipse alternative epistemic perspectives.

I now propose a second candidate for a suitable epistemology: coherentism, or rather holism. It will obviously not be possible to spell out a detailed formulation here, but I hope to show, albeit in schematic form, that coherentism constitutes a promising epistemology for feminism, for it can be interpreted as giving a strong role to values without forfeiting a realist account of empirical belief. We might think of such a coherentist position, first, as providing a suitable epistemological background for Harding and Longino's arguments for the rejection of value-neutrality; and second, as fleshing out the weak interpretation I have offered of Donna Haraway's position. It depicts belief as normatively constrained both by reality and by a process of rational self-criticism, and thus it can satisfy the realist requirement as well as the two epistemological desiderata specified at the outset. We might also note the further advantage that coherentism can meet these requirements while staying flexible as to the precise *degree* of independent influence which the world is said to exercise on belief, thereby remaining open to more or less realist interpretations. I am proposing a certain kind of coherentism, then, as an epistemological framework with promise for diverse kinds of feminist development, both with regard to its realism, and more particularly with regard to the exploration and analysis of the influence of social factors on the determination of belief.

A suitable model to start with is Quine's (Quine 1980). Despite being an empiricist theory, Quine's holism pictures knowledge as a *construct*, as a network of beliefs which is empirically pinned down only at the periphery. The belief-system as a whole, then, is pictured as *partially* constrained by reality. This kind of coherentism therefore incorporates what Helen Longino called 'the underdetermination thesis', which says that theory, while accountable to experience, is not fully determined by it. The result is that there is much 'latitude of choice' in theory construction, and this allows us to see values of various kinds as primary influences on the epistemic conventions operative within that latitude. In this sense, holism supports feminist arguments undermining the ideal of value-neutrality. Quine gives a 'naturalistic' account of our epistemic conventions, but the naturalistic view lacks socio-political focus. Holism, then, invites socio-political development regarding the different ways in which knowledge is situated, i.e., the ways in which socio-political values, among others, mediate data and theory. It should be added, however, that if our realism is to be of a non-naive variety, then the data themselves must be theorized as conceptual, and thus our modes of conceptualization are also proper objects of socio-political analysis.[8] But the more specific advantages of holism most relevant here are as follows.

A strong role for values

Holism's underdetermination thesis enables us to explain how we may claim that enquiry necessarily invokes values, where sometimes these values are socio-politically loaded. Opinions about which ones are in fact socio-politically loaded are bound to change over time. It is relatively recently, for example, that we have come to recognize the limitations and perhaps androcentricity of the 'adversary paradigm' in philosophy (Moulton 1983), and no one can predict what new revelations the future may hold. Analyses of which values are being invoked where, therefore, must be constantly evolving, as must our positive arguments for deciding to invoke certain values and not others in theory construction (in as far as we succeed in making ourselves aware of them).[9] These decisions will – as in Longino's position – inevitably have to be argued for at the time on moral/political grounds, but this consequence of holism provides no cause for embarrassment. Since political *interest* has been discovered at the heart of epistemic practice, it is only appropriate that political *argument* should be inserted at the heart of epistemology. What other way could there be, after all, to regulate the unavoidable influence of socio-politically relevant values?

A dialectic of facts and values

I said earlier that political and empirical beliefs – facts and values – stand in dialectical relation, so we need an epistemology which can incorporate that interdependence. Holism achieves this in two distinct ways. It allows us to assert that values, socially relevant or otherwise, influence our beliefs not singly, but through the belief-system as a whole. This has the result that, while some beliefs will be more directly influenced by values than others, no belief can remain immune in principle from the influence of values.[10] And this means that there is no sharp categorical distinction between empirical beliefs along the periphery and political beliefs further towards the centre; there can be no sharp distinction between facts and values.

105

The second and more substantial way holism supports the claim that political and empirical beliefs are interdependent is through the coherentist theory of justification which accompanies it: all beliefs in the system are logically interdependent, for their justification depends upon their coherence with the rest of the system. A change in one belief therefore resonates through the system so that it may recommend a change in others. Thus when a United Nations report declared in 1980 that women constitute half the world's population, perform nearly two-thirds of its work hours, receive one-tenth of the world's income and own less than one-hundreth of the world's property, the absorption of this empirical information may have entailed adjustments to the reader's political beliefs elsewhere in the system.

A realist account of empirical beliefs

Quinean holism is an empiricist theory. It pictures our belief-system as normatively regulated by publicly available stimuli emanating from sources out in the world – 'The edge of the system must be kept squared with experience' (Quine 1980: 45). This supplies the realist account of the empirical which I have argued to be required by feminist politics itself (though this is clearly an area for further development, since the kind of experience of which feminism ultimately requires a realist account involves far more than mere physical stimuli). Likewise it supports the implicit realist assumption made by both Harding and Longino. We might also note that holism's principle of coherence preserves the proposed supplement to Haraway's weak thesis, namely, the regulatory ideal of a unitary truth, and that it does so without positing any belief as absolutely (or 'totally') true in the sense of being above revision.

The empirical dimension to holism means that the values which inevitably play a substantial role in our practices of belief-justification do not have *carte blanche* in constructing knowledge. We might say that reality anchors our belief-system, for it provides substantial empirical constraints on what we may believe. These constraints, however, become weaker the further towards the centre of the belief-system we go. That is to say, empirical constraints obviously restrict empirical beliefs *more*, and more directly, than they restrict, say, political beliefs, though we have already noted that holism permits no sharp distinctions here.

A normative role for empirical data

Reminding ourselves for a moment of the two epistemological restrictions specified at the beginning of this paper, we should ask whether coherentism provides norms for belief. This question is already answered in the section above, for if coherentism can afford a realist account of empirical belief by depicting it as normatively constrained by the world, then *a fortiori* we have norms for empirical belief. Moreover, norms are supplied by the degree to which different beliefs are answerable to empirical matters; by the dual principle of coherence and simplicity; and, it has been argued, by mediatory values of various kinds.

A self-critical practice

Moving to the second of the two initial epistemological restrictions, the final feature to recommend coherentism is that it can provide an account of reflective self-criticism in our epistemic practices. The essence of the standard Quinean account is that in order to evaluate and perhaps revise any given area of the belief-system, we must provisionally take up an attitude of unquestioning acceptance towards the rest of the system in order to have a position from which to criticize the section under review. Neurath's well-known metaphor, often cited by Quine, of the sailor rebuilding his ship while at sea gives lucid expression to this idea.

This account of self-criticism and revision within the system can be adapted to our purposes, since it can be extended to explain how marginalized groups can initiate rebellion against a given epistemic hegemony. Neurath's metaphor explains how it is possible that feminists have been able to observe the (often unconscious) sexist biases in many fields of study, including science and philosophy. The gap of underdetermination between empirical data and theory explains how there remains room for self-interested manoeuvre in theory construction and in epistemic practices generally, so that powerful groups can use values to fashion belief to serve their interests. But by the same token, this theoretical context equally provides room for less powerful groups to rebel – to rock Neurath's boat, so to speak. Holism gives marginalized groups the epistemological licence to assert their own perspectives and to force revisions piecemeal in the collective belief-system, though the *actual* success of this process will depend upon the political climate or, in my terms, on whether a methodology of openness prevails.

It is true that on this account we can never question or revise all our beliefs at once but only in small groupings, but this does not prevent us from gradually following through the implications of our revisions throughout the whole system. And where revision depends on a many-sided ongoing debate, it seems more appropriate to think of it as progressing step by step, rather than as hurtling towards infinite partiality. It is no special disadvantage to feminist critical practices that we can never step off Neurath's ship. On the contrary, feminist arguments to the effect that knowledge inevitably involves value-judgement independently advise us that the very idea of stepping off onto some neutral *terra firma* is a pernicious myth. Thus holism provides an epistemological context in which to place both feminist deconstructive critiques and reconstructive proposals, since these are a radical instance of holism's more general capacity for the self-critical revision of belief.

In summary, holism and the underdetermination thesis provide a theoretical model which can explain how values permeate even our most rigorous forms of enquiry, and it achieves this without forfeiting the realist account of empirical belief in which I have argued our very politics is anchored. The construction necessary to bridge data and theory means that it is both epistemologically legitimate and politically imperative that feminist and other progressive politics should contribute to the architecture of epistemology.[11]

NOTES

1 Genevieve Lloyd (1984) provides a useful study spanning Plato to Simone de Beauvoir of the association of 'woman' with phenomena deemed enemies of reason, such as passion, the body, nature and 'immanence'.

2 'Empirical' here is intended in its broadest sense, to include not just experience of the material world, but also experience of which the content is morally or politically coloured.

3 Longino does not discuss exactly what conception of 'data' she is working with, but I presume she would wish to avoid any conception which fails to acknowledge that data themselves are theory-laden. See, for example, Donald Davidson (1973).

4 This sympathy arises largely out of her criticisms of the essentialist tendency in standpoint theory, but it should be noted that the more recent book enacts a *rapprochement* with standpoint theory as Harding defends it against the charge of essentialism.

5 See, for example, Richard Rorty's arguments for pragmatism as an ally of feminist politics, in which he says that what it is 'pragmatic' (and thus, on his view, true – though not 'True') to believe depends on the *interests* of one's particular social group. Political interests, then, are said to determine true belief (1991: 234).

6 I borrow this phrase from a later article by Donna Haraway, 'Situated knowledges: the science question in feminism and the privilege of partial perspective' (1988).

7 In the later article, 'Situated knowledges' (1988), Haraway explicitly distances herself from what she calls 'the strong program in the sociology of knowledge', though she proposes an analysis of objectivity which is again given exclusively in terms of partial perspective: 'only partial perspective promises objective vision' (1988: 582–3). This analysis therefore remains perilously close to what I have identified here as an unfortunately strong position.

8 See those articles in *Feminism and Science* (Tuana 1989) which critically examine the ways in which biological phenomena have been conceptualized by scientists.

9 See, for instance, Helen Longino's remark that she and her research partner, Ruth Doell, chose to invoke a model of human beings as capable of self-determination, and that this decision was an aspect of their feminism (Longino 1989: 211).

10 See also Elizabeth Potter: '[the "Network Model"] makes it clear that even good scientific theories, by all the traditional criteria, can be androcentric or

sexist in the sense that a sexist or androcentric assumption constrains the distribution of truth values throughout the system' (1989: 144).

11 Many thanks to Sabina Lovibond and to Kathleen Lennon for their comments on earlier drafts of this paper.

REFERENCES

Davidson, Donald (1973), 'On the very idea of a conceptual scheme', *Proceedings and Addresses of the American Philosophical Association*, vol. 67 (1973–4), pp. 5–20.

Garry, Ann and Pearsall, Marilyn (1989), *Women, Knowledge and Reality: Explorations in Feminist Philosophy*, Boston: Unwin Hyman.

Haraway, Donna J. (1988), 'Situated knowledges: the science question in feminism and the privilege of partial perspective', *Feminist Studies*, vol. 14, no. 3, pp. 575–99.

Haraway, Donna J. (1990), 'A manifesto for cyborgs: science, technology and socialist feminism in the 1980s' in *Feminism/Postmodernism*, ed. Linda J. Nicholson, New York and London: Routledge, pp. 190–233 (first published 1985 in *Socialist Review*, no. 8).

Harding, Sandra (1986), *The Science Question in Feminism*, Milton Keynes: Open University Press.

Harding, Sandra (1991), *Whose Science? Whose Knowledge? Thinking from Women's Lives*, Milton Keynes: Open University Press.

Harding, Sandra and Hintikka, Merrill B. (eds) (1983), *Discovering Reality: Feminist Perspectives on Epistemology, Metaphysics, Methodology, and Philosophy of Science*, Dordrecht: Reidel.

Lloyd, Genevieve (1984), *The Man of Reason: 'Male' and 'Female' in Western Philosophy*, London: Methuen.

Longino, Helen (1989), 'Can there be a feminist science?' in *Women, Knowledge and Reality: Explorations in Feminist Philosophy*, ed. Ann Garry and Marilyn Pearsall, Boston: Unwin Hyman, pp. 203–16 (also in *Feminism and Science*, ed. Nancy Tuana, Bloomington and Indianapolis: Indiana University Press, pp. 45–57).

Moulton, Janice (1983), 'The adversary method' in *Discovering Reality: Feminist Perspectives on Epistemology, Metaphysics, Methodology, and Philosophy of Science*, ed. Sandra Harding and Merrill B. Hintikka, Dordrecht: Reidel, pp. 149–64.

Nicholson, Linda J. (ed.) (1990), *Feminism/Postmodernism*, New York and London: Routledge.

Potter, Elizabeth (1989), 'Modeling the gender politics in science' in *Feminism and Science*, ed. Nancy Tuana, Bloomington and Indianapolis: Indiana University Press, pp. 132–46.

Quine, Willard Van Orman (1980), 'Two dogmas of empiricism' in *From a Logical Point of View: Nine Logico-Philosophical Essays*, Cambridge, MA: Harvard University Press, pp. 20–46 (first published 1953).

Rorty, Richard (1991), 'Feminism and pragmatism', *Michigan Quarterly Review*, vol. 30, no. 2, pp. 231–58 (reprinted in *Radical Philosophy*, no. 59 (Autumn 1991), pp. 3–14).

Tuana, Nancy (ed.) (1989), *Feminism and Science*, Bloomington and Indianapolis: Indiana University Press.

7

WOMEN'S AUTHORITY IN SCIENCE

Diana Sartori

I

If one looks at that area of thought and study generally called 'gender and science', the most obvious thing one notices is that in the last ten to fifteen years, particularly in Anglo-American work, there has been a quite significant development in this area, at least when one looks at the longer and longer bibliographies one has to quote. These are made even longer by the most recent, and often quite contrasting, efforts to organize the existing material, and to define exactly the state of the field. During these years, I have been reflecting on gender and science, trying to relate what has emerged within Anglophone discussions to the terms of the Italian debate closer to home, and my attitude has gone through several phases. Initially, I felt an optimistic curiosity, which turned to distance and distrust, and now, recently, I have become more interested again. These phases were marked, for me, by two 'signs', which I shall try to explain.

I came across the first sign in 1988, reading Barbara Imber and Nancy Tuana's summary of the points which emerged in the contributions to *Hypatia* republished in the collection *Feminism and Science* (Tuana 1989). Imber and Tuana started off by saying that 'there is consensus... that science is not value-neutral, that cultural/political concerns enter into the epistemology, methodology and conclusions of scientific theory and practice' (Imber and Tuana 1988: 139). I was struck by such an explicit affirmation of the importance of politics in science and in reflection on science. It seemed to me, on the contrary, that this reference to politics and to the way in which it permeates and determines scientific activity owed more, in the current debate, to an unreflective reference to the Marxist tradition and critical theory, on the one hand, and on the other to the more recent tradition of epistemological criticism of positivism, rather than being a real self-questioning about the meaning, direction and effectiveness of women's politics. As a result, the political possibilities of feminism ended up being dependent on these two critical traditions, while the issue of women's politics remained completely obliterated by the traditional concept of poli-

110

tics. I thought it would be difficult to conceive of a dialogue between this kind of tradition and the one to which I am attached, which was growing in Italy at that time and whose most fundamental root was its link with the reflection and political practice of the women's movement. Consequently, my attitude towards the Anglo-American debates on gender and science became marked by the idea that there was an almost insuperable distance between us.

The second sign I mentioned confirmed my judgement, but also had the effect of modifying my attitude. In fact, some of the positions which have emerged more recently within that debate seem to me to be giving the discussion a real change of direction, so that the distance does not appear so great. This makes it easier for me to imagine the possibility and even the value of looking at what our debates might have in common. This beneficial shift was promoted by the woman who has perhaps contributed most to the development of the debate on science, Evelyn Fox Keller, and who has facilitated the widespread discussion, among American feminists, of the question of conflicts between women.[1] Her co-edited book, *Conflicts in Feminism*, includes, as well as discussion of political conflicts, a lucid article on conflicts in science, written by Helen Longino and Evelyn Hammonds. It is in this article, and in the context of scientific conflict, that I found the most precise 'sign' of the possibility that the two traditions I mentioned might converge.[2]

Helen Longino starts from the intuition that the conflicts taking place within the gender and science debate conceal the real ground of the argument. While on the surface there is disagreement between epistemological or philosophical options, in reality the matter concerns disagreements of a political nature, particularly about whether one intends to change science from the 'inside' or from the 'outside'. However, these differences are not confronted as such; they should preferably not be mentioned. Why is this? All of Longino's hypotheses suggest the same explanation: conflicts are 'refracted through the father's eye' (Hirsch and Keller 1990: 176) so women are divided between themselves by traditional male divisions, and fight over the one and only place next to the man. The appeal in her final paragraph invites us to look at how new our arguments are, to free ourselves from the narrow limits imposed on us by traditional categories – while recognizing that this will not mean the elimination of disagreements among women – and is equivalent to an invitation to escape submission to the image 'refracted through the father's eye'. To leave Helen Longino, and using the language of the tradition I am familiar with, I could say, submission to the paternal symbolic order.

The intervention by Helen Longino (like that of others such as Fox Keller, Hammonds, Teresa de Lauretis or Jacquelyn Zita) indicates an awareness of the necessity to connect the perspectives of women's research, in this case, epistemological and scientific research, to the more properly political dimension of feminist reflection of the last few years. Such an approach characterizes the style of Italian feminism (as many have recognized, for instance at the international Feminist Theory Conference in Glasgow, July 1991), which has always sought to maintain a strong connection between theoretical elaboration and political practice, unlike what has happened to feminist movements in other countries, where political debate and 'academic' research, under the aegis of women's studies, have sometimes diverged (although the latter necessarily derives its power from its commitment to benefiting women). On this issue I believe that some of the Italian debates, particularly the work of the Milan Women's Bookstore Collective, and the 'thought of difference' theorized by the women's philosophical community, Diotima, might be useful. In particular, the problem represented by *women's authority* needs to be looked at in relation to the crucial area of science.[3] I think in fact that the problem of *authority* represents the central node of the complex interweaving of elements which create the present situation of conflict (and in certain ways, of impasse) in the sphere of women's theoretical and political reflection on science. Let me try and explain this more clearly.

II

Science, modern science at least, has to do, in a very specific way, with authority. In the process (well described by Hannah Arendt[4]) of a progressive weakening, in the modern era, of authority in its classical forms, the only form of authority that still maintains its strength and moreover has ended by encapsulating and replacing the others, is that of science. This remains true, even if the crisis of science has been talked about for more than a century, even if there is an exacerbated acceleration of the tendency away from authority in so-called postmodern society. This does not seem to have changed the social investment in scientific knowledge as a source of authority: in spite of having been demythified and its often poor showing, science maintains such an aura (it has perhaps even increased it) that it has the last word. So, science has authority. Even more, it *is* authority. I think it's important to look at how this happens and what its consequences are.

Historically, if we look at the time in which science in its modern sense takes shape, at the 'scientific revolution', it is easy to see how, at the origins of modern science, a problem of authority arises. On the one hand, there is a question of principle, in fact it is the 'argument from authority' that is Galileo's target. On the other hand, there is the question of the redefinition of *de facto* authority, as the Church well understood. The famous abjuration by Galileo was not enough to restore the breach in the old order of authority; it enacted the submission by the scientist as an individual to the institutionalized political and religious authority, but the authority of science was no longer in Galileo's hands or tied to his destiny; it lay in the impersonal power of scientific method. Since then, it is said to be the method that legitimates the authority of scientists; they enjoy a cognitive authority deriving from the scientific method which is authoritative, and it is to method alone that they refer when assessing the validity and meaning of their activity. In this way, the elimination of other human factors, such as social relations, ideals, religious and political convictions, becomes not only permissible, but in fact required by the constitution of science and of the subject of science.

Besides this question of method, there are many aspects accompanying the origin and development of modern science as we know it which determine the criteria of authority: above all, its universality and its connection to truth. It is because of the idea that scientists, thanks to method, have a special access to universal knowledge and to the truth, that we are prepared to attribute so much authority to them. Both these factors put them in a position of distance, superiority and at the same time, irresponsibility towards the world and their fellows, where they affirm both the mythology of the autonomy of science and that of the freedom of research, as implicit guarantees of the justifiability of the scientific enterprise as well as of everyone's freedom. The concepts of objectivity, neutrality and scientific realism also belong to such a circuit between the authority of things and the authority of science, via the method, and the aim of truth. Evelyn Fox Keller observes:

> The question of whether scientific knowledge is objective or relative is at least in part a question about the claim of scientists to absolute authority. If there is only one truth, and scientists are privy to it (i.e. if science and nature are one), then the authority of science is unassailable. But if the truth is relative, if science is divorced from nature, and married instead to culture (or 'interests'), then the privileged status of that authority is fatally undermined.
>
> (Tuana 1989: 40)

I come now to the second point, which is the enormous extent of the consequences of that authority, and especially where the relation of women (scientists or not) with science is concerned. Among the elements to bear in mind regarding the extent and significance of the effects of scientific authority, the most important is that although it represents itself as autonomous and independent of social and intellectual conditioning, science is itself a social enterprise which is influenced by and also determines the discursive and relational structure of the social form of which it is part. The figure of the autonomy of science is the particular modality according to which such a social-symbolic order produces a socially effective authority. As I've already mentioned, most feminist scholars have directed their criticism to the presumed neutrality of science, and its claims to be value-free, so that this critique now appears to be generally accepted. It has some unarguable merits, among them that of demythifying science and revealing its inbuilt sexism, showing how it is at the level of science's inbuilt epistemology and its images that prejudices take root and get reproduced. However, this critique runs the risk of remaining within the boundaries of a reactive position which has little substantive effect.

I have already pointed out that, in my opinion, this limitation is connected to the failure to look at the problem of authority. It's not that the analysis is unaware of the relevance of the element of authority within science, but often feminist critique views this authority from an exclusively antagonistic point of view, with the more or less explicit intention of proceeding to a challenge of its legitimacy *tout court*. The critique then runs the risk of sounding quite simply anti-scientific, and alienating the women who love and practise science. The justified critique of scientific authority as it now is (falsely neutral, sexist, both authoritarian and irresponsible) needs to be connected to an autonomous consideration of the problem of authority, which can bear in mind on the one hand the fact that women are both involved in science but also extraneous to it, and on the other, the difficulty and the necessity of thinking women's authority within science. It is here that it can be useful to refer to the theoretico-political work that women have been doing on the crucial problem of women's authority.

In fact, one of the most significant contributions of the Italian feminist debate of the last few years has been to locate the main obstacle to women's freedom in their lack of authority, their lack of symbolic authorization, rather than in male oppression. The political experience of the feminist movement has shown how a problem exists in relation to authority, so that, for example, a woman has a particular difficulty both in exercising authority in her own name and in acknowledging the authority of another woman. On the symbolic level, authority remains bound to the name of the father, adhering to the masculine symbolic order, and when it is a woman's body that bears the authority, she presents herself as a 'substitute', continuing to refer to the paternal order. What brings it about that having authority and being a woman are perceived as fundamentally contradictory is the refusal to recognize sexual difference, and the absence of the symbolic figure of an authority of female origin, that is, of the mother's authority. Female authority is the only thing which can authorize a woman to escape the image 'refracted through the father's eye'. The aim of the 'practice of relation between women', privileging female mediation in its various forms, is to re-establish the greatness of the mother figure and 'female genealogy' through the mother and daughter line.[5] Perhaps the most important mediation, surely the most discussed in the Italian debate, is *affidamento* or entrustment, a relation between two women which functions as a means of mediation with the world, in which disparity and the authority of the other are recognized. This makes possible the reconciliation with the mother at a symbolic level, and the constitution of an order of relations between women at a political level (see Muraro 1991).

Returning to what was said earlier, I think that if we bear in mind this lesson, which comes from the more properly political dimension of the feminist debate, it is possible to shed light on a series of problems in the sphere of women's research in science, and to understand better the nature of the critical points where the problems get stuck. On the one side, authority is invested in the scientific enterprise, it is the determining characteristic of the symbolic and social power of science as men have wanted it; on the other side, that of the enterprise of women's freedom, authority appears as the crucial transition to the determination of what women are able to want for themselves. It is clear, then, that the convergence of the two sides creates a high level of potential conflict. If, in other words, our essential problem is authority, and science presents itself as the main locus of authority, then there is no doubt that science is a problem which concerns us essentially.

III

Reflecting with other women, both scientists and non-scientists, who belong to Ipazia (Hypatia) (which we intentionally call a 'scientific community' and not a 'group'), I have reached the conviction that there is a need for women to have scientific authority, and this must be the aim of the political work that needs to be done. The statement that women need to have authority in science is, in view of what was said in the previous section, likely to meet with considerable disagreement, first of all because of how scientific authority is currently understood, but also because of how women, including declared feminists, feel about scientific authority. There are two different reasons for this, which reinforce each other: first, the representation given by science of its own authority is taken to be correct; second, women themselves have difficulty effecting a reorientation towards a different symbolic reference of authority and acknowledging women's authority. Some women maintain that they cannot countenance women's authority, because they fear it will simply be a mirror-image of what they know male authority to be. Such a reaction shows, besides a suspicion of women's authority, how deep-rooted is the traditional image of authority – defined as neutral, objective, univocal, value-free etc. On the contrary, we must remember that these are the ingredients, the criteria, the ideals, which maintain and justify our scientific authority as a social and symbolic structure. They correspond to some justified requirements: the need that there should be a scientific authority, and that it should act within self-imposed limits on arbitrariness or deception. But they also express some clear purposes, imposed historically in relation to specific subjects, wishes, interests, metaphysical and epistemological commitments, not the least of which is that of claiming the pre-eminence of one sex, by means of a strategy of making it the only sex, and denying the significance of sexual difference. Putting forward such a model is not without consequences: in fact it cuts, along the line of principle, the umbilical cord which connects scientific knowledge to what gives birth to it, in principle and in fact; in a similar way to that in which the work of the mother remains unrecognized, with the contradictory result of seeking to eliminate the ineliminable, namely the necessary continuity between the two levels, without which knowledge is dead.

Neutrality, universality, truth, objectivity link arms, forming the circle of the authority of science. Both the logical and the material structure of this device for the production of scientific authority join to maintain and reinforce each other, cutting themselves off from their source and referring only to themselves. The criteria which constitute such a structure are none the less at one and the same time a particular form of mediation with that from which it cuts itself off, i.e. the vital and social context. It is for this reason that it is rather ineffective to focus on regulating science by criteria external to it, appealing to criteria and values that belong to a domain whose relevance is denied and neutralized *in principle* by the way in which the circle of scientific authority is drawn and closes on itself. This doesn't mean that there is no external regulation; it takes both tacit pathways, and also, when it is congruent with internal criteria, it takes the highway. These routes align themselves with the might and power of the existing order. This does not mean that they are ruled out as routes to women's freedom; women are not completely powerless and have, by necessity, learnt to make use of the existing structures for their own ends. There remains though an obstacle of principle which blocks the highway, that of the definition of the constitutive criteria which, because of the ways in which they define the nature of authority, disallow the very idea of female scientific authority. Women's authority requires therefore a new and autonomous definition of the criteria of scientific authority. This work still has to be accomplished. However, I believe that it is possible at least to indicate some of the elements that this work should undertake.

I believe that in order to rethink the supporting criteria of scientific authority, we should seek first of all to overcome the model of science as a self-enclosed domain, and look beyond the traditional approach (which corresponds to science's vision of itself) which sees an opposition between science and politics or between truth and *senso*.[6] One of the limits of the critical approach is that one is immobilized by the dilemmas of this polarity; one is forced into a blind alley in which 'value-free' is replaced by 'political correctness'. The key point is that of the relation between truth and *senso*. I have already explained that truth is the main criterion among those contributing to the establishment of scientific authority in its present form; in this version, science would be authoritative in so far as it is tied to truth, where truth is defined *a priori* as not belonging to the domain of *senso*. From this perspective, then, the scientific enterprise is thought of as the social enterprise producing truth. Given the centrality of the category of truth in our present conception of knowledge, I feel that in saying this, it might seem I am saying a lot, perhaps too much. On the contrary, I am convinced, with Nancy Cartwright, that 'truth doesn't explain much' (Cartwright 1983) and that there exists a real overestimation of the value of truth in science. The criterion of truth, at least the traditional criterion of truth as correspondence, is, I believe, inadequate to describe either the effectiveness of the model or the explanatory value of the theories.

By this I do not wish to place myself among those who criticize science's claim to truth with the aim of weakening it. On the contrary, the quest for truth does not appear to me to be an excessive demand, or an unrealistically high aim. Instead I think that it is not enough. Not enough, anyway, when we consider the authority that accrues to those who profess the quest for scientific truth. Consequently I don't think it is necessary to weaken scientific authority, and even less do I think that this would be to women's advantage. I believe instead that we should think rather of raising the requirements for authority – which, at the moment are limited in principle to competence, and *de facto* to the observation of the rules for membership of the community of professional scientists – and develop criteria which could overcome science's self-enclosure. This would mean first of all reconnecting the dimension of truth with that of *senso*.

In addition, the criteria of truth which are constituted internally to an order of *senso* have a different value for those who are fully part of that order, because they have constructed it, and those – women – who are, fundamentally, outsiders. Cutting off truth from *senso* may be acceptable to those who share *senso*. On the contrary, for those who are unable to share it, the quest for truth remains, quite literally, senseless. This is the contradiction complained about by many women who are engaged in scientific research, and yet are extraneous to it. We should add also the impossibility of women acceding to authority, which confirms how illusory it is to put one's faith in the current legitimating criteria for scientific authority. Even if the scientific enterprise is willing to recognize the formal authority of competence, and even if its institutionalization tends to invest authority in whoever has a function in it, there is no real authority unless there is a real connection to the *senso* of the enterprise of which one is part, whether scientific or otherwise. For these reasons, I see the problem of women's authority in science as insoluble, unless we bring about a change in the symbolic order, i.e. a reconfiguration of the horizon of *senso*, so that the qualification 'women's authority' is no longer subordinate but constitutive, able to reformulate the very criteria of scientific authority. It is not a matter of 'mental' change, even if it certainly implies something similar to a revolution of the mind. Just as the criterion of truth is not formal but bears all the materiality of the relation with reality, so the criterion of *senso* brings with it all the concreteness of the relation with the community with which it is shared. To transform *senso* requires a revolution in relationships as well.

If what I have affirmed up to now is at least in part well-founded, then for a woman to have authentic scientific authority requires various conditions and changes and in the first place, the one that has made me put the adjective 'authentic' before authority, i.e. the awareness of the substantial inappropriateness of the authority offered by science as it is at present. By this, I don't mean that if, for instance, a woman is a scientist, she should reject, in the name of loyalty to her sex, whatever authority accrues to her from membership of the scientific community. When I speak about female scientific authority, I am referring to a higher stake: that of going beyond the alternative implicit in the choice between identity as a scientist and identity as a woman. If a woman refuses to submit to this choice, if she truly loves both science and herself, if she wants to abandon neither science nor her own desires, but does not wish to restrict herself to complaining, an effective acknowledgement of this situation will mean a move in the direction of transforming the idea of scientific authority. Which can mean a number of different things: it would certainly mean looking at science with a different eye, but equally it would mean looking in a different direction, and looking towards one's fellow women. If in fact it is inevitable that registering the contradiction in science between the ineliminable fact of being a woman and having the authority of a scientist will create some change in the *senso* to be given to science itself; it is equally inevitable that if one wants to find a new *senso*, the starting-point will have to be that ineliminable fact. If being a woman is the factual bedrock, then the symbolic reference to those who share the fate of that factual determination will be indispensable in the shared creation of *senso*. Turning away from 'the reflection in the eye of the father', I shall have to turn my glance towards other women, and first of all towards those with whom choice, desire or chance has brought me into contact.

This was the suggestion made by Helen Longino; it implies an alternative that she has described elsewhere as a choice concerning the community to whom we hold ourselves 'accountable' (Longino in Hirsch and Keller 1990: 54). In Italy, some women have in contrast spoken of a conflict between the different communities to which one 'belongs', either to the scientific community, or to one's own sex or to the feminist community. I am not satisfied with either of these two formulations. Instead, in order to define the crux of the alternative we are talking about, I would like to use the term *affidabilità*, trustworthiness. I prefer this term, not for aesthetic reasons, but because it suggests the idea of a bond with someone to whom one is loyal, while expressing at the same time an essential characteristic that science should possess. I see in fact in trustworthiness the special quality and primary aim of knowledge that can be defined as scientific: in uncertainty, to be able to have a trustworthy knowledge. This has been traditionally interpreted in the sense of the quest for truth, certainty or objectivity, and the scientific method has structured itself as a guarantor of these aims. However, trustworthiness has a much wider and deeper significance than these criteria have. The latter derive from scientific method, and are mostly centred on the object and on the methodological rigour of the research. Whereas trustworthiness reminds us of the tie not only to the object under investigation and the mode of investigation, but also to the subject, and further to a subject who is not identical with the one who is researching, and who seeks knowledge. It reminds us that this tie is carried into the very heart of the scientific enterprise, it is internal to it. From this perspective, for instance, the women of Ipazia (to which I belong) have suggested that one meaning of scientific community is: those who practise the relation competents/incompetents.

The authority of science and authority within science are, after all, nothing other than what springs from that essential need for trustworthiness; there they have their first roots. Authority turns on trustworthiness, and this happens in a relation in which, no matter how unequal the reciprocal acknowledgement, a recognized community of *senso* has to exist. Women do not have authority in science because there, as in other places, this primary pact on which the community of *senso* rests was a pact between men, and the consequent regulatory ideals (competence, rigour, control, objectivity, etc.) are valid within that pact and not outside it. We may respect them but we were not part of the community which created them.

For this reason I believe that the alternative I referred to earlier – between faithfulness to scientific method and its rules and faithfulness to one's own sex – has to be considered from the perspective of trustworthiness. For, when we look at it from this point of view, certain clues come to light. The first: that with science as it is, there is no possible relation of trustworthiness, unless one understands the latter in its impoverished meaning of mere competence and the formal acceptance of scientific criteria. The second: that the reference to one's fellow women, in terms of trustworthiness, can go beyond simple solidarity, extending as far as outlining the possible source of a new female authority in science, but also to the wider sphere of the structure of social relations. In this respect, to focus on a principle of trustworthiness is, I feel, potentially fruitful from a methodological point of view, because, as scientific criteria have been able to do, it seems able to act not only as a regulatory and demarcating principle, but also to indicate a method and an effective practice: a method and practice involving the redefinition of relations between women within the scientific community, but also between these women and those who are outside it, with all that this can mean with respect to demarcation and the function of the scientific community.

Here, on the terrain of the practice of trustworthiness, we return to the complex interweaving of elements in women's politics which I mentioned in the first section, and to the question of the 'how' which Helen Longino identified as the central issue of women's debate on science. The alternative appeared to be 'from the outside' or 'from the inside', an alternative which is paralysing but not inevitable. It only appears inevitable if one goes no further than the rigid self-descriptions with which science and sometimes also feminist politics represent themselves. I think that the practice of women's authority and trustworthiness with regard to one's fellow women could avoid that apparently inevitable dilemma, if only by confusing the tracks of the paths marked 'inside' and 'outside'. However, it isn't a route that leads us outside science; indeed, I am convinced of the opposite, namely that it leads towards its centre. A woman who, practising science, makes herself trustworthy *vis-à-vis* her fellow women, brings in fact a seed of trustworthiness and therefore of authentic authority to science itself.

Translated by Emmanuela Cervato with Margaret Whitford

NOTES

1 First in her essay 'Competition and feminism: conflicts for academic women' in Keller and Moglen (1987), and then in her co-edited collection *Conflicts in Feminism* (Hirsch and Keller 1990).

2 Helen E. Longino and Evelynn Hammonds, 'Conflicts and tensions in the feminist study of gender and science' in Hirsch and Keller (1990).

3 See the Milan Women's Bookstore Collective (1990), Diotima (1987, 1990). A longer version of the present essay can be found in Ipazia (1992). See also Bono and Kemp (1991) for a useful anthology of Italian feminist debates.

4 At various points in her thought. See in particular Arendt (1958, 1968).

5 The concept of genealogy comes from the thought of Luce Irigaray. See in particular Irigaray (1987), which has been very influential in Italy.

6 [We have kept *senso* in Italian, since it has a range of different meanings for which it was difficult to find a single English equivalent, and yet for which it seemed important to retain a single term, as in Italian, because of the centrality of the concept to the argument of the paper. *Senso* can mean: sense, sensation, feeling, sentiment, judgement, understanding, meaning, import, direction, way. Diana Sartori provides the following gloss: 'The term includes, at one and the same time, the semantic field, the value and the symbolic and cultural relationships attributed to a concept. Therefore you cannot determine "truth" unless you have reached a previous statement of *senso*. *Senso* establishes the conditions within which "truth" can be determined. As far as science is concerned, *senso* refers to the possibility of an explanation' – Eds.]

REFERENCES

Arendt, Hannah (1958), *The Human Condition*, Chicago: University of Chicago Press.

Arendt, Hannah (1968), *Between Past and Future: Eight Exercises in Political Thought*, New York: Viking Press.

Bono, Paola and Kemp, Sandra (eds) (1991), *Italian Feminist Thought*, Oxford: Blackwell.

Cartwright, Nancy (1983), 'Truth doesn't explain much' in Nancy Cartwright, *How the Laws of Physics Lie*, Oxford: Clarendon Press, pp. 44–54.

Diotima (1987), *Il Pensiero della Differenza Sessuale*, Milan: La Tartaruga.

Diotima (1990), *Mettere al Mondo il Mondo*, Milan: La Tartaruga.

Diotima (1992), *Il Cielo Stellato dentro di Noi*, Milan: La Tartaruga.

Hirsch, Marianne and Keller, Evelyn Fox (1990), *Conflicts in Feminism*, New York and London: Routledge.

Imber, Barbara and Tuana, Nancy (eds) (1988), 'Feminist perspectives in science', special issue of *Hypatia*, vol. 3, no. 1.

Ipazia (1992), *Autorità Scientifica, Autorità Femminile*, Rome: Editori Riuniti.

Irigaray, Luce (1987), *Sexes et parentés*, Paris: Minuit. Trans. as *Sexes and Genealogies*, trans. Gillian C. Gill, New York: Columbia University Press.

Keller, Evelyn Fox and Moglen, Helen (1987), 'Competition and feminism: conflicts for academic women', *Signs*, vol. 12, no. 3, pp. 493–511.

Milan Women's Bookstore Collective (1990), *Sexual Difference: A Theory of Social-Symbolic Practice*, Bloomington and Indianapolis: Indiana University Press.

Muraro, Luisa (1991), *L'Ordine Simbolico della Madre*, Rome: Editori Riuniti.

Tuana, Nancy (ed.) (1989), *Feminism and Science*, Bloomington and Indianapolis: Indiana University Press.

8

WOMEN, POWER AND TECHNOLOGY

Annette Fitzsimons

Elizabeth Grosz argues that the aim of feminist theorizing is to construct alternative theoretical strategies and that there is a need to go beyond simply critizing either existing theory or practice. She states:

> if it remains simply reactive, simply a critique, it ultimately affirms the very theories it may wish to move beyond. It necessarily remains on the very ground it aims to contest. To say something is not true, valuable, or useful without posing alternatives is, paradoxically, to affirm that it is true, and so on.

> (1990: 59)

By focusing on gender and technology, I want to examine the extent to which the feminist critiques of technology construct either theory or strategies for change, or to what extent they produce the type of negative or reactive project discussed by Grosz. The feminist critique of science and technology which stresses the male dominance of science would appear to reproduce and thus affirm the theories which it criticizes, and I will argue in this essay that this occurs because of the concept of power and dominance which characterizes these critiques. The debates on gender and science have structured the debates on gender and technology, as technology is rarely discussed without reference to science. As Judy Wajcman explains:

> The development of a feminist perspective on the history and philosophy of science is a relatively recent endeavour. Although this field is still quite small and by no means coherent, it has attracted more theoretical debate than the related subject of gender and technology . . . feminists pursued similar lines of argument when they turned their attention from science to technology.

> (1991: 1)

The feminist critique functions on a number of levels. One dimension concerns the articulation of the scientific project, scientists' own conception of their enterprise. Elizabeth Fee in her article 'Critiques of modern science:

the relationship of feminism to other radical epistemologies' (1986) provides a number of examples of this bias, including the now infamous statement from Richard Feynman who called the idea that inspired the work for which he won a Nobel prize an

old lady, who has very little that's attractive left in her, and the young today will not have their hearts pound when they look at her anymore. But we can say the best we can for any old woman, that she has become a very good mother and has given birth to some very good children. And I thank the Swedish Academy of Science for complimenting one of them.

(Fee 1986: 45)

Moreover, the emphasis on objectivity and a specific idea of rationality within scientific methodology legitimates not only scientific knowledge but also men's involvement and women's exclusion from science and technology. From the emergence of modern science, science has been conceived as the control of nature. The characteristics which denote science in our culture link the high status of scientific knowledge with men and the control of nature. Men are characterized as closer to culture versus women as closer to nature. Men and science are deemed rational in contrast to women who are defined as emotional and irrational, illogical. As Weininger (1906) stated:

A being like the female, without the power of making concepts, is unable to make judgments. In her 'mind' subjective and objective are not separated; there is no possibility of making judgments, and no possibility of reaching, or of desiring, truth. No woman is really interested in science; she may deceive herself and many good men, but bad psychologists, by thinking so.

(cited in Tuana 1989: vii)

The masculinity of science has not only been manifest in its conceptualization of itself; scientific knowledge has been used to legitimate the confinement of women to the sphere of the 'natural' not simply because of mistaken male bias and lack of understanding but, according to some writers, in order to control and dominate women. According to Cockburn (1985), Corea (1985), Faulkner and Arnold (1985), this involves male dominance in the real sense of actual men having power and control of women, and the use of scientific reasoning and practices to legitimate this control. For some writers, the problem of science and therefore technology would be solved by the involvement of more women in the scientific community – the 'adding women on' approach. For others (Harding 1986, Rose 1986) the problem is much more fundamental and requires a reassessment of scientific methodology.

The issue I want to concentrate on is the link between the feminist critique of science and the feminist critique of technology in relation to male dominance and male power. In the literature on women and technology, there appears to be a borrowing of, and concentration on, the idea that technology is used by men to subordinate and control women, and the conflation of science with technology. As Wajcman states: 'technology, like science, is seen as deeply implicated in the masculine project of the domination and control of women and nature' (1991: 17). To deal with the question of power, I want to begin by providing some examples from the literature to demonstrate the notion of power which underpinned the feminist critique of science and technology.

For example, Margaret Low Benston in *Inventing Women* writes that

> power is the most important message that male use of technology communicates. Power over technology and the physical world is just one aspect of men's domination of this society. . . . Male power over technology is both a product of and a re-enforcement for their other power in society. Even at the household level, every time a man repairs the plumbing or a sewing machine while a woman watches, a communication about her helplessness and inferiority is made.
>
> (1992: 37)

As I indicated earlier there is a long list of books and articles which discuss women's relationship to the power of science and technology in these terms (see Corea 1985, Arditti *et al.* 1984, Cockburn 1985). The problem with this is that women are positioned as passive victims of male dominance and male control. Women are cast as the dominated, as powerless. 'Power is associated firmly with the male and masculinity. Commentators on power have frequently remarked on its connections with virility and masculinity' (Hartsock 1990: 157). The discourse around technology is thus shaped by these masculinist discourses on science and power. So, for example, when feminists write about 'power over our bodies', 'power over our lives' they are using the concept of power and domination which pervades the traditional discourses on power. Thus there is, as Grosz argued (see above), an affirmation of this conceptualization of power rather than the posing of an alternative. It provides little, if any, room for manoeuvre from conceptualizing the relationship between women and technology in ways other than those of domination, and hinders the creation of a strategy for change. The notion of power used to theorize the gender, science and technology debates imitates the traditional, 'masculinist' approach best exemplified by the work of Steven Lukes in his book *Power: A Radical View* (1974). Power is viewed as repressive, as emanating from the top downwards, either through governmental and social elites, state and/or class interests. Foucault says of conceptualizations of power such as these, that:

it allows power to be only ever thought in negative terms: refusal, delimitation, obstruction, censure. Power is that which says no. Any confrontation with power thus conceived appears only as transgression. . . . The manifestation of power takes on the pure forms of 'thou shalt not'.

(1979: 53)

Starting from his critique of this way of formulating power in society, Foucault outlines a different way of thinking about power. If power is always about domination posed

only in terms of constitutions, sovereignty etc., hence in juridical terms; [and] on the marxist side, in terms of the state apparatus [, then t]he way in which it was exercised concretely and in detail, with its specificity, its techniques and tactics was not looked for; one contented oneself with denouncing it in a polemical and global manner, as it existed among the 'others' in the adversary's camp: power in Soviet socialism was called totalitarianism by its opponents, and in western capitalism it was denounced by marxists as class domination, but the mechanics of power were never analysed.

(1979: 34)

Rather than concentrating on the negative, repressive aspects of power, Foucault argues that if this was the only story about power it cannot explain what he terms the productivity of power. The way power 'produces things . . . induces pleasure . . . forms knowledge . . . produces discourse' (1979: 36). Foucault's critique of this formulation and his analysis allows a more emancipatory analysis of power which enables the establishment of a framework for examining women's relationship to technology.

Feminists have long talked about power in much more diverse ways than those discussed within mainstream academia. By talking about gender-relations in terms of power, feminists put on the agenda the idea that the whole of social relationships involves notions of power. This includes the recognition that whenever two or more people are engaged in some activity, power conflicts and struggles are involved. This means, however, that women are also involved in the exercise of power. Rather than viewing power with unease, or in terms simply of male dominance, as coercion, as a negative concept, the fact that women have and exercise power means that power cannot simply be located with men. Foucault's 'new' concept of power provides the possibility of enabling a productive discourse on power which could be used to explore the empowerment of women in ways that could be progressive and liberating. Nancy Fraser (1989) also puts forward a positive reading of Foucault on power, arguing that his analysis enables power to be analysed at the micro-level, at the level of everyday practices, and turns the focus away from power residing with the state or with the economy. Jana Sawicki (1991) makes very similar points in her discussion of Foucault and power. She analyses the ways in which his concept of power differs from traditional conceptions, which concentrate on power as dominance, or repression, and discusses the exercise and productivity of power in relation to identity and sexuality and the body.

In the second part of this chapter I want to perform a similar exercise in relation to gender and technology. In order to begin to recast this debate, it is necessary to separate analytical science and technology. As was explained at the beginning of the piece, much of the literature uses the debate around science to discuss technology. This has meant that the same restrictive analysis of power and dominance which pervades the debate on science also saturates the debates on gender and technology, and as I hope to demonstrate, both limits and restricts our understanding of technology.

If you take a long historical view you find that women were closely involved with the earliest technologies both in terms of technique, e.g. knowledge and knowhow, and also in terms of design and use. The historical evidence would appear to suggest that women in western industralized societies, continued, up to and during the industrial revolution, to be as involved as men were with technology. Gradually they were moved out of this arena either because women were deemed to be unable to cope with technology or because women's skills were not recognized and/or the concept of technology narrowed, so that only male activities were designated technological and women's activities and skills were devalued. It would appear then that, though Cynthia Cockburn is correct to argue that '[t]echnological competence is a factor in sex-segregation, women clustering in jobs that require little or none, men spreading across a wider range of occupations which include those that call for technical training' (1985: 9), this is only correct in relation to a specific historical period. It only represents one dimension of women's relationship to some kinds of technology and obscures the more complex involvement of women both historically and in the present day. The history of computing provides a clear example that women can take the lead in technological involvement. Women were the first computer programmers (Kraft 1977, Lloyd and Newell 1985, Wajcman 1991), though as has been pointed out, in what is both a history of this occupation and an analysis of the process of deskilling which has been in progress within this particular labour process:

It is one of the ironies of programming that women pioneered the occupation, largely by accident, only to make it attractive to men once the work was redefined as creative and important. The further irony, however, is that the men who followed the women pioneers – and effectively eased them out of the industry – eventually had their work reduced into something that was genuinely like clerical labour.

126

It was at this point that women were allowed to re-enter the occupation they had created.

(Kraft 1977: 5)

These women worked in the Department of Defense for the American government, and in my own research on computer programmers I interviewed women who did similar programming work for the British Ministry of Defence. It is only when the importance of computer programming was recognized, and thus status entered into this occupation, that the type of changes referred to by Cockburn occur. In other words it is not technological competence which is paramount as such, but the status, power and control which goes with this competence. It follows then that Cockburn is incorrect to argue that 'only very recently have women begun to aspire to technical training and work' (1985: 8). The historical picture is much more complex.

Following the models proposed by Keller (1992) and Long and Dowell (1989, cited in Keller 1992) I would propose that technology has moved through a number of stages historically. First, the craft stage, where product invention and use were designed for a specific purpose and women were part of all of these three processes. This stage can be put on the long historical path from hunting and gathering societies through to the beginnings of industrialization. Women had the techniques and the knowhow. Cockburn (see her discussion 1985: 21) would disagree with this picture, as she argues that women were excluded from craft production, but the historical evidence from Stanley (1983) and Griffiths (1985) would appear to indicate that women were engaged in specific crafts and trades, and that during this stage women designed, made and used technology. Cockburn's analysis of this stage is, I would argue, based on a limited use of the term 'technology'. Three different layers of meaning are identified by MacKenzie and Wajcman (1985) (see also Wajcman 1991 and Bush 1983). These are: technology as a form of knowledge; technology as a form of practice; and finally technology as physical objects. The debates on gender and technology have tended to concentrate on the first layer of meaning, on knowledge and knowhow. Cockburn uses technology in this limited way to refer to a very specific type of technological knowledge which she terms 'essentially a transferable knowledge, profitably carried from one kind of production to another' (1985: 26). Ironically it seems that she is using a definition which refers to a later stage (applied science) where technological knowledge is exclusively the property of a small number.

The second stage is characterized by the 'Engineering' model, which excluded most women in terms of technique and use, though some historical examples are available of women who were involved in both. For example the work of Lillian Moller Gilbreth (Trescott 1983) in engineering, and the first women computer programmers who work on ENIAC –

127

Electronic Numerical Integrator and Calculator (see discussion above) could be included in this stage. Gender and technology in the present day is shaped by the 'Applied Science' model. Essentially technology and science during this stage are controlled mainly by rich white men which excludes practically all women and the majority of men, in terms of technique but not of use. The latter categories include the consumers and users of technology. As Cockburn writes: 'women are to be found in great numbers *operating* machinery, and some operating jobs are more skill-demanding than others. But women continue to be rarities in those occupations that involve knowing about what goes on inside the machine' (1985: 11). Many times in the literature on women and technology the role of women as 'simply' consumers and users of technology is discussed, and this is usually presented in a negative way. However, if we pay attention to the historical relationship of women to technology and understand technology so as to include all three layers of meaning we can see that there is no *necessary* antagonism between women and technology; and that women's relationship to technology is not necessarily that of passive victims.

This historical perspective aids our project of redefining women's (actual and potential) relationship to technology via reconceptualizing the relationship between technology and power. It is here that we need to make use of a concept of power alternative to that associated with control and domination.

In light of the arguments outlined above about the micro-practices of power, in terms of pleasure and control, and the importance of these micro-dimensions of power in upholding a macro-level of power, it is important to acknowledge some element of personal power within the 'user' relationship to technology. For example, people who can drive a car, an aeroplane, a tractor, who can work a computer, a camcorder, a mixing desk, seem to have more control, authority and autonomy than those who are unable to use these technologies. Highlighting the pleasure and power which can be exercised through the use of technology prepares the ground for a distinct way of theorizing around gender and technology which is specific to technology and marks out the distinction between science and technology. Through the identification of technology with applied science, and a particular mode of conceptualizing science, women are constructed as passive recipients of technology. In this model women who don't make, control or understand technology are thus dominated and controlled by it. This simplifies the reality of the different ways in which women relate to technology, and by encouraging this particular discourse, feminist analysis is perpetuating the myth of a female subject who is situated within the discourse of technology as a controlled and passive user. The implication of my argument for a feminist analysis of technology is that a fundamental starting-point needs to be the specific social interests that structure the knowledge and practice of particular kinds of technology. Incorporating the conceptualization of power suggested in this essay could provide a framework for a positive theory of power, unlike the traditional approach which views power as negative, as aggressive, as destructive, as 'male', and which excluded women from participation in the exercise of power in areas of social life.

This is not to deny the exclusion of women from the exercise of power at a macro-level or to deny the ambiguity of Foucault's analysis of power for women. He never discussed the gendering of power, but then again, according to Meaghan Morris and Paul Patton (Foucault 1979: 8–9), Foucault's aim was never to provide a theory of power but rather a description of the various techniques of power. From these descriptions, this 'genealogy' of power, one can extract a positive discussion, even an optimistic discussion of power. Foucault does not dispute the coercive and repressive aspects of power but whilst accepting these dimensions he also explores what he calls the 'productivity' of power. As he says:

> If power was never anything but repressive, if it never did anything but say no, do you really believe that we should manage to obey it? What gives power its hold, what makes it accepted, is quite simply the fact that it does not simply weigh like a force which says no, but that it runs through, and it produces things, it induces pleasure, it forms knowledge, it produces discourse; it must be considered as a productive network which runs through the entire social body much more than as a negative instance whose function is repression.
>
> (1979: 36)

I would argue that whilst it is true that Foucault's analysis does not provide in any way a complete or properly theorized analytical model of power which feminists can use, he does, however, provide a framework from which one can start to build an analysis, a model, if you like, of gender and power, which may help to recast the debate on gender and technology. This framework would enable the construction of alternative feminist strategies rather than continuing to use theories of male dominance based on a notion of power which

> is limiting because it detemporalized the process of social change by conceiving of it as a negation of the present rather than as emerging from possibilities in the present. In so doing, it restricts our political imaginations and keeps us from looking for the ambiguities, contradictions and liberatory possibilities.
>
> (Sawicki 1991: 86)

REFERENCES

Arditti, Rita, Duelli-Klein, Renate and Minden, Shelley (eds) (1984), *Test Tube Women: What Future for Motherhood?* London: Pandora Press.

Benston, Margaret L. (1992), 'Women's voices, men's voices: technology as language' in *Inventing Women: Science, Technology and Gender,* ed. Gill Kirkup and Laurie Smith Keller, Oxford: Polity Press with Open University Press, pp. 33–41.

Bleier, Ruth (ed.) (1986), *Feminist Approaches to Science,* New York: Pergamon Press.

Bush, Corlann Gee (1983), 'Women and the assessment of technology: to think, to be; to unthink, to free' in *Machina Ex Dea: Feminist Perspectives on Technology,* ed. Joan Rothschild, New York: Pergamon Press, pp. 151–70.

Cockburn, Cynthia (1985), *Machinery of Dominance,* London: Pluto Press.

Corea, Gena (1985), *The Mother Machine,* London: The Women's Press.

Faulkner, Wendy and Arnold, Erik (eds) (1985), *Smothered by Invention: Technology in Women's Lives,* London: Pluto Press.

Fee, Elizabeth (1986), 'Critiques of modern science: the relationship of feminism to other radical epistemologies' in *Feminist Approaches to Science,* ed. Ruth Bleier, New York: Pergamon Press, pp. 42–56.

Foucault, Michel (1979), *Michel Foucault: Power, Truth, Strategy,* ed. Meaghan Morris and Paul Patton, Sydney: Feral Publications.

Fraser, Nancy (1989), *Unruly Practices: Power, Discourse and Gender in Contemporary Social Theory,* Oxford: Polity Press.

Griffiths, Dot (1985), 'The exclusion of women from technology' in *Smothered by Invention: Technology in Women's Lives,* ed. Wendy Faulkner and Erik Arnold, London: Pluto Press, pp. 51–71.

Grosz, Elizabeth (1990), 'Contemporary theories of power and subjectivity' in *Feminist Knowledge: Critique and Construct,* ed. Sneja Gunew, New York and London: Routledge, pp. 59–120.

Hanmer, Jalna (1983), 'Reproductive technology: the future for women' in *Machina Ex Dea; Feminist Perspectives on Technology,* ed. Joan Rothschild, New York: Pergamon Press, pp. 183–97.

Harding, Sandra (1986), *The Science Question in Feminism,* Milton Keynes: Open University Press.

Harding, Sandra (1991), *Whose Science? Whose Knowledge? Thinking from Women's Lives,* Milton Keynes: Open University Press.

Hartsock, Nancy (1990), 'Foucault on power: a theory for women' in *Feminism/Postmodernism,* ed. Linda J. Nicholson, New York and London: Routledge, pp. 157–75.

Hekman, Susan J. (1990), *Gender and Knowledge: Elements of a Postmodern Feminism,* Oxford: Polity Press.

Keller, Laurie Smith (1992), 'Discovering and doing: science and technology, an introduction' in *Inventing Women: Science, Technology and Gender,* ed. Gill Kirkup and Laurie Smith Keller, Oxford: Polity Press with Open University Press, pp. 12–32.

Kirkup, Gill and Keller, Laurie Smith (eds) (1992), *Inventing Women: Science, Technology and Gender,* Oxford: Polity Press with Open University Press.

Kraft, Philip (1977), *Programmers and Managers: The Routinisation of Computer Programming in the United States,* New York: Springer Verlag.

Lloyd, Anne and Newell, Liz (1985), 'Women and computers' in Anne Lloyd and Liz Newell, *Smothered by Invention: Technology in Women's Lives,* London: Pluto Press, pp. 283–51.

Lukes, Steven (1974), *Power: A Radical View*, London: Macmillan.
MacKenzie, Donald and Wajcman, Judy (eds) (1985), *The Social Shaping of Technology*, Milton Keynes: Open University Press.
McNeil, Maureen (ed.) (1987), *Gender and Expertise*, London: Free Association Books.
Nicholson, Linda J. (ed.) (1990), *Feminism/Postmodernism*, New York and London: Routledge.
Rose, Hilary (1986), 'Beyond masculinist realities: a feminist epistemology for the sciences' in *Feminist Approaches to Science*, ed. Ruth Bleier, New York: Pergamon Press, pp. 57–76.
Rothschild, Joan (ed.) (1983), *Machina Ex Dea: Feminist Perspectives on Technology*, New York: Pergamon Press.
Sawicki, Jana (1991), *Disciplining Foucault*, New York and London: Routledge.
Scutt, Jocelynne (ed.) (1990), *The Baby Machine: Reproductive Technology and the Commercialisation of Motherhood*, London: Green Print.
Stanley, Autumn (1983), 'Women hold up two-thirds of the sky: notes for a revised history of technology' in *Machina Ex Dea: Feminist Perspectives on Technology*, ed. Joan Rothschild, New York: Pergamon Press, pp. 5–22.
Stanworth, Michelle (ed.) (1987), *Reproductive Technologies*, Oxford: Polity Press.
Trescott, Martha Moore (1983), 'Lillian Moller Gilbreth and the founding of modern industrial engineering' in *Machina Ex Dea: Feminist Perspectives on Technology*, ed. Joan Rothschild, New York: Pergamon Press, pp. 23–37.
Tuana, Nancy (ed.) (1989), *Feminism and Science*, Bloomington: Indiana University Press.
Wajcman, Judy (1991), *Feminism Confronts Technology*, Oxford: Polity Press.
Zimmerman, Jan (1986), *Once Upon the Future: A Woman's Guide to Tomorrow's Technology*, New York and London: Pandora Press.

9

THE KNOWING BECAUSE EXPERIENCING SUBJECT

Narratives, lives and autobiography

Liz Stanley

INTRODUCTION

The phone went when I was fast asleep Saturday night. It was Alan[1] [my brother][2] to say Mum was in hospital, might have had a stroke, had been found that evening by a neighbour & John [my cousin] I thought he said but that was wrong. . . . I rang the hospital. . . . It was a stroke, a bad one they thought, & the next 48 hours would be critical. . . . Not much sleep. About two troubled hours, & lying there with all kinds of things going through my head. Hoping that it somehow wasn't true, just all a dreadful mistake; not being able to believe it; hoping that she would die & not linger paralysed like Mr Humphrey [her neighbour] did. . . . And so on, round & round. . . . We drove down the 300 miles with me in a complete daze . . . all practical things going round & round in my mind but behind them a dull dazed horror. I wanted to wail, but it seemed too dramatic and too premature and anyway it's difficult to react like that when you're watching yourself for signs of in/appropriateness. . . . I was so shocked when I saw Mum. She looked so different from when I saw her on Wednesday that I wouldn't have recognized her or only with difficulty. . . .

(Monday 3 September 1990)

I really did expect to be summoned last night, but again nothing after 8 or is it 9 or 10 days [since the last stroke]. . . . But no, on & on she goes. I feel exhausted, drained; until today she's looked better than I do. I spent much of yesterday by the bedside reflecting on the nature of 'life' & 'not-life' and where one begins and the other leaves off, the puzzle of human consciousness or whatever it should be called. Whatever 'it' is . . . progressively – regressively – 'it' has faded, departed. Today for the first time she actually looks like she's dying, her skin colour and tone, but also something much harder to specify, just the way she looks.... I seem to be in a perpetual British Rail waiting room ... but one echoing all the time with this dreadful breathing, so laboured that it exhausts me because I find myself breathing each breath with her and willing it to be the last, and a kind of feeling that I shall stop breathing when she does....

(Monday 9 March 1992)

In this chapter I explore some aspects of a feminist epistemology (a theory of knowledge) and its relationship to a feminist ontology (a theory of being); I do so by engaging with debates concerning how we should understand and theorize the notion of 'self' inscribed in autobiography. The autobiographical has recently proved a rich seam for academic feminism to mine (Jelinek 1980, 1986; Stanton 1984; Benstock 1988; Brodzki and Schenck 1988; Personal Narratives Group 1989; Heilbrun 1988); and the richer the seam, the more a variety of poststructuralist, deconstructionist and postmodernist tools have been employed to work it. However, I consider that feminist postmodernist writing about 'the self' and autobiography is insufficient on a number of grounds, in particular because narrative is the key to the complexities of the self and not something to be excised, as this approach suggests, from the feminist analysis of lives. 'The self' is immensely complex and feminist conceptualizing of it, within as well as across conventional discipline boundaries, needs to be correspondingly complex. Biography and autobiography are not only intertextually referential of each other, but also 'self' does not exist in isolation from interrelationship with other selves and other lives; it is grounded in the material reality of everyday life, and a key part of the constitution of this material reality is formed by the narrations of selves and others that figure so importantly in everyday talk as well as being a 'hidden' component of much academic writing.

My principal concern is the narration of lives which constitutes the 'bio' in 'auto/bio/graphy' (self-life-writing). The narrative focus of the large majority of autobiographical accounts – spoken as well as written – has been castigated by some feminist analysts as naively referential and such experiential claims treated as not only problematic epistemologically, but also as unamenable to analytical and theoretical investigation because closing off contrary argument. I shall argue, against this, that narrative is highly complex and its referential claims frequently exist to repair what is actually an awareness of ontological complexity and fragmentation; that experiential claims are no less but certainly no more problematic than other kinds of knowledge-claims; and that both narrative and 'experience' are suitable ground for analytical investigation.

FEMINISM, POSTMODERNISM AND 'THE SELF'

Postmodernism (in which, for the sake of shorthand, I include poststructuralism and deconstructionism) I characterize as a set of ideas, 'postmodernist theory' or 'postmodernism', and distinguish from 'postmodernity', a claim concerning a particular kind and degree of postulated social change. Among other things, postmodernism constitutes a set of ideas concerning 'the self'. Conventional ideas about the self are depicted as bourgeois humanist ones which are apparently totalizing but in practice assign selfhood to only a specific kind of person. This traditional grand narrative of the self is seen as an ideology which promotes its supposed coherence and linearity, its temporal development and significance, and which must be challenged and replaced by an understanding of the actual fragmentation, polyphony and atemporality of the self. In postmodernist theory the self is instead positioned in relation to situated knowledges and presentations, as contextually and temporally specific rather than as static and unitary.

There are different feminist ways of reading postmodernist theory. One is to see it as the exposition of interesting, challenging and crucial ideas which imply and hopefully herald an end to the hegemony of 'science' – ideas which challenge and encourage demolition of the totalizing grand narratives of 'theory'. Another equally plausible way to read it is as the return of the recently displaced 'great men' in their new guise as apparently 'dead authors'; as the replacement of one tribal totem of male social theory – 'Marx–Weber–Durkheim' – with another – 'Derrida–Baudrillard–Foucault–Barthes–Lyotard'; and as itself a meta-narrative, but a de-politicizing and anti-feminist one.[3] There is a middle ground, of course, but those feminists who inhabit it[4] largely accept the critique while arguing that the ideas are too important not to support.

Rather than debate the pros and cons of such arguments abstractly, I look at them through the feminist use of postmodernist ideas in analysing women's autobiographical writing. There have been a number of important feminist collections on autobiography with a strong theorizing editorial presence, of which Estelle Jelinek's (1980) *Women's Autobiography*, Domna Stanton's (1984) *The Female Autograph*, Shari Benstock's (1988) *The Private Self*, and Bella Brodzki and Celeste Schenck's (1988) *Life/Lines*, are perhaps the best known. These promote 'a canon' of women's autobiographical writing, formed largely by 'good' women writers: the names of Zora Neale Hurston, Maxine Hong Kingston, Maya Angelou, Alice James, Colette, Mary McCarthy, Audre Lorde, Simone de Beauvoir, Virginia Woolf, Djuna Barnes, Emily Dickinson, running like ink between them. This canon-establishing writing rejects the narrative conventions by which 'a life' is typically inscribed in autobiography by deconstructing the claimed referentiality between a life and writing about a life as mere textual rhetorical artifice. The strongest exposition of this is in Domna Stanton's editorial, which argues that 'bio' should be removed from auto-bio-graphy, refocusing the emphasis from the writing of one's *life*, to the *writing* of one's *self*: 'autography'.

I have a number of problems with such a line of argument. Narrative – in this case, in the form of the story of a life – is neither so simple nor so easily dismissed as this argument suggests, and nor is referentiality. It needs to be pointed out that the statement of this theoretical approach is itself narratively produced. Moreover, it is not only theorists – feminist, postmodernist or any other – who have an analytic awareness of the complexities, silences, fractures and changes of 'the self', and a good many of such ontological complexities are expressed and explored in autobiographical writing that is narratively and temporally expressed and which is strongly referential.

In an earlier discussion (Stanley 1992) I analysed such complexities contra this canonical writing by reference to a range of autobiographical writing, particularly spiritual narratives written by three black Methodist women in mid-nineteenth century America, collections of 'coming out' stories by lesbian women, and the diaries of Hannah Cullwick (which I had earlier (Stanley 1984a) edited). These autobiographical writings take a clear 'this and then that' narrative form in which the life of the self, and thus the writing self also, is constructed by means of strong referential claims. But – and what an important 'but' it is – they do so in awareness of the 'inner' fragmentations of self as also expressed in outward behavioural and interactional form, positioning the writing of a narrative of a life as a means – one means – of constructing coherence and identity for self; they also inscribe something of the distinction and tension between versions of the 'I', the self, not least the tension between the self as an experiencing subject and the imposition on this self of constructions of 'it' as 'a woman'.

Here I provide my response as an *autobiographer*, turning analytic attention towards my own 'intellectual autobiography' (Stanley 1984b, 1985, 1988, 1990b, 1992; Stanley and Wise 1990, 1992, 1993), my own uses of narrative, sense of the fragmentations and the coherences of self, as I go about the business of understanding the ontological and epistemological status of a self apparently in dissolution. In doing so I make three broad arguments, concerned with self, with narrative and with the referentiality or otherwise of this autobiographical depiction of (aspects of) 'my life', which I return to in the conclusion. My data is composed by transcribed tapes of some fifty or so hours of conversations with my mother, but particularly by a research diary I kept from when my mother had a very severe cardio-vascular arrest (CVA or 'stroke') until her death nineteen months later.[5] I use these autobiographical materials to address four themes which bear upon my understanding of self, narratives and lives: my mother's changing 'self', my changing constructions of this, my changing relationship to 'my Mum' and referential and anti-referential currents in my diary-writing about these matters.

MY MOTHER'S CHANGING SELF

The tapes I made with my mother were produced in the context of my father's death in August 1984, after a six-year period in which he suffered (I use the word advisedly) many minor strokes, the cumulative impact of which left him almost without language, partly paralysed in one leg, confused and for most of the time very angry with those of us who tried in any way to constrain his behaviour (Stanley 1988, 1990c). Among other matters, on the tapes my mother talks about family histories on both 'sides', her own and my father's; working-class life in Southern (where my parents lived their lives) between the wars and as compared with working-class life for their parents' generation, and many other matters. On them she also reflected a good deal about 'the meaning of things', all the things that had happened during her life.

In September 1984, in a conversation about her parents and siblings and their deaths, my mother said 'I don't exist any more'. In October 1986, when discussing family holidays shared with two of her sisters, their husbands and children, and the subsequent deaths of all those of her generation, she said 'they're all gone, so have I really'. On the same topic, in December 1989 she said 'there's no point in my being alive, well, I'm not really, I'm just waiting'. I read these remarks, made when my mother was fully 'a self' as we culturally understand this, as indicating that she held a view of her self as one shared in common with an age cohort that centred on her family and friends. Hers was a non-unitary and anti-individualist self: a collective self, and one which had 'gone' and was in her just 'waiting' after this collectivity had, through death, departed from her life. What was left was a strong-willed and determined woman, but withal a woman who lived in the past – this was what mattered to her, intellectually and emotionally.

In the early hours between 31 August and 1 September 1990, my mother had a stroke of such severity that she was not expected to survive, but did. For three months I spent about seven hours a day being with my mother on the hospital 'female elderly acute' Nightingale Ward she went to following the stroke, and then the ward for long-term elderly female patients, the Gaskell Ward at Queen Charlotte Hospital. During this period of time I was, daily, hourly, by the minute, forcibly struck by the complexities of my mother's post-stroke self. Her stroke brought with it a demolition of the apparatus of self as we culturally understand it: my mother could not speak because of her inability to comprehend the spoken word apart from in occasional broad outline; she also lost her ability to interact with others, in the sense of her behaviour responding to that of other people. None the less, the complexities of my mother's self, following the demolition of these apparatuses of self, were considerable:

> Nothing ... could possibly convey ... how changed she is. ... CVA brain damage for Mum ... [makes her] react more on internal assessments, thoughts & so on, not in the ways we learn as interactionally appropriate. Yes that's it I suppose, it's really something about being an entirely solitary self, a Warty Bliggins[6] who knows that all the world centres on him and his toadstool. For Mum 'intersubjectivity' in Schutzian terms doesn't really take place: I enter her domain on her terms and her terms alone.
>
> (Wednesday 3 October 1990)

A few weeks later I commented that:

> Mum now has an 'I' of steely strength, an absolute, and an imposition on all who engage with her [some examples follow, including of her infantilising consultants on ward rounds by chucking them under their chins, playing with their lips and hair, and kissing them]. ... This self insists each minute on *its* identity, *its* reality, *its* needs & demands, pleasures and pains, & those of others do not exist at all. It also recognizes 'the past' but excises it. ... This absolute I is aware (is it? how to tell the difference between aware and not?) of its gaps & fractures & displacements ... 'bio' exerts its primacy over & against those fractures & splits that Mum seems at some level to know exist but refuses to allow into this domain of her self as she now creates and controls it.
>
> (Saturday 20 October 1990)

These two lost indicators of self may have been closely related to each other, products not only of my mother's changed sense of self but also of her perception of the patterns of interaction and communication around her. I picture her self as a small ball of light at the centre of a hazy foggy landscape of coming and going, muttering and mumbling, in which some faces, voices, sounds, were recognized but others not, and with time collapsed at the heart, in the mind, so that yesterday's acquaintances and her lifelong-loved nephew and daughter were each equally glowing pools of kindness, all surface and for the moment alone. This is how I 'picture' it, but there are no maps or guides and precious few clues to 'know' in any of the usual senses of knowing. Another picture: my mother as an often fractious, sometimes sunny, very elderly baby, with her often perplexed but increasingly loving and motherly daughter in tow.

MY CHANGING UNDERSTANDINGS OF THIS

Whatever, my mother's 'response' was typically unrelated to any interactional events around her. Sometimes I might eventually get an
impression of what occasioned this 'response', but more usually, and more
frequently as time passed, I would not. There seemed to be nothing external
to the workings of her mind that could give me any clue, any insight,
into 'why', however strong the impact of 'what' because of my mother's
determined insistence that I take cognizance of and action about her
feelings.[7]

Once the first shock of the suddenness and finality of what had occurred
to my mother – her right-side paralysis and blindness, her extreme brain-
damage – had become familiar, I felt as though *my* mother, my *real* mother,
had gone, died almost, and that the person who was left was much like
the husk of a former living experiencing interacting self. I expressed it
like this:

> Mum continues to elude me, or rather I can't completely accept that
> she *is* my Mum, who seems both to be there & gone from that poor
> woman in the hospital. . . . I want *that* woman, that shell with confus-
> ing vestiges of Mum, to die – partly for her sake, for the pathos &
> tragedy of it, but also for my own, for the amount of time, energy,
> emotion, thought, & above all responsibility that I have to give to
> this situation. I want to be free of parents & the compelled links we
> have with them. . . .
>
> (Friday 30 November 1990)

This is, however, only one dimension of how I experienced the changes
in/to my mother. On other occasions, I felt that her stricken and attenuated
self, as the above diary entry construes her, was actually the concentrated
essence of what a self is:

> Mum . . . incorporated me into the flow of things as soon as I arrived
> – as though I had never been away. There was no acknowledgement,
> not even the merest sign, that I had arrived, that I had been away,
> that I was welcomed, that I was anything other than there & so
> available . . . it seemed as though it might have only been a few
> minutes since I was last there . . . how on earth does John cope, going
> every day; he'll vanish. . . .
>
> (Saturday 2 February 1991)

These puzzlings and mullings of course say as much about me and the
epistemological stance these events were understood within as they do
about the ontologies of the self/selves that was/were my mother. Continually my interactions with her puzzled and at times dumbfounded me as I
struggled to comprehend the nature of this changing evolving self. These

138

puzzles, as I have termed them, were grounded in many hours of 'just being' with my mother, attending to her gestures and expressions, holding her hand, touching her face, brushing her hair, wheeling her about the hospital, tidying her clothes, speaking of cats and birds and flowers – all things nice – and all the while conveying as much loving attention as I could. This round of small satisfying/annoying/confusing intimacies gave me not only a sense of the emotional bond between us, but also of how much her ordinary pre-stroke self she still was: her hair, eyes, hands, body, looking the same 'now' as they had 'then', in moments of stillness when we simply 'were' together. I lurched from these moments to those of utter incomprehension as my mother gesticulated, cried, laughed and poked and prodded at my arm with her forefinger, compelling me by her anger or her grief endlessly to sort through her underwear, skirts, blouses and toiletries, and dump vests or knickers or soap or whatever in the ward wastebins. Then her anger or laughter or despair as I secretly tried to rescue them. On such agitating and upsetting occasions I would leave the ward exhausted, perhaps most of all by the nagging suspicion that somehow somewhere my mother as I had previously known her was still 'there', 'inside' and 'beneath' or 'behind' or 'beyond' *this* self. While intellectually 'knowing better', emotionally I retained a sense of the 'false' and the 'real' selves of my mother.

MY CHANGING RELATIONSHIP TO MY MOTHER

In late October 1990 it became apparent, financially, legally, that someone had to take charge of my mother's 'affairs' – her house, her pension and so on – and also to assume some degree of responsbility for my mother herself, her welfare and her long-term good. With my relatives' and the ward consultant's agreement, I gained my mother's power of attorney. Then in October/November 1991, following more strokes and the onset of epileptic fits, this was registered with the Court of Protection.[8] Soon after gaining the power of attorney, a conversation with Mr Court, my mother's solicitor, considerably startled me. In discussing my position regarding major decisions about finances but also regarding the hospital service, he had said that in the eyes of the law to all intents and purposes I had 'become my mother' financially, and had effectively become so regarding her legal existence more widely. I found this very unsettling:

> Since Mr Court said it, I have been reflecting on 'you are your mother'. How very strange it is, indeed totally disconcerting, to have it said so baldly. What does it mean, to be another person?
>
> (Friday 29 November 1991)

> 'I am my mother', or rather 'you are your mother' as an attribution by someone or something else.... I both want such a status, to

stop ... anyone ... from doing things that will hurt & upset Mum, and I also feel highly resistant to & resentful of it. The resentment is easier to express: Why *me*, why should I have to shoulder this enormous responsibility for another person? ... The resistance is harder to express. ... I feel invaded ... in various parts of my emotions, where I can no longer respond as *me* but must do so as Liz-and-Mum – indeed as Mum-and-Liz ... it *feels* odd ... being leashed in in myself & having to express emotion as though I were another.

(Saturday 30 November 1991)

It was then at an emotional level that the ontological reverberations of the changing relationship with my mother were expressed. Largely, as this diary extract suggests, this was because I felt the need to repress, to leash, my own emotional responses and instead express as 'Mum-and-Liz'; however, at times I also felt constrained by my responsibility to this 'other' persona to express emotions 'I' did not exactly feel. The most notable of these occasions occurred around two linked events. The first was when my mother, without my knowledge or consent (or that of any other family member), was moved to a private nursing home the day after I left the country for work reasons. When I returned, I visited my mother all unawares of this:

I arrived on the ward to find Mum's bed in a different place. Mum was so pleased to see me, she was fairly bright, but kept crying at various things ... in the book was the alarming information from John that on 22 September he'd gone to see her after his holiday and she wasn't there, was in a nursing home, & when he went there she was desperately unhappy, & that by 25 September he'd raised a commotion & got her back on the ward. I went immediately to talk to the sister. ... According to the sister – & not said in this order, I pieced it together by making her say it slowly so I could write it down & then checking the dates with her – on 13 Sept [I left Britain on 12 September] Dr Smith & the ward staff decided she should go to [the nursing home] 'for a break'; Smith has control over it & uses various of its beds as an extension of the ward ... & she was back on 25 September ... John was horrified when he visited – Mum was in an 8' x 6' room with no window, a TV (which she can't see or understand), a bed, a commode chair on which she was sat all day, & locked in. Not surprisingly, she was distraught, weeping etc, banging her head against anything near. He went straight to the ward & luckily Susie was on duty & she agreed Mum could come back. ...
At various points we almost broke into open rows but I kept clamping my tongue between my teeth, about how much Mum understands being the main thing: the sister claims she understands everything –

'they told her it all & she agreed to go' – stupid cow. 2-second interactions with Mum & there she is saying that I must respect her 'expert opinion' and that 'she knows best'. She nearly fell over when I said if that was so she must respect my 45 years of knowledge about my mother. . . . My greatest rage and hurt about all this was that they did it just the day after I left the country, when they knew I was leaving, & I wasn't here to help Mum. . . . Thank heavens the power of attorney is going through the Court of Protection.

(Monday 11 November 1992)

The second followed my written complaint and insistence on the legal need for 'the hospital' at the very least to inform and consult me about such major and consequential changes in my mother's life. As a consequence a formal case conference – the very first there had been since my mother first entered hospital – was called by the consultant and ward sister:

It seemed to me I was somehow being tested by them, & if I came up to scratch, they would oblige. The atmosphere completely changed when I got upset about Mum at [the nursing home] – from distant & formal, to smiles & niceness, & a complete *lightening* of how I felt they were responding to me.

From interrogation – 'what is your assessment of your mother', 'how do you see her comprehension', to supportive statements – 'it's been very upsetting for you', 'I dread something similar happening to my mother', 'what do you think we can do to help'. . . .

(Friday 29 November 1991)

I cried over Mum's misery while at [the nursing home]: it was partly me, partly me putting myself in Mum's place, but partly, even mainly, it was because I knew it would impress them & make them feel more sympathetic. Then I stopped the emotion in its tracks because I knew Mum would be wheeled in & she would have been upset if she realised I'd been crying (as per her reactions that time I cried about Dad – her ability to cope was hinged to mine . . .) . . .

(Saturday 30 November 1992)

CURRENTS IN MY DIARY WRITING

So far I have provided an account of the major dimensions of a debate or enquiry I experienced consequent upon my mother's stroke and its aftermath. This concerns 'the self' in general, my mother's and my own in particular, and I have presented various extracts from my diary in which I attempted analytically to come to grips both with these events and also with the ontological problematics engendered by them. I have used these diary entries in a basically referential way, assuming that they do indeed refer to a set of real events in the material world, the interpretation of which may differ between myself and other participants but the reality of whose occurrence would be shared. However, the diary extracts themselves question their own referentiality. Indeed they centre differences of understanding and interpretation, between myself and my mother, myself and my niece Jennifer, myself and the ward sister, myself and Dr Smith, about these events and also about the nature of 'self', of 'consciousness' and of the interactional means by which we judge the character and extent of this. Overwhelmingly as I read my diary over the period from my mother's first stroke to her death, it is concerned with the *absence* of referentiality, between my understanding and that of other people, between my writing and the events this writing is ostensibly 'of'. It is from this that its abiding concern with referentiality derives: the need to establish 'a point of view' that seems consonant with 'the facts' as seen from this point of view, because without this there were multiple disjunctures, 'puzzles' as I typically referred to them.

I have also used these diary extracts to construct a narrative – to 'tell a story' – around a set of ontological problematics (what did all this mean, regarding my mother's self, regarding myself, regarding selves and consciousness in general) with epistemological consequentiality (what did all this entail for how I, we, understand what it is to have knowledge about another person, about one's self). At this point I want to shift my analyst's gaze from such problematics and consequentialities, and turn it towards the writing and recording process itself. I want to suspend assumptions of, and querying of, referentiality within my diary, and instead focus on 'the diary', so as to treat writing as transformative in its own right – to recognize that the act of writing constructed – not reconstructed – these events and mis/understandings by making them, recording them, differently from how they were first experienced.

In this chapter I have constructed 'a narrative', at its most simple a story with a linear development, the denouement of which is the attention here to the writing process itself. Some feminist commentators, as I noted earlier, tend to treat autobiographical narrative as fundamentally, essentially, both referential and essentialist because seen to claim that 'there are real events of which this is a true record with an almost one-to-one relationship to them'. Above, I questioned the apparent referentiality of diary-writing: in my case, referentiality was striven for because in life there was little referentiality between my experience and how I construed that of other people, or between my own experience on different occasions; and overwhelmingly the diary is concerned with these 'puzzles' about ontological and epistemological complexities, confusions. Here I want to focus upon the question of narrative.

Reading back through more than eighteen months of my diary, I find both a focused attention to providing narrative detail and structure – I experienced this as a need, an imperative almost – and a continual questioning and probing of this. The 'narrative imperative' was one in which my diary was composed by 'descriptions' (glosses, summaries) of each day, written as soon as I woke up:

> A beautiful but cold day – such a change after the last 2 days of mud, cloud & torrential rain. I woke at 6.30. . . . I wrote – ploddingly – on my chapter yesterday morning until just before midday. Then changed & went to [a pub] for lunch & read. . . . At the hospital Mum still much the same – not angry, but not as she was either. Much more difficult to be with, & I think understands less. Yesterday after the first hour or so I found it difficult to concentrate when she was trying to communicate something to me – I just wanted to sit quietly & passively while she struggled noisily & actively. . . . I just couldn't figure it out. . . . When I got back I arranged for the house to be valued, 3 different estate agents . . . first I rang . . . then. . . . David rang – a time for the Department meeting on Friday. . . . It's 8.15 now & I'm fretting about dates when I can get home. If only I could just take her back [to a hospital in Manchester] it would all be so very much easier. . . .
>
> (Tuesday 1 November 1990)

I often mulled over why I wrote the kinds of things I did, although these mullings were actually infrequently inscribed within the diary itself. One occasion when I did so, I wrote:

> In between other things . . . my mind returns to the puzzle between what I write in this diary & the rest of my life. The diary contents . . . don't act in a 1 to 1 nor even a 1 to 10 relationship with the rest – rather it is at a skew to the rest, a part of it, but like a distorting mirror. My mind & the flow of events both (but differently) contain so many more varied things; & anyway the diary is focussed on rather odd things . . . a set of flat what purport to be descriptions of usually dull or trite things, or if they aren't either dull or trite in themselves (like 'Mum & the hospital', a favourite glossing phrase) nevertheless how I write about them is. This leaves me wondering why I bother. . . .
>
> (Saturday 23 March 1991)

What particularly bothered me was less the 'triteness' or the non-referential 'skewed' nature of what I wrote, much more a sense that a diary written around physical dissolution and the encroaching possibility of death 'should', 'ought', to be somehow different from this, but in which ways I was not clear about; however, even if I had been clear I could not have written like it, for I experienced precisely an 'imperative' to write in the way I did. I derived satisfaction from somehow 'emptying ' a part of my mind, my self, each morning. I was consciously using my diary-writing in not so much an anti-referential way as one which selected only some things to write about and did this in an evening-out way – 'flat' was the word I used earlier – a way that removed the peaks and troughs, the cadences of the days and weeks:

> The relentless narrative of what I write fascinates me when I think back. My thoughts are circular & concerned with the possibilities & their consequences. But what comes out on paper is linear & chronological, with a few more reflective paragraphs, tho' very few of these. And yet I know what appears in these narrations is a selection only, that all the thoughts & feelings – mine, & what I think are other people's – that make it contingent and consequential reality rather than brief actually decorticated writing are absent. . . .
>
> (Wednesday 12 September 1990)

The main reason was my felt need to record and to tell, to myself, 'a story'. This 'story' was one in which my immersion in the telling of small stories of everyday life was linked to the silence that comprised my mother. Always, for all of my life, my mother had been the source of an apparently endless, and after my father died, almost daily, supply of tales from the minutiae of her (past, present) life:

> I've thought a good deal about Aunt Flora [one of my mother's sisters, who had just died] since Saturday. I didn't know her at all, & now I've lost the chance of knowing what Mum made of her over the years & why the breach between them. These lost histories have been much in my mind recently – things I want to be told about, to listen to tales of people & places, & I never will again.
>
> (Tuesday 19 March 1991)

It wasn't the lost chance of knowing Aunt Flora that concerned me, but the lost possibility of *my mother telling me about* Aunt Flora. My mother had been the bearer of histories for me, the provider of accounts of a (sometimes shared, more often not) familial past. As time moved on so my diary took on this quality: a historiography (competing historiographies) of events that were closed to conversation about them with my mother.

HISTORIOGRAPHIES, LIVES AND NARRATIVES

At this point I return to the three broad arguments introduced at the start of this chapter, concerned with self, narrative and 'bio' or life, to draw together an argument already implicit – and at points explicit – in the preceding sections and the diary extracts located within them.

The ordinary self, the conscious and experiencing subject, is much more complexly constructed and more aware of its internal fractures, is more knowingly a social self composed through many overlapping patterns of interrelationship, than feminist postmodernist commentary on autobiography allows. Having in earlier work explored this self through the route of biography, I have examined it here by autobiographical means. The spoken and written accounts of the past we all produce, which constitute a major element in the fabric of our lives, certainly trade on and are typically structured by means of referential assumptions and claims. However, they do so because people are well aware that these are indeed historiographies – accounts – and not history itself; and the process of 'accounting' that autobiographies constitute is an important means of making real and present what we all know is actually memory and past. Autobiographies are works of the imagination, of art and artifice, certainly predicated on what once (was said to have) happened, but in a creative way, one often shared by or debated between former co-participants and present co-authors of such accounts. I came to think about, and write about, the complexities of self, its entwined fragility and indomitability, not through reading academic feminist texts, but through living and experiencing the illness, dissolution and death of people close to me. This is, I would suggest, the common conclusion of such experiences, rather than simple referentiality.

These everyday historiographies of ordinary lives typically take narrative form, as have both my autobiography within my diary-writing and this piece of writing itself. 'A narrative' is a story told by structural and rhetorical means in which there is an unfolding, a development or progression, a denouement and/or conclusion. In other words, in which there is a beginning, a middle and an end. Among other possibilities, narratives can be structured temporally, logically, argumentatively. The narrative of this chapter, for instance, is argumentatively structured, rather than temporally or (in the formal sense) logically. Moreover, narratives of lives, in diaries, letters and memoirs as well as 'autobiography' strictly speaking, can have similar structural form and yet adopt different rhetorical 'voices', construct different relationships between writer and readers, make different claims to referentiality, and also use the notion of time in very different ways.

The narrative form is appealing for good reason, as is the referentiality often associated with it, not because autobiographers are naive or lacking in analytic sophistication concerning the minutiae related to the broad sweep of their lives. These good reasons lie in the centrality of stories and of time in our lives. Our lives have beginnings, hopefully middles and inevitably ends, and we endlessly tell stories about each of these for ourselves and others. Narrative is a sinuously plastic form capable of subtlety as well as power. It has the hold that it does because its basic form reflects the symbiosis of time and the tides of our lives, and our perception of the impinging reality of these. Some feminist analysts of autobiography imply that a complete anti-referentiality in autobiographical writing is both possible and desirable. Certainly it is important to be aware of the intertextuality of images and realities and of the issues surrounding referentiality. It is equally important to note the actually 'referential' nature of anti-referential arguments, which are tantamount to a declaration that 'the *real* reality is that there is no single real reality', an account that is as rhetorically loaded as those being critiqued. It is also important to acknowledge that a real world and real lives do exist, howsoever we interpret, construct and recycle accounts of these by a variety of symbolic means.

All writing derives from, is the product of, helps to construct, lives – even that kind of writing which is apparently most abstract and least connected to flesh-and-blood living and breathing people. The current tide away from 'experiential' statements and writings perceives and evaluates these in relation to a perceived alternative, a binary, a dichotomy. But against this, my conviction is that by whatever rhetorical means the experiential basis of knowledge is denied or silenced, none the less all knowledge of the world is rooted in the knowledge-production processes engaged in by enquiring and experiencing and therefore knowing subjects. Autobiographical writing centres the knowing subject and makes the basis of its knowledge-claims available for analytic scrutiny. Of course these are accounts, historiographies, and not the past of a life itself; and of course they should be evaluated in such terms. But to recognize this does not entail rejecting the form or denying its very real interests and attractions, and most certainly nor should it entail dismissing its ability to provide analytically sharp, albeit experientially derived, theory.

POSTSCRIPT

Mum died at 10 to 12 [midday]. I got there early that morning at 2.45 am. A long long night but now she & I are free at last. I caught her last breath & opened the window to let it go. And now this diary is definitely closed.

(Tuesday 10 March 1992)

I thought I probably wouldn't write a diary again for a while – but one of the first things I did when I left the hospital was to buy this new notebook. . . .

(Wednesday 11 March 1992)

The thing I miss the most is the responsibility, the way my life and my thoughts were organized around Mum, the fortnightly cycle of visits, all the time on the trains, dreading going but then missing being there. But more than that, at some point it will really sink in that I'm now living in a world without Mum, without 45 years of loving care, but also ... of feeling totally responsible for Mum. No love but no responsibility ....

(Tuesday 21 April 1992)

NOTES

1 All names in this chapter, including those of institutions and wards and cities as well as persons, have been changed. My brother Alan and his wife Betty live in the north of England, in a small town near where I live. My cousin John lives in Southern, where my mother lived. Two nieces live in a town a few miles away from Southern; my brother and sister-in-law's other children live in different places.
2 Square brackets indicate later additions to help present readers.
3 For a discussion of these points in more detail, see Stanley (1992: 2–19, 240–56).
4 See for example Alcoff (1988), Morris (1988), Soper (1990), Grosz (1990), Brodribb (1992). Like probably many other academic feminists, I variously adopt all three responses, depending on time, place and circumstances. Of those mentioned in this footnote, Alcoff is the most supportive of postmodernism and Brodribb the most critical; none the less even Brodribb is highly influenced by the debates and, most of all, the conceptual language associated with this discourse.
5 The tapes were part of a research project known as 'Our mothers' voices' (Stanley 1985), in which I and a number of other feminist sociologists who were working class by birth collaboratively explored with our mothers the complexities and nuances of 'class' when looked at experientially. We sought to contrast these complexities with what we felt were highly unsatisfactory academic feminist investigations of women's class (read 'working class', for there are few feminist investigations of other class groups), for among other problems these deny the investigators' own class location and understandings and the part these play in how other women's class is understood. The research diary is one I have kept, off and on, for the last fifteen years or so.
6 Warty Bliggins, a toad who construes his toadstool as the plumb centre of the universe, is the subject of a poem by Don Marquand in his wonderful series of poems about Archie the reincarnated free-verse poet and currently a cockroach, Mehitabel the cat but formerly Cleopatra of Egypt, and others.
7 For instance, a repeated stab stab stab stab stab in my upper arm from a determined forefinger, with a smile or tears or an enquiring look accompanying this, going on and on and on as I sat at her side until I did something deemed appropriate or acceptable or, increasingly, evasive.
8 As explained by my mother's solicitor, the power of attorney certainly gives the attorney full legal ability to act on behalf of another in all financial aspects of their life, and possibly broader powers as well. Registering the power of attorney with the Court of Protection gives the attorney almost total powers to act for the other person, subject to the Court, which acts on behalf of the person the attorney represents.

REFERENCES

Alcoff, Linda (1988), 'Cultural feminism versus post-structuralism: the identity crisis in feminist theory', *Signs*, vol. 13, no. 3, pp. 405–36.
Benstock, Shari (ed.) (1988), *The Private Self: Theory and Practice of Women's Autobiographical Writing*, London: Routledge.

Brodribb, Somer (1992), *Nothing Mat(t)ers: A Feminist Critique of Postmodernism*, Melbourne: Spinifex Press.

Brodzki, Bella and Schenk, Celeste (eds) (1988), *Life/Lines: Theorizing Women's Autobiography*, Ithaca: Cornell University Press.

Grosz, Elizabeth (1990), 'A note on essentialism and difference' in *Feminist Knowledge: Critique and Construct*, ed. Sneja Gunew, London: Routledge, pp. 332–44.

Heilbrun, Carolyn (1988), *Writing a Woman's Life*, London: The Women's Press.

Jelinek, Estelle (ed.) (1980), *Women's Autobiography: Essays in Criticism*, Bloomington: Indiana University Press.

Jelinek, Estelle (1986), *The Tradition of Women's Autobiography: From Antiquity to Present*, Boston: Twayne Publishers.

Morris, Meaghan (1988), *The Pirate's Fiancée; Feminism, Reading, Postmodernism*, London: Verso.

Personal Narratives Group (ed.) (1989), *Interpreting Women's Lives: Theory and Personal Narratives*, Bloomington: Indiana University Press.

Riley, Denise (1988), *'Am I That Name?' Feminism and the Category of 'Women' in History*, London: Macmillan.

Soper, Kate (1990), *Troubled Pleasures: Writings on Politics, Gender and Hedonism*, London: Verso.

Stanley, Liz (ed.) (1984a), *The Diaries of Hannah Cullwick*, London: Virago and New Jersey: Rutgers University Press.

Stanley, Liz (1984b), 'How the social science research process discriminates against women' in *Is Higher Education Fair to Women?*, ed. Sandra Acker and David Warren Piper, London: Nelson, pp. 189–209.

Stanley, Liz (1985), 'Our mothers' voices', paper given at the Third International Interdisciplinary Congress on Women, Dublin.

Stanley, Liz (1988), 'Behind the scenes during the creation of a social services department statistic', *Research, Policy, Planning*, 5, pp. 22–7.

Stanley, Liz (ed.) (1990a), *Feminist Praxis: Research, Theory and Epistemology in Feminist Sociology*, London: Routledge.

Stanley, Liz (1990b), 'Feminist praxis and the academic mode of production' in Liz Stanley, *Feminist Praxis*, London: Routledge, pp. 3–19.

Stanley, Liz (1990c), 'A referral was made' in Liz Stanley, *Feminist Praxis*, London: Routledge, pp. 113–22.

Stanley, Liz (1992), *The Auto/biographical I: Theory and Practice of Feminist Auto/Biography*, Manchester: Manchester University Press.

Stanley, Liz and Wise, Sue (1990), 'Method, methodology and epistemology in feminist research processes' in Liz Stanley, *Feminist Praxis*, London: Routledge, pp. 20–60.

Stanley, Liz and Wise, Sue (1992), 'Feminist ontology and epistemology: recent debates in feminist social thought', *Indian Journal of Social Work*, vol. 53, no. 4, pp. 343–65.

Stanley, Liz and Wise, Sue (1993), *Breaking Out Again: Feminist Ontology and Epistemology*, London: Routledge.

Stanton, Domna (ed.) (1984), *The Female Autograph: Theory and Practice of Autobiography from the 10th to the 20th Century*, Chicago: University of Chicago Press.

10

THE PERSONAL IS INTERNATIONAL

Feminist epistemology and the case of international relations

Kimberly Hutchings

The study of women in the international system seems to be designed to turn our attention away 'from the state and its power as a unit of analysis' to the needs and interests of women as 'an identity group'.

(Coker 1990: 23)

I fear that many feminist theorists of international relations may follow the currently fashionable path of fragmenting epistemology, denying the possibility of social science.

(Keohane 1991: 46–7)

But feminists, like those attempting to draw on cultural traditions that have been eclipsed by the pretensions of the most powerful, are always in danger of relapsing into claims of privileged access, of reproducing the cultural arrogance they seek to undermine.

(Walker 1988: 151)

KNOWLEDGE, IDENTITY AND DIFFERENCE

The three quotations given above are all by male theorists from within the discipline of international relations, reacting to the intervention of feminism into a subject area that has been even more male-dominated than most of the social sciences. The introduction of feminist concerns and feminist theories into international relations is of a very recent date. In Britain the arrival of a feminist input into international relations literature was first signalled as significant in a special edition of the journal *Millennium* in 1988, much of the material from which has been incorporated into a book, *Gender and International Relations* (see Grant and Newland 1991). By and large, the existing literature on feminism and international relations is in the form of articles rather than books, and dates from the mid-1980s.[1] Nevertheless, it is already possible to see the implications of feminist

149

contributions to debates in international relations, in terms of both the object of study and how that object is to be explained and understood. By insisting on the recognition of gender as both constituting and being constituted by international political and economic reality, feminist scholars necessarily raise questions about the validity of traditional conceptions of international political and economic reality which render gender invisible. More than this, however, feminist scholars raise questions about how the relationship of the knower to the object of knowledge has been traditionally understood within international relations research. This kind of questioning is not peculiar to feminist critics; within international relations similar questions are also being raised from a variety of other theoretical perspectives, most notably the two labelled 'critical theory' and 'postmodernism'.[2] Thus the feminist contribution to thinking about the science of international relations involves both an encounter with a fundamentally empiricist orthodoxy and with a complex debate between two other radical alternatives. At the same time, the feminist intervention is by no means monolithic and reflects ongoing arguments within feminist epistemology itself. In this paper, I will be arguing that looking at international relations in the context of feminist epistemology, and looking at feminist epistemology in the context of international relations is a peculiarly fruitful exercise in pointing the way forward to new accounts of both knowledge and the international realm.

In the western philosophical tradition of epistemology, whether rationalist or empiricist, we are presented with an ideal model of knowledge which still shapes the claims of both natural and social science today. One of the key premises of this model is the presumption of the absolute difference between the subject-knower and the object of knowledge, and the unproblematic self-identity of the two 'sides' involved in the process of knowledge acquisition. The ideal standard of what knowledge ought to be according to this tradition is an identity of this absolute difference, in which the subject erases itself in order to provide a pure and unsullied mirror in which the object is perfectly reflected. The erasure of the subject is the project of method, the techniques by which scientists back up claims to objective truth. Practising scientists, social scientists and philosophers of science are rarely convinced that they attain the ideal of knowledge. However, even the most sceptical arguments about the status of scientific or social scientific knowledge remain haunted by ideals of objectivity and truth, which, if they cannot be attained, at least succeed in debasing the value of what can be achieved. The logic of the traditional model of the relationship between knower and known is dictated by the conception of identity/difference that underlies it. If the difference between subject and object is absolute, then knowledge can only be possible if this difference is erased; epistemological idealism and realism are a testimony to this necessity. Only by subsuming the object under the subject or the subject under the object can knowledge become possible. If this subsumption is impossible then the ideal of knowledge is also impossible. It is the impossibility of the absolute identity of difference that inevitably forms the starting-point for attempts to rethink the traditional model of knowledge. Two such attempts are to be found within international relations theory in critical theory and postmodernism. It is my contention, however, that neither of these attempts succeeds in challenging the traditional logic of identity/difference, so that both end up, for different reasons, with a reassertion of the impossibility of knowledge.

If we turn to feminist interventions in international relations, we find very similar arguments to those of the critical theorists beginning to develop, but the implications of those arguments suggest a more effective challenge to the logic of identity/difference than is presented by the other radical alternatives. In order to appreciate the dangers and possibilities of feminist theorizing in international relations it is necessary to look first at the reasons why other critical traditions fail to overcome the logic of traditional epistemology.[3]

TRADITIONAL AND ALTERNATIVE EPISTEMOLOGIES IN INTERNATIONAL RELATIONS

Christopher Coker's response to the introduction of women as a legitimate object of study within international relations, quoted above, is premised on orthodox ideas about both knowledge in general and what counts as knowledge in international relations in particular. For Coker the introduction of women into international relations analysis is a distortion of what social science ought to be, since it premises knowledge-claims on specific identities and interests. More specifically, the introduction of women onto the scene distracts attention from what international relations is properly about, i.e., the state and its power. Coker is defending not only a model of the way the knower ought to relate to the object of knowledge, but also a definition of the object of knowledge itself, a definition that corresponds to the realist tradition in international relations theory.[4] According to this tradition the international is constituted by a system of states which relate to one another in a context of anarchy. The proper way to understand this system is via concepts of power, security and rational self-interest, and through detailed examination of the world of governments, diplomats, foreign policy and so on. Underlying realism is a series of assumptions about the nature of the political as opposed to both the moral and the economic, which include specific ideas about who or what counts as an actor in the international realm. According to realist presumptions women have very little relevance to the international sphere, since, as a consequence of the way in which it is conceived, they very rarely appear in it. More generally, gender is an irrelevance in realist thinking because the motivations for and constraints on action in the international context are conceived as ungendered and universally applicable. Looking back at the kind of social science of international relations Coker is advocating, we find the logic of the traditional model of knowledge inscribed within it. The subject and object of knowledge are absolutely different self-identical poles. The difference between subject and object is ideally transcended through the use of methods and concepts which ensure the erasure of the subjectivity of the subject and ground objective knowledge-claims.

The realist paradigm has not gone unchallenged in the years in which it has dominated research in international relations. However, it is only recently that the epistemological assumptions underlying realism have been brought into question.[5] Both critical theory and postmodernism have offered radical critiques of the realist conception of the nature of the subject and object of knowledge within the social science of international relations. This has involved attempts to reconceptualize the subject/object polarities of the epistemological tradition and new claims about the possibilities and impossibilities of knowledge about the international realm. The schools of thought labelled as 'critical' and 'postmodernist' in international relations theory can be located in broader theoretical/philosophical traditions. Critical theory borrows from the social theory tradition of the Frankfurt School, particularly the work of Habermas (see Linklater 1982 and Hoffmann 1987). Postmodernism owes a debt to the work of Derrida and Foucault in particular (see Ashley 1988 and Walker 1989). Although the two schools of thought have a critique of traditional international relations which overlaps in many respects, their conclusions are overtly antithetical. Critical theorists see postmodernists as undermining the possibility of meaningful claims to knowledge, and postmodernists see critical theorists as returning to the project of grounding true knowledge in a way that has been demonstrated to be untenable. On examination, however, it appears that the conclusions of the critical theorists and postmodernists may have more in common than they themselves suppose.

Critical theorists argue for an essential connection between knowledge and interest. According to critical theory the realist theory of international relations was born out of and continues to serve the interests of those who want to maintain the international *status quo* and close off the possibility of change (see Hoffmann 1987: 338–41). It is claimed that critical theory, by premising its understanding of the international sphere on the possibility of and interest in emancipation, will produce a different and more adequate knowledge (344–5). Underlying this assertion is a claim that understanding from the viewpoint of the subjugated is epistemologically privileged, in some sense less blinded or ideologically loaded than that of the powers that be (see Brown 1988: 466). When it comes to the conceptualization of the object of knowledge in international relations, critical theory undercuts many of the presumptions of the tradition. The definition of the political in abstraction from the moral and the economic is challenged. Critical theorists argue that the apparent abstraction of the political sphere disguises a deeper reality in which the political is inseparable from the economic and the relation between them is ethically loaded. The analytic separating out of the political serves the interest of those who wish to claim its unchanging status. The greater emphasis on the link between the system of states and global political economy in critical theory has implications for traditional notions of who is to count as an international actor. Moreover, concepts of power, security and rationality, rather than being seen as neutral conceptual tools, are identified as being used in morally and politically loaded ways. What critical theory shares with traditional views about knowledge in international relations is the idea that a true account of the international sphere is possible. However, for the critical theorist, this true account is premised on a critical stance and an emancipatory interest (an identification with the oppressed) rather than on what is claimed to be value-free social scientific method (Brown 1988: 472).

The model of knowledge at work in critical theory cuts against the traditional model in its account of the subject and object of knowledge and the relationship between them. According to critical theory the subject is not erased through social scientific method; rather it is disguised. The object is fashioned in the interests of the subject, so that objectivity becomes the guise of subjectivity and the knowledge of the object is false knowledge. The way forward to true knowledge in which the object is understood in its objectivity is argued to be through entry into a new and uncontaminated subjectivity, the subjectivity of the oppressed, which illuminates the object in a non-ideological way. This radical rethinking of knowledge in international relations appears fundamentally to challenge the traditional account. However, on reflection it is clear that the traditional ideal of knowledge has not been subverted. The critique of the existing grounds of knowledge-claims is based on the failing to achieve the absolute identity of difference through method; that this is the ideal is not itself questioned. Instead, critical theorists suggest a new way of achieving the impossible, by starting from the standpoint of the oppressed. The position of the subjugated comes to do the work of method in erasing subjectivity from the scene in order to allow truth to shine through.

There are no grounds given as to why emancipatory interest should be any more effective than social scientific method in achieving the logical impossibility of true knowledge. Like the critical theorists, the postmodernists in international relations challenge the realists' distinction between knower and known and the relation between them. Unlike the critical theorists, for the postmodernists there is no privileged stance from which truth or objectivity can be claimed. On this account, all knowledge is discursively constructed; it does not reflect reality so much as constitute it. However, the reality that is constituted is not closed either by the empirical facts or by the specific interest of the knower. Postmodernists invite the deconstruction of the traditional conceptual logic of the discipline of international relations and privilege difference over identity in both the subject and object of knowledge. Thus, what seemed a stable epistemological relationship becomes fluid and problematic. The knower is no longer the neutral social scientist, neither is he/she a subject with a specific oppressive or emancipatory interest. Both knower and known are complex constructions constituted by a logic of binary oppositions which contains the possibility of its own subversion (see Walker 1989: 43). Postmodernists in international relations focus on unsettling conceptual hierarchies that have been taken for granted traditionally. Thus the orthodox view of the international realm as fundamentally anarchic is demonstrated to be unsustainable by the conceptual logic which supports that very view (see Ashley 1988: 227–62). It is argued that knowledge-claims are never free from a power dimension, concepts are never neutral and that there is no sense in which truth can be claimed over against power as the critical theorists wish to do. Where both traditional and critical theorists acknowledge an ideal of the absolute identity of difference, postmodernists put all identities into question and celebrate the proliferation of difference with the impossibility of truth with a capital 'T'.

It is clear that the postmodern theory of international relations goes a lot further than critical theory in challenging orthodox epistemology in international relations. Where critical theory condemns traditional theory by its own standards of value-freedom and then suggests a new way of grounding objective truth, postmodernism undermines the old idea of objective truth completely. However, looking carefully at the nature of the postmodern critique of both orthodoxy and critical theory it can be seen that it is itself little more than a confirmation of the impossibility of the logic that drives the traditions it is criticizing. The impossibility of the identity of absolute difference required by the traditional ideal of knowledge is confirmed by postmodernism; the mutual exclusivity of identity and difference is not itself in any way challenged. Thus postmodernism in international relations becomes not a new way of thinking about knowledge, but at best a problematizing, at worst a denial of the possibility of knowledge at all. Meaningful claims about the international sphere cannot be distinguished from meaningless ones and orthodox and critical theorists join in accusing the postmodernists of undermining the conditions for any social scientific research.

Contemporary debates over theorizing in international relations display a peculiar pattern of alliance and hostility. While critical theory and postmodernism both criticize orthodoxy for universalizing a partial and interested construction of the international realm, orthodoxy and postmodernism are united in denying the epistemological privilege claimed by critical theory for the standpoint of the oppressed, and critical theory and orthodoxy are united in condemning postmodernism for its subversion of the possibility of objective knowledge. Behind these identities and differences, I have argued, lies the traditional identity/difference logic of the ideal standard of what knowledge ought to be. The impossibility of the erasure of the difference between subject and object opens up orthodox social science to critique. However, as long as the critiques operate with the same ideal concept of knowledge, they are inevitably destined either to struggle against that impossibility and open themselves up to the same kind of criticism, or to affirm that impossibility and deny knowledge. It is at this point that the third radical intervention in international relations theory, the feminist intervention, needs to be considered. I will now go on to examine the extent to which feminist critiques of orthodox theorizing also remain caught in the logic of an impossible ideal of knowledge, and the extent to which they may offer an opportunity for a more fundamental rethinking of identity and difference and the subject/object relation.

FEMINISM AND INTERNATIONAL RELATIONS THEORY

The three quotations cited at the beginning of this chapter indicate the range of dangers that feminist thinking in international relations is seen to represent, not only by orthodox theorists but by representatives of more radical traditions. Along with disrupting the ideal of neutral social science, feminists are also suspected of either falling into the pit of postmodern fragmentation or setting up a claim to epistemological privilege akin to that of the critical theorists. It is certainly the case that although there are common themes to feminist writings on the international, approaches and concerns are diverse, as is illustrated by the range of work in the 1988 edition of *Millennium*[6] mentioned above. However, while the articles in this volume vary widely, they do have in common a deep dissatisfaction with existing orthodox approaches to the understanding of the international, a dissatisfaction with both theoretical and practical dimensions. On the one hand, traditional approaches are seen as perpetuating actual discrimination against women in both economic and political spheres, and on the other hand those same approaches are seen as incapable of yielding a proper understanding of the international sphere itself.

At the same time as engaging with orthodox international relations, many of the feminists writing in this area are placing themselves within the debates of feminist theory and epistemology. The most striking thing about the feminist contributions in this respect is the extent to which the epistemological stance favoured by almost all of the writers corresponds most closely to what Harding has identified as 'feminist standpoint theory' (see Harding 1991: 105–37), a position which emerges in most cases from an encounter with orthodoxy which leads to a deep mistrust of empiricism and in some cases is bolstered by an equal distrust of theoretical positions that prioritize difference and undermine claims to objective truth (see Newland 1988: 513–15). Thus feminist work in international relations is self-consciously engaged in dialogue with all three of the traditions discussed above. Epistemologically it appears to be most closely aligned to critical theory, in that it argues for understanding from the viewpoint of subjugated woman. It is this fact that inspires Walker's comment quoted at the beginning. It is this fact that seems to imply that my claim that feminist thinking may liberate the social science of international relations from the shackles of traditional epistemological logic must fall to the ground. However, if we look closely at the version of feminist standpoint or critical theory at work in some of the feminist writing on the international it seems to me to imply an alternative conceptualization of identity/difference and subject/object, which is not always followed through, but which could form the basis for a genuine rethinking of the traditional concept of knowledge. This will be demonstrated through an examination of one feminist theorist of international relations who argues for a version of the standpoint approach to knowledge (Ann Tickner 1988: 429–40). Tickner's project in the theory of international relations is clear from the title of her article in the special issue of *Millennium*, 'Hans Morgenthau's principles of political realism: a feminist reformulation'. In this article Tickner takes Morgenthau's principles and the concepts embedded in them and discusses the way they have been problematized by feminist theorists. In particular, Tickner challenges Morgenthau's concepts of power and the political, which she argues are foundational to masculinist international relations theory. As Tickner sees it, Morgenthau's concept of power is a one-sided concept, meaning 'power over' the other. Tickner argues that this concept of power is a reflection of masculine experience and therefore neglects alternative senses of power which emerge from female experience, the concept of power as 'power with' or 'empowerment' (1988: 434). Similarly Tickner argues that the traditional assumption of the autonomy of the political from ethical and economic spheres in international relations rests on male identification with the public sphere, which itself rests on the masculinist distinction between private and public. Women's experience leads to a recognition of the political within the supposedly private sphere and therefore undermines the masculinist conception of the public/private divide and what follows from it (438). Throughout her argument Tickner is not proposing that her feminist reformulation of Morgenthau is the basis of a new alternative international relations theory. Instead Tickner claims that the feminist critique is a step on the way to a new universal science of the international in which both feminist and masculinist insights would be incorporated (438). In another recent essay in which she looks at the sister discipline of international relations, global political economy (1991: 191–206), Tickner puts forward a similar argument:

A feminist perspective on international political economy might begin, therefore, by constructing some alternative definitions of concepts, such as rationality, security, and power – concepts that have been central to our understanding of the field, but, as I shall argue, have been embedded in a masculine epistemology.

(203)

Taking the concept of rationality, which in its traditional meaning within international relations signifies commitment to the maximization of self-interest, Tickner redefines it thus: 'A feminist definition of rationality would, therefore, be tied to an ethic of care and responsibility' (203). In explaining her concept of rationality, Tickner locates the feminist definition in the experience of women under capitalism and the public/private split that goes with it. The feminist concept of rationality therefore, comes out of the disjuncture of experienced realities and a theoretical tradition that excludes those realities and their significance. Tickner argues that the old concept of rationality helps to impose a reading of the international and of history which has given itself the status of an eternal, universal truth on an historically contingent and partial basis. The feminist concept of rationality Tickner has formulated opens up new avenues in the analysis of global economic realities, since it enables recognition of rationality in activities that are not simply tied to profit-maximization. When the feminist and masculinist insights are both given equal credence, then a fully human science of international politics and economics will be possible.

Arguments like Tickner's add a new twist to debates in international relations theory since they posit the concrete identity/experience of the knower as crucial to the substantiation of claims to knowledge. Tickner clearly shares with critical theory and postmodernism a critique of orthodoxy that focuses particularly on the ungrounded nature of its claims to objectivity and universality. However, Tickner goes further than the critical theorist who asks for an abstract identification with the viewpoint of the subjugated as the key to knowledge, and unlike the postmodernist, Tickner is committed to the retention of the possibility of an 'ungendered or human science' (1988: 438) which will replace the old partiality. If we go back to traditional epistemological logic, then, it seems that Tickner is attempting to ground the impossible identity of absolute difference between subject and object (which is true knowledge) on the coming together of two different subjective identities, which are masculinist and feminist. There are two sets of problems that are immediately obvious here: first, how are masculinist and feminist subjectivities going to be able to provide a mutual ground for knowledge? Second, how are these identities themselves grounded and accorded their epistemological privilege? It appears from what Tickner herself argues that the former question can only be answered by a relapse into a new dualism, since the concepts grounded by the different identities are scarcely complementary. The second question poses even more problems. According to Tickner's own account the orthodox conceptual tools of international relations are grounded in masculine experience under western capitalism in the modern era. The feminist reformulation of these concepts follows from women's experience under the same regime. While it seems quite plausible that the position of women under capitalism may well give different insights into global politics and economics than those of the tradition, it is unclear why these insights should be epistemologically privileged. Why should we accept that modern western male and female experience between them are any more capable than social scientific method or an emancipatory interest of delivering the ideal of truth?

Tickner's argument thus appears to fall prey to Robert Walker's warning against 'cultural arrogance' and to arguments formulated by other feminists about the significance of differences between women as well as differences between men and women.[7] The problems of generalizing on the basis of western experiences are particularly evident in a discipline like international relations. The women oppressed under capitalism in Europe over the past three hundred years are identified as oppressors by many non-western women and have had genuinely good reasons for endorsing the way the global economy has operated and operates to exclude, marginalize and impoverish others, both men and women. What is the epistemological status to be accorded to these other experiences? The new universalism which is offered by Tickner is threatened by two alternatives, that of setting up an unsustainable claim to objective truth, or that of collapsing into the validation of all claims to knowledge grounded in different experiences, without any way of judging between them. We are back with the alternatives offered by the 'malestream' debates between false knowledge and no knowledge at all.

The analysis of the problems posed by Tickner's argument leads us to a familiar dilemma in feminist epistemology about the legitimacy of claims to know. If traditional methodology and its claims to erase the subject and make objective knowledge possible are to be rejected as impossible, what can make knowledge possible? Given that one of the key criticisms of tradition is that its subject is not erased but disguised, and that that subject is an oppressive patriarchal subject, then the idea of a new subject as the key to true knowledge is appealing. The new subject will provide a different and clearer view of the object because of the nature of its experience and interests. At once, however, the difficulty arises that there is a plurality of subjectivities amongst the oppressed and that oppressors and oppressed cannot always be distinguished. Nor is it clear why oppression aids the clarity of vision of the subject-knower, helping her to recognize the object of knowledge as it is in itself. The logic of the feminist standpoint itself seems to push us into a plurality of viewpoints, yet the abandonment of the idea of a standpoint leaves us without anchor in a sea of contending narratives, with no possibility of distinguishing between those that are meaningful and those that are not. The pattern of the relation between orthodoxy, critical theory and postmodernism described in the previous section seems to be repeated. Indeed, I would claim it is repeated as long as the feminist epistemologist clings to the old ideal of knowledge and the logic that implies it. If this logic is accepted then the impossibility of knowledge will be continually confirmed, either through fundamentally problematic claims to have transcended the absolute difference between knower and known, subject and object, or through a confirmation of that absolute difference. I wish to go on to argue, however, that in Tickner's version of the feminist standpoint, in the context of international relations, it is possible to discern a more radical challenge to traditional epistemological logic and therefore the beginnings of a new concept of knowledge.

The radical potential of Tickner's argument, and indeed of that of any feminist theorist asserting the relevance of subjective identity to the identity of difference that is knowledge, lies in the way that that assertion invites a closer examination of the concept of knowledge itself as an identity of subject/object difference. The claim is that the feminist standpoint brings the scientist closer to the truth of at least some aspects of international reality. When feminists are called upon to justify the claim that the absolute gap between subject and object has been bridged it is clear that they cannot do so. This failure, however, is premised on the absoluteness of the divide between the subject and object of knowledge; what happens when we start by challenging that divide rather than the bridge which crosses it? Is there an absolute difference between the knower and what they seek to know, the reality so often qualified by the word 'external'? This is where the concreteness of Tickner's attempt to spell out a feminist standpoint directly contradicts the idea of a separation between knower and known. The basis of Tickner's feminist reformulation of concepts in international relations theory is the reality that certain women have lived, and this in turn is part of the object of knowledge of her putative social science. Does this then imply some simple identity between knower and known, taking us back to an extreme form of subjectivism? Clearly it does not, since this identity is one of a partial relation, a relative identity, in which subjects fail to recognize themselves in their international reality, but also do not encompass the whole of what constitutes that reality. Does this then take us back to a mere plurality of narratives? Clearly it does not, because just as reality is mediated by subjectivity, so subjectivity is mediated by reality, forming partial, relative identities before ever a conscious effort to ground a claim to knowledge is made. Meaningful claims to knowledge are neither what can be absolutely proved to be true, nor are they any coherent assertion; they are the product of a complex dialectical interrelation between subjects and objects which is already dynamically at work prior

159

to scientific enquiry and which can never be negated by that enquiry. The idea of the feminist standpoint is the beginning of the acknowledgement of that pre-existing relation which enables knowledge. If this is recognized, then the notion of absolute epistemological privilege in relation to standpoint cannot make sense. The idea of the feminist standpoint as the key to objective truth, or the idea of a combination of standpoints as the keys to objective truth is incompatible with the radical rethinking of the subject/object relation. Knowledge has to be redefined as a partial and tentative thing, because the subject/object of knowledge is never complete and is always shifting. As Jennifer Ring puts it:

> The choice is not between a world with no distinctions at all and a world of dichotomies. Rather a dialectically conceived world is one where anyone who looks carefully and thoughtfully can see *both* the connections and the distinctions, the intangibility and the tangibility of thought and life, and will recognise the inconclusiveness of a detached, Archimedean perspective.[8]

CONCLUSION

A feminist approach to international relations can never repeat the infinite ambition of realism, which claims to have captured the eternal truth of inter-state relations from an objective standpoint. The idea of the feminist standpoint is the acknowledgement that we can only know from the standpoint of who we are and our identity in difference with the reality we seek to understand. This implies paying attention to who and what we are not, as well as who and what we are, and means that our knowledge-claims will be inevitably tentative. There is no need to apologize for this tentativeness, since it is all that knowledge can ever be. In the context of international relations in which all subjective identities are implicated in global political, social and economic relations, there is no absolute closure between the identity in difference of subjects seeking to understand the international sphere from what may be experienced as radically different, or even opposing, standpoints. This is not going to make a universal theory of the international possible, but it does ground the possibility of a meaningful dialogue, because the relation is already concretely in place, mediating both the subject and object of knowledge. This is very well illustrated by Cynthia Enloe in her exploration of the way in which gender constructs the international, and gender is constructed internationally (see Enloe 1989). In the complex processes that Enloe traces, the political, social and economic activities of men and women continually identify and differentiate men and men, women and women, women and men. According to Enloe's picture there can be no simple identification of women across the world; instead she demonstrates how local and global patterns of hierarchy and oppression mediate and are mediated by women as buyers and labourers, wives and prostitutes. What Enloe's analysis brings home is that neither international political, social and economic structures, nor the subjectivities that are implicated in them are absolutely divided from subject-knowers who seek to understand the international realm from whatever standpoint; this is what makes knowledge about the international realm possible.

In conclusion, then, I contend that the feminist intervention in international relations theory does succeed in suggesting a way beyond the deadlock of the debates between orthodoxy, critical theory and postmodernism discussed above. It does this by forcing a rethinking of the logic of identity and difference in the relation between the subject and object of knowledge as traditionally conceived. A feminist approach to international relations acknowledges the identity in difference of the subject/object of knowledge, rather than asserting the victory of identity over difference or of difference over identity. The mutual mediation of the subject and object of knowledge in feminist international relations is a complex and dynamic process. The project of understanding global reality can never be completed or closed to the claims of other situated knowledges (see Goetz 1988: 491), but this doesn't detract from the significance of the truth it will be able to offer. As a counter to the three masculine comments at the beginning of the chapter I will end with a quotation from a female international relations theorist putting forward an idea of knowledge which seems to me most productive for a feminist social science.

> The commitment to engage with difference in an ongoing 'conversation' entails a view of knowledge and politics as a continuously evolving process. Engaging in endless revision and reformulation – and thereby being responsive to the aims and activities of those social categories of subordinated women with which it identifies – a feminist consciousness committed to embracing difference without diminishing it may be able to produce a more politically adequate epistemology.
>
> (Goetz 1988: 492)

NOTES

1 There are some notable exceptions to this; see Elshtain (1987).

2 For an account of critical theory in international relations see Hoffmann (1987). For an example of a postmodernist approach see Ashley (1988).

3 Martin Hollis and Steve Smith recently claimed critical theory, postmodernism and feminism as the three main alternative positions in international relations. According to Hollis and Smith these three approaches appeal to separate, self-contained groups of adherents. It seems to me, on the contrary, that the three approaches have much in common and much to learn from one another. See Hollis and Smith (1991: 393–4).

4 Realism as a theoretical approach within international relations should not be confused with epistemological realism. For an account of realism as a paradigm for understanding the international sphere see Tickner (1988: 430–1).

5 Realist/neo-realist paradigms along with a strongly positivistic methodological approach have dominated the study of international relations since World War II. There are alternatives to realism, such as approaches utilizing the concept of international society, but these do not differ radically from realism in their account of how the international is to be known. It is only with the advent of critical theory and postmodernism that the epistemological presumptions of the discipline of international relations have been fundamentally challenged. See Hoffmann (1987) and Ashley (1988).

6 Some of the articles in this volume focus on questions of policy, others on theoretical debates. The areas covered include development and global political economy as well as the more traditional terrain of political inter-state relations. See Tickner (1988), Brown (1988), Goetz (1988), Ashworth (1988) and Newland (1988).

7 The work of Gayatri Spivak demonstrates very clearly the problematic nature of the universal claims of western feminism. See Spivak (1987).

8 See Ring (1991: 123). Ring's account of knowledge, like my own, owes a substantial debt to Hegel and his explorations of the relation between the subject and object in knowledge and the logic of identity and difference. See Hegel (1977) and Hegel (1969).

REFERENCES

Ashley, Richard (1988), 'Untying the sovereign state: a double reading of the anarchy problematique', *Millennium*, vol. 17, pp. 227–62.

Ashworth, Georgina (1988), 'An elf among the gnomes: a feminist in north-south relations', *Millennium*, vol. 17, pp. 497–505.

Brown, Sarah (1988), 'Feminism, international theory, and international relations of gender inequality', *Millennium*, vol. 17, pp. 461–75.

Coker, Christopher (1990), 'Women and international relations', *The Salisbury Review*, vol. 8, no. 4, pp. 23–7.

Elshtain, Jean Bethke (1987), *Women and War*, Brighton: Harvester.

Enloe, Cynthia (1989), *Bananas, Beaches and Bases*, London: Pandora.

Goetz, Anne Marie (1988), 'Feminism and the limits of the claim to know: contradictions in the feminist approach to women in development', *Millennium*, vol. 17, pp. 477–96.

Grant, Rebecca and Newland, Kathleen (eds) (1991), *Gender and International Relations*, Milton Keynes: Open University Press.

Harding, Sandra (1991), *Whose Science? Whose Knowledge? Thinking From Women's Lives*, Milton Keynes: Open University Press.

Hegel, G. W. F. (1969), *The Science of Logic*, trans. A. V. Miller, London: George Allen and Unwin.

Hegel, G. W. F. (1977), *Phenomenology of Spirit*, trans. A. V. Miller, Oxford: Oxford University Press.

Hoffmann, Mark (1987), 'Critical theory and the inter-paradigm debate', *Millennium*, vol. 16, pp. 331–49.

Hollis, Martin and Smith, Steve (1991), 'Beware of gurus: structure and action in international relations', *Review of International Studies*, vol. 17, pp. 393–410.

Keohane, Robert (1991), 'International relations theory: contributions of a feminist standpoint' in *Gender and International Relations*, ed. R. Grant and K. Newland, Milton Keynes: Open University Press, pp. 41–50.

Linklater, Andrew (1982), *Men and Citizens in the Theory of International Relations*, London: Macmillan.

Newland, Kathleen (1988), 'From transnational relationships to international relations: women in development and the international decade of women', *Millennium*, vol. 17, pp. 507–16.

Ring, Jennifer (1991), *Modern Political Theory and Contemporary Feminism: A Dialectical Analysis*, Albany: SUNY Press.

Spivak, Gayatri Chakravorty (1987), *In Other Worlds: Essays in Cultural Politics*, New York and London: Methuen.

Tickner, J. Ann (1988), 'Hans Morgenthau's principles of political realism: a feminist reformulation', *Millennium*, vol. 17, pp. 429–38.

Tickner, J. Ann (1991), 'On the fringes of the world economy: a feminist perspective' in *The New International Political Economy*, ed. C. N. Murphy and R. Tooze, Boulder, CO: Lynne Rienner Publishers, pp. 191–206.

Walker, Robert (1988), *One World, Many Worlds: Struggles for a Just World Peace*, Boulder, CO: Lynne Rienner Publishers.

Walker, Robert (1989), 'The Prince and "The Pauper" in the theory of international relations', *International/Intertextual Relations: Postmodern Readings of World Politics*, Lexington, MA: Lexington, pp. 25–48.

11

FEMINISM, SUBJECTIVITY AND PSYCHOANALYSIS

Towards a (corpo)real knowledge

Caroline Williams

> Up until now, in the field of knowledge nothing has been conceived which did not participate in the fantasy of inscribing the sexual relation.
>
> (Lacan 1975, cited in Roustang 1990: 94)

> No praxis is more orientated to that which, at the heart of experience, is the kernel of the Real than psychoanalysis.
>
> (Lacan 1979: 53)

INTRODUCTION

The metaphysical critique of western forms of knowledge as allied with and contributing to patriarchal domination has long been a theoretical and political concern of feminism. That the epistemological and ontological assumptions underlying philosophy's claim to hold the truth has come under attack in recent years, particularly by poststructuralism, is of no surprise to either feminism or psychoanalysis. Both, in different ways, have long viewed the omnipotent cries of the Cartesian knowing subject as based on both the exclusion and repression of the feminine.[1]

Indeed, these two theoretical practices share a common interest in the epistemological plight of the metaphysical subject as split, fragmented and decentred in relation to knowledge and the social world.[2] Nevertheless, dialogues between the two, in particular the criticisms levelled by feminist theory toward psychoanalysis, have created, I wish to argue, a philosophical or more specifically, a binary impasse which itself falls prey to a masculine logic, juxtaposing the symbolic and the imaginary as masculine and feminine respectively.[3]

Psychoanalysis is at its most disruptive when forced to challenge its own authority: feminist rereadings of Freud and Lacan help it to do just this. I wish to argue that psychoanalysis can be seen as an epistemological device

164

for revealing the bodily roots of all claims to knowledge, truth and representation. If we exclude psychoanalysis from debates concerning knowledge (what is it, who has it, what gives it meaning) and subjectivity (what does it mean to know, to think and create systems of knowledge), we also deny access to the male imaginary and its role in procuring the present 'crisis of the subject', the so-called death of man, through the suppression of the body.

This chapter will situate the work of the poststructuralist and psychoanalyst, Jacques Lacan, within this theoretical space of crisis.[4] It will question the compatibility of feminism and psychoanalysis. Its specific aim is to consider the feminist critique and rereading of Lacan's work in the context of the knowing subject of philosophy. It will assess the contribution feminist psychoanalytic theory can make to an understanding of the knowing subject. My main thesis is that feminist theory is able to take Lacan's theory to its limit by focusing on the category of *the real*. Those writers who emphasize the imaginary and symbolic dimensions of his work do so to the detriment of the real which remains ignored, reified or misrecognized.[5] It is precisely the real which leads us to confront 'the sexualization of discourse' and the corporeal roots of that knowledge which seeks to exclude the feminine and 'fix' objectivity in complicity with masculine norms. This, I will maintain, is most clearly theorized in the work of Luce Irigaray.

PSYCHOANALYSIS AND EPISTEMOLOGY

The relationship between the knowing subject and all philosophical attempts to ground truth, demarcate and limit the world as a rational, self-reflective order has rested on the epistemological primacy of the all-perceiving, self-purposive subject of Cartesian logic. The ontological structure of this consciousness posits a subject *a priori* to the world, privileging *sight* as the yardstick to measure practico-empirical claims to truth. That is to say, the subject becomes identical with knowledge, and knowledge comes to reflect the rational constitution of the subject. Truth is represented as a unitary and stable form of reasoning.[6] It is adjudicated by a subject able to differentiate good from evil, certainty from mere impulse, and the permanence of the object of investigation over and above the fluctuating, discontinuous claims of nature.

Feminist rereadings of our philosophical heritage – particularly the discourse of Enlightenment – have seen the repetitive identification of man with reason and transcendence and woman with irrationality and the fall from Grace, to be illustrative of the gender-specificity of the knowing subject (see for example Hodge 1988). Woman is effectively the other of reason, often associated with the mythical, the mystical and the maternal. Stability in representation may be signified by the masculine but it is internally supported by viewing the feminine as inherently *unstable*. These binary oppositions (nature/reason, rational/irrational, subject/object, mind/body, masculine/feminine) ground masculine theories in what Irigaray calls the Logic of the Same: that is, they are all steeped in a masculine order of discourse, that which we may call or name phallogocentrism.[7]

It is clearly through the instrument of psychoanalysis that feminism has been able to develop these claims. Both Freud and Lacan have deconstructed the philosophical position occupied by the Cartesian subject, emphasizing that it is the unconscious of the knowing subject which should be our focus. Psychoanalysis proposes that we reconsider the thought-processes of the sovereign subject to reveal beneath its fixed abstractions the complex dynamics of libidinal energy which order unconscious activity and represent sexual instinct in the mind.

> This illusory fixed point is not the whole of rationality, nor does it sum up what thinking is about. . . . Thinking is the means of grasping the fluid mass of the affects which animate the body as a libidinal space. . . . The process of theorization – like every other gesture of creation – is the art of transforming lived experience, of representing it (to oneself) through the play of the imagination.
>
> (Braidotti 1991: 31–2)

In other words, we are suggesting a symptomatic reading of philosophical texts, one which treats the process of abstraction, *Vorstellung*, as the means by which unconscious drives are organized and harnessed for their outward manifestation in knowledge. Thus binary oppositions are seen to have a very complex structuration. Stability in representation is a result not *only* of the suppression of the second term (the feminine) but also of a *desire* for continuity, coherence and a pathological insistence for order. Western forms of knowledge, it will be argued, constitute the masculine ego and its object, whilst the feminine ego has no means of representation. In Lacanian terms we are asserting that the imaginary foundations of knowledge are dominated by masculine drives. This monopolization of both truth and reason by knowledge provides for a state of constancy, conformity, and this in turn affords the masculine ego its narcissistic desire to repeat itself, to mirror itself and moreover to create (the illusion of) stability. As Jane Flax comments, 'the pathology of systematic philosophy extends beyond its "male-ordered" contents and methods to its intolerance of ambivalence, disorder and ambiguity and its dominating and relentless desire for closure, finality and certainty'.[8] This desire for closure and certainty corresponds to the *méconnaissance* of the (masculine) subject. The stability of systematic thought is maintained only by excluding the real and repressing the feminine as the ground upon which theories of knowledge develop. Feminists thus have a particular interest in the disruptive and creative potential of the real, in so far as the latter is both allied with the feminine (in its exclusion), and destabilizing of masculine representations of knowledge.

Despite the significance of psychoanalysis as an epistemological starting-point for critiques of knowledge and subjectivity, feminist theory often appears wary of being duped by a science which has as its *raison d'être* the subject of woman. Can psychoanalysis succeed in its quest to privilege what is *missing* from masculine discourse when its aim has always been – and in some circles continues to be – the explanation of female hysteria, her lack of the phallus and her status in the symbolic order? Psychoanalysis must be seen as a double-edged weapon (Wright 1989: 142). On the one hand (as ally), it has great explanatory capacity, demystifying traditional conceptions of natural sexual difference and emphasizing the social construction of sexual identity. On the other hand (as adversary), it falls victim to its own brand of essentialism, again reducing female identity to her genitalia. It will be a matter of continuing debate how far feminists can utilize psychoanalysis to serve feminist interests. However, the dilemma outlined above serves only to blur their intimate relationship. It is not a question of *either* embracing *or* rejecting psychoanalytic theory. Psychoanalysis is an 'inescapable' discourse which aligns psychic energy, primordial drives and unconscious fantasy with the repression of the maternal site of origin. Feminist theory must move towards a critical intervention in this discourse. I want to argue that it is through a closer reading of Lacanian theory, in particular an understanding of the real and its role in the construction of knowledge that this move can be initiated.

Lacanian theory offers a way out of the dominant form of knowledge which establishes the self-certainty and truth of the subject through its relation to the object. This Cartesian identification, or correspondence, of subject and truth will always be a partial relation. The subject, we must remember, can represent only a *symbol* in language and not the thing itself. In Lacan's theory of the mirror-stage, it is the objectification of both subject and object, and the ontological break, *Spaltung*, with the pre-discursive realm which affords the rational subject its claim to mastery. I will turn now to consider a feminist analysis of the psychoanalytic structure of knowledge, viewed through the category of the real.

SO WHAT'S REAL?

I shall argue in this section that it is the real (rather than the imaginary) which signals the impossibility of complete rational self-purposive thought. It thus remains a fundamental concept for a feminist epistemological critique of foundationalist theories of truth. As we shall see, it signals that a dynamic libidinal structuration will dominate the subject's relation to itself, the other and the social world.

Lacan's discussion of the real can at best be described as elusive. There is no systematic or definitive study of the concept, rather it is present throughout his *oeuvre*, its meaning given always in relation to its structural partners: the imaginary and the symbolic. (The three are said to form a 'Borromean knot'.[9]) It is clear however that his work problematizes standard concepts of reality and it is perhaps easier to begin by establishing what the Lacanian real is *not*. It is not the real world, nor its historical representation;[10] it is not the discursive construction of the social, nor the subject's *lived relation* to that order. Neither can it be the subject's immediate relation to itself.[11] In other words the real does not correspond to that view of reality generally adopted by existential, phenomenological and social-constructionist theories where the subject's 'experience' of the real is either immanent in consciousness or uncontestable.

For Lacan, the real is a dimension beyond and behind the symbolic, yet it is also resistant to symbolization. Prior to the constitution of both subject and object, it seems to disrupt and confuse their imaginary and symbolic construction.[12] As Lacan writes: 'The Real is that before which the Imaginary falters and the Symbolic stumbles' (1977: x, translator's note). It represents a state of *primal discord*, one where there are no boundaries, no limits, no symbolic language. Indeed this domain would appear to be inaccessible to the subject-as-signifier, one who exists only in, and through, language. It comes very close to the event of death in the subject's life,[13] indicating that all that is *prior* to the symbolic order has been masked, hidden and excluded. Death is rooted in the 'inarticulate strivings of the body' (Boothby 1991: 102), those unbound, psychic energies which by their *non*-assimilation tend towards the disruption of both imaginary and symbolic life. The death-drive can be seen here as the 'unprocessed real' (101), that which remains unsymbolized, lacking an adequate signifier to enter speech. It 'represents' – and seeks to adjudicate – the tensions and conflicts between the imaginary and the symbolic, by binding tendencies towards fragmentation and lack of fixation on the part of the ego. To quote Lacan,

> When we wish to attain in the subject what was before the serial articulation of the symbol and what is primordial to the birth of symbols, we find it in *death, from which his existence takes on all the meaning it has.*
>
> (1977: 105, my emphasis)

However, if the real is to be identified with a *pre*-discursive space, its definition is problematic. The real seems to challenge the way we 'think' about formulations of knowledge. If it 'exists' as a category (outside of language/meaning), the construction of the definition is problematic (even contradictory). Here feminists have a choice: to relinquish an apparently irrational concept, or investigate its bodily roots. It is my argument that the real is inextricably 'bound' (in the Freudian sense) to the bodily roots of knowledge, and the biological pre-discursive subject.

We can begin to deal with these questions by exploring the theorization of the real in Lacan's Seminars, in particular its resonance within the analysis of the symptom (trauma, hysteria, neurosis and fantasy), and significantly its meaning in relation to a psychoanalytic conception of knowledge. Lacan's reading of the real corresponds in several ways to his own philosophico-theoretical development.[14] This, for the purpose of explanation, can be divided into three distinct periods.[15]

In the 1950s, a period one could associate very loosely with idealism, Lacan sees both the subject and his/her desire as rooted in the natural or the biological. All attempts to satisfy biological needs (hunger, thirst) ultimately fail, in that they occur within the subject in an endless mechanical repetition.[16] In this instance, the real is 'a brute pre-symbolic reality' (see Ragland-Sullivan in Wright 1992: 375). It is the object (or thing) that determines need, and is also the one that imposes a 'lack' in the subject and orders the radical impossibility of fulfilment. It thus ricochets the traumatized subject into a quest for satisfaction in the Other, be this a form of auto-eroticism, identification with an-other, or the objectification of the self in language. At this stage in his work, the real is for Lacan an object beyond comprehension. It is both no-thing and some-thing. Like the Kantian thing-in-itself, it is 'unconceptualized, but nonetheless an absolute' (375). This seems to signal, at one and the same time, Lacan's import of philosophical idealism *and* his criticism of it. The subject's unrelenting desire to come to 'know' the object will always lead it to posit some definitive view of the real within the symbolic and call it truth itself. The act of signification for Lacan creates a gap between the real and the symbolic wherein the subject takes root.[17] There can be no *absolute* truth or knowledge. To the extent that the subject attempts to express the real, to fix and name it as a signifier, the real is transferred to the realm of fantasy and self-deception. According to this view, all efforts to posit a rational *episteme* produce anxiety in the subject because bits of the real will always infect the purity of perception and burden the subject with an 'excess' which must be reformed and contained within both identity and representation. Hence the alienation of the subject in the symbolic.

In the second period (the 1960s and early 1970s), a time some commentators associate with the 'structuralist' Lacan, a number of conditions are given to the real. In accordance with structuralist anti-humanism, the symbolic is ordered by language and comes to function independently of subjectivity. The real here has no linguistic form or expression outside the authority of the paternal metaphor; it can only speak through its agency. Whilst we view the real in itself as impossible, it is present in its effects (Žižek 1989: 161). These receive amplification in the symbolic realm, either in a latent form to be uncovered through the (psycho)analysis of the symptom, or through the utterances of the psychotic subject.[18] In this phase, the real can be seen as an entity which can be reconstructed through analysis. However, as a structural relation in this schema the symbolic also functions by signifying the lack of the subject. It binds, subdues, coerces and reforms the real, delimiting its effects and bringing the subject into line with the norms of everyday life.

However, I think it is within Lacan's later work, his 'third period' (late 1970s), that the 'Logic of the real' is made apparent.[19] It is marked both by Lacan's critical return to idealism and by the development of his views on feminine sexuality within *Encore*. Here Lacan's views take on an increasingly complex formulation: the issue at stake is 'the impossible goal of maintaining consistency' (Ragland-Sullivan in Wright 1992: 376), of achieving oneness, of recognizing the other, of satisfying our desire, of *knowing* the object. What appears to be implied here is that the subject – and the real – will always remain incomplete and outstanding, hence signalling the impossibility of absolute truth and certainty. Yet at the same time, in his theorization of Woman, Lacan seems to be giving certain characteristics – and arguably 'possibilities' of disruption – to the feminine, which overlap and intersect with his analysis of the real. The real thus appears to be coded as feminine. Let us examine this logic in greater detail.

In Lacanian theory, Woman, as such, cannot exist in the symbolic order defined in relation to the phallus as transcendental signifier.[20] Moreover, she is the missing element in discourse. Unable to take up her place as signifying subject, the female subject is the excluded other, outside grammatical language. As Lacan writes: 'There is Woman only as excluded by the nature of things which is the nature of words' (Mitchell and Rose 1985: 144). For Woman to achieve representation she must be *de*-naturalized or objectified in language. It is only as man's other that Woman enters the process of signification (68). Through the objectification of Woman the masculine subject maintains his self-coherence and disguises his origin in the real. Woman's role then, is to represent the unrepresentable real. To the extent that she succeeds in this masquerade of truth, Woman takes on the function of a fetishized object for man, she becomes man's symptom,[21] and represents for him a state of phallic *jouissance* and consistency (affirmation of his own subjecthood).[22] Within this relation, Woman remains mute, unable to express her own organic needs (pleasure, desire, love, her relation to the world), the immediacy of her body as rooted in the maternal, or her *real* relation to knowledge (founded on non-singularity, non-fixity and non-closure). Each of these facets of Woman remain, like the real, unrepresentable, impossible.

It is this logic which forms the basis of Lacan's assertion of the myth of the sexual relation, the absence of a signifier to represent both genders. It precludes the possibility of oneness and also signals death, if by death we mean, in Lacanian terms, a loss or unbinding of the form and coherence of the imaginary.[23]

However, to some extent, Woman escapes this destructive knot formulated by the (masculine) subject's desire for completeness, *jouissance*. For Lacan, she has no ontological being, and must exist as an effect in the symbolic order.[24] This lack of ontological essence is by no means a disadvantage. If following Lacan, we wish to argue that ontology springs up as a result of the *Spaltung* (splitting) of the subject and has as its form durability, self-identity and singularity (see Irigaray 1991a: 88), then its status is also one grounded upon the repression of the feminine. Woman's *lack* of essence links her strategically with the play of *jouissance*,[25] the proximity to the death-drives and an excess in meaning which resists and refuses binary logic: that is, the real, *par excellence*.

It should be clear from my exposition of the real that each period in Lacan's *oeuvre* contains an implicit reference, an illustration of Woman as excluded from and yet the determinant of all claims to truth and objectivity. Moreover, the three conceptions of the real offered above (as engendering lack, producing anxiety as symptom and disturbing the ego-centricity of discourse), all resonate in the immediate, imaginary existence of the subject. These effects are present in symbolic and imaginary structures. Arguably, it is *Woman* as biological mother who engenders this lack in the subject. Similarly, it is *Woman* who masquerades as man's symptom, and *the feminine* which subverts the unity of speech and image. How far does Lacan's account of the real coincide with his views on the feminine and his description of the non-existence or impossibility of Woman? It has been argued above that thinking establishes the stability and equilibrium of the (masculine) subject *only* by excluding the real, by mistaking images of wholeness for the real thing. In *Encore*, Lacan seems to be indicating that the feminine subject neither succumbs to complete alienation from the real, nor enjoys – or indeed desires – so full an association with the symbolic as does the masculine subject.[26] Woman is, at one and the same time, associated with excess and impossibility. It is at this point in Lacan's account that the subversive nature of the real can be used as an instrument of feminist criticism. The feminine subject, by her very proximity to the real, is a disruptive force upon the symbolic order and the reigning paternal metaphor that defines the relationship between knowledge, subject and social world.

However, generally, feminist interpretations of Lacan have not tended to take up these issues. For example, a number of feminist theorists claim that Lacan's system, whilst invigorating Freudian psychoanalysis with an emphasis on language and culture in the creation of gendered subjects, rests upon an anatomical view of woman as lacking in her sexual form. Feminist critiques and rereadings of Lacan have tended to focus – predominantly – on the discursive construction of the feminine and her imaginary alienation from the established phallocentric symbolic order. To this extent, his system is misread as closed, universal and totalizing in its effects. This, as noted in my introduction, can often lead to a theoretical impasse: the imaginary and the symbolic are established in a relation based purely on their *opposition*. This binary trap creates masculine and feminine identities within a static, secondary order which can be described, criticized but never *real*-ly understood. Ragland-Sullivan neatly sums up this problem: 'No feminist or political theoretician will succeed ... in dismantling the real power implicit in the impasses, singular desires or ego fictions that emanate from the unconscious by using tactics of oscillating ambiguity aimed at smashing the binary' (Ragland-Sullivan 1989: 52). Thus feminism submits its *own* theoretical argument to phallocentric logic when the real is ignored. This accounts for the rather unfair caricature of French feminism as essentializing woman, reducing the debate to the biological and returning the feminine to a chaotic pre-symbolic. Whilst the real enmeshes the natural/biological, it cannot be reduced to this alone. Neither can it be wholly associated with the unconscious. It houses the *energetics* of the libido and the death-drive which becomes repressed when the subject attempts to recognize an object as an image of him/herself. Language will always express inchoate desires and libidinal energies, *irrespective* of the subject's desire to master them by designating them irrational, unscientific or subjective. This has a profound effect for any theory of knowledge which views the construction of the object to be the agency of the knowing subject. As Lacan has shown, the materiality of language, the creation of discourse, is rooted in the real of the pre-discursive body and not consciousness *per se*.

LUCE IRIGARAY AND THE POLITICS OF THE (CORPO)REAL

I want to argue that it is in the work of Luce Irigaray that the relationship charted above between the feminine, the real and attempts to ground truth and certainty, is given critical expression. Moreover, Irigaray, on several accounts, exposes the phallocentric logic which seeks to claim (all) knowledge as its own, and draws our attention to the masculine subject's suppression of the real, in its many and multiple forms. In this way, her work illustrates how the political containment and epistemological suppression of the real function ultimately to signal the impossibility of the subject's completeness and the *real* possibility of symbolic disruption on the part of the feminine.

Whilst the category of real is not often explicit in Irigaray's texts, its meaning resonates in her discussions of subjectivity, the maternal and its origin[27] and the role of death in the constitution of the social symbolic order.[28] In particular, Irigaray is creating a critical dialogue (on the level of epistemology) with the psychoanalytic community, as well as situating the question of the real within the wider field of western forms of knowledge. It is these two dimensions that I propose to focus on.

Irigaray is both psychoanalyst and philosopher. Her debt to Lacan is immense, although her role as analyst has been that of an outsider to the community which operates on the basis of normal (masculine) science.[29] Her work was viewed as an anomaly by the Ecole Freudienne; in 1974 she was expelled and has maintained an independent and critical voice, questioning whether psychoanalysis can take place when subjected to a science of completeness (Irigaray 1991b). Psychoanalysis is not the privileged *episteme* that Lacan throughout his life imagined: Irigaray submits psychoanalysis, along with all other discourses of philosophy and science to a rigorous epistemological critique. 'Who, according to our epistemological tradition', she asks, 'provides the keystone to the order of discourse?' (Irigaray 1985c: 77). This question, for Irigaray, cannot be answered by any discourse of knowledge, which has always-already been appropriated by the masculine imaginary, very often under the guise of a rationalism, a universalism: science *par excellence*. It is the knowing subject underlying these claims, the one who positions the world before himself and reconstitutes it in front and outside of himself who is of interest here. What 'schize' does science bring about? What desire is at play? (75, 83). How is the subject of science and philosophy constructed?

It is through her critique of Lacan that these answers are developed. Irigaray rejects the theory of the subject's interpellation into symbolic life initiated by the mirror-phase. This flat mirror can only be used for the reflection of the masculine subject in language. She writes:

> Women, starting from this flat mirror alone, can only come into being as the inverted other of the masculine subject (his alter-ego), or as the place before the emergence and veiling of the cause of his (phallic) desire, or again as lack.
>
> (Irigaray 1985b: 129)

The metaphor of the mirror can likewise be extended to the sphere of knowledge. The flat one-dimensional imago reflected by the mirror coincides with the dominant characteristics of the male imaginary: order, form, visibility, unity and erection (Irigaray 1985c: 77). Psychoanalysis is a masculine science; the myth of Oedipus operates as universal law. It invades the space of neutrality and scientificity and is illustrative of the repression of the (M)other, the feminine in western discourse, a fear of fusion, disequilibrium and difference; ultimately it can be reduced to a certain relation with death. It is the death-drive for Irigaray which represents the 'crisis of civilization' (Irigaray 1991b: 97). To the extent that the subject sublimates the tension caused by the 'real' experience of death and its symbolic 'absence', the social order will remain one which will forever privilege hierarchy and hence restrain the progress of the feminine.

This perspective may be transposed into the debate concerning the foundation of philosophical Reason and Enlightenment. In *Speculum*, Irigaray examines and exposes the western (patriarchal) unconscious as it materializes in the discourse of philosophy. This search for the repressed reveals that the subject is a narcissistic male and the Other, woman, has not yet acceded to subjectivity.[30] Irigaray's aim is to theorize the terms on which the female imaginary can assume an identity which will not be colonized by the male. She wants to offer women some version of their own mirror, so that women may become the subjects of science too, and create their own space in the symbolic order.

The female imaginary which Irigaray wants to invoke in both speech and writing appeals to the metaphors or motifs of the female body. As we have seen, the transcendental (masculine) subject of language appropriates only a fantastical image of the (feminine) body, namely one that can be accommodated within the Order of the Same. The corporal realm of the feminine, articulated by Irigaray in *This Sex Which is not One* and 'When our lips speak together' (1985b: 23–33), points towards a pre-discursive space hitherto ignored in the construction of knowledge. Preceding ontology, prior to phenomenological experience, lies the open, unstable and mobile site of feminine desire. This is a residue which is not comfortably contained in knowledge. It lies exposed, but beyond appropriation, in the real.

However, for many of her commentators, this metaphoric recourse to the female body is seen to render an essentialist view of Woman's body and nature, reinscribing binary oppositions in a form complicit with masculine theories of knowledge (i.e., man as identity, unity and women as non-identity, plurality (see for example Stanton 1986)). But like Lacan's Phallus, the 'Lips' (which are *discursively constructed* by Irigaray) also function when veiled, as the following extract illustrates:

> She is not closed up or around one single truth or essence.... And she does not oppose a feminine truth to a masculine truth.... If the female sex takes place by embracing itself, by endlessly sharing and exchanging its lips, its edges, its borders, and their 'content', as it ceaselessly becomes other, no stability of essence is proper to her.
>
> (Irigaray 1991a: 86)

Irigaray's emphasis on the female genitalia is a strategic play.[31] She rejects the male–female dichotomies of traditional epistemology. Her critics and commentators fail to see that the pre-discursive corporeal realm is an expression of a *real* relation to knowledge. When Irigaray equates fluidity with the flow of blood and the mucous membranes, and the feminine sex with an 'excess with respect to form' (1985b: 110), she is utilizing the subversive potential of the real, bringing to language a *parler-femme* that was previously repressed, and illustrating that woman's relation to knowledge is diffused 'according to modalities scarcely compatible with the framework of ruling symbolics' (106). In other words, the underside of feminine sexuality is used to transgress and confuse the boundaries between the real and the symbolic in the articulation of knowledge.

Using these double-edged strategies, Irigaray relates the categories and ruptures of masculine forms of knowledge *back* to the necessities of the self-representation of phallic desire in discourse (see Irigaray 1985b: 77). In reply to some of her psychoanalytic (and also some feminist) critics, she writes that these texts do not

> imply a regressive retreat to the anatomical or to a concept of 'nature'. . . . It is more a question of breaking out of the autological and tautological circle of systems of representation and their discourse so as to allow women to speak their sex. The 'at least two' lips no longer corresponds to [your] morpho-logic; nor does it obey Lacan's model of the 'not all' to which the One is necessary. There is something of the One, but something escapes it, resists it, is always lacking; there is something of One, but it has holes, rifts, silences which speak, murmur to and and among themselves, etc. [Can this be] *something of the real rebelling against all laws, but already produced under the empire of the law?*
>
> (1991b: 97, my emphasis)

'Just ask yourselves', Irigaray continues, 'whether the Real might not be some very repressed-censored-forgotten "thing" to do with the body' (86). It is the feminine body which Irigaray is here linking explicitly with the real. When psychoanalysis censors the body (its blood, circulation, air and respiration (95)), it makes its representations of desire with a certain violence to the body, denying its origin and relation with death.

The real, after all, precedes and sanctions gender. It stands for 'all that actual human possibility and relation to others that is excluded by the Oedipal account of our relations with ourselves, the Other and language' (Cornell and Thurschwell 1987: 147). It stands outside the dyadic couple, symbolic and imaginary, it reminds us of a different way of being in an unstable language, pre-Oedipal, or perhaps post-patriarchal, unfixing gender and releasing the feminine from its binary position as the Other of Man.

It is women themselves who must take part in the releasing of the real from its point of systemic closure, to create a new Symbolic. This involves for Irigaray (following Derrida here) using the tactic of mimicry or mimesis:

> To play with mimesis is thus, for a woman, to try to locate the place

of her exploitation by discourse, without allowing herself to be simply reduced to it. It means to resubmit herself ... to ideas, in particular to ideas about herself that are elaborated in/by a masculine logic, but so as to make 'visible' by an effect of playful repetition, what was supposed to remain invisible: recovering a possible operation of the feminine in language.

(Irigaray 1985b: 76)

This tactic of disrupting the symbolic order by a strategic use of the feminine relation to the real is central to Irigaray's political vision. By recalling and recuperating the feminine in language, the ontological security of the (masculine) epistemological subject is called into question. The feminine subject's proximity to the real can pose a challenge to the primacy of the knowing subject of philosophy. That the real is also structurally related to (his) psychic constitution ensures that these disruptive tactics will not be a worthless labour.

Hence, Irigaray focuses on 'those blanks in discourse which recall the places of [Woman's] exclusion' (1985a: 142), the gaps, the bits and pieces of the feminine subject that are excluded from masculine reason. It is 'a game of specular/speculative reflection of the inner Logic of phallo-logo-centric discourse' (Braidotti 1986: 9), the hidden instance of the maternal. In the phallo-symbolic, the mother of infancy is repressed and reconceived, revalued as the castrated, unknowable other and located in the real. The following extract seems to situate Irigaray's disrupting strategies directly to the real:

The substratum is the woman who reproduces the social order, who has made this order's infrastructure ... isn't there a fluidity, some flood, that could shake this social order? ... if we make the foundation of the social order shift, then everything will shift.

(Irigaray 1991c: 47)

CONCLUSION

In conclusion I want to assess the implications of the Lacanian assertion that the real is impossible. It poses some problems for Irigaray's analysis of the real (its recuperation and *possible* political role in the transformation of the symbolic), and for a dynamic critique of phallocentric forms of knowledge. Again Irigaray sums up the primary obstacle which is 'a certain not taking into account of the subject's search for himself' (1985c: 82). It is, let us remember, the continuous attempts, and repetitive failure of the subject to name, define and incorporate the real into his symbolic universe that structures Lacan's theory and sends the subject-as-signifier on an endless journey in search of the object within knowledge.

An alteration in the order of discourse demands that the epistemological subject renounces its own narcissism and neuroses which affect discursive mastery, lets go of the object which undermines the status of the feminine and embraces its own finitude over the certainty of the world. These changes require no less than an extension of the Copernican revolution in scientific knowledge to the corporeality of the human subject (see also Irigaray 1985a: 133 and 1985c: 83). It requires that the taboos and myths which organize life in civil society *and* the epistemological assumptions upholding the knowing subject of philosophy are reconstituted with reference to the feminine. Such myths and taboos have already supported a patriarchal genealogy. Irigaray notes the universal matricide which gave rise to the myth of the primordial father portrayed by Freud in *Totem and Taboo*. In political and scientific life, the result is synonymous: women have been represented as other to reason and truth, unable to claim (the object of) knowledge as their own. By using its laws/myths to uncover its logic of exclusion as unconscious desire, Irigaray opens up the domain of the (corpo)real subject. This brings the subject into naked contact with the real, death and the immediacy of his/her desire.

Nevertheless, for Lacan and his followers the real is impossible. It is inaccessible; our subjectivity arises as its structural effect. Symbolic closure separates the subject from his/her 'experience' because the pre-discursive real has no linguistic representation (except in analysis). Those Irigarayan strategies outlined above, that seek to disrupt this logic and transform the symbolic from phallomorphic singularity into a multifarious arena of languages where both sexes can speak with different voices, are seen by some to be misplaced solutions. For in this Lacanian view the symbolic and the imaginary must always subsume the real if we are to avoid 'nothingness', psychosis, death itself.[32] Prior to the Name-of-the-Father, feminine subjects remain mute, without subjectivity. Woman must be content to remain the engendering force of the symbolic order. Is this an impasse or a difficulty constitutive of the real itself?

Lacan and Irigaray offer conflicting responses to this problem. For Lacan, the real is an absolute which resists recuperation on all fronts. Unformalized, without foundation or linguistic expression, it circumscribes a place which can only lie outside of meaning and representation. The following statement sums up Lacan's position quite clearly:

> From a psychoanalytic standpoint, there is an aspect of the relation to the primordial object of satisfaction that remains irretrievable. There is always a remainder, a left-over.... This something-always-beyond cannot be recuperated in a dialectical reconciliation with the Other.
>
> (Boothby 1991: 215)

Irigaray would agree that it is precisely because of the *un*formalized existence of the real (as death-drive, psychic energy, bodily fluids and organic residues) that it cannot be assimilated to the symbolic. The drives, like the feminine, have no language of their own, although we can argue that it is Irigaray's project (*parler-femme*) to devise such a language. Her strategies of subversion are political in their quest to present a different symbolic organization of discourse, and to unsettle the existing order by disrupting the self-constitution of form through exclusion of the real.

Identifying the real represents a danger which is best translated as an ethical problem.[33] The real is an unstable, open and communicative category. It both compels the subject to search for truth and simultaneously constructs and disrupts its attempts. For the real to become truth itself, knowable by the subject, would be a grave and destructive mistake. It requires symbolic containment and translation; unsymbolized and unsublimated it remains extremely dangerous.[34] These effects by necessity are also present in the realm of knowledge. Psychoanalysis cannot aspire to absoluteness unless it seeks to represent the real, in much the same way that the knowing subject of philosophy seeks to represent the object as a reflection of himself. Lacan, after all, called for 'a limping truth' which defies any grounding in knowledge. Hence Lacan was aware of the limits of the real, although his formulations sometimes distorted this.

The issues discussed in this chapter revolve around the status of the feminine in modern conceptions of knowledge. Using the category of the real, feminists, I have argued, are able to perform a meta-epistemological critique of knowledge, drawing attention to the impossibility of absolute truth and certainty by employing the feminine to subvert the ground of phallogocentric logic. This theoretical project is clearly a valuable and revealing one. As some essentialist readings of Irigaray illustrate, when feminists *misrecognize* the real, they only reinstate binary oppositions, recapitulating claims to truth and certainty in similar fashion to masculine forms of knowledge. A similar misreading follows for those feminist interpretations of Lacan that view his system as totalizing, universal and closed: false claims of authority resurrect a phallogocentric symbolic structure without reference to the necessary effects, again ignoring the political resonances of the real.

Clearly, feminism occupies a complex position in this debate which requires careful negotiation. It must recognize and resituate its *own* desire for the representation of the repressed in phallogocentric knowledge. To reclaim the feminine as the Other of the Same can only produce a reified theory of knowledge. Similarly, to appropriate the real as feminist would be a genuine catastrophe, given its proximity to death. Hence it remains rather more significant for feminists to recognize the limits that the real encapsulates, its sources (as feminine, excess, residue of form), and its structural relation to symbolic and imaginary forms of knowledge. A new ethical sensibility should thus be created which can account for the female subject's structural relation to the real, and the masculine subject's suppression of it. It is in this direction that a feminist epistemology may fruitfully develop.

NOTES

1 For psychoanalysis, of course, this repression has always been linked to the Oedipus complex in a natural relationship; feminists, as we will see, have drawn on this repression more critically.

2 Contemporary feminist conceptions of subjectivity have their roots in psychoanalytic theory. See for example the work of Julia Kristeva (1980, 1982) and Luce Irigaray (1985a, 1985b). For Anglo-American developments, see Braidotti (1991), Jardine (1985) and Flax (1990).

3 Criticisms often raised in relation to Kristeva's 'reliance' on Lacan. See for example Hekman (1990).

4 It is not easy to pinpoint the philosophical influences on Lacan which remain many and varied. For different perspectives see Macey (1988), Borch-Jacobsen (1991) and Boothby (1991: ch. 5). There is also a useful selection of essays in Smith and Kerrigan (1983).

5 It is ironic that Lacan has defined the real in terms of a psychoanalytic encounter that will always remain 'a missed encounter' (Lacan 1979: 55).

6 For a critique of the primacy of sight in the constitution of knowledge, see Derrida (1974).

7 For definition and commentary on this term, see the entry 'Phallogocentrism' by Paul Smith in Wright (1992: 316–18).

8 See 'Philosophy' by Jane Flax in Wright (1992: 323–7, esp. 326).

9 Most glossaries accompanying Lacan's work use this definition. See for example Lacan (1977).

10 This is Fredric Jameson's understanding of the Real; see Jameson (1977). For criticism of his position, see Jardine (1985: 123).

11 It cannot be seen to correspond to the regulative, tolerative tendencies of the Freudian reality-principle.

12 This clearly sets up the Real in correspondence to the theorization of the abject in Kristeva's work; see Kristeva (1982). Boothby (1991: 65), also makes this link.

13 We do not speak here of literal (mortal) death, but an 'imaginary' death or death-drive, signified by the endless return of castration anxiety and misrecognition in language.

14 This is not a definitive statement. I agree with David Macey's comments that there is little point in searching for the 'final Lacan'; his *oeuvre* defies this project. See however the recent study by François Roustang (1990), where he offers an extremely sophisticated and well-researched argument for the claim that Lacan's reading of the Real *throughout* his work is dominated by the quest for scientificity.

15 See 'The real' by Ellie Ragland-Sullivan in Wright (1992: 374–6).

16 This perspective is reminiscent of the Hegelian dialectic, the unceasing mediation of nature and spirit. It also supports a quasi-scientific reading of Lacan; see Roustang (1990).

17 See Juliet MacCannell's comments on the relation between truth and the pre-symbolic in MacCannell (1986: 48).

18 For Kristeva, psychotic speech is an expression of the *True-Real*. See her essay in Moi (1986: 214–37). According to Roustang (1990), Lacan also viewed

psychotic speech as illustrating a fundamental law defining every human being (70–1). This view is confirmed by Lacan's usage of metonymy and metaphor to understand unconscious language.

19 I take this title from Žižek (1991: 101).

20 The phallus is the privileged signifier, the *point-de-capiton* of the symbolic order. It also serves to represent the lack of the subject, and to this extent it always fails. The phallus only functions as a signifier when it is veiled. See Mitchell and Rose (1985: 80, 82).

21 For an elaboration of this point, see 'Symptom' by Slavoj Žižek in Wright (1992: 423–7).

22 I take heed of Jane Gallop's comment on the problem of defining/translating *jouissance* (1984). I would emphasize, however, that phallic *jouissance* must reinstate and assure the masculine subject of stability. It is a form of satisfaction and thus requires constant repetition and reordering in relation to the death-drive. For a thorough account of *jouissance* and its relation to feminism, see 'Jouissance' by Juliet MacCannell in Wright (1992: 185–8).

23 Boothby (1991: 94). Boothby also states:

> If the death drive, instead of being a literal force of death leading to the demise of the organism, is understood as the assertion of the instinctual as such against the bound structure of the ego, than at certain moments in the development of the ego sexuality itself must be seen to constitute a force of death.
>
> (94)

24 Lacan writes: 'There is no such thing as *the* Woman ... of her essence she is not all', in Mitchell and Rose (1985: 144). For more of the same, see Mitchell and Rose (chs 6 and 7).

25 Lacan says that Woman can experience a supplementary *jouissance*; she moves beyond the phallus, and yet, he writes, she can know nothing of this *jouissance*; see Mitchell and Rose (1985: 145).

26 Both Silverman (1983) and Montrelay (1978) make this claim.

27 I will not pursue the relation between the maternal and the Real here; suffice it to say that for Irigaray (1985a), and according to the logic of Oedipus, the image of the mother and the maternal site of origin lie *outside* the hom(m)osexual symbolic order in the Real of the biological body. The mother–child dyad must be overcome if the subject is to become a rational self-reflective creator of knowledge. See also, for example, Berg (1991) and Braidotti (1991: 31).

28 Whitford (1991) draws on these aspects of Irigaray's work, relates them to Lacanian concepts and implicitly to the Real (66, 67). However, when the Real is explicitly dealt with in the text, it is untheorized (94) or subsumed into the characteristics given to the imaginary (89). In this way, Irigaray's radical reading of the Real – mainly in its epistemological formulations – remains undeveloped and largely unacknowledged.

29 I take this term from Kuhn (1970). For some commentators, the 'psychoanalytic community' headed by Lacan followed scientific precepts and was organized in an authoritarian manner; see Borch-Jacobsen (1991) and Roustang (1990).

30 To this end Irigaray would agree in a strategic sense with the poststructuralist claim that 'Woman does not exist'; see her comments in Irigaray (1985b: 122, 156).

31 Essays by Berg (1988, 1991) and Fuss (1989), support this point.

32 See notes 13 and 18 above.

33 See Rajchman (1991) for a reading of the Real as an ethical category. 'Our idealised identities as moral beings are built up from something in our familial and social existence that we can never fully idealise: our bearings in relation to "the real" ' (60).
34 Margaret Whitford (forthcoming 1994) makes a similar point.

REFERENCES

Berg, Maggie (1988), 'Escaping the cave: Irigaray and her feminist critics' in *Literature and Ethics*, ed. Gary Wihl and David Williams, Toronto: University of Toronto Press, pp. 62–76.
Berg, Maggie (1991), 'Luce Irigaray's "Contradictions": post-structuralism and feminism', *Signs*, vol. 17, no. 2, pp. 50–69.
Boothby, Richard (1991), *Death and Desire: Psychoanalytic Theory in Lacan's Return to Freud*, New York and London: Routledge.
Borch-Jacobsen, Mikkel (1991), *Lacan: The Absolute Master*, Stanford: Stanford University Press.
Braidotti, Rosi (1986), 'The ethics of sexual difference: the case of Foucault and Irigaray', *Australian Feminist Studies*, no. 3, pp. 1–13.
Braidotti, Rosi (1991), *Patterns of Dissonance: A Study of Women in Contemporary Philosophy*, Cambridge: Polity Press.
Cornell, Drucilla and Thurschwell, Adam (1987), 'Feminism, negativity, intersubjectivity' in *Feminism as Critique: Essays on the Politics of Gender in Late-Capitalist Societies*, ed. Seyla Benhabib and Drucilla Cornell, Cambridge: Polity Press, pp. 143–62, 185–9.
Derrida, Jacques (1974), *Of Grammatology*, trans. Gayatri Chakravorty Spivak, Baltimore and London: Johns Hopkins University Press.
Flax, Jane (1990), *Thinking Fragments: Psychoanalysis, Feminism and Postmodernism in the Contemporary West*, Berkeley: University of California Press.
Fuss, Diana J. (1989), ' "Essentially speaking": Luce Irigaray's language of essence', *Hypatia*, vol. 3, no. 3, pp. 62–80.
Gallop, Jane (1984), 'Beyond the *Jouissance* principle', *Representations*, no. 7 (reprinted in Jane Gallop, *Thinking Through the Body*, New York: Columbia University Press 1988, pp. 119–24, 132–3).
Hekman, Susan (1990), *Gender and Knowledge: Elements of a Postmodern Feminism*, Cambridge: Polity Press.
Hodge, Joanna (1988), 'Subject, body and the exclusion of women from philosophy' *Feminist Perspectives in Philosophy*, ed. Morwenna Griffiths and Margaret Whitford, London: Macmillan, pp. 152–68.
Irigaray, Luce (1985a), *Speculum of the Other Woman*, trans. Gillian C. Gill, Ithaca and London: Cornell University Press.
Irigaray, Luce (1985b), *This Sex Which is not One*, trans. Catherine Porter with Carolyn Burke, Ithaca and London: Cornell University Press.
Irigaray, Luce (1985c), 'Is the subject of science sexed?', trans. Edith Oberle, *Cultural Critique*, vol. 1, pp. 73–88.
Irigaray, Luce (1991a), *Marine Lover of Friedrich Nietzsche*, trans. Gillian C. Gill, New York: Columbia University Press.
Irigaray, Luce (1991b), 'The poverty of psychoanalysis', trans. David Macey with Margaret Whitford in *The Irigaray Reader*, ed. Margaret Whitford, Oxford: Blackwell, pp. 79–104.
Irigaray, Luce (1991c), 'Women-mothers, the silent substratum of the social order',

trans. David Macey in *The Irigaray Reader*, ed. Margaret Whitford, Oxford: Blackwell, pp. 47–52.

Jameson, Fredric (1977), 'Imaginary and symbolic in Lacan: Marxism, psychoanalytic criticism and the problem of the subject', *Yale French Studies*, nos. 55–6, pp. 338–95.

Jardine, Alice A. (1985), *Gynesis: Configurations of Woman and Modernity*, Ithaca and London: Cornell University Press.

Kristeva, Julia (1980), *Desire in Language: A Semiotic Approach to Literature and Art*, trans. Leon S. Roudiez, New York: Columbia University Press.

Kristeva, Julia (1982), *Powers of Horror: An Essay on Abjection*, trans. Leon S. Roudiez, New York: Columbia University Press.

Kuhn, Thomas (1970), *The Structure of Scientific Revolutions*, Chicago: Chicago University Press, (first published 1962).

Lacan, Jacques (1975), *Le Séminaire livre XX, Encore (1972–3)*, Paris: Seuil.

Lacan, Jacques (1977), *Ecrits: A Selection*, trans. Alan Sheridan, London: Tavistock Press.

Lacan, Jacques (1979), *The Four Fundamental Concepts of Psychoanalysis*, trans. Alan Sheridan, Harmondsworth: Peregrine Press.

Lacan, Jacques (1988a), *The Seminar of Jacques Lacan, Book I: Freud's Papers on Technique (1953–1954)*, trans. John Forrester, Cambridge: Cambridge University Press.

Lacan, Jacques (1988b), *The Seminar of Jacques Lacan, Book 2: The Ego in Freud's Theory and in the Technique of Psychoanalysis (1954–1955)*, trans. Sylvana Tomaselli with notes by John Forrester, Cambridge: Cambridge University Press.

MacCannell, Juliet Flower (1986), *Figuring Lacan: Criticism and the Cultural Unconscious*, London: Croom Helm.

Macey, David (1988), *Lacan in Contexts*, London: Verso.

Mitchell, Juliet and Rose, Jacqueline (eds) (1985), *Feminine Sexuality: Jacques Lacan and the Ecole Freudienne*, trans. Jacqueline Rose, New York: W. W. Norton.

Moi, Toril (ed.) (1986), *The Kristeva Reader*, Oxford: Blackwell.

Montrelay, Michèle (1978), 'Inquiry into femininity', trans. Parveen Adams, *m/f*, no. 1, pp. 83–102 (reprinted in *The Woman in Question*, ed. Parveen Adams and Elizabeth Cowie, London: Verso, 1990, pp. 253–73).

Ragland-Sullivan, Ellie (1986), *Jacques Lacan and the Philosophy of Psychoanalysis*, London: Croom Helm.

Ragland-Sullivan, Ellie (1989), 'Seeking the third term: desire, the phallus and the materiality of language' in *Feminism and Psychoanalysis*, ed. Richard Feldstein and Judith Roof, Ithaca and London: Cornell University Press, pp. 40–64.

Rajchman, John (1991), *Truth and Eros: Foucault, Lacan and the Question of Ethics*, New York and London: Routledge.

Roustang, François (1990), *The Lacanian Delusion*, trans. Greg Sims, Oxford: Oxford University Press.

Silverman, Kaja (1983), *The Subject of Semiotics*, Oxford: Oxford University Press.

Smith, Joseph and Kerrigan, William (eds) (1983), *Interpreting Lacan*, New Haven: Yale University Press.

Stanton, Domna C. (1986), 'Difference on trial: a critique of the maternal metaphor in Cixous, Irigaray and Kristeva' in *The Poetics of Gender*, ed. Nancy K. Miller, New York: Columbia University Press, pp. 157–82.

Whitford, Margaret (1991), *Luce Irigaray: Philosophy in the Feminine*, New York and London: Routledge.

Whitford, Margaret (forthcoming 1994), 'Irigaray, utopia and the death drive' in

Engaging with Irigaray, ed. Carolyn Burke, Naomi Schor and Margaret Whitford, New York: Columbia University Press.

Whitford, Margaret (ed.) (1991), *The Irigaray Reader*, Oxford: Blackwell.

Wright, Elizabeth (1989), 'Thoroughly postmodern feminist criticism' in *Between Feminism and Psychoanalysis*, ed. Teresa Brennan, New York and London: Routledge, pp. 141–52.

Wright, Elizabeth (ed.) (1992), *Feminism and Psychoanalysis: A Critical Dictionary*, Oxford: Blackwell.

Žižek, Slavoj (1989), *The Sublime Object of Ideology*, London: Verso.

Žižek, Slavoj (1991), *For They Know Not What They Do: Enjoyment as a Political Factor*, London: Verso.

Part II

KNOWLEDGE, DIFFERENCE AND POWER

12

POSTMODERN EPISTEMOLOGICAL POLITICS AND SOCIAL SCIENCE

Anna Yeatman

Postmodernism is a contested zone. However, many and maybe most commentators agree that it represents a crisis of authority for the western knowing subject posed by the refusal to stay silenced on the part of those whom this subject had cast as Other: natives, colonials, women and all who are placed in a client relationship to expert, professional authority. By insisting on their own voice and status as subjects, these erstwhile objects of modern western knowledge have disrupted the epistemological order of domination inscribed within modern, western knowledge. They have caused a major crisis of legitimacy for this order, while, simultaneously, there has been a series of strategies mounted by the gatekeepers of modern social science to maintain both its authority and its ongoing licence to assert itself as subject over those placed as objects to its knowing gaze.

Postmodernism, then, can be interpreted from the standpoint of what I shall call the master subject contemplating the issues of legitimacy for his authority which arise from the refusal of those cast as other to stay silent. Or, it can be interpreted from the standpoint of those who are placed as the disruptive and challenging voices of the Other.

It is important to recognize that postmodernism is quite different depending on which of these standpoints is adopted. For the former, postmodernism is a general sea-change, reflecting the combined impacts of various social, cultural and technological changes. The revolt of the Other is acknowledged in an overgeneralized, abstract way. It remains unspecified and uninvestigated. It is immediately drowned within an acknowledgement of the increasingly globalized context of social science, and a reinstatement of the social scientist's authority as 'observer' of these general patterns and dynamics of change.

From the standpoint of those who are contesting their status as Other, postmodernism appears as the efforts of the modern imperial, patriarchal master subject to manage the extent and direction of the crisis for his authority. Postcolonial and anti-racist intellectuals such as Edward Said and Cornel West (see West 1988, 1989) respectively quite evidently view postmodernism as without any emancipatory dynamics of its own: it is 'reaction' of the kind that seeks to pre-empt and co-opt. It is a reaction which accommodates by de-politicizing the challenges to the order of the modern master subject (see Said 1989: 222–3). Indeed, the silence of contemporary social science on post-war liberation movements, on how they have interpellated and cross-referenced each other, and on how they have undertaken as a fundamental strategy the contestation of colonized subjectivities, has been deafening. I refer here not only to the various national liberation and anti-colonial movements but to the women's, gay and black liberation movements within the metropolitan and semi-metropolitan national contexts.

The relationship of feminism to postmodernism is more complex. Contemporary feminist theorists working within the politics of difference are making postmodernism over to their own agendas. This becomes a very different postmodernism from the quietist, pragmatic versions championed by such as Lyotard and Baudrillard. Postcolonial and feminist theorists of difference converge however in their insistence on a nexus between knowledge and power, and in their sustained contestation of how this nexus works to maintain and reproduce domination within modern social science. It is necessary to say something of the epistemological politics they espouse. In so saying, I am constructing an ideal-type of this politics which would be evidenced to a greater or lesser extent by those who could be reasonably regarded as postcolonial and feminist theorists of difference. It is evidenced most in the work of feminist theorists of difference who are either also situated as postcolonials (e.g. John 1989 and Mani 1989), or as 'living on borders and in margins' in respect of two or more cultures. The phrase comes from Gloria Anzaldúa, a lesbian Chicana who grew up on the border of (US) New Mexico and Mexico:

> The actual physical borderland that I'm dealing with in this book is the Texas–U.S. Southwest/Mexican border. The psychological borderlands, the sexual borderlands and the spiritual borderlands are not particular to the Southwest. In fact, the Borderlands are physically present wherever two or more cultures edge each other, where people of different races occupy the same territory, where under, lower, middle and upper classes touch, where the space between two individuals shrinks with intimacy.
>
> (Andalzúa 1987: Preface)

I

These oppositional intellectuals agree with what is arguably the core feature of postmodernism: the critique of epistemological foundationalism. Put simply, this critique is based in a rejection of mirror theories of knowledge, where knowledge, if it is to be true or accurate knowledge, mirrors an order of being outside itself (see Rorty 1980). In such accounts of knowledge, all that matters is that the knower is trained correctly to use the techniques and methods which permit him direct, 'objective' access to reality. These techniques and methods combine experimental or quasi-experimental modes of empirical investigation with logical rigour. The experimental orientation presupposes that knowledge-claims are testable in some sense in relation to a reality which is external to the knower, and which the knower thereby encounters as a facticity he must respect. The logical criterion of truth or accuracy presupposes the existence of universal reason in that it assumes that logical modelling by its own preferably mathematical precision is self-evidently true. Such a truth-claim depends on a metaphysical assumption concerning the existence of universal reason.

A rationalist metaphysics of this kind turns out to be a rationalist version of the divine right of kings. The rationalism ensures a particular authority to intellectuals as rational knowers of reality. Since they can discern the laws of social-historical being, it is their knowledge which is to provide the rational basis for the law and policy of governments. All putatively objective knowledge acquires the authority of such access to being. Their science permits them 'objective' knowledge of the nature of those who are subjected to government. They thereby assume the authority of modern professionals who know the real needs of laypersons better than these people do themselves. Thus, the scientific revolutionary who designs a political project based on the real as distinct from the false (i.e., 'expressed') needs of the people is no different in this respect from the profession of doctors who understand their expertise as authorizing them to discern the real as distinct from the expressed needs of their patients. We can see here how the authority of a foundationalist science ensures that the voice of the scientists not only prevails over but silences all those who are not scientists.

Moreover, this monocultural rationalism not only maintains a clear distinction between those who legitimately wear the authority of science and those who cannot do so, but ensures very clear membership rules for access to the club of scientists. The authority of a foundationalist science constitutes the scientist as Subject to all those who, brought under the regime of the scientist's observation, are constituted as Object. They are objectified *in order to* produce the subjectivity of the scientist surveying the universe.

This means that individuals who belong to groups which are consistently objectified by modern science – women, blacks, colonials, peasants and other groups typified as stupid, prejudiced or ignorant – are admitted to the scientific club only as exceptions to the norm for their group. There is a price for their admission: assimilation. They are admitted to the club of scientists only if they combine an appropriate training in the procedures of foundationalist science with the adoption of the persona of the rational sovereign subject. In adopting this persona, 'minority group' scientists are always to place loyalty to 'the' community of scientists over loyalty to their origins. However, if on occasion they should contravene the scientific norms of disembodied, detached proceduralism and commit an emotional excess of some kind, this will be forgiven as an inevitable flaw which confirms their status as somewhat less than real scientists – as subaltern scientists. The flaw is even required. That is, subaltern scientists are allowed to orient their science in terms of values which pertain to their origins, as long as these values are not elaborated so as to call into question and to politicize the scientific enterprise itself.

Feminist and postcolonial intellectuals who refuse to be assimilated on these terms place themselves in a contestatory relationship to the authority of modern, foundationalist science. Because they do so, it is obvious from the standpoint of modern foundationalist science that they are not proper scientists. Hence, as far as social science goes, their contestation and knowledge-claims are consigned to the soft, discursive world of the humanities, or to the post-disciplinary nether worlds of cultural studies, women's studies, black studies, etc.[1]

Feminist and postcolonial intellectuals develop a critique of foundationalist theories of knowledge. They adopt the Nietzschean/Foucauldian proposition that we know reality only via our representations of reality. These representations are not simply historically and culturally variable, or, rather, their multiplicity reflects difference in representational perspective. This difference arises out of differences in the *positioning* of knowing subjects in relation to the historicity of interconnected relationships of domination and contestation.

This idea of positioning is both relational and political: i.e., the positioning of a knowing subject is located within the time- and space-specific politics of particular relationships of contested domination. Thus, this perspectivalist account of knowledge is to be distinguished from pluralist accounts of culturally relative knowledge. Where the latter maintain the ideological fiction of a horizontally integrated community of differently value-oriented intellectuals, postfoundationalist accounts deal in a politics of knowledge where principles of vertical integration are challenged but not supplanted by those of horizontal integration.

In short, where feminist and postcolonial intellectuals proceed beyond cultural relativism is in their insistence on contested representations within what are putatively singular or common cultures. They refuse to accord a discursive formation coherence through any other effects than those of power, of domination. Feminist theorists carry over this idea into an account of their own identity as positioned subjects. Indeed, precisely because women are positioned as Other to the integrity of the masculine subject, they are not required, nor do their circumstances readily permit, a sense of their own subjective identity as an integral, bounded, coherent entity (see De Lauretis 1990). For feminist intellectuals still measuring their identity and worth in relation to the master subject's integrity, this appears – just as the master subject has always said – a lack (lack of maturity, lack of development in respect of the higher levels of social and ethical life). However, this project of 'seeking assimilation and a place for women within hegemonic discourse, within "the ideology of the same" ' (De Lauretis 1990: 132) has been displaced by a feminist politics of difference informed by a postfoundationalist epistemology.

It will be clear that these oppositional intellectuals also refuse the effect of cultural integrity that an uncritical acceptance of national or local boundaries generates, an effect on which the idea of a collective conscience depends. Instead they insist on the interconnections between how national, class, gender, race and ethnic differences are produced and reinvented in order to maintain and expand a globally integrated network of relationships of domination. This is a series of networks rather than a closed system, an historically contingent socio-cultural-economic formation, which looks and operates differently depending on where one is positioned within it (see Haraway 1988). To the degree that the system is contingently integrated through techniques of discursive management, these operate to distinguish those positioned as the international elite of managers of this system and those who are positioned as the objects and instruments of their regime. The mainstream social sciences provide the intellectual foundations of this system of global management.

Feminist and postcolonial intellectuals thereby enjoin a *politics* of representation. Central to this politics is the twofold strategic question: whose representations prevail? Who has the authority to represent reality? To put the question differently: who must be silenced in order that these representations prevail? Whose voice is deprived of authority so that they may prevail? This is a politics of representation which insists on the material effects of discursive power, and which contextualizes the institutional politics of the western university within the world-historical dynamics of western capitalist-patriarchal-imperial domination and its contestation.

This is a representational politics which refuses legitimacy to the consensual community of rational scientists which both Karl Popper and Jürgen Habermas invoke in their respective conceptions of science and rational discourse. Feminist and postcolonial intellectuals make visible the structure of domination on which the 'we-ness' of that community, and the possibility of such consensus, are dependent. In short, they show how the consensus depends on the systematic exclusion of those who would dissent if they were given voice, which they are not.

Feminist and postcolonial intellectuals are clearly attempting to open up contested epistemological spaces. Theirs is a narrative which is ordered by metaphors of struggle, contest, forced closure, strategic interventions and contingent opening of public spaces for epistemological politics. There is no illusion that, just because the dominant epistemological order is subject to contest, the material force of this dominant order will not prevail. After all, the dominant epistemological order is inscribed in the material institutions and relationships of modern capitalism and imperialism. In this context, the response of master subjects who recognize the crisis of authority, and who recommend the development of non-foundationalist, intellectual 'conversation' is a familiar liberal's attempt to get the raucous and dangerous mobs off the streets by tempting some of their leaders into safely cloistered, polite conversation in civilized comfort with the decision-making elite.

By disrupting the we-ness of the community of knowers and locating all knowledge-claims within the politics of contested domination, the epistemological force of the politics of difference is to refuse any vantage point for knowledge outside or beyond this field of contested domination. There is no place outside an ideological positioning within this field, and there can be no innocence in respect to how knowledge-claims enter into the politics of modern capitalist-patriarchal-imperial domination.

Edward Said indicates how this must mean an ongoing crisis for the discipline of anthropology, situated as it is as the knowledge-discipline which has informed and legitimized the modern western project of civilization/colonization on a world system scale. As he points out, this is a crisis not simply for those stages of anthropology which represent its service to the colonial regimes of direct and indirect rule. If, in the era of independent statehood, anthropology no longer serves this kind of colonial governmentality, it still serves western empire by continuing to exoticize, to 'other', non-western peoples – not least by representing them as legitimate objects for the scientific gaze of the western observer. Said's (1989: 212) insistence on 'the problematic of the observer' is crucial:

> Look at the many pages of the very brilliant sophisticated argument in the works of the metatheoretical [anthropological] scholars, or in Sahlins and Wolf, and you will begin perhaps suddenly to note how someone, an authoritative, explorative, elegant, learned voice, speaks and analyzes, amasses evidence, theorizes, speculates about everything – except itself. Who speaks? For what and to whom?

The problematic of the observer allows us to see how modern social science constructs the object of the observer's gaze so as to make it appear that the observer has nothing to do with the dynamics of the object itself. When those who are objectified for the purposes of modern social science speak, their voices are heard not as interlocutors placed within a shared field of dialogical contestation and negotiation with the social scientists.

Instead their voices are maintained as voices of the object by being treated as further evidence to be studied by the social scientist who keeps his identity firmly outside this objectified and subordinated community (see Fabian 1983). As Said (1989: 219) puts it:

> the Western Africanists read African writers as source material for their research, Western Middle East specialists treat Arab or Iranian texts as primary evidence for their research, while the direct, even importunate solicitation of debate and intellectual engagement from the formerly colonized are left largely unattended.

II

The crucial epistemological shift for postfoundationalist, critical social science concerns its entering into the politics of intellectual authority. In so doing it can build on an earlier tradition of critical social theory, a sociology of the knowledge-producers – the intellectuals – as the new class (Gouldner 1979; Konrad and Szelenyi 1979). New class theory enquires into how the interest of the knowledge-producer as a knowledge-producer impacts on knowledge (Szelenyi and Martin 1988: 649). It attributes a distinctive interest to intellectuals as monopolists of cultural capital in both the conservation of this monopoly, and in the extension of the capacity of cultural capital to translate into money capital and political capital. Where new class theory maintains a Marxist (materialist) exteriority of the class's interest to its ideology (knowledge in this case), postfoundationalist critical theory insists on the mutually constitutive character of this relationship. Intellectuals are constituted precisely through the relationship of knowledge-producers to those who are the objects of knowledge, and, thus in so far as they enter the domain of knowledge, are produced by knowledge. This relationship *is* the cultural capital of the intelligentsia.

Put differently, it is this relationship which constitutes the authority of the intellectual. As a general rule, the politics of intellectual authority concerns its maintenance as an unproblematic expression of objective, foundationalist knowledge, on the one hand, and the various challenges to such an account of knowledge which insist on its constitutive, value-ridden, interested and political characteristics. Within earlier epistemological debates concerning the politics of intellectual authority, positivism has expressed the resistance among mainstream intellectuals to the politicization of their bid for power, while anti-positivism has expressed the variously oriented intellectual challenges to positivistic renditions of intellectual authority as objective science (see e.g. Adorno *et al.* 1976).

Subaltern intellectuals are those who are admitted into the class of intellectuals on just the same terms as women have been educated to make good wives and mothers, and colonials have been educated to rule on behalf of the metropolis within the colonies: namely, as intellectuals whose authority as intellectuals is qualified by, and indeed subjected to, their lack of authority in being positioned as subordinates. Because subaltern intellectuals are those who are refused entry to the new class elites, and to the ruling levels of the institutions which gatekeep intellectual authority, they are tempted to regard themselves as unable to claim new class cultural capital even if they wanted to. However, it is clear they are constituted as bearers of cultural capital in relation to their own subaltern constituencies, namely the non-intellectual Others with whom they are identified as women and/or postcolonials. They are thereby vertically integrated into a stratified system of cultural capital and accorded the role of mediating and domesticating the claims of these constituencies by turning them into intellectualized claims subject to techniques of rational administration. This happens, for example, when postcolonial intellectuals are inducted into western development theory and when feminist western intellectuals theorize 'women's' claims in ways that make them subject to legal adjudication and public policy.

Vertical integration of this kind is destabilized when the subaltern intellectuals simultaneously surrender illusions of upward mobility within the stratified system of cultural capital *and* discover the power of horizontal ties among themselves. Such horizontality tables difference of positioning amongst subaltern intellectuals, and forces them into an empirical awareness of their different perspectivally oriented knowledges, differences that cannot be 'resolved' by being subsumed within some transcendent ideal of a scientific community. The current politics of representation which postcolonial feminists and 'women of colour' have opened up in respect of what they have perspectivally constituted as the limited and interested ideology of 'western' feminism is a case in point (see Haraway 1988, Ong 1988 and Mohanty 1988).

III

Subaltern intellectuals are positioned in a contradictory relationship to intellectual authority. As intellectuals, and as evidenced especially when they are directing their intellectual claims upwards as it were, i.e. to the ruling elites of academe, they are drawn within the culture of intellectual authority and use its conventions unproblematically. At the same time, as subaltern intellectuals, they are not only positioned as outsiders in respect of these ruling elites, which can foster a tendency to call into question the reliance of these elites for their status on intellectual authority, but they are positioned with loyalties and ties both to fellow subaltern intellectuals who lack access to the institutionalized capital of the new class, and to subaltern non-intellectuals.

Thus, when a subaltern intellectual, who is well-credentialled in terms of levels and kinds of degrees and in terms of academic appointments, publication access and networks, publishes an oppositional piece within a mainstream, elite journal, this is communication upwards. Accordingly, even if it eschews an objectivist (foundationalist) epistemology, it is likely to be dressed up in the arcane, technically precise, esoteric language of the intellectual elite. The privilege of this elite may be recognized by there being no requirement of its members to communicate with anyone outside the elite: thus, for example, the highest circles of the metropolitan Academy are insulated from the *demos*, namely anyone less initiated than the brightest Ph.D. aspirants among the graduate students.

While there can be no doubt that technically precise language permits certain types of ratiocination impossible without it, and intellectual knowledge would be deprived of insight and depth without this, the subaltern intellectual is one who is positioned as having actually to accord status to that familiar question – why can't you put your ideas in language which ordinary people can understand? This is because the subaltern intellectual is positioned across audiences. Her audiences comprise not just those who may arbitrate and foster her academic career, but women who want to be introduced to university-based feminist ideas in order to become not necessarily graduate students in women's studies but the kinds of service-delivery practitioners they want to be, as well as women within the general community. Moreover, she may be placed in significant peer relationships with black and/or postcolonial feminist intellectuals who either cannot get access to the Academy and its publication institutions, or who choose to maintain communicational links with their own constituencies, i.e., women who share their non-intellectual 'origins' in ways which require different types of publication outlet. bell hooks, for example, is an important black feminist theorist in the US, who refuses to use esoteric language and who publishes her work through a non-academic, politically oriented press. To be sure, she has an academic position in a good liberal arts college, but her positioning operates to orient her as an oppositional intellectual seeking to communicate with black women, and to contest the implicit racism of white, western feminism, as is evident in this statement:

> It is essential for continued feminist struggle that black women recognize the special vantage point our marginality gives us and make use of this perspective to criticize the dominant racist, classist, sexist hegemony as well as to envision and create a counter-hegemony. I am suggesting that we have a central role to play in the making of feminist theory and a contribution to offer that is unique and valuable. The formation of a liberatory feminist theory and praxis is a collective responsibility, one that must be shared. Though I criticize aspects of feminist movement as we have known it so far, a critique which is sometimes harsh and unrelenting, I do so not in an attempt

to diminish feminist struggle but to enrich, to share in the work of making a liberatory ideology and a liberatory movement.

(1984:15)

Monocultural rationalists who maintain the idea of the possibility of a neutral, non-positioned, non-perspectivalist knowledge, perceive the contemporary politics of representation as threatening the very idea of science. As indeed is the case if by science is meant a foundationalist conception of knowledge and its procedures, namely an orientation to 'truth'. Postfoundationalist knowledge surrenders this orientation, but it is still science in the sense of objectifying for its purposes whatever is deemed to come under its ambit. How the objectification proceeds is subject to a politics of method. This notwithstanding, such objectification is subject to reflective evidential and logical procedures which by their adoption distinguish the scientist from the non-scientist.

This point is worth labouring because both foundationalist and postfoundationalist scientists too readily participate in a game where the former get to wear the mantle of 'science' and the latter the mantle of 'politics'. This permits the former to complacently insulate themselves in the face of the threat the latter represent. Perhaps more dangerously it permits the latter to smuggle into their postfoundationalist intellectual claims a moral species of foundationalism. Their claims are right because they are more virtuous, more in line with contemporary standards of justice.[2] This is a righteousness almost impossible to abjure by those intellectuals who are positioned as marginals within the Academy.

As to scientific methods of objectification, if postfoundationalist intellectuals must as intellectuals adopt these methods, their positioning makes it likely that some among their audiences will question their observer role. That is to say, the problematic of the observer becomes an open problematic for these oppositional intellectuals: they cannot escape or evade it. This injects a tension into their intellectual work, a tension that produces a vulnerability to demands for accountability of their work to non-academic intellectual and to non-intellectual audiences. For these intellectuals, there are unresolved tensions between demands for accountability to the academic authorities for the quality of the academic performance their work represents, and demands for accountability to the subaltern constituencies in which their politics is entailed.

It is common for foundationalist intellectuals to reject postfoundationalist knowledge politics for its inevitable subscription to and complicity with the nature of intellectual authority.[3] Postfoundationalist intellectuals, as those who embrace an open politics of representation, are vulnerable to this kind of charge only if and when they deny it. It is too much to expect that the contradictions and tensions in their positioning will not operate sometimes (often?) to encourage such denial. None the less, there is an emergent postfoundationalist epistemology which is oriented in terms of the premise that knowledge-claims are irresolvably multiple, and comprise historically specified fields of contested claims. As knowledge, these claims have no more status than the historicity of their discursive positioning.

No amount of good intentions, then, will obviate the postfoundationalist, as the foundationalist, intellectual's assertion of the domination which is inscribed in the knowing subject/object relationship. What distinguishes the postfoundationalist from the foundationalist intellectual is the former's positioning within a contradictory pull of demands for accountability, some of which both problematize and challenge her use of the intellectual's authority.

Acceptance of these types of demands for accountability probably rule out all types of field-work which involve an observer objectifying others for the sake of the former's research. They do not rule out various forms of action research where the objectives, methods and reporting of the research are all situated within a dialogical relationship between the intellectual and the community for whom the research, allegedly, is designed. Evidently, action research does not obviate the problematic of what thereby becomes a professional/client relationship, but a mobilized polity around a particular research project can require of this professional a genuine accountability for their methods of procedure and findings.

It is a good measure of academe that, when research ethics and methods are taught, it is objective rather than action research that is in question. For good reason, the problematic of the observer is occluded, and students are inducted into the authority of the intellectual. To use Veblen's phrase, they have trained incapacity in respect of competing and conflicting demands for accountability to different types of audience.

IV

Up until now, oppositional intellectuals have been intellectuals who hold on to their authority as intellectuals, but place it in service to non-dominant groups or classes. They have espoused the old, genteel professional ethic of 'service'. The democratizing claims of the social movements of the 1960s, 1970s and 1980s have problematized the intellectual's authority as well as that of the professional. In this context, a profession of oppositional values is not sufficient to indicate an intellectual's support for these democratizing claims. What matters is how they practise their authority as an intellectual and whether they open it up to being both problematized and made accountable to different audiences.

Profession of critical values and good intentions, indeed, serves to uphold the intellectual's authority. It reinstates a *communitas* of intellectual virtue shared, at least ideally, by all intellectuals. Within such a community of virtue, differences are rendered a matter of individually professed values and are not allowed to sunder the shared commitments to foundationalist epistemological procedures. Postfoundationalist epistemological procedures deconstruct the transparency of good intentions and the sovereignty of authorship. Thus, when they invite an open contest of differently positioned knowledge-claims, they are doing something other than reinventing an intellectual liberalism.

Liberalism always presupposes rational closure of debate, whether the idea of closure is held to be an operational possibility or an ideal. A politics of representation is premised on the ideas that not only is there no possibility of resolution of contesting claims, but that they are complicit with each other in ways that are not at all transparent in respect of their authors' intentions. The positioning of those who make the claims is a function of this field of discursive contestation. That is, it cannot be declared in advance, but emerges within the perspectivally oriented differences that constitute this field.

It follows that it is important to work to open up the Academy – admission and assessment policies, methods of teaching, academic publishing and means of communication in general – to a politics of representation. In particular, this means doing what is situationally appropriate to open up space for non-resolvable dialogues between those who are differently positioned in relation to this politics of representation. It is to develop the polity that any particular and contingently bounded community engaged in a politics of representation comprises.

Once this point is made it necessarily begins to implicate the relationship of intellectuals to those they constitute as non-intellectuals (see Bauman 1987: chs 1 and 2). Oppositional intellectuals, who are willing to work with the problematic of intellectual domination, are likely to see themselves as committed to extending access into the credentialling authority of the academy. They are also likely to be interested in and committed to working with non-intellectuals to develop an experimental practice of partnership in harnessing knowledge to the needs of the polity they together comprise.

In the Australian context, the first of these implicates policy issues which extend access into higher education through a number of means, including effective articulation arrangements with TAFE (Technical and Further Education). Essentially, it is a cluster of practical efforts – which must include practice within the classroom as well as curriculum – to ensure that the credentialling hierarchical levels of the education system are as close to an open admissions policy as they can be.

The second of these is predicated on a model of differentiated contributions to political practice and struggle. Here the oppositional intellectual has a responsibility which goes beyond working their side of the relationship between theory-based knowledges and practice-based knowledges, as occurs, for example, when intellectuals work with policy-makers, programme managers and professional service-deliverers to apply their (theory-based) knowledge. If policy makers etc. are, in a real sense, practice-oriented intellectuals, the requirements of their practice environments impose first loyalties to something other than 'knowledge'. This positions them as those who put the authority of applied knowledge in the service of the state or of a single profession. To the extent that state and professional authority are represented as based in knowledge, the bids for power of intellectuals, policy-makers and professional service-deliverers converge. They all partake of what can be termed professional domination – the determination of the needs of others by those armed with professional knowledge – in relation to those constituted as the objects of professional knowledge (non-professionals). This convergence should not be allowed to occlude the significance of the differences in how they are positioned in relation to the whole world of the generation, transmission and application of professional knowledge.

Oppositional intellectuals cannot advocate for non-professionals without abandoning their deconstructive insights into their own membership of the new class, where this class's bid for power operates to empower professionals at the expense of non-professionals. What they can do is cooperate with non-professionals who contest professional domination of their needs, and of the services which provide those needs. Such cooperation would mean accepting this contest, and working with its presence within what is constituted as a polity of contested professional domination.

This, then, is a politics of accepting the non-resolvability of what Said termed the problematic of the observer. Where Johannes Fabian, who has contributed an important work in understanding the problematic of the observer (Fabian 1983), seeks to overcome the problematic (Fabian 1990), postfoundationalist feminist and postcolonial intellectuals can contribute to showing over and over again this non-resolvability and its irrefragable nature.

Foundationalist epistemologies de-problematize and naturalize the knowing subject-object relationship by making epistemological procedures appear in line with the nature of things. They thereby de-politicize this relationship, and the most they may require of an epistemological politics is a confession of values on the part of the sovereign author, which once made is safely sequestered from science. Foundationalist epistemologies actively legitimize the bid for power of the new class, and deeply implicate it in the modern western state-centric imperialist and capitalist system of domination.

At a time of unparalleled assertion of difference, foundationalist social science is regrouping so as to accommodate difference within the politics of vertical integration. It does this by revamping liberal pluralism, the methodological individualist equivalent of which is the rational actor's preferences. As is well known, pluralism occludes not only inequality – some are more plural (equal) than others – but also how such inequality is a function of interconnected relationships of domination. Pluralism renders the contemporary politics of difference into a level playing field of special interest groups, and uses market appeal as the central criterion of whether a group has sufficient presence or power to be accorded existence.

Revamped pluralism indicates, in fact, that the project of foundationalist social science is complete: all that can be done under the pressure of contemporary political demands is put new wine in old bottles. What this declares is the irreconcilability of foundationalist epistemologies with a politics of difference, a proposition that makes good logical, even tautological, sense.

Thus, contemporary foundationalist social science has two options whereby to theoretically orient itself: (1) to enter into a classicism in respect of its founding texts, with such acknowledgement as is made of the possibility of their anachronism in respect of contemporary politics drowned out by a deferential conversion of them into the origins or foundations of the discipline; (2) to acknowledge difference but quickly convert it to become the formal difference of individualized preferences, the subject of neo-classical ('modern') economics, and generalizing the model of *homo economicus* to the whole realm of social action. Neither of these options excludes the other. Both maintain the liberal fiction of the sovereign subject/author, where the idea that there is an origin of knowledge logically maintains the idea of a foundation for knowledge (see Ryan 1989). Moreover, both declare that the project of modern social science is a completed one. It is doomed to repetition and to endless technical refinement.

Postfoundationalist social science confronts the challenges that I have identified. It also confronts those who come to it as intellectuals trained in the modern disciplines of social science with what appear at first as formidable requirements of new learning. Significantly these demand full immersion in what can be regarded only as an extraordinary wealth of new social and political theorizing, coming of course from non-disciplinary directions.

NOTES

1 Charles Lemert's (1988: 803–4) sympathetic portrayal of contemporary challenges to 'the most fundamental categories of social thought' reproduces this exclusion:

> the epistemological uppitiness of feminist theory may well be one of its more important contributions to feminist theory. The fact of exclusion from the disciplines is, presumably, the political as well as the organisational condition for the clarity and probity of much feminist theory. Many feminists in institutionally marginal programs, often in other than first-rank universities, subjected to well-known secret doubts about the 'objectivity' of their knowledge have been forced to develop a theory and

practice of knowledge consistent with the social experience of exclusion. Hence the critical difference of feminist theory.

Lemert here is uncritically reproducing the binary opposition of inner and outer; nowhere is this more evident than in the familiar trick on the part of the powerful (the 'included') in conferring on the excluded the status of being more moral (more innocent, more idealistic, etc.).

2 Spivak's (1989: 217–18, emphases in the original) comments are apt here:

It is *in the interest of* diagnosing the ontological ruse, on the basis of which there is oppression of woman, that we have to bring our understanding of the relationship between the name 'woman' and deconstruction into crisis. If we do not take the time to understand this in our zeal to be 'political', then I fear we act out the kind of play that Nietzsche figured out in *The Genealogy of Morals*: in the interest of giving an alibi to his desire to punish, which is written into his way of being, in other words in the interest of a survival game, man produces an alibi which is called justice. And in the interests of that alibi, man has to define and articulate, over and over again, the name of man.

3 One of the nastiest moves to discredit Said, for example, has been to point out that he shares in the authority of the metropolitan intellectual elite by his institutional position within one of the metropolitan elite universities (for discussion of this see Marcus 1990: 7). As Marcus points out, where Said is positioned as a Palestinian, a less than innocent signifier in the current setting, those who attack him in this way never position themselves (see e.g. Turner 1989).

REFERENCES

Adorno, Theodor, *et al.* (1976), *The Positivist Dispute in German Sociology*, London: Heinemann Educational Books.

Anzaldúa, Gloria (1987), *Borderlands: La Frontera*, San Francisco: Spinsters/Aunt Lute Company.

Bauman, Zygmunt (1987), *Legislators and Interpreters: On Modernity, Post-Modernity and Intellectuals*, Ithaca: Cornell University Press.

De Lauretis, Teresa (1990), 'Eccentric subjects: feminist theory and historical consciousness', *Feminist Studies*, vol. 16, no. 1, pp. 115–51.

Fabian, Johannes (1983), *Time and the Other: How Anthropology Makes Its Object*, New York: Columbia University Press.

Fabian, Johannes (1990), 'Presence and representation: the other and anthropological writing', *Critical Inquiry*, 16, pp. 753–73.

Gouldner, Alvin (1979), *The Future of Intellectuals and the Rise of the New Class*, London: Macmillan.

Haraway, Donna J. (1988), 'Reading Buchi Emecheta: contests for women's experience in women's studies', *Inscriptions*, nos. 3–4, pp. 107–27.

hooks, bell (1984), *Feminist Theory: From Margin to Center*, Boston: South End Press.

John, Mary (1989), 'Postcolonial feminists in the western intellectual field: anthropologists *and* native informants', *Inscriptions*, no. 5, pp. 49–75.

Konrad, George and Szelenyi, Ivan (1979), *The Intellectuals on the Road to Class Power*, New York: Harcourt, Brace and Jovanovich.

Lemert, Charles (1988), 'Future of the sixties generation and social theory', *Theory and Society*, no. 17, pp. 789–807.

Mani, Lata (1989), 'Multiple mediations: feminist scholarship in the age of multinational reception', *Inscriptions*, no. 5, pp. 1–25.

Marcus, Julie (1990), 'Introduction: anthropology, culture and post-modernity' in *Writing Australian Culture: Text, Society and National Identity*, ed. Julie Marcus, *Social Analysis*, no. 27, pp. 3–16.

Mohanty, Chandra Talpade (1988), 'Under western eyes: feminist scholarship and colonial discourses', *Feminist Review*, no. 30, pp. 61–89.

Ong, Aihwa (1988), 'Colonialism and modernity: feminist representations of women in non-western societies', *Inscriptions*, nos. 3–4, pp. 79–94.

Rorty, Richard (1980), *Philosophy and the Mirror of Nature*, Oxford: Blackwell.

Ryan, Michael (1989), *Politics and Culture*, London: Macmillan.

Said, Edward (1989), 'Representing the colonized: anthropology's interlocutors', *Critical Inquiry*, 15, pp. 205–26.

Spivak, Gayatri Chakravorty (1989), 'Feminism and deconstruction, again: negotiating with unacknowledged masculinism' in *Between Feminism and Psychoanalysis*, ed. Teresa Brennan, London and New York: Routledge, pp. 206–23.

Szelenyi, Ivan and Martin, Bill (1988), 'The three waves of new class theories', *Theory and Society*, no. 17, pp. 645–67.

Turner, Bryan (1989), 'Research note: from orientalism to global sociology', *Sociology*, no. 23, pp. 629–38.

West, Cornel (1988), 'Interview with Cornel West' by Anders Stephanson in *Universal Abandon: The Politics of Postmodernism*, ed. Andrew Ross, Minneapolis: University of Minnesota Press.

West, Cornel (1989), 'Black culture and postmodernism' in *Remaking History: Dia Art Foundation Discussions in Contemporary Culture*, no. 4, ed. Barbara Kruger and Phil Mariani, pp. 87–97.

13

WHOSE LANGUAGE?[1]

Alessandra Tanesini

Questions about the notion of 'woman' have become central to feminist and so-called postfeminist thinking. It is quite common to hear feminists argue that we ought to give up the notion of gender in favour of a multiplicity of identities. However, accepting this fragmentation seems to lead to political paralysis. How could feminist movements continue a struggle to end women's oppression if the meaningfulness of the concept 'woman' is called into doubt?[2] It was not long ago that feminists started questioning the universality of theories and concepts which are part of the intellectual tradition of the West. Their research showed that a hidden male bias operated in this tradition. Their work made it possible, for the first time, to ask questions such as 'whose reason?', 'whose science?', 'whose language?' The research of these feminists, whom I call gender theorists,[3] relied on the idea that it is possible to employ the notion of 'woman' as a useful analytic category. However, the utility of such a category has now been questioned; it is argued that it is both essentially embedded in misogynist discourse and conducive to exclusionary practices. There is no doubt, I believe, that the history of the notion of 'woman' is embedded in misogyny and that, even within feminist thinking, it has been instrumental in the exclusion of certain groups. However, I also believe that the concept has sometimes been usefully employed in some emancipatory projects and that, furthermore, the negative history of a concept does not always constitute sufficient grounds for excluding the possibility of future progressive use of that concept.

In this chapter I would like to consider this issue from the perspective of language. From this perspective one understands the position of gender theorists as saying that the meanings of some words, such as 'reason', present a gender bias. In the first section of this chapter I look at how, according to these theorists, words can have a gendered meaning, and discuss some of the criticisms their position has rightly received. In the second and third sections I provide an account which is not, I hope, open to the same kind of criticisms. In the fourth section I show how my account can be applied to the meaning of the word 'woman' itself. I argue that this account shows how it is possible to continue talking about woman without being committed to any form of essentialism. Finally, I would like to mention some of the consequences that the position presented in this chapter has for epistemology.

What results from this project is an argument for the usefulness of the notion of 'gender' as a theoretical category. However, in this as in every other case, the usefulness of a concept will depend on the purpose of the enquiry. Therefore, I do not claim that gender is always a useful notion, but only that it is useful in some projects. In the context of this essay, I argue that it is useful for understanding how meanings and concepts are produced. I take it for granted that gender is a concept grounded in social relations.[4] No one is a woman outside the framework of relations that constitute a society. However, it is not clear how the grounding in social relations of the concept of gender is to be understood. In some sense one could read this chapter as attempting to provide a partial answer to this question.

THE GENDER THEORISTS' APPROACH TO GENDER AND MEANINGS

In the late 1970s and early 1980s many feminists found the notion of 'gender' to be a useful tool for uncovering previously hidden aspects of the history and culture of our society (see for example Chodoron 1978 and Keller 1985, among others). These gender theorists argue that the exclusion of women in society is deeper and subtler than a mere suppression of the voices of past women from the official canons of various disciplines. They claim that theories and concepts which are presented to us as universal and transhistorically valid embody male biases. That, if one studies these theories and concepts using gender as an analytic tool, one discovers that the supposedly universal concepts and theories are, in fact, gendered concepts and theories. Gender theorists focus their analysis on normative concepts such as reason, science and knowledge. These concepts are short-hands for clusters of judgements about, for example, how one ought to think, collect data in a laboratory and formulate hypotheses. Normative concepts, then, express values and embody ideals. The central insight of gender theorists is that these concepts which are used to prescribe and evaluate behaviour do not express universal values and ideals but male ones.

In the late 1980s feminist thinkers started criticizing gender theorists for making mistakes similar to those made by the male theorists they criticized. Spelman, for example, claims that the 'dominant Western feminist thought has taken the experiences of white middle-class women to be representative of, indeed normative for, the experiences of all women' (Spelman 1990: ix). Gender theorists are thus accused of working with a notion that, whilst it presents itself as being universally applicable to all women, is at most adequate as a characterization of white middle-class women. There are good reasons for criticizing some of the existing accounts of oppression that use the notion of 'gender' as an analytic category. It is true that at least some of these accounts look at the ways in which white middle-class women have been marginalized and use their results to explain the plight of all women.

More recently, however, the criticisms that this practice has attracted have taken a new epistemological turn. These criticisms are embodied in an epistemological position that Bordo has called gender scepticism. It is 'a new scepticism about the use of gender as an analytic category' (Bordo 1990: 135). Gender sceptics claim that racist, heterosexist and classist biases are part of the logic of the concept of gender. In other words, they claim that it is conceptually impossible to use the notion of gender without engaging in exclusionary practices. They hold that, if one is attentive to differences of ethnic origin, sexual orientation and class, the notion of gender disintegrates into fragments and cannot be employed any more as a useful category.

Both gender theorists and their feminist critics adopt the view that there are no universal standards or norms with an objective and transcendental existence. Instead, they hold that normative concepts are to be viewed as historically and culturally embedded in communities and social practices. Some gender theorists provide an explicit interpretation of how normative concepts are embedded in social practice. According to them, normative concepts are descriptions of those values, actions and claims which are endorsed by the tradition. They take central normative concepts to express male values because they codify the endorsement of practices whose endorsement is also codified by the norms regulating masculinity. An account of the gendered character of concepts along these lines has some initial attraction. However, as various critics have shown, this kind of account cannot do the work that it is supposed to do.

First of all, as Fraser and Nicholson notice, these thinkers 'have continued to theorize in terms of a putatively unitary, primary, culturally universal type of activity associated with women, generally an activity conceived as domestic and located in the family' (Fraser and Nicholson 1990: 29). Fraser and Nicholson rightly claim that such theorizing, which assumes a certain cross-cultural stability in facts about gender, is not substantiated by evidence (31). Another problem with gender theorists' accounts is that they assume that it is possible to neatly separate social facts about gender from facts about race, class and sexual orientation. But, as Spelman writes,

> If it were possible to isolate a woman's 'womanness' from her racial
> identity, then we should have no trouble imagining that had I been

Black I could have had just the same understanding of myself as a woman as I in fact do. . . . To rehearse this imaginary situation is to expose its utter bizarreness. . . . It is thus evident that thinking about a person's identity as made up of neatly distinguishable 'parts' may be very misleading.

(Spelman 1990: 135–6)

According to their critics, gender theorists fail because they assume cross-cultural stability and separability of facts about gender. But, they continue, it is only in virtue of these assumptions that gender theorists can make those generalizations about gender that allow them to talk about gendered concepts. According to their critics, this move hides the fact that their generalizations embody racial, classist and heterosexist biases.

LANGUAGE

Gender theorists and their critics share two assumptions about the logic of normative concepts. The first assumption is that claims about the gendered character of meaning must be descriptions of the uses of certain terms, and, specifically, descriptions that bring to light how these uses are related to facts about gender. Thus, they assume that claims about meanings explain how words are used. The second but closely related assumption is that normative concepts function as descriptions of the endorsements of a society. That is, this is an analysis that attempts to explain concepts as determined by past usage. Both gender theorists and their critics, for example, assume that 'reason' is a term that describes the ways of thinking endorsed by society and that when we talk about the meaning of the word 'reason' we are describing how the word is used.

I question both assumptions. One of the main problems with an account of normativity like the one offered both by gender theorists and their critics is that it does not allow the possibility of disagreement from within a community and its conceptual schema. This is an account which declares *a priori* that concepts with an oppressive history must be abandoned since they cannot be put to progressive use. I believe that any account with such consequences cannot be adequate. Wittgenstein, and more recently Brandom and Lance,[5] have developed an account of meaning and normativity that avoids these problems. I shall not defend here the theoretical adequacy of their account, since they have already done so better than I ever could. Instead, I limit myself to a presentation of the account followed by a brief outline of its advantages over other competitors.

According to the account I endorse, understanding concepts is understanding their practical social significance. The practical social significance of concepts is given in terms of the significance of the claims they figure in. The significance of claims is not to be understood in terms of their truth-conditions, but in terms of their inferential-justificatory role, that is, in terms of their justificatory conditions and of their inferential relations to other linguistic and non-linguistic expressions. Hence, the content of expressions is to be explained in terms of their role in a linguistic practice. The inferential-justificatory role of kinds of expressions can also be understood as indicating the purpose for having expressions of that kind in the language. Applying this approach to normative expressions one discovers that their purpose is not that of describing anything, not even what the society endorses. Rather, their purpose is that of proposals about how we ought to proceed from here. That is, normative expressions function either as emendations of current linguistic or non-linguistic practices or as endorsements of the *status quo*. Hence, if I say that one ought to do *x*, I make an assertion whose purpose is not to describe anything. Its purpose is to influence the evolution of ongoing practices (Lance 1992: 12).

Normative assertions have an inferential-justificatory role in linguistic practice. This role can be seen as constituted of two aspects: commitment and entitlement. This is so because in making an assertion we are undertaking a commitment to respond to certain appropriate challenges. Furthermore, if we succeed in discharging such responsibility, we gain an entitlement to that assertion. For example, abolitionists who asserted that one ought not to enslave people undertook the commitment to respond to those challenges which relied on the permissibility of slavery in society. Abolitionists gained entitlement to their assertion by answering to those challenges, and thereby discharging their responsibility. These dimensions of responsibility and authority constitute the inferential-justificatory role of the assertion.

The next point to notice is that, according to Wittgenstein, meaning is not use, but correct use.[6] That is, to make a claim about the meaning of a certain word is to make a claim about how the word ought to be used, it is not to describe how the word is used. Meaning claims, then, are normative claims. For example, consider the following claim: ' "Strega" in Italian means witch'. This is a claim about how one ought to use the Italian word 'strega'. When I make that assertion, I am undertaking the commitment to justify the claim, and, if I succeed, my claim becomes epistemically authoritative, since I will become entitled to reassert that claim, to use it as a premise in an argument and to license others to assert it or to use it in arguments. Meaning-claims then do not perform any explanatory role; their purpose in language is that of prescribing emendations or preservations of current practices. In particular, their function is not that of describing the inferential-justificatory role of any linguistic expression. That is, they do not explain the content of an expression. Instead, meaning-claims are proposals about emendation or preservation of the roles of expressions; these claims become prescriptive, if one is entitled to make them. As proposals

207

for influencing the evolution of ongoing practices, meaning-claims are grounded in social practices.

My interpretation of this grounding, however, is different from the one offered by gender theorists. When I say that normativity is rooted in social practice, I do not mean that normative claims are about objective features of common usage. Since I endorse the account I have described above, I reject the view accepted by gender theorists that normative words describe the values endorsed by a society. Furthermore, I reject the view according to which to say that meanings are gendered is to describe how words are used and show that this use presents a gender bias. Instead, I suggest that normative words have a certain inferential-justificatory role and a prescriptive function. Furthermore, I hold that to make claims about the meanings of words is to engage in an evaluation of the linguistic practice. There are various aspects of this account of normativity in general, and of meaning in particular, that make it different from other accounts.

First, it rejects a transcendental view of normativity, but it also rejects a relativist view according to which what ought to be done is determined by past practice. Instead, it suggests that we view normative claims as based upon practice in so far as normativity emerges from the game of undertaking commitments and gaining entitlements. Thus, it views normative claims as vehicles for proposing how our practices should go on in the future. In particular, it views claims about meaning as means for saying how we should use words in the future. Similarly, one level up, the account suggests that we understand epistemic norms as arising out of our justificatory practices. Thus, there are no absolute norms about what counts as a valid argument or what counts as evidence for a claim. Instead, making a claim about epistemological norms is to advance a proposal about how we ought to reason in the future. Second, the account advances a view of content as determined by inferential and justificatory relations between linguistic and non-linguistic acts. Thus, it radically departs from the traditional western view that content is a matter of representation. Third, according to this account, emendations of linguistic use are made by gaining entitlement to assert certain claims, where gaining such entitlement depends on discharging a certain commitment. Thus, since how well one performs in all these tasks depends on many political factors, the account partly explains how the political structure of a society causally influences which linguistic practices are available within that society. Fourth, the account puts epistemology at the centre of language. It is by means of a certain epistemic game that claims about meaning perform their role. So the epistemic game will influence which kinds of meanings are produced by a certain society.

MEANINGS AND GENDER:
A DIFFERENT APPROACH

According to the approach I have outlined above there are two different kinds of enquiry concerning the content of normative words such as 'reason', and 'knowledge'. On the one hand, one can attempt to explain their content by looking at the inferential-explanatory role these words have in current practice, and at how this role is shaped by social facts. Presumably, to engage in this project is to provide a sociological theory of linguistic practice. On the other hand, one can use these concepts in subversive ways. That is, one can attempt in various ways to change the inferential-justificatory role of these concepts. One of these ways is by means of making claims about the meaning of these concepts. What results from this is that whilst it might be true that gender is not a useful sociological category, it does not follow that it cannot be useful when trying to influence the creation of new meanings in a certain society. As I see it, to ask whether a certain notion has a gendered meaning does not consist in describing certain features of that meaning and showing that those features are grounded in objective social facts about gender. Rather, since meaning-claims are normative claims, to ask that question is already to engage in one kind of evaluation of those concepts. A similar point can be made by saying that to claim correctly that the meaning of a certain term is gendered is not to point out gendered features of that meaning which were already there. Rather it is mainly a matter of changing the inferential-justificatory role of that concept. It is a matter of influencing the evolution of our social practice concerning the use of certain terms.

To influence changes in the usage of words and claims is particularly important when those terms and claims are themselves normative claims. Normative claims, I hold, function as proposals about how to develop many of our social practices, e.g., practices concerning the production of knowledge. Normative claims, thus, if endorsed by a community, license individuals to do certain things; they function as premises to practical inferences. It is important to evaluate those actions which are licensed by normative claims, and ask whether these actions should be allowed. If we conclude that they shouldn't, then it is important to modify the normative claim that licenses doing them. One way of modifying these claims is by arguing that the way in which the claims are used is not the way in which they should be used. To argue in this way is to make a statement about the meaning of those claims. In particular, to argue that a certain normative concept has a gendered meaning is to claim that the way in which it is used is, at least in part, a way in which it ought not to be used because of reasons that have something to do with gender. For example, the Cartesian concept of Reason embodies judgements about how one ought to think. Because of this, it functions as a premise for practical inferences

209

about how to do something – namely, thinking. The adoption of this concept is justified on the basis of its leading to results that are good from a cognitive point of view, and on the basis of its prescribing ways of thinking in which everybody can think. To claim that this concept is gendered is to hold that we ought to change at least some uses of the concept. Such a claim is justified by pointing out that the inferential-justificatory role of the concept contains contradictions with regard to the issue of gender. In particular, this concept is used to license practices that exclude at least some women, whilst its justification requires the impossibility of such exclusions. Hence, there are epistemic reasons for claiming that how this concept is used is not how it should be used. In other words, there are reasons for claiming that the community is wrong about the meaning of the term in question and for suggesting ways in which the term ought to be used. In this example, those reasons are provided by the internally contradictory structure of the inferential-justificatory role of this term.[7]

The advantages of viewing content in terms of an inferential-justificatory role, and meaning-claims as proposals for the emendations of practices, are various. First, it suggests that meanings are not things which one either totally adopts or completely rejects. Rather, meanings are always corrigible and modifiable. Hence, a concept with an oppressive history can be given future progressive uses. For example, saying that reason is male does not require that one rejects reason *tout court*, rather it entails that one rejects some of the claims about how one ought to think which are licensed by the traditional concept. Second, it claims that the contents of normative terms and assertions are given by the role these expressions play in a framework of justifications and practical inferences. Hence, the actions these expressions license are, in part, constitutive of their content. Therefore, when one talks about the meanings of these expressions – i.e., when one evaluates whether they are used as they ought to be – one ought to consider whether the actions licensed are consistent both with the justifications provided for that usage, and with those epistemic norms, available to the community, which are not at the time under scrutiny. What results from these claims is that the social practices instituted by normative expressions are viewed not as a result of the application of these concepts, but as constitutive in part of the concepts themselves. Furthermore, these claims entail that there are epistemic reasons why some of the social and political implications of the uses of expressions are crucial to an evaluation of the role of these expressions in linguistic practice. Finally, the account suggests that when we use the notion of gender in meaning-claims, we are trying to modify some aspects of important concepts by allowing new inferences to be made, new evidential standards to be created.

I believe that it is because claiming that meanings are gendered opens up a new conceptual schema, makes new ways of thinking possible, that for so many of us reading the works of gender theorists has been an illuminating and liberating experience. The account I am encouraging you to adopt views the creation of new meanings as part of a game of giving and asking for reasons, a game that all people have engaged in, albeit from different positions of power. It is important not to forget the role played by past women in this game. For example, as Atherton (1993) argues in 'Cartesian reason and gendered reason', seventeenth-century French philosophers Mary Astell and Damaris Masham employed the Cartesian account of reason to claim rationality for women. Their employment of this notion is subversive since they both reject the view, held by Descartes, that reason encompasses only one way of reasoning. Furthermore, they claim that reason should not be understood in terms of transcendence from the senses, but as that on which the proper functioning of emotions is dependent (Atherton 1993: 27–31). To some extent their work, even if it is mainly forgotten, has contributed to the formation of some of the inferential aspects of the concept of reason.

The fact that more of these analyses, at least along the lines of class, sexual orientation and race, are needed, does not prima facie undermine the utility of a gender-analysis because the latter does not depend on the pre-existence of facts about gender. However, some critics have held that using the concept of gender always involves endorsing heterosexist biases. A criticism along these lines is provided by Butler, who claims:

> The internal coherence or unity of either gender, man or woman ... requires both a stable and oppositional heterosexuality. That institutional heterosexuality both requires and produces the univocity of each of the gendered terms that constitute the limit of gendered possibilities within an oppositional, binary gender system.
>
> (Butler 1990: 22)

This is a criticism of a different kind from those traditionally raised against gender theorists. Whilst those were criticisms about the empirical adequacy of gender as a sociological category, this is a criticism about gender as a normative concept which is taken to be inherently heterosexist. Wondering whether Butler's criticism is correct requires us to move from thinking about gender and meaning to thinking about the meanings of gender.

THE MEANINGS OF GENDER

When we ask whether there are women we might mean different things by that question. Even if 'woman' is understood as expressing a social concept – that is, a concept whose meaningful use presupposes the existence of a certain set of social relations – there remain ambiguities about the ontological status of the concept. Thus, some people have held that there are some intrinsic characteristics, such as being a caring person, that are essential to being a woman. Others have rejected essentialism and endorsed a position according to which there are no intrinsic properties that are essential to being a woman. For example, according to Alcoff, 'woman' is a concept that must be characterized as a family of relations rather than as a set of intrinsic attributes (Alcoff 1989: 323).

What is common to all these accounts of 'woman' is that they all take the normative notion of 'woman' to be descriptive of a set of social facts or relations. However, there is plenty of empirical evidence to show that there are no suitable isolated social facts or relations which provide the basis for those attributes or relevantly similar relations constitutive of woman. Hence, it appears that 'woman' has no characterizable content and no reference. One can read much of the postmodern criticisms of the notion of 'woman' as saying that such a notion is not descriptively adequate. Spelman, for example, says:

> And if we examine the use of 'woman' in particular contexts, then we might be encouraged to ask when descriptions of what-it-is-to-be-a-woman really are descriptions of what-it-is-to-be-a-woman-in-culture-X or subculture-Y. Being a woman, as we surely know by now from cross-cultural studies, is something that is constructed by societies and differs from one society to another.
>
> (Spelman 1990: 136)

Spelman is not the only example of this kind of criticism; other thinkers have complained that because the notion of 'woman' imposes unity over an empirical plurality, it must be rejected as inadequate (see Flax 1990: 56 and Fraser and Nicholson 1990: 35).

These criticisms take 'woman' to be a notion that describes arrangements of social relations. However, as we all know too well, 'woman' is primarily a normative notion, a notion which summarizes a cluster of judgements about how one ought to behave, judgements that have acquired prescriptive force in many societies. We might agree that, because 'woman' is neither a natural nor a social kind term, it cannot be usefully employed as a transcultural sociological category. However, this agreement does not provide an answer to the feminist question concerning 'woman'. It is certainly important to realize that 'woman' is a normative notion and that, as such, it is not a description of any facts. In other words, there are no facts or relations, not even social ones, which constitute somebody's being a woman. In so far as postmodernists have made this latter claim, their criticisms of the notion of 'woman' have been extremely helpful.

Where at least some of these critics have gone astray is in the derivation from their insight of the claim that the notion of 'woman' is fictional. To discover that there are no facts about being a woman should not be taken as showing that there is no meaningful notion of 'woman', but only as showing that the point of having the concept is not that of describing anybody. The way in which 'woman' is used is as a concept that licenses inferences about how one ought to be and behave.

One can certainly attempt to provide a description of how the concept is used; to do so is to attempt a sociological account of various linguistic and non-linguistic practices. This is a legitimate enquiry, but it is one that does not allow any generalizations along the lines of gender. There is, I believe, already enough empirical evidence to show that there is no significant overlap between the ways in which the concept has been used in different times and cultures. However, it is also legitimate to give an account of how the concept of woman ought to be used. The latter is an account of the meaning of 'woman'. When we do so, we provide proposals about where to go from here; these are proposals for the emendation of current practice. To propose emendations is to attempt giving to 'woman' a different inferential-justificatory role. I believe that it is important that feminists contribute to the construction of new uses for the concept of 'woman', instead of abandoning the concept altogether.

There are political reasons for wanting to appropriate the notion of 'woman'. It is useful that those people to whom the concept is taken to apply are those who take charge of the claims about how the concept ought to be used, and about which normative judgements it ought to license. This is the strategy adopted with positive political effects by some other minority groups. For example, the word 'queer', which was originally used as an insult, has been appropriated by homo-affectionally-oriented people. By adopting that word, they have attempted to claim for themselves the right to decide how that word ought to be used. Thus, they are striving to change the meaning of the word.

There are also epistemological reasons for a feminist analysis of the meaning of 'woman'. The way in which this word is used is full of contradictions and tensions which justify the claim that the word ought to be used in different ways. Above all, this is a notion which gender theorists would say has a gendered meaning. It has a gendered meaning, they would say, because it expresses male biases about how we ought to be. It is, therefore important to expose the contradictions present in the concept of 'woman', to analyse why they have been ignored and to propose how the concept ought to be used.

I am not suggesting here that feminists should legislate and impose on everybody their own proposal about how the word 'woman' ought to be used. The meaning of 'woman' is a matter of negotiation, something that can be developed in many and unforeseeable ways. It might also be the case that at some future point our practices will have developed in such a way that this concept will lose its purpose in the language. For the time being, however, the concept of 'woman' could be a useful instrument of social critique if, after having exposed its normative content, we take charge of deciding how it should and should not be used. I would like to return to Butler's claim that the concept of 'woman' is inherently heterosexist. I think she is right in so far as she is pointing out that this concept is used in a way that prescribes heterosexuality. However, she is mistaken if she thinks that because of this we must stop using the notion of 'woman'. Instead, we must expose the oppressive uses of 'woman', and provide arguments for the claim that these uses must be abandoned. Feminists, I believe, must not abandon woman, they must make her anew in many different coexisting ways.

EPISTEMOLOGICAL REFLECTIONS

Let me conclude with a brief reflection on epistemology. The central notions of epistemology are normative notions like 'knowledge', 'justification' and 'reason'. These are notions that embody epistemic norms. Many feminists have produced important critiques of the ways in which these concepts have been used in traditional western philosophy. They have criticized those who view these notions as embodying universally valid standards. These criticisms are certainly correct. More recently, however, some feminist and non-feminist thinkers have opted for abandoning these concepts altogether, and settling for a time and culture-specific description of current practices. Rorty, for example, seems to hold that 'there is nothing to be said about either truth or rationality apart from descriptions of the familiar procedures of justification which a given society – ours – uses in one or another area of inquiry' (Rorty 1991: 23). It should be clear that I think that Rorty is wrong in thinking that normative concepts are entirely explained by current practices. I think that he is terribly mistaken in saying that what is justified is what our culture takes to be justified, and then using this claim to reject epistemology altogether.

Instead, I believe that we ought to engage in the epistemic game of giving and asking for reasons. Epistemology is neither a matter of describing transcendental norms nor of describing current practices; rather, it consists in advancing and defending proposals for how to develop our epistemic practices. In a sense, we make up epistemology as we go along since there are no unrevisable standards. Epistemology, then, is a practice; it is something we do. What we do, when we do epistemology, is create new norms. Feminists should not abandon this normative enterprise in favour of describing current practices; what we should do is engage in the production of new and progressive epistemic norms.

NOTES

1 An earlier version of this chapter was presented at the Society for Women in Philosophy (SWIP) conference on Gender and Language held at Warwick in March 1993. I would like to thank Kathleen Lennon for helpful comments.

2 This dilemma is sharply presented by Alcoff (1989: 295–326).
3 I borrow this term from Bordo (1990).
4 I do not want to be taken as implying that whilst gender is a social concept, sex is a natural one. I believe, instead, that the concept of sex should also receive a social analysis, one which is closely connected to, but separable from, an analysis of the notion of 'gender'. For a similar claim, see Haslanger (1993: 117).
5 See Wittgenstein (1968), Brandom (1983), Lance (1990 and 1992).
6 See Wittgenstein (1968: 99, §289). This point was brought to my attention by Lance (1992: 1).
7 However, reasons of other kinds can also be used as evidence that how a word is used is not how it should be used. Furthermore, since even the usage of the notion of 'evidence' is subject to emendations, it is also possible to challenge the epistemic standards on the basis of which a certain claim is taken to be evidence for another claim.

REFERENCES

Alcoff, Linda (1989), 'Cultural feminism versus poststructuralism: the identity crisis in feminist theory' in *Feminist Theory in Practice and Process*, ed. Micheline R. Malson, Jean O' Barr, Sarah Westphal-Wihl and Mary Wyer, Chicago: University of Chicago Press, pp. 295–326.

Atherton, Margaret (1993), 'Cartesian reason and gendered reason' in *A Mind of One's Own*, ed. Louise M. Anthony and Charlotte Witt, Boulder, CO: Westview Press, pp. 19–34.

Bordo, Susan (1990), 'Feminism, postmodernism and gender scepticism' in *Feminism/Postmodernism*, ed. Linda J. Nicholson, New York and London: Routledge, pp. 133–56.

Brandom, Robert (1983), 'Asserting', *Nous*, 17, pp. 637–50.

Butler, Judith (1990), *Gender Trouble: Feminism and the Subversion of Identity*, New York and London: Routledge.

Chodorow, Nancy (1978), *The Reproduction of Mothering: Psychoanalysis and the Sociology of Gender*, Berkeley: University of California Press.

Flax, Jane (1990), 'Postmodernism and gender relations in feminist theory' in *Feminism/Postmodernism*, ed. Linda J. Nicholson, New York and London: Routledge, pp. 39–62.

Fraser, Nancy and Nicholson, Linda J. (1990), 'Social criticism without philosophy: an encounter between feminism and postmodernism' in *Feminism/Postmodernism*, ed. Linda J. Nicholson, New York and London: Routledge, pp. 19–38.

Haslanger, Sally (1993), 'On being objective and being objectified' in *A Mind of One's Own*, ed. Louise M. Anthony and Charlotte Witt, Boulder, CO: Westview Press, pp. 85–125.

Keller, Evelyn Fox (1985), *Reflections on Gender and Science*, New Haven: Yale University Press.

Lance, Mark (1990), 'The grammar of meaning' in *Wittgenstein: Towards a Re-Evaluation*, ed. R. Haller and J. Brandl, Vienna: Verlag Holder-Pichler-Tempsky, pp. 156–60.

Lance, Mark (1992), 'Where do we go from here?: toward a Wittgensteinian conception of normative judgment', unpublished typescript.

Rorty, Richard (1991), 'Solidarity or objectivity?' in Richard Rorty, *Philosophical Papers vol. I: Objectivism, Relativism and Truth*, Cambridge: Cambridge University Press, pp. 21–34.

Spelman, Elizabeth V. (1990), *Inessential Woman: Problems of Exclusion in Feminist Thought*, London: The Women's Press.
Wittgenstein, Ludwig (1968), *Logical Investigations*, Oxford: Blackwell.

14

MORAL DIFFERENCE AND MORAL EPISTEMOLOGY

Janna Thompson

When advocates of a 'feminine ethic' say that women speak with a different voice on ethical matters, they want to claim something more than that women sometimes reach different conclusions from men about moral problems. They are suggesting that women reason differently about moral matters, or have a distinct and different moral perception of the world. This amounts to a claim that the difference is an epistemological one: that it has to do with the way that ethical beliefs are acquired and applied, or how ethical judgements are justified.

Carol Gilligan's studies of the moral decision-making of women led her to make substantial criticisms of accounts of ethical rationality which take male reasoning as standard (1982, 1987), and to insist that the 'perspective of care' should be regarded as equally important as the 'justice perspective' favoured by philosophers and psychologists.[1] Noddings (1984) and Ruddick (1989) have developed an alternative 'feminine' ethics which centres on care or maternal love, and Okin (1989) and Young (1990) aim to show how discourse about justice must be altered in order to take into account the point of view of women and other marginalized groups.

Gilligan contrasts the way in which women make moral decisions with the idea of ethical reasoning embodied in Kohlberg's account of moral development. But Kohlberg has been criticized by many philosophers for having a conception of moral reasoning which presupposes the superiority of a particular morality, namely the Kantian idea of moral duty. I will therefore begin by presenting a model of ethical reasoning which doesn't seem to privilege any particular ethical theory, and will then consider what aspects or assumptions of this model feminists are questioning, and whether they are justified in doing so.

The model I will use as a point of reference is found in Rawls, 'Outline of a decision procedure for ethics' (1951).[2] In this early account of ethical decision-making, Rawls conscientiously models ethical reasoning on inductive method. Correct judgements in ethics, as in science, he believes, are most likely to be made by competent investigators following the correct procedure.

He first defines a class of competent judges – individuals who have characteristics which are most likely to enable them to make reasonable judgements. The person must be reasonably intelligent, knowledgeable, endowed with common sense and not affected by fixed ideas or prejudices. Because of the nature of moral enquiry, the judge must also have 'a sympathetic knowledge of human interests' and be capable of imaginatively appreciating the standpoint of others. The judge must be impartial: 'he must not consider his own de facto preferences as a necessarily valid measurement of the actual worth of those interests which come before him' (179). He must consider them as if they were his own.

Rawls then specifies the conditions under which these judges can make considered judgements about particular cases. Competent judges, adjudicating between parties with conflicting interests, must, of course, have available to them relevant knowledge, and this includes knowledge about the desires, goals, feelings of those whose case is being judged. Everyone must be given a fair opportunity to represent his or her side of the case (182). Judges are most likely to reach a correct conclusion, Rawls thinks, if they can make independent decisions – if they do not stand to gain from their judgement and are not subject to pressure. A judgement is also likely to be more trustworthy if the case in question is reasonably straightforward – if it is not an unusual case or one of enormous complexity.

By bringing together and explicating their opinions concerning a number of particular cases, competent judges, Rawls claims, should be able to formulate general ethical principles which can then be tested by determining how well they are able to deal with more difficult cases. The more competent the judges and the more ideal the circumstances, the more reason we have to believe that their judgements are correct judgements, and that the principles they arrive at by generalizing from the total range of these considered judgements are correct principles. Once principles are confirmed by this testing procedure, we can then use them in making judgements about particular cases.

The following features are essential to Rawls's decision-procedure for ethics, and to others like it: (1) it regards ethical reasoning as being a matter of making general moral hypotheses and testing them; (2) it requires that rational moral agents, when determining their moral principles, be concerned with the interests and needs of all individuals and treat everyone equally; and (3) that the agents themselves be free of bias and the influence of particular relationships or sympathies. Feminist critics have different ideas about which of these requirements should be rejected. I will first try to show that many of the common objections do not succeed in challenging Rawls's procedure in a substantial way. This discussion will put us in the position to determine exactly what is objectionable about the method and its assumptions.

Some critics reject the idea that ethical reasoning involves formulating general hypotheses. Gilligan notes that many of the women and girls she tested were unwilling to make ethical judgements by subsuming a particular problem under a general principle. They wanted to find out more about the facts of the case, and seemed to feel that moral judgement had to be context-dependent. Lawrence Blum (1988) contends that for Gilligan 'moral action itself involves an irreducible particularity – a particularity of the agent, the other, and the situation' (475). A principle like 'Protect children from harm', he says, does not tell us what harm means in a particular situation (486). Similarly, Noddings doubts whether it is possible or desirable to generalize in the way that Rawls recommends: when we abstract from concrete human predicaments the qualities which are supposed to be the same, 'we often lose the very qualities or factors that gave rise to the moral question in the situation' (1984: 85).

However, Blum and Noddings overstress the particularity of ethical judgement. The women in Gilligan's studies were often concerned about how their judgement of one case compared to the way they judged others, and about whether they could give a general justification for what they regarded as relevant. They sometimes made generalizations based upon their experiences: e.g. 'You should keep your responsibilities to others'; 'You have a responsibility to yourself'. They worried about whether and how these generalizations could be applied to particular cases, and whether they were being consistent in their judgements. They attempted to justify their generalizations, both by references to views about how to live an ethical life and by reference to the possible consequences of their decisions.

Rawls's procedure should be regarded as a method for answering these questions about justification. It does not demand that we always make judgements by subsuming particular cases under general principles (indeed it depends upon our being able to make good judgements without reference to principles). On the other hand, Rawls can be accused of ignoring the difficulties of applying general principles to particular cases. Ethical principles can no more be expected to tell us what to do in a particular case than scientific laws can be expected to tell us exactly how to build a bridge in a particular spot. Dealing with particularities always requires rational creativity. But this consideration does not amount to a rejection of his model. It is compatible with Rawls's procedure to regard principles as mere guidelines for dealing with particular cases: something that can be used to draw attention to factors that are relevant to making a judgement, and not something that determines in a logical way what the decision should be. It is also compatible with his method (if not his later theory of justice) to believe that ethical principles are always low-level generalizations, not grand, all-inclusive theories.

The second assumption of Rawls's method – that we should regard individuals impartially – has been challenged by those who believe that the care perspective requires us to favour those to whom we are related:

our children, lovers, friends, etc. Noddings points out that the duties of care are always to specific people, and Blum suggests that our moral perspective depends upon our relation to these particular others. It is a parent's understanding, he says, which enables her to view a scene of children playing in a park and recognize that one child is being too rough with another. Another adult who doesn't have this caring concern is likely not to see that harm is being done (1988: 485).

Blum seems to confuse two senses of 'caring'. Care can mean 'caring about': having a sympathetic appreciation of the needs and situation of others. A perceptive stranger observing the children playing is capable of appreciating that a child is being hurt by a rough game. Rawls's decision-procedure requires that competent judges exercise care of this kind: they must be able to recognize the needs of others and understand when they are being hurt or disadvantaged. Being able to care about others is a prerequisite for moral judgement, but it is not in itself a moral point of view. On the other hand, care can mean 'caring for': an attitude of loving attention, involvement and feeling of responsibility which a person might have for children or friends. Rawls's method does not exclude the possibility of such duties of partiality. Treating people fairly does not mean that we have to regard our obligations to everyone as being the same.

What Rawls does require is that we make impartial judgements about duties of partiality. What this means, first of all, is that we have to acknowledge the universality of these duties. If I think I have a special duty to my children, then Rawls's method requires me to recognize that so do all other mothers and fathers. If my special duties to my children entitle, or require, me to use most of my own resources for their benefit, then others cannot make demands on me that interfere with this entitlement, but neither can I make such demands on them. It means, second, that the belief that we have such a duty has to be justified by means of the ethical decision-procedure. Some of those who believe in the existence of duties of care may insist that justification is not needed, that duties to children or lovers are simply basic. But this is not a satisfactory position, especially for a feminist. Not only does it leave us in the lurch when people come into conflict because of different ideas about their special duties, but it also leaves us no room to argue that these duties are predicated on roles which are oppressive for women. Care may be important in any human life, but who we ought to care for and what relationships we should strive to preserve are matters for critical reflection. It is this critical thought which Rawls's procedure, and its requirement of impartiality as fair treatment, promotes.

However, Rawls's model, and other similar models of ethical decision-making also require that moral agents can and should discover, assess and weigh everyone's preferences, needs and interests in an unbiased way. By claiming that ethical action is 'irreducibly particular in respect to the agent',

Blum seems to be denying the possibility of impartiality in this sense. Similarly, Young (1990: 97ff.) argues that the ideal of impartiality is 'an idealist fiction' that has had pernicious consequences for women and other oppressed groups.

Young's complaints about the consequences of a procedure which depends upon the judgements of competent judges are not difficult to appreciate. The idea that some people, because of their social position, education, psychological make-up or sex, are better at making impartial moral judgements than others, has been used to justify the authority of the educated and wealthy over the poor, colonists over those they colonize and men over women. Men have often been regarded as the legitimate moral guardians of women. However, supporters of the Rawlsian model would argue that the fact that people sometimes have biased views about who can be a moral authority is no reason for rejecting the claim that Rawls's decision-procedure – or something like it – defines what ethical rationality is. Any procedure can be abused.

However, Young has an epistemological, as well as a political, objection to the ideal of the competent judge. The ideal of impartiality is impossible, she says. It 'expresses a logic of identity that seeks to reduce differences to unity' (97). By abstracting from the particularities of a situation, it ignores important differences in situation, represses the feelings which attach to our experiences and reduces all forms of subjectivity to one. But these 'particularities of context and affiliation cannot and should not be removed from moral reasoning' (97). The main problem with Rawls's method, and others like it, is that it is 'monologic' – it assumes that a judge can determine for himself or herself what is right or wrong, good or bad, independently of the judgements and opinions of others. In its place she advocates a procedure which requires that subjects, through communicative interaction, determine their moral relations. This procedure, she claims, is more congenial to a democratic politics than an 'elitist' ideal like Rawls's.

Like Noddings and Blum, Young can be accused of overstressing the importance of particularity. All ethical judgement, whether done by an individual or by a collective, involves some abstraction from a situation. But this doesn't mean that ethical judges cannot pay serious attention to the needs, feelings and interests of particular individuals. Indeed, Rawls insists that they do so, and he allows that the individuals themselves should represent their interests before the tribunal of judgement. Nor is it necessary, as far as his method is concerned, that a few be the judge of the affairs of the many. In our everyday life all of us are required to make moral judgements as best we can.

Our best may not be good enough. It may be impossible for anyone to be completely unbiased in their judgements. All of us are affected by our situation; no one can know everything about the situation or needs of others.[3] But this is not an objection to Rawls's procedure any more than the bias of scientists is an objection to scientific method. Rawls is presenting an ideal to which we can aspire. His method guarantees that the more impartial the reasoner, the less affected by prejudice, the greater his/her ability to appreciate the situation of others, the more likely to be correct the judgement. Given that all human judges are limited by their situation, it might be impractical to rely on any individual to arbitrate the moral affairs of others. Discourse and collective decision-making may be the best way of ensuring that everyone's point of view is taken into account. But this practical reason for preferring dialogue to monologue does not constitute a rejection of Rawls's procedure.

Young believes that difference of situation is a reason for rejecting impartiality even as an ideal, but does not make it clear why this is so, or how collective decision-making can manage to overcome the difficulties associated with difference. What is needed is an epistemological enquiry into what it means to regard moral judgements or moral theories as 'correct'. If people differ in their moral point of view, then what conclusions should we draw about moral knowledge?

For Rawls, moral disagreement means that something has gone wrong with the judgement or reasoning of one or more of the judges. Either they do not know all of the facts of the matter, or they are making mistakes in reasoning, or they are prejudiced in their moral assessments of the facts. He assumes that if people were more knowledgeable and rational and less biased, they would be more like an ideal judge, and their judgements would be similar to the judgements of such a judge and therefore similar to each other. This means that difference in situation has to be regarded as a source of error. It is this idea which leads him in *A Theory of Justice* to suppose that if individuals were behind a veil of ignorance and did not know their situation – e.g. what class or race they come from – they would make unbiased, and therefore correct, judgements about the principles of justice. And it is this way of regarding difference which Young and others are objecting to. But what is it about difference of situation which makes it resistant to Rawls's treatment?

A number of the criticisms I have earlier discussed have raised the possibility that women and men differ in a basic way in their moral way of seeing. Gilligan sometimes presents the difference between the female and male point of view as a difference of Gestalt (1987). But whether this idea (if true) can be used to challenge standard ideas of ethical knowledge depends upon how the analogy should be spelt out. Gilligan claims that women and men can, and sometimes do, learn how to see the world from each other's perspective, and that it may be possible to 'marry' the two perspectives (1982: 174). Okin supposes that such a marriage is possible when she claims that agents behind Rawls's veil of ignorance who are ignorant of their sex, but aware that the family and the gender system of their society can affect the life chances of individuals, will be able to arrive at moral principles valid for everyone (1989: 101). If the perspectives can be brought together in this way, then differences in the way of seeing pose no substantial difficulty for the application of Rawls's decision-procedure. But if women and men cannot fully appreciate each other's perspective, or if the perspectives cannot be reconciled, then a gap opens up between the 'ideal' perspective of the competent judge and the perspectives which individuals use to make ethical judgements about particular cases – a gap which cannot be filled in a non-arbitrary way using Rawls's procedure.

Gilligan's claim that women have a different voice can be understood as a claim that Rawls's view of moral disagreement is wrong. If it is, then his decision-procedure is also brought into question. It can clearly not be saved by insisting that one voice ought to prevail. To think that the existence of different responses to ethical problems means that some ethical reasoners are not competent judges is to beg the question. Rawls's way of identifying competent judges must be independent of the judgements they arrive at; otherwise our choice of competent judges would be biased in favour of choosing judges who arrive at particular kinds of judgements: e.g. judges who respond to ethical problems in a way more typical of men. On the other hand, we cannot simply assume that moral disagreements between women and men must be understood as arising from a basic difference of moral perspective. We have to determine whether differences are the result of error or prejudice, or are the consequence of having a different moral point of view.

Gilligan sometimes uses Nancy Chodorow's (1978) theory about the development of female and male personalities to back up the idea that the difference in perspective of women and men is a deep and persistent difference (1982: 7ff.). Others have suggested that bodily differences between women and men, and what they entail, result in different moral and political outlooks (O'Brien 1981). These hypotheses may be false. Or it may be the case that differences between the perspectives of men and women are peripheral and minor compared to differences between people of different races and cultures. But the idea is that a difference in perspective exists if there is reason to think that differences in judgement have to do with the very identity of individuals, with basic aspects of their personalities and their approach to the world. If individuals with these different perspectives were placed behind the veil of ignorance, they would still make different judgements about moral matters – simply because they are the people they are.[4]

This way of understanding the distinction suggests some practical tests that can be used to distinguish error and prejudice from a difference in moral perspective. If a person's judgement is affected by lack of knowledge then it is reasonable to suppose that once the lack is overcome, his or her judgement will change. If an individual reasons in an illogical way, refuses to take into account the views of others, makes no effort to appreciate their position, or subject his/her own view to criticism, then there are grounds for saying that he/she is prejudiced. In practice it may be difficult to be sure that accusations of prejudice are not question-begging. But since there are some tests of rationality which do not depend upon any particular moral point of view (e.g. standards of inductive and deductive argument), and ways of telling whether agents are seriously engaging in moral reasoning, it is not impossible in practice to make the distinction between a prejudice and a perspective. (A white racist who habitually condones the actions of whites and condemns the behaviour of blacks is a clear example of someone with a prejudice.) But if arguments and references to the facts cannot persuade people that their views are wrong, and there is no reason for thinking that they are irrational or insensitive, then the accusation of prejudice becomes hard to sustain. In other words, if people seem to satisfy the conditions for being a competent judge but yet continually and systematically disagree about a whole range of questions, then it is reasonable to think that the disagreement is the result of a real difference of moral perspective.

We can admit the existence of different ethical voices and yet rescue Rawls's decision-procedure by conceding that ethical judgement is always culturally specific. Those who hold this position can continue to advocate the use of the procedure within groups or cultures, but have to acknowledge that it cannot be used to arrive at principles valid for everyone. The different ethical perspectives of the communities create different ethical universes, and intercourse between them has to be a matter of negotiation. There is no overarching, universal ethical knowledge. This is the direction that Rawls himself has taken in his recent works (1985, 1988).

When Young advocates a communicative approach to ethical decision-making she could be understood as holding this position. Since no competent judge(s) can make a decision for everyone, conflicts may have to be decided by parley. But this way of understanding ethical discourse does not seem to do it justice. As we usually understand it, ethical rationality is supposed to provide us with knowledge; it is supposed to determine what our ethical duties really are – and not merely what we have to agree to in order to make a truce. It is this idea that is behind Rawls's decision procedure, and also Habermas's communicative ethics (1989–90) which Young basically endorses (106). Either we have to acknowledge that our usual understanding is wrong, or we must look for an account of ethical knowledge which is capable of comprehending different ethical perspectives. I think that this can be found by bringing into question the Cartesian premise of Rawls's method – an assumption generally endorsed by cultural relativists or subjectivists as well as 'universalists': that ethical knowledge is the knowledge of individuals, something each person can either intuit or arrive at by a process of reasoning.

If ethical knowledge exists, but is not something that individuals can determine by themselves, then communication has to be regarded as the way of obtaining it, and not merely a means for making a truce between individuals with their different convictions. What counts as ethically correct, in so far as this is possible to determine, is *defined* by the compromises which individuals manage to reach under certain conditions. These compromises are not, according to this view, the arrangements that individuals have to make with each other because they are not able to overcome bias or do not have time to settle the issue by argument. The compromises are themselves the closest we can get to truth on matters of morality. Ethical decision-making is inherently a collective matter, and individuals, recognizing this, will regard it as rational to accept the collective decision even if this decision is not in accordance with the conclusion they would have come to by themselves. This conception of communicative ethics is similar in some respects to that of Habermas and Young. But both of these philosophers seem to assume that discourse is a way of reaching a consensus by getting each individual, by means of argument and interpretation of needs, to recognize the validity of general principles. They continue to cling to the Cartesian assumption about ethical knowledge, or at least have not clearly departed from it. What I have tried to show is that those who hang on to this assumption have no good reason for rejecting Rawls's conception of ethical rationality.

As a feminist meta-ethic, the view I am considering has a number of features to recommend it. It takes ethical disagreement seriously; it allows that this disagreement can go very deep; and it does so without falling into a relativist or subjectivist position. It insists that there is such a thing as ethical knowledge and that we can collectively achieve it, or at least approach it. There are, however, two obvious objections to the collectivist approach. How viable this approach turns out to be, and how compatible with feminist priorities, hinges on whether these objections can be answered. In what follows I will merely indicate how I think they could be dealt with.

The first objection is that a collective method of ethical decision-making seems to undermine an idea which has played an important role in western thought – and in feminist movements: that an individual, because of her personal understanding of what is right or wrong, is justified in objecting to the morality and behaviour of her social group. Most feminists would not want to have to accept the idea that a woman's personal decision about something like abortion could be overruled because of the points of view of others.

The second objection is closely related. Compromises can be made in all sorts of ways: by use of force, by throwing dice, by voting, etc., and these different methods are likely to lead to different results. In negotiations the stronger party is usually capable of obtaining a more favourable outcome. Inconsistent results reached in an arbitrary way can hardly be called knowledge, and feminists, along with many others, would object to the idea that just any compromise counts as a satisfactory moral decision. But if a person is entitled to make a judgement about the fairness of a compromise – if there are good reasons for favouring some outcomes and not accepting others – then it seems that it is also necessary for a person to have an authoritative view about what moral decision is correct. The Cartesian assumption seems indispensable.

Advocates of communicative ethics argue that to have a valid result, discourse must allow each participant an equal voice: each person's needs and point of view must be equally represented and weighed.[5] Let us assume that identifying the circumstances that are likely to prevent participants from speaking or being heard is simply an empirical matter. Nevertheless, the moral insistence on equality that is contained in the requirement needs a justification. If all we have to appeal to are the results of communication or the moral perspective of individuals, then it seems that we are either arguing in a circle or abandoning the collective approach. But if the premise can't be justified, then the insistence on equality seems arbitrary. Why not say that the people with power are the ones entitled to determine what is ethically correct?

In order to prescribe the form discourse takes, it seems to me that the basic moral premise of communicative ethics has to be something that all individuals, reflecting on the nature of ethical perception and rationality, will acknowledge as a starting-point for their collective reasoning. A communicative ethic thus requires a meta-ethical consensus, and if it turns out that people on reflection cannot agree about this basic assumption of discourse, then they have no common concept of what ethical knowledge and rationality are, and their communication about moral matters, to the extent that they find it worthwhile to engage in it, can be nothing better than a means of making a truce.

What, then, is the meta-ethical justification for the assumption that ethical knowledge should be determined by a discourse in which everyone is an equal participant? If ethical belief were simply a matter of individual conviction, then there would be no point in discourse about ethical matters. The fact that it is possible to argue about moral matters is a basic presupposition of discourse. But if ethical perceptions were always, and in every respect, subject to universal standards of rational criticism, then there is no reason why the ideal competent judge, who is supremely rational, could not in principle make a decision for everyone. Discourse is needed as something more than a measure for correcting the decisions of judges who are less than ideal if individuals do have irreducibly different ethical perspectives. This means that the collective approach to ethical decision-making depends both on the assumption that ethical judgements and individual needs can sometimes be subject to generally accepted standards of rational criticism, and that there is something about an ethical perspective that eludes such rational critique. Given that these assumptions are true, it seems that we can justify the idea that each individual should participate equally in discourse. Each individual has something to add to the discourse that no one else can provide. Her moral point of view cannot even in principle be represented by others.

The criticisms by feminists and others suggest that the presuppositions of the collective approach to ethical decision-making are correct. People do seem to have basically different ethical perspectives but nevertheless believe that their ethical beliefs can often be subject to rational criticism. If so, this gives some support to a collective approach to ethical knowledge. However, abstract discussions of equality may not allay the fears of feminists who do not like the idea that a woman's personal convictions about what is right may be overruled by a collective decision. I want to suggest that this possibility is not as objectionable as it first appears.

Suppose that I find myself to be pregnant. I do not want a child, and I feel that I do not want to continue the pregnancy. Having an abortion seems to me the right thing to do. On the other hand, my partner very much wants to be a father, and he feels that we ought to have the child. Though we are both sympathetic to each other's point of view, I cannot truly understand how he feels, and he cannot really understand my position. However, neither of us has good reason to believe that his or her own perspective must be right. We both recognize the limits of our point of view. So we discuss our motivations, the implications of each alternative, our circumstances, etc. and eventually reach a decision. What exactly we decide in the end will depend upon what compromise satisfies both of us in a situation where each of us has reason to believe that our feelings and the reasons for them have been taken seriously. I may still not truly understand his perspective or he mine, but we are both convinced that the compromise we have made is as good a decision as we can make, and are prepared to abide by it. We have not only maintained our relationship, but we have made an ethical decision that deserves to be called rational. A feminist might argue that no satisfactory compromise can be reached in a society where women are oppressed. This may be so, but it is not an objection against collective rationality, rather a reason for changing our social institutions so that women can really be equal participants in moral discourse.

A collectivist conception of decision-making will affect the way in which individuals approach moral problems. Those who accept it will not only refrain from laying down the moral law or insisting that their moral convictions be regarded as the truth. They will also be concerned to work out as best they can what a good compromise might be in the circumstances. Above all, those who take a collectivist stance will be concerned

227

to ensure that people are and remain in a position to discuss, argue and make satisfactory compromises.

It is notable that the approach to ethical reasoning of the women whom Gilligan studied resembles the approach of the collectivist. These women were not inclined to think of themselves as judges or moral arbiters. They were more inclined to regard their view as a contribution to a discussion, as one opinion among many, and were anxious to maintain the relationships in which a reasonable solution could be found. I am not saying that these women actually held a collectivist view of ethical reasoning; but it does mean (if this position is indeed correct) that the women had a rational approach to solving ethical problems.

NOTES

1 The collection *Women and Moral Theory*, edited by Kittay and Meyers (1987), is largely devoted to interpretations and discussions of Gilligan's data by philosophers. *Feminist Ethics*, edited by Card (1991), and *Women's Consciousness, Women's Conscience*, edited by Andolsen, Gudorf and Pellauer (1985), also contain views about her work.

2 I choose this procedure rather than the one that Rawls presents in his later *Theory of Justice* (1972), to escape some of the criticisms which feminists, as well as others, have made of the idealizations which Rawls embodies in the 'original position' (for example Benhabib 1986). The earlier procedure maintains a closer contact to the way in which we ordinarily make ethical judgements. However I discuss below how Rawls's earlier and later procedures are related.

3 Young (1990: 213ff.) argues that it is impossible to grasp the subjectivity of any person, even of ourselves. This may be so, but it doesn't mean that a competent judge can't make good enough judgements about the needs and interests of others in a particular situation.

4 Darwall (1983: ch. 1) recognizes that perspective affects judgement, and argues that it too must be eliminated by the veil of ignorance in order to ensure universal agreement about principles. But Young rightly argues (1990: 103) that if an individual were separated from her perspective, she would not be able to make a moral judgement at all.

5 For a discussion of what democratic decision-making requires, see Young (1990: 184ff.).

REFERENCES

Andolsen, Barbara Hilkert, Gudorf, Christine E. and Pellauer, Mary D. (eds) (1985), *Women's Consciousness, Women's Conscience: A Reader in Feminist Ethics*, San Francisco: Harper and Row.

Benhabib, Seyla (1986), *Critique, Norm and Utopia: A Study of the Foundations of Critical Theory*, New York: Columbia University Press.

Blum, Lawrence A. (1988), 'Gilligan and Kohlberg: implications for moral theory', *Ethics*, vol. 98, pp. 472–91.

Card, Claudia (ed.) (1991), *Feminist Ethics*, Lawrence, Kansas: University of Kansas Press.

Chodorow, Nancy (1978), *The Reproduction of Mothering: Psychoanalysis and the Sociology of Gender*, Berkeley: University of California Press.

Darwall, Stephen (1983), *Impartial Reason*, Ithaca: Cornell University Press.

Gilligan, Carol (1982), *In a Different Voice: Psychological Theory and Women's Development*, Cambridge, MA: Harvard University Press.

Gilligan, Carol (1987), 'Moral orientation and moral development' in *Women and Moral Theory*, ed. Eva Feder Kittay and Diana T. Meyers, Totowa, NJ: Rowman and Littlefield, pp. 19–37.

Habermas, Jürgen (1989–90), 'Justice and solidarity', *Philosophical Forum*, vol. 21, nos. 1/2.

Kittay, Eva Feder and Meyers, Diana T. (eds) (1987), *Women and Moral Theory*, Totowa, NJ: Rowman and Littlefield.

Noddings, Nel (1984), *Caring: A Feminine Approach to Ethics and Moral Education*, Berkeley, Los Angeles and London: University of California Press.

O'Brien, Mary (1981), *Politics of Reproduction*, Boston and London: RKP.

Okin, Susan Moller (1989), *Justice, Gender and the Family*, New York: Basic Books.

Rawls, John (1951), 'Outline of a decision procedure for ethics', *Philosophical Review*, vol. 60, pp. 177–97.

Rawls, John (1972), *A Theory of Justice*, Oxford: Oxford University Press.

Rawls, John (1985), 'Justice as fairness: political not metaphysical', *Philosophy and Public Affairs*, vol. 14, no. 3, pp. 223–52.

Rawls, John (1988), 'Priority of right and ideas of the good', *Philosophy and Public Affairs*, vol. 17, no. 4, pp. 251–76.

Ruddick, Sara (1989), *Maternal Thinking: Towards a Politics of Peace*, Boston: Beacon Press.

Young, Iris Marion (1990), *Justice and the Politics of Difference*, Princeton: Princeton University Press.

15

SHOULD THE FEMINIST PHILOSOPHER STAY AT HOME?

Anne Seller

INTRODUCTION

Let me begin by explaining why this question came to haunt me. In 1990 I was invited to spend six weeks in a women's university in India, giving guest seminars and helping them to develop their curriculum. The university had no philosophy department and the invitation was at short notice, so that there was little time for me to find out about the background to women's studies, or feminism, in India. But neither of these conditions seemed overwhelmingly problematic: we would, I thought, develop a dialogue, discussing the differences and commonalities in our feminist beliefs. After all, the university, Mother Teresa Women's University (MTWU), had only recently been founded, with the explicit aim of raising the status of women in India; its motto is 'Towards Equal Status', and it is entirely devoted to women's studies. This bespoke not only a whole continent of common ground, but also, for me, a political idyll; an entire institution committing its research and teaching programmes to the cause of women. I used the short preparation time I had thinking up questions and short statements that would most fruitfully prompt dialogue, and took off committed to what I call a democratic epistemology.[1]

This is an account of knowledge which insists that everybody's experience is valid and to be listened to, that the higher-educated do not have a privileged access to the truth which the rest can only accept on trust. I had developed my views in response to the feminist dilemma of appearing to have to claim either that every woman's view is equally right (including those supporting patriarchal structures), or that some women (feminists?) know better than others, thus repeating the age-old claim that women don't really know what they want or what is in their interests. I appealed to the idea of dialogue to overcome this dilemma, arguing that the way to develop knowledge is through comparing experiences and beliefs with others who share at least some of our meanings and values. I argued that this obviated the need to choose between realism, the view that there is an objective order of reality which can be known (and mistaken) by the human observer, and relativism, which claims that all views are equally good, because in any particular case, the holders of either view would have to appeal to the same community in the same way to articulate and confirm their particular knowledge-claim. Thus knowledge is not so much an achievement as a process, an ongoing engagement in a conversation with a community in which we both discover and recreate our world. With these views, I assumed that our first task would be to set an agenda and exchange reading materials. Primarily I saw myself in the attitude of a listener; I would listen, listen, listen, and together we would develop a dialogue across our two different cultures, maybe creating a space from which we could think together about each of them. A view no longer from the margins so much as from another place.

What follows is not in the usual form of a philosophical paper, but more in the form of a meditation upon the experience, explicitly from my perspective. Ideally, I should have liked it to have been a joint project, but difficulties of distance and communications make that impossible. This means that often the chapter reads as a western subject thinking about Indian women as 'other'. Indeed, much of the chapter is about the breaking down of those categories *in a particular context*. For stylistic reasons, I do not always indicate that the women I am responding to are members of MTWU. But it would obviously be absurd to generalize from my experience at MTWU either to other Indian universities (they vary enormously), or to Indian women as a whole. (The immensity and diversity of India ought not to need commenting on.) The chapter should thus be read as an account of a western feminist struggling to come to terms with a particular experience.

THE FEMINIST PHILOSOPHER'S DILEMMA

As a philosopher, I think I have an intimate knowledge, not merely of my own culture, but of the way that it talks to itself. As Cavell has put it, philosophy captures a society whispering to itself. I work at the assumptions not normally heard, the justifications taken for granted, pulling apart the categories within which we normally conceive of ourselves and our world. In doing this, I am necessarily engaged with the culture; I need to be both committed to it, in order to understand those whisperings, tease out their sense and at the same time, distanced from it to hear the strangeness of the obvious. So, to develop the skills and technique to do this work, you need the kind of knowledge that is only likely to come from being immersed in a culture. I haven't said what 'a culture' is; it can be something as narrow as British malestream academic philosophy, where my point might be most forcefully made, since much of the time only the members of this culture seem capable of understanding each other, and indeed only seem able to listen to each other. Or it can be as broad as 'enterprise' or 'The Market' culture, where at least a set of linked concepts, rules of behaviour and values are understood in such diverse places as New Delhi and Market Harborough, Tokyo and Tennessee. We belong to more than one culture, and they are nothing if not permeable to each other. In this lies our chief hope, and I shall discuss this further in the chapter. But at this stage I want to note two things: (1) This is *not* the same as claiming that we all share some basic or fundamental culture. One of the major issues for feminists is whether or not we should abandon the pursuit (either as discovery or construct) of a shared culture. (2) The term 'culture' is commonly understood to mean a community or society, and often identified with a nation-state. British academic philosophy is in some sense parasitic upon British culture (although a British philosopher might have more in common with an Australian philosopher than with an East-End firefighter). Whatever we mean by the term in this sense, it is to this that we most often refer when we speak of being marginalized or alienated. We are marginalized or alienated from something, some scheme of things, that we feel we have some claim on, and which makes some claim on us. To claim that we are alienated is to imply a proper state of affairs where we would be at home, and similarly with marginalization. Even though I don't really want to be part of malestream academic philosophy, my claim of marginalization amounts to a claim *on* that community. I'm not *simply* an outsider, I have a right to belong, to insist on changes to make a space for me and my concerns. Most feminist criticism, and indeed much philosophical criticism, is written from that perspective. Further, if these cultures constitute the meaning of my activities and judge them, then merely by living within these cultures, I am engaged in a conversation with them, however one-sided, about the meaning and value of my activities.

Now the problem of the feminist philosopher abroad looms clearly. If she does not know or understand the culture that she visits, does not understand it conceptually, how can she do her work? I spent a lot of time simply not understanding, not hearing what was said, because I did not understand how the concepts worked, what meaning words had in this changed context. Women's studies was a new departure for the British Council, and I found myself envying all those shadowy biochemists who come directly into a familiar vocabulary, or literary critics who work with an established canon. We had to create and recreate a vocabulary between us, explaining and re-explaining our terms to each other, with no agreed canon to work upon, particularly since I was resisting their pressure to base our discussions on western feminist texts.

But not only does the visiting philosopher lack the immersion necessary for her work, her alienation or marginalization from the culture becomes problematic because of that. She is *simply* an outsider, with no right to belong. And so what right does she have to be critical? Especially if she is a member of an ex-colonial power. But the critical and the analytical activities are inseparable. Indeed, the questioning intended to develop the necessary understanding can itself be seen as critical analysis. So the problems of the feminist philosopher abroad are that she lacks both the understanding and the right to do her work. She seems only able to work with her own culture, and I began to feel, particularly in a country with such great needs, that the money spent on getting me there would have been better invested in income-generating schemes for women. The feminist philosopher should stay at home.

These might be academic reasons for explaining my sense of failure to myself. Having written them down, they sound more like a rationalization of the sense of failure and frustration that I returned with than a statement of a problem to be solved. Reading them, I think, 'Well, all you needed was more time, more attention, more patience. Six weeks is not long enough.' That wouldn't resolve the question of the right to be critical (would giving time and attention, acquiring understanding, confer such a right? Does it confer membership? Is this the language we need?). But my experience was that I couldn't separate out asking critical questions from acquiring understanding. I could not *simply* listen, not only because I could not develop a dialogue through silence but also because to be a witness is to change a situation, especially in the institution that I entered. What were the thoughts of the women I was going to meet? To be a British witness in India is to have an impact that I would have preferred not to have, but which I had to learn to recognize. The day before my arrival, all the members of the university were exhorted to ask intelligent questions, and at least one lecturer spent the night before my first seminar sleepless with anxiety that she, and hence India, would not make a good showing. Conversing, being with people, inevitably means engagement, and that means both commitment and judgement. For example, listening to a young woman describe her refusal to allow her brothers to determine her future calls for a response, which is bound to be based on my values and commitments. Perhaps only tourists and anthropologists have aspired to enjoy and observe without changing anything, and both have notoriously failed in this. Their aspiration is, perhaps, to be invisible. Mine was for us to jointly explore our world.

STUMBLING BLOCKS TO DIALOGUE
FROM MY PERSPECTIVE

I begin with problems that I stumbled over: problems which initially I saw as problems for me because of what the university and its members were like. They could, of course, equally be seen as problems because of what I was like.

Understanding the language

Everyone spoke English, and it was the language-medium that the university used, but not only were there words whose specific history and meaning I had to learn (for example, 'uplift',[2] 'awareness creation') but, of course, familiar words have different meanings in different contexts. For example, in our discussions of the family, my concept remained centrally that of a voluntary and contractural relationship, which could in principle be dissolved at will by individuals, and/or structurally reformed to meet needs differently. It is a model that does not so much deny such needs and values as nurturance, affection, loyalty, etc., as not talk about them, focusing instead on structure. For many of the women I spoke to, the family represents their deepest and dearest values, and it is these, rather than a particular way of structuring relationships, which are the focus of any debate. You can imagine how such conceptual differences would bedevil discussions of autonomy and independence.

The rejection of feminism

I had presumed that although we might define this very differently, we would share a commitment to feminism. Indeed, I had imagined our dialogue would be about our differing understandings of what this meant in our different societies. The first thing that women I met said to me was: but we're not feminists.[3] I learnt that they rejected feminism because it represented what they perceived as some of the worst vices in western culture and character: egoism, selfishness, individualism, sexual perversity, promiscuity, loss of valued feminine traits and virtues and most important of all, an attack on the family. Now this is a litany that most western feminists are familiar with, and have learnt to argue with at home. But at home, we are out to change and persuade. I felt it would be fruitless, foolish and arrogant to adopt that attitude after only a week in India. More importantly, the women at the university were not the anti-feminists I was familiar with. These were lecturers and students in women's studies, committed to raising the status of women. Their work covered such familiar feminist areas as a programme to eliminate sexist stereotyping in school textbooks, making visible women's contributions to national history and culture, making women aware of their rights and ways of securing them.

Women's studies and the lack of theory

In the West, we developed women's studies out of our discontent with male-dominated education. At MTWU women's studies consisted in the application of the disciplines they had learnt (economics, sociology, education, etc.) to the problems of women, and this meant primarily bringing

234

women into the development process: literacy drives, income-generating schemes, etc. Over and over I heard the motto: 'Uplift a man and you uplift one individual. Uplift a woman and you uplift a whole family.'

The main consequence of this was a lack of interest in theoretical or philosophical issues. I am intensely interested in such issues because of my struggle to make sense of my life and my thought within theories that have proved inadequate. But such an interest seemed to be absent at MTWU. These academics had not come to women's studies out of a sense of the inadequacy of the theory they had been taught; they were not struggling to find ways in which they could express and make sense of their lives (and indeed many would see that as typical western self-indulgence). They felt no need to develop critiques of the society as a whole; on the contrary, they saw their own activity as a continuation of a tradition of reform by government, in full co-operation with, and often initiated by, men. So when asked about patriarchy, they would say: 'but we don't hate men', or 'Men don't oppress us'. And then we would go round and round in a familiar groove, for they seemed unwilling to recognize structures of oppression, while I would try to hold on to my anger as I heard victims being blamed for their failure to claim the rights that independence had won for them. Our respectively different histories made us not only look in different places for the causes and cures of women's sufferings, but also unwilling to admit different hypotheses, certainly to each other, and probably to ourselves.[4]

University as pragmatic institution

If I was wrong to expect women's studies to provide an intellectual and political forum, I was also mistaken in my assumptions about the sort of intellectual space that the university was providing. I have grown up in a tradition that treats universities as primarily places of thought and talk, and only secondarily as institutions of social policy or practical activity. Working abroad, I discovered how much I still believe in that official ideology of 'disinterested' knowledge and my right to pursue whatever research interests me, and the extent to which in Britain I am allowed to work on that assumption. At MTWU there was a repeated demand for pragmatic solutions to problems.

I knew that the university was primarily a research institution. I only gradually became aware that every single piece of research had to be justified by its demonstrable benefit to the women of Tamil Nadu. So every research report or paper ended with a list of recommendations, which often baffled me in their range from moral exhortation to pragmatic detail, and which often gave no indication of how the recommendations were to be put into effect, or what effects they might have. My immediate response was to want to engage them in the theoretical and philosophical issues that their studies raised, but they were not really interested in these, and I felt that I could not get past a barrier of terms that blocked my questions. Every discussion seemed to end with the proposed palliative of 'awareness creation'. Initially, I assumed that this would be similar to consciousness-raising, but that was the wrong translation. Consciousness-raising is the beginning of a line of enquiry: who does the raising, what is the process, why do we count the latter stage as raised rather than different, how can the subject conceptualize herself through these changes... and so on. We also see it as the beginning of a life of conflict (see Bartky 1977). Awareness creation seemed to be the end of a line of enquiry, and seemed to consist of discussing ways and means of making women aware of certain rights (e.g. to own property) or of certain techniques (e.g. of how to avoid child diarrhoea, how to cultivate mushrooms as a source of income) or of changing moral attitudes. Conflict was eschewed. Awareness creation was, I think, the name for the programme of taking an agreed-upon policy to 'the people', and as such the contrary of consciousness-raising. But I only grasped this by going outside the university. Within it, I kept battling away at what I thought was the major business of universities and what I knew how to do: primarily theoretical and critical discussion.

I learnt by going to Gandhigram: an institution (now with university status) founded on Gandhian principles of going to the villagers, and developing what they need for (more or less) economic autonomy, whilst at the same time learning from them. So, for example, they will devise water-collection systems which use the local resources and conditions, or new recipes adapting new resources (such as the mushrooms mentioned above) into traditional dishes. Although the particular institution I visited has developed more conventional degree programmes, and the students I talked to were more interested in their own careers than the Gandhian ideals, through Gandhigram, I saw what MTWU was trying to do. In British universities, we tend to look at empirical detail, in order to generalize from it. For example the justification of a sociological study lies in the general or theoretical points that can be concluded from it. On the whole, at MTWU, the justification lay in what could be done *for the group that had been studied*. This was the 'really useful knowledge', which I was committed to generating in British universities, with a vengeance. Further, the knowledge-production process itself was hierarchical and authoritarian. The consequence was, I felt, a closure of the exploratory and critical approach that I have come to identify with women's studies. Thus a return visitor to Canterbury asked in exasperation: 'You've discussed pornography three times in this University. But what are you *doing* about it?'

The university as authoritarian

This was my biggest stumbling block. The physical arrangement of the main seminar room where we met reflected the structure and functioning of the university: a U-shaped table with long arms, fixed to the floor. The main speaker sat at the apex, professors closest to her, and down the arms in descending order of status, the rest of the academic staff. The youngest and humblest were furthest away. Behind them, in serried rows, equally ordered, were research assistants, Ph.D. and M.Phil students, and right at the back, the lowest of them all, the MA students. So physically, the lower in the hierarchy, the harder it was to ask a question or make a contribution. They were there, primarily, as observers.

I blundered through this, trying to rearrange furniture with little notion of the assault I was mounting on the system. I simply wanted people to feel that they could speak freely, to overcome any inhibitions they might have about entering the discussion, but it was a struggle to generate discussion. Students and young academics came to me privately, freely discussed a wide range of issues and raised telling questions, but said that they could not do so in the seminar, because they would be identified as of bad character, or as troublemakers. The seminar could not be a forum for discussion, or a place of dialogue, because people felt it was too risky to say what they thought, because (as I discovered through trial and error), our explorations were mined with unmentionable topics, and because everyone was looking to me to tell them things which they could simply incorporate into their body of knowledge. Two examples of what I mean: the Ph.D. student conducting research into single parenthood, who could not include unwed mothers in her work, because they are unmentionable, and the young lecturer who in discussion courageously suggested that battered women should leave their husbands, and was reported to the Vice-Chancellor for recommending divorce. I was surprised to discover within myself a commitment to liberal principles so deep that I was at a loss when they were not being used to define my working space, for I made my own critique of liberalism, long ago, when I became aware of the ways that voices can be silenced and problems hidden in its name. I was beginning to suspect that neither creative critical thought, nor dialogue, were possible without those liberal premises, and at the same time I was beginning to see that my attempts (albeit unwitting at first) to put them into practice could be a piece of cultural hegemony. A consequence of this experience however was to see the way that an interest in generalizing (that is not directly related to practice consequences) combined with freedom of expression, is necessary for the development of critical thought, and at the same time, the way that abstract thought develops and strengthens freedom of expression. Without these I felt that the conditions for the dialogue I had dreamt of did not exist.

I have a commitment to self-expression: making women's voices heard, creating the spaces in which they define and make sense of their own life. Again, a western liberal interest. The women I met were more interested in improving the severe physical constraints on others than in their own self-expression, so they talked about changing *other* people's awareness, not their own, without any questions about self-determination. They seemed uninterested in their own lives as topics of discussion. So, for example, occupying radically different roles as academics and wives and mothers, no question of identity arose for them. ('I just am a mother at home, an academic here.') And although they spoke strongly about the double burden, the conclusion was 'We just suffer'. Their subject-matter was other women's lives, not their own.

Given the acute problems of poverty in India, this focus on immediate and pragmatic solutions felt like a moral imperative. So I vacillated between feeling that my insistence on discussion and dialogue was a cover for arrogantly imposing my own cultural assumptions (egoism, liberalism, materialism, self-interest) and suspecting that they shared my liberal commitment, and that I was simply not understanding what was going on. I now want to discuss the stumbling blocks that I threw up to dialogue for them.

STILL FROM MY PERSPECTIVE: STUMBLING BLOCKS TO DIALOGUE FOR THEM: MY POWER AND OUR HISTORY

I was so eager to create an atmosphere in which talk could flow freely, so anxious about the power relations between others, that it was a long time before I realized how I was inhibiting the dialogue. Indeed, I became aware of much of what follows only on my return to Britain, when I was amongst people who had enough nerve (power? strength?) to say: 'But look at you. Did you enjoy your power?' I am impressed by the way that power generates ignorance, for I was oblivious to my position for as long as it inhibited others; which means for as long as I remained isolated in the university, the only European.

A scene that recurs in my memory: I am on a visit to the nearest city, walking along the street with an American acquaintance and a young Indian woman. We are discussing the wearing of the sari: all women in South India wear it, and many of the women I knew felt it to be an inconvenience at times, physically restrictive, but none the less wanted to wear it. The Indian was saying that her brothers liked her to wear it, and the American immediately asked whether they wore the lungi (the traditional male dress). 'No, they prefer trousers.' 'Then so should you, don't you tell them that if it's all right for them to wear western dress . . .', etc. I was impressed by her certainty; she never missed an opportunity to point out the evils of arranged marriages, to 'raise consciousness'. But I was also appalled by her didacticism, by that very same certainty. I felt that it silenced, so that the only voices that could be heard were those of western feminists, analysing Indian practices. I also felt much less certain: hearing the way that the marriages of women I knew had been arranged (rather in the way that a US student and parents might select a university), hearing the ambiguities and fears of some of the young single students about their own marriages, and detecting a pragmatic approach to the choice of husband, I wondered whether it was any worse than the romantic gamble (gambol?) that passes for choice in the West. Only wondered, for I also saw some of the costs of the system and felt that the connection with dowry death[5] needed thinking through, but I felt no certainties, and I did not want my seminars to turn into a western feminist analysis of Indian institutions. This translated itself into a controlling anxiety. I would counter remarks like: 'I think we are at the stage that you were at fifty years ago' with 'No, no, there is not one way for women to progress, one history with stages'. In short, I refused to allow them to tell me the things that they thought I believed, or to express their own discontents within the vocabulary of the western feminist movement. Note that 'I wanted . . .' 'I refused . . .', and ask, as I did not: 'But whose seminar is this?'

At the same time, as I have already indicated in the previous section, I refused to allow them to simply repeat back to me what I was beginning to identify as the university ideology: that basic Indian institutions are sound, and the need is to stop the abuses within the system. I wanted them to at least raise the issue of patriarchy, and with that, I wanted to challenge the model of knowledge that they were using.

Finally, I was refusing to tell them how to do this, for I feared that they would take my words, write them down and give them back without critical reflection.[6] In short, in the interests of an open and equal dialogue which was to be both critical and creative, I effectively closed off all of the means available to them for expressing a view. And I did not notice what I was doing. Looking back, it is a testimony to their wit and pride that we broke through the resounding silences I was busily building.

It was my position of power which made it possible for me to create these difficulties. I simply presumed my right to determine the quality of our exchanges, behaving like a teacher whilst refusing to be one, and actually teach. This behaviour was determined by both oversensitivity, and blindness to our colonial heritage. I insisted on Indian forms of feminism rather than a discussion of western feminist texts, because I feared the latter would be uncritically adopted, and would be an imposition on a radically different situation. I failed to notice that the English-language legacy in India means that many Indian thinkers want to pursue their discussions in relation to western conceptual categories, and I failed to notice that the form of discussion I aspired to was an idealization of western liberalism. I had unwittingly fallen into seeing the women in the seminar as radically 'other', paralleling this with an unreflective ideal of autonomous thought as wholly independent of outside influences, whilst being highly critical of both these positions in the abstract. The situation was saved, I suspect, only because of relationships outside the seminar.

COULD DIALOGUE BE ACHIEVED?

The form I insisted upon for the seminars was derived from the combination of epistemological and political beliefs referred to in my introduction: that solutions to problems (my version of truth) are best found through discussion rather than the application of a particular philosophical method, that the silencing of anyone is a philosophical *and* political error, and perhaps most importantly, that the point of our activities is to create intelligible and livable worlds for all of us (Seller 1988). Indeed, I was unconsciously (or maybe semi-consciously) mounting an assault on an institution which I felt precluded the creation of such worlds. So it seems that I was coming to the dialogue with truths to communicate, although I did not fully realize that at the time, perhaps because I assumed that those truths were already shared.

But, of course, this creates a dilemma. If I merely treat it as a means of communicating my truths, I am engaged in patient monologue rather than dialogue. I may not pronounce on the ideology of less liberal institutions, but I certainly judge them in trying to change them. When equals set about trying to change each other's minds, something like dialogue emerges; indeed the difficulties I have written of seem to imply that dialogue is only achievable between peers within a community of shared values. Not only were we not equal, but we seemed not to share those very values which I deemed essential for meaningful dialogue. Furthermore, every time I explained some illiberal or incoherent claim to myself by reference to either history or poverty, I seemed to be claiming that I understood them in ways in which they could not understand themselves, to be claiming a superior knowledge which precluded dialogue. I seem to be trapped: the conditions do not exist for dialogue, and if I try to create them, I preclude the dialogue. The imperialistic history of my birthplace would seem to require that the feminist philosopher should stay at home, or at least stay away from ex-colonies. But if we are ever to unpick the legacy of that accursed history, we need to talk to each other.

A way may be found in the following considerations. Sometimes when I did not understand, I thought that they simply had different values to mine, without any inclination to judge. For example, every woman I talked with put a high value on compromise, on the maintenance of harmony within the family, and saw confrontation as a failure, much as some historians tend to see armed conflict as a failure of the diplomatic processes.

Thus one described to me the ingenious and at times hilarious devices she used to get her husband to help with the laundry: at no point did she confront him with the inconsistencies between his assumption of a right to clean clothes, and his avowed commitment to equality. To do so would be a betrayal of her values, like a pacifist shooting a warmonger. I could not decide whether this was a failure to think things through, an unreflective acceptance of a bit of the culture of the submissive wife or a value difference of the sort I experience when arguing with those who believe in revolution by violent means. I was vacillating between assuming a 'superior' understanding or meeting someone who finds different things of greater importance than I do. I think I felt that confusion because I could see the appeal (value) of her position, while finding it unworkable in my own life. Here is one way of ordering relationships, and a good way.

This contrasts with those cases where I reached immediately for the judgement that they had not thought things through. For example, the concern with the abuse of women, the ambition to give women self-esteem and economic independence, combined with the wholly uncritical attitude toward the family, that I have already mentioned. Again and again, I would blame their lack of theory for a failure to see contradictions and consequences, and it would be like running into a wall: beating wives is wrong and divorce is wrong, dowry deaths are wrong and the unmarried woman is to be pitied.

There were many reasons for our inability to move over these contradictions, ranging from the constraints on saying certain things in public (and hence what sometimes felt like a crazy denial of facts: there is no sex outside marriage and no child sex-abuse, and yet there is child prostitution in Bombay and there are illegitimate children), to an unwillingness to suggest to a representative of an ex-colonial power that there could be anything fundamentally wrong with the Indian system. But there is another view of it: I am a pacifist, and this means that by refusing to consider violent solutions to problems, I am forced to think harder about non-violent ones. As long as the simple solution of violence is available, it operates as a block to re-visioning the world. Couldn't Indian women be engaged in a similar intellectual manoeuvre with the family? I don't know: but private conversations on the one hand showed significantly more doubt and transition than was ever publicly admitted, and on the other that the family was so woven into their lives and identities that it was impossible to think outside it. (For example, when talking about life-plans, ambitions, decisions, 'we' rather than 'I' was invariably used, and 'we' referred to the family. As in 'We could only afford one dowry, so we decided to use it for my sister, and that I would become an academic'.) I began to feel the appeal and value of this approach, as a topic to be talked around. *But as long as I reached for theoretical inadequacy as an explanation, I was blind to it*. Incidentally, these examples also show how form and content cannot be distinguished. What we choose to see as contradictions, rather than thoughts in transition, reveals our values.

These thoughts suggest ways in which dialogue can emerge, ways which were made evident to me through experiences outside the university. I spent a few days with a group of Gandhian workers, and was taken by them to visit some village projects. The immediacy and obviousness of needs shattered any inclination to think about conceptual schemes or systems of thought. We shared an emotional world, swept by hope and despair, fatigue and anger. We were on the same political side, in opposition to some of the most powerful interests in our respective societies. Because we could see how each other's lives were committed to social transformation, we could understand each other's compromises. And most importantly, we became friends who laughed together and tried to support each other. Because I shared a wide range of responses with the Gandhians (for example, to the bullying of people, whether by poverty or authority or brute force), I could return to MTWU and recognize the responses we shared there.

On my return, we had what felt like a real breakthrough, when we discussed autonomy. Interpreted as an element within western feminism, many of the women saw it as at best a mistake, at worst morally corrupt. They saw it as a denial of the dependencies and obligations of the family, as a selfish insistence on getting one's own way, an example of that typical western egoism that they so deplored, and that in their view had left western women childless, lonely and unhappy. I suggested that the ideal had more in common with *swaraj* than egoism. *Swaraj* was the term used for independence, or self-rule, and as developed by Gandhi, included the idea of responsible self-determination by communities and individuals. (As he put it: 'We shall have failed if we replace the British raj by an Indian raj.') So it includes both the ideas of mutual dependence and answerability, and the idea of not being ruled by others, for others. The suggestion got some interest, but did not generate the examples I hoped for, exploring the differences between self-denying and self-fulfilling commitments. But the next day, 'Can there be swaraj at MTWU' was written on the blackboard when we entered the room. I don't know whether this was a comment on my control of the seminar or on the university, and perhaps neither did the writer. But it showed me that in insisting on a certain type of forum, I was also insisting that certain values were values. I was being as didactic as my American friend. Or was I? I was certainly delighted with the response, and subsequently recognized it as one of our points of breakthrough to the beginnings of dialogue, for at least one student began to play with ideas of egoism and altruism and self-denial in terms of different kinds of institutions: 'They may be egoists in families, but they give themselves to their causes' she said with an air of enlightenment. 'We are altruistic in our families, but selfish outside', and she went on to describe how, on a recent railway journey she had witnessed a family take over a railway carriage, throwing out the other passengers, which led to a heated discussion of the public/private spheres.

There were several reasons that I considered this a breakthrough. First, because of the quality of the discussion: real questions were being asked, for example about the care of the elderly (seen, with much justification, as one of the shames of the West), and about the meaning of selfishness and independence. Second, I felt that suddenly I was no longer such an enigma to them, that they began to understand me, a childless woman living on her own and insisting that I was not miserable with that. And this was mutual enlightenment, for I saw why life without the family was unimaginable to them: there was, literally, no other social space for them to inhabit. I felt that we could begin to talk about our differences, and what they mean. Third, they were talking about themselves, about the significance and value of their own lives, instead of about other poorer women and what could be done about them. It was the kind of discussion I had hoped for. I believe that it was partly (and only partly) my position of power that made this possible. Was I so excited by such occasions because they came round to my way of discussing things?

I was insisting on certain conditions for dialogue, but at the same time I was beginning to recognize apparently conflicting values as familiar and shared. For example, we shared a fundamental commitment to gender equality, but differed over how that equality should be expressed and lived out. I do not believe any theory or method can deliver correct decisions over such issues. At best, such theories provide a platform from which to view the problem. At worst, they obstruct rather than facilitate dialogue. I was also beginning to recognize that the more abstract and theoretical our formulations, the more culturally specific they become.[7] Intuitively, I had expected the opposite.

A dialectic was underway, of friendship, shared concerns and political alignments. I was not in dialogue with a system of thought, nor even with an institution. It had been my fundamental error to think in those terms. I was talking to people, who had varying degrees of commitment to, and discontent with, the institution that paid their wages, and very different hopes for its future course. I am not simply saying: people, not systems, have dialogues. Rather, that people engage in the world, developing and changing identities, commitments and concerns. The way that we bear those commitments and concerns determines whether or not dialogue is possible. Hence a lot of breakdown can be expected, but given patience, it is rarely terminal. I found myself in political alliances, and those alliances revealed to me the multiple selves that we all are.

In summary I broke out of my isolation, and they broke through the silence because of friendship, because of some shared political commitments and loyalties, and because sometimes we were in the same emotional world.

CHANGING THE METAPHORS

I have already suggested that the metaphor of a system of thought is misleading, suggesting as it does enclosed and self-sufficient cultures or systems of belief. If this metaphor is dominant, it tends to make us think that we can probably only understand and judge people who think like ourselves, and it was because of that metaphor that I felt I had to put my beliefs into abeyance when I went to India. I now want to explore some alternative metaphors.

I have spoken in this chapter about being forced into a place that was prepared for me, a position of power and authority within and by the university, and by our colonial pasts. This isn't simply a matter of facts, of course, but of a world understood and organized according to certain theories. The same is true of my initial assumptions about the nature and functioning of the universities. Theories prepare places for us to go to. I often think of theories as maps: they give a wider view than can be had from personal experience, explain puzzling appearances, help us to chart a course. This is true both of the more or less tacit theoretical understanding we have of our daily institutions, as well as the more articulate theories (e.g. Marxism) that we develop to explain them.

Maps, of course, can be mistaken, can grossly mislead us (as many East-European and Soviet citizens now feel about Marxist-Leninism), or can be misread (as many West-European socialists feel the old Soviet leadership did with Marxism). So it's always difficult to know when to discard one, even when you are falling into streams that shouldn't be there.[8] Maps also represent different features, political or geographical, for example, and come in different projections. Such differences enable us to see different kinds of features, or to see the world in a completely different perspective.[9] In this respect too, theories prepare places for us to go to, enable us to see certain things whilst hiding others from us. This metaphor can only be pushed so far, but I want to draw out three suggestions from it:

1 It shows the importance and usefulness of theory, but also the limitations and risks.

2 It implies that no single theory could fully represent a society. (Imagine a map representing *all* the features of a country: it would be horrendously confusing. Imagine one simultaneously using several projections: could you find your way with it?) But, of course, maps are drawn for different purposes: some to find our way with, some to hang on walls to remind us of our loves or conquests, some to contemplate and so on.

3 Reading a map is not the only way of coming to know a land. The

traveller who fails to lift her eyes from the map is liable to meet with catastrophe, and if she survives, might as well have stayed at home. So I want to suggest a different metaphor for coming into a country.

Imagine feeling your way through a forest or up a mountain, all your senses tuned to the lie of the land, the sound of water. Any decent hike is like this, and when I do it, I feel that the land responds. I am in a process of continuous discovery of its contours, and it sings to me. I don't understand it, so much as find out how to be with it, and if I do it sensibly and intelligently, I can move around unknown country even without a map. Reflecting on my experience in India after my return, I found this a rich metaphor for some of my best moments there. What I was discovering was a way of being with others whose immediate understandings were not my own. This required a full engagement, with *all* of my skills and values in play, helping me to feel my way.

I'm not suggesting these metaphors as alternatives to each other; we need to both use maps and make journeys without them. Together the metaphors may throw light on the question of 'the right to judge'. The question only makes sense if we think of ourselves as members of different rights-conferring systems. 'As a Briton I have no right to judge Indian ways' and 'As a woman I have a right to judge patriarchal oppression' are crude summaries of the kind of unhelpful dispute that tends to be generated by the question. But such disputes are oblivious to the fact that judgement cannot be avoided. As I have repeatedly pointed out, being who I was, doing things in the way I knew, meant that I judged, even when I didn't intend to. Further, the friendships I made, my engagement in and responsiveness to others' lives necessarily involved my emotions and concerns, my values. To feel your way through a countryside, you must have feelings. The only way to avoid judgement is to totally lose identity, and to be completely unresponsive to the world around you. So what is the dispute about? You might argue that we have a collection of maps, and according to some maps we have the right . . . according to others not . . . but that makes the dispute an irresolvable academic issue. The dispute is generated, not because people judge, but because some people have had the power to impose those judgements on others: they *sentence*. Our anxiety about judging, within the British feminist movement, has more to do with a concern with our collective guilt as members of a colonial[10] power than with worries about neutrality, and it is easier to pretend not to judge than to try to change our lifestyles. The language used in discussions about the right to judge other cultures pushes us unreflectingly straight into seeing the world split into 'us' and 'them', and does this because it is dependent on the metaphor of cultures as systems, with individuals as functional parts. It blinds the participants to the question of who the subjects and objects of their sentences might be and how these might shift around, just as the first part of this chapter does. But if I use the metaphors of maps and of discovering a country, then I see that subjects and objects of my sentences change according to the map that I am using, and who is looking at it with me (we Gandhians, for example, judging those communalists), and I see the ways in which I might use a variety of maps to help me feel my way through, or into, the country. I replace the pointless (because impossible) injunction: 'Don't judge' with a series of questions about what I should say to ... how I should respond to.... That is, my attention is focused on my relationships to the people that I am with, and if I am fortunate, we can find our dialogue.

CONCLUSION

Should the feminist philosopher stay at home? My answer is no, not because of what I gave or taught but because of what I received and learnt.

I began to learn how to be with people who were radically different to myself. This was not a matter of finding agreed ways of seeing things, but of seeing the value of things in their lives that I would find unworkable in my own. I also learnt about the ambiguous nature of my power, which forces me to endorse some knowledges at the expense of others, which enables me to act in the world, but at the expense of some of the relationships I would like. And I learnt that having and exercising power is neither wholly voluntary nor wholly automatic, but a matter of institutional position and personal willingness, intermittent because of that.

Because of these features, I learnt that it is a mistake to aim for *a* dialogue, which will generate agreement out of two systems of thought or cultures. I discovered that people, not belief-systems, have dialogues, and that these dialogues occur, intermittently, on the basis of common concerns. These concerns, a combination of belief and emotional response, can be over anything from children to architectural styles. So we can be engaged in a wide variety of dialogues with a wide variety of people: I could recognize 'my kind of people' in what appeared to be a wholly alien culture as I recognized common concerns, and I could see how these could break down as we discovered other, different concerns. I also learnt that there are other ways of being with people, apart from having dialogues: namely through that whole complex process I have tried to encapsulate in the metaphor of feeling your way into a country. My time in India sparkled with small acts of inclusion, by people who often had only a few words of English, from the housekeeper's invitation to share her *puja* to the students' invitations to watch television. Perhaps at the end of the day, the most important gifts are those small acts of inclusion.

On my return to Britain, I asked myself 'How shall I live the rest of my life?' For I felt that we shared one world. This doesn't mean thinking about how to solve 'their' problems (what can I suggest to improve the income of head-loaders?), but rather, rethinking my own problems within a context that includes them (how can I continue to enjoy my life of wealthy ease in a world that contains head-loaders?). I think it is not so much a question of whether to stay at home, as of learning how to travel.

NOTES

1 This view is more fully argued for in Seller (1988).
2 Which initially seemed similar to consciousness-raising, but lacked any connotation of liberation or alienation from the dominant ideology.
3 Of course, there are Indian feminists, but MTWU was at pains to separate itself from them. For a view of Indian feminism, see *Manushi* (but note also the article by its editor and founder, Kishwar 1990). See also Bhasin and Khan (1986), Kishwar and Vanita (1984), Suma (1988) and Kalpagam (1986).
4 In India, improving the status of women was an integral element in the Independence Movement. Thus middle-class Indian women developed their traditions of political struggle in opposition to colonial rule, while British women developed theirs against their own state. As one Indian woman put it: 'We feel angry on your behalf.'
5 These occur when young brides are killed or driven to suicide by husbands or in-laws who are dissatisfied with the dowry payments. Such deaths are on the increase: as one Indian remarked to me, you only have to visit the acute burns ward in the local hospital to see the problem. Because cooking is often done on kerosene stoves and saris easily catch fire, murder can be covered up, and the commonest deaths are by burning.
6 Indian educational practice seems to be largely based on rote-learning. This is in part colonial inheritance, and in part an economical way of guaranteeing a minimally uniform standard of education over vast social and geographical distances.
7 For example, at the moment, I cannot imagine how a highly abstract and theoretical book like Judith Butler's *Gender Trouble* (1990) could quite literally make sense to the Indian women I knew, not because they lack 'theoretical understanding', but because it fits into such a specific, and I suspect, enclosed, dialogue.
8 See the past twenty years' discussion of Karl Popper's theory of falsification. And with thanks to Caroline, who taught me that the blue lines on US maps represent not water-ways but minor roads.
9 E.g. look at Peterson's projection.
10 I still regard Britain as a colonial power: the political status has changed but not the economic one.

REFERENCES

Bartky, Sandra Lee (1977), 'Toward a phenomenology of feminist consciousness' in *Feminism and Philosophy*, ed. Mary Vetterling-Braggin, Frederick A. Elliston and Jane English, Totowa NJ: Littlefield, Adams and Co., pp. 22–34.
Bhasin, Kamla and Khan, Nighat Said (1986), *Some Questions on Feminism and its Relevance in South Asia*, New Delhi: Kali for Women.
Butler, Judith (1990), *Gender Trouble: Feminism and the Subversion of Identity*, New York and London: Routledge.

Eck, Diana L, and Jain, Deraki (eds) (1986), *Speaking of Faith*, London: The Women's Press.

Ghadially, Rehana (ed.) (1988), *Women in Indian Society*, New Delhi and London: Sage.

Kalpagam, U. (1986), 'Gender in economics: the Indian experience', *Economic and Political Weekly*, vol. 21, no. 43 (25 October), pp. 60–6.

Kishwar, Madhu (1990), 'Why I do not call myself a feminist', *Manushi*, no. 61 (November-December), pp. 2–8.

Kishwar, Madhu and Vanita R. (eds) (1984), *In Search of Answers*, London: Zed Press.

Manushi: A Journal about Women and Society, New Delhi.

Seller, Anne (1988), 'Realism versus relativism: towards a politically adequate epistemology' in *Feminist Perspectives in Philosophy*, ed. Morwenna Griffiths and Margaret Whitford, London: Macmillan, pp. 169–86.

Suma, Chitnis (1988), 'Feminism: Indian ethos and Indian convictions' in *Women in Indian Society*, ed. Rehana Ghadially, New Delhi and London: Sage.

16

OPENNESS, IDENTITY AND ACKNOWLEDGEMENT OF PERSONS

Meena Dhanda

INTRODUCTION

In this chapter I shall restrict the discussion to the idea of 'openness to' persons rather than 'openness of' persons. The latter has been emphasized by several 'postmodernist' enthusiasts[1] and has also come under severe criticism from many philosophers who are suspicious of the untimely 'goodbye' to self-determination.[2] I shall discuss the idea of openness to persons in the context of ethical disagreements. The aim is to describe what might be considered appropriate personal conduct in the face of ethical conflict with others, and in the process, offer theoretical reasons for addressing difference and diversity, with openness.

In the course of a discussion on objectivity in ethics,[3] Bernard Williams has asked:

> If an ethical disagreement arises, must one party think the other in error? What is the content of that thought? What sorts of discussion or exploration might, given the particular subject-matter, lead one or both of them out of error?
>
> (Williams 1991: 10)

What I have to say about 'openness' in discussions of ethical differences turns out to be partly a response to the questions raised by Williams. It may therefore be seen as a contribution to the 'theory of persuasion' which is Williams's suggested alternative to the search for a theory of our common ethical nature in which the hopes of the ethical objectivist are mistakenly invested. In the absence of an objective value that could settle a matter in favour of one or the other disputants to an ethical claim, what we need is

> only something more restricted, the idea of the acceptable answer to this disagreement, an answer that might be reached in actual historical circumstances: an answer or the refusal of an answer, to which the parties could honourably agree.
>
> (Williams 1991: 10)

249

An honourable agreement is akin to an outcome of a negotiated settlement, in that it may not be final. It is renegotiable. But again any subsequent renegotiation of the ethical agreement would depend upon, among other things, a mutual understanding that to an extent the conditions of the initial agreement have been met with. The problem of what might be counted as an honourable agreement and the answer to it 'belongs to what might be called a theory of persuasion' which would be 'itself an ethical discussion: a discussion of the proper role of rhetoric, and loyalty, and disinterestedness, and the value of truth – plain truth, the truth of historical and social truthfulness, rather than the phantasm of ultimate ethical truth' (Williams 1991: 10).

The ethical disagreement that I shall discuss is one about what it is to be a particular person with a particular identity. I shall do it in a specific case, with an example which is reflective of actual historical circumstances. I shall assume[4] that ascription of identity is in part a normative task. This will also be evident from the example itself. I shall therefore treat disagreements about identities as in part ethical disagreements. In the course of the following discussion I hope to suggest an answer to 'the ethical question of how in dealing with ethical disagreement we should best conduct ourselves' (Williams 1991: 10).

AN EXAMPLE

A, B and C live in Britain, and consider it their home. A claims to be a Sikh. A's friend B (who is not a Sikh herself) knows that Sikhs are prohibited from smoking and do not approve of others smoking in their presence and that they have an obligation not to cut their hair. B acknowledges A to be a Sikh by not smoking in the presence of A, and when A gets her hair cut one morning by exclaiming 'So! Given up being a Sikh?!' 'Of course not!' replies A, 'I am very much a Sikh even now'. B is left puzzling over what it is to be a Sikh, while a couple of hours later A runs into another friend C (who also claims to be a Sikh) and is shot with a disbelieving look coupled with the remark 'How could you do this? How could you betray Sikhs like this?' A protests 'But I am still a Sikh, I have not betrayed anyone'. 'Don't say that you are a Sikh, you stopped being a Sikh when you cut your hair', says C. 'Well, I never kept long hair under any obligation to do so but only because I liked it that way. I am as much a Sikh now as I was when I wore my hair long, because I believe that what is essential to being a Sikh is living by the values the Gurus taught, of equality, commitment to the oppressed in one's society and collective struggle and I consider myself as bound to these values now as I was a couple of hours ago.' 'A lot of other people too say that they have these values', C promptly points out, 'what is the difference then in being a Sikh and not being a Sikh?' A replies: 'With those who in any case believe what I believe, I see no point in asserting that I am different. I need to assert my difference only when others refuse to grant that I have a right to live by the values that I share with other Sikhs and to show my reverence to the Gurus who have inspired me. At these times I need to assert that I am a Sikh. And I have a right to be one.'

AN ANALYSIS:
KNOWLEDGE AND ACKNOWLEDGEMENT

The imaginary bits of conversations[5] presented above as an example, may be analysed in the following way: A's claim that she is a Sikh, from her point of view, is a claim about what she believes and values. It is not a claim directly about what she does, like wearing her hair long or not smoking. From her point of view being a Sikh is not a simple fact. Since B acknowledges A to be what she claims, in the new situation when face to face with the short-haired A, it is her simple understanding of what it is to be a Sikh that undergoes a challenge rather than her recognition of A. B does not doubt the genuineness of A's claim, but only her own understanding of what it involves.

In C's case, the situation is reversed. C doubts the genuineness of A, while remaining certain about her understanding of what A claims. For C, given her own understanding of the claim made by A to be a Sikh, there is no way A could be making a true claim. There are only two ways C can see A, viz. either as a traitor or else as a self-deluded person. C does not recognize A to be what she claims. In other words, C does not acknowledge A.

To be more precise, in seeing her as a traitor, C does not contest that A *is* a Sikh. What she contests is her way of being a Sikh. A is alleged to be a traitor, precisely, because she is still considered as belonging to the fold. Whereas in seeing her as self-deluded, it is being alleged that she is not and never was a Sikh. Any claims to the contrary only arise from delusion about her true nature.

In the above case, the lack of acknowledgement of A by C does not imply that some fact about A is being missed by C. The case therefore suggests that absence of acknowledgement does not entail that a fact about the person is not being acknowledged, which in turn suggests that acknowledgement of facts about a person is not *ipso facto* an acknowledgement of the person.

Let us, therefore, ask: is C failing or refusing to recognize some fact about A? Or is she, despite recognizing all the relevant facts about A, failing or refusing to affirm that she does so recognize these facts? Or is C acknowledging the relevant facts about A, yet failing or refusing to acknowledge A?

We can grant that C knows A well enough to believe in the sincerity of the claims she makes about her values and their source of inspiration in the Gurus, up to the point when the change in her personality occurs. C is from then onwards suspicious of A. The fact that may be hardest for C to recognize is that in the past A kept long hair not because of any inspiration from the Gurus but simply because she liked it that way. C may be reluctant to accept this fact, but let us grant that she does recognize it for a fact too, because for all practical purposes A 'was' a Sikh. Is there any other relevant fact about A that C does not recognize? Perhaps C finds it difficult to accept that A is not mistaken in making her claim and that her knowledge or understanding of Sikhism is not inadequate. But ascertaining the level of someone's understanding of something is a matter of judgement, not of finding out a fact. It may be concluded therefore that there is no fact about A that C does not recognize. And we know that nevertheless C does not acknowledge A. That establishes that acknowledgement of facts about a person is not *ipso facto* an acknowledgement of the person.

This conclusion sets my approach to the question of how best to deal with difference slightly apart from an approach such as S. Benhabib's, that stresses that 'more knowledge rather than less contributes to a more rational and informed judgement' (Benhabib 1987: 93). In one sense this is clearly tautologous, if more 'rational' and more 'informed' means having more 'knowledge'. But there are other ways of being 'informed', such as, for example, by sharing to a degree a 'social space' in Bernard Williams's use of the phrase. This gives 'some shared understanding of the psychological bases of moral agreement and disagreement themselves: a sense of the virtues, of expected conduct, or of public principle, and with these we work, in seeking to articulate and perhaps resolve disagreements' (Williams, 1991: 10). On my understanding of Williams's concept of sharing a social space it cannot be confined to sharing or increasing 'knowledge'. It would have to be a more complex education than sharing 'knowledge', if one can educate oneself to acquire a place in the 'social space' of 'others'.

We are left with the problem: what is this failure to acknowledge a person if not a failure to acknowledge some fact(s) about the person? What prevents C from acknowledging A to be what she claims to be?

It may be said that A and C are not differing about facts but about the right interpretations of facts. A believes that one ceases to be a Sikh only if one stops believing in and valuing the politico-ethical teachings of the Gurus. Her contention is that cutting off one's hair does not of itself amount to ceasing to be a Sikh, because keeping long hair is of no intrinsic value. C believes that a Sikh must be recognizably a Sikh. She therefore considers cutting off one's hair tantamount to losing one's identity as a Sikh. There would be no quarrel between A and C if A accepts, as C would like her to, that she is a renegade or if C concedes that in exceptional circumstances it is acceptable that a Sikh may not keep long hair and that

A's case is such an exception. There is a problem here because neither A nor C concedes that much to the other.

C's lack of acknowledgement of A is a problem for A, and I shall argue that it is a problem for C as well, even if C does not perceive it as such in any obvious sense. I shall also suggest that what prevents C from acknowledging A to be what she claims is the implication of that acknowledgement, namely, that C's own claim to be a Sikh needs to be re-examined. C's failure (refusal) to acknowledge A is a failure to undertake a re-evaluation of her acknowledgement of herself.

There is a way in which one may try to block this implication of C's acknowledgement of A. This way may be offered as a resolution to the problem of lack of acknowledgement. I shall try to show that taking this way does not lead to a satisfactory resolution.

The problem of lack of acknowledgement may apparently be made fairly easily resolvable if seen, as I considered a moment ago, as one of interpretation of facts. It may be suggested that if A and C grant that there can be different ways of interpreting facts, then that would provide a good reason for each to appreciate the case for adopting the other's point of view, and appreciating the other's point of view is all that is needed in order to acknowledge the other. In other words it may be said that one can acknowledge the other by appreciating the other's point of view. To my mind this only delays the solution of the problem of acknowledgement, by pushing it one step back. For now we are left with the equally insurmountable difficulty of appreciating that the other has a point of view. Since the difficulty persists, albeit in another form, I consider the suggested way out to be unsatisfactory.

It is questionable whether one needs to recognize that the other has a point of view at all in order to acknowledge the other. I would like to turn the problem around and suggest that *one needs to acknowledge the other because it is often not possible to appreciate the other's point of view.* Acknowledgement of persons must be possible despite the inability to appreciate the other's point of view. (In my example such an acknowledgement corresponds to B's acknowledgement of A.) I say that it *must* be possible, because discussions are simply better than quarrels, and acknowledgement of the discussants is necessary to prevent the metamorphosis of a discussion into a quarrel. Acknowledgement of persons may not by itself move a discussion forward, which for the lack of appropriate terms of debate may have come to its limits, but it may keep a debate in limbo for a possible renewal, thus preventing an equally possible degeneration into a quarrel, or worse still an all-out fight.[6] Acknowledgement of persons is thus the appropriate attitude within situations of disagreements, and one that acts as a bridge to move from disagreements to possible agreements, sometimes simply agreements to disagree.

It is necessary for acknowledgement that one grant that there may be a point of view other than one's own. It is not necessary to grant that the other *has* another point of view, but only that the other may (or may not) have another point of view which I cannot decide in advance. Since the possibility of the other's point of view being another point of view is only speculative, there is no question of appreciating the other's point of view. There is instead a need to be open about one's own point of view, and to allow the possibility that one's own point of view may not hold together and that the process of acknowledging the other may take one to adopt a different point of view from the one that is currently held. This new point of view might only *incidentally* be the other's point of view or might be close to the other's point of view.

Such an attitude is somewhat like the liberal ideal of realizing 'the relative validity of one's convictions' and yet, standing for them 'unflinchingly'. But the crucial difference is that there is both a greater and lesser confidence than is necessary to make the claim of 'relative validity' and 'unflinching' commitment. In my view, on the one hand, one is completely convinced of the soundness of one's convictions, which is a sign of greater confidence. On the other hand, one is totally prepared to re-evaluate one's convictions, so that one cannot be so resolute as to be unyielding in situations of conflict. An important consequence of this willingness to negotiate with others would be that in judging others with whom one is in conflict, one would have to abandon the idea of 'false consciousness'.

It is relevant to suggest that at this point 'openness of' persons intersects with 'openness to' persons. The idea of an ideal coherence and stability of the acting subject, such as Sabina Lovibond upholds, in her defence of the Enlightenment ideals of autonomy and integrity (Lovibond, 1989), does not sit very well with the temperament of tentativeness, an 'openness to' persons (including oneself) that I have suggested above. But then I do not find an alternative to the idea of 'openness to' persons in Sabina's criticism of the decentred subject (of the 'openness of' persons). She considers the 'loss of confidence in the idea of false consciousness' one of the 'large concessions' that feminism has made to the 'anti-rationalist mood of the times' (Lovibond 1989: 25). It might be relevant to have recourse to the idea of 'false consciousness' if it helps oneself and works as an invitation to others to embark on an examination of what respectively each one of us identifies with. But the use to which this idea has been put, historically speaking, is to politically discredit those with whom one has chosen not to communicate. As an attitude towards 'difference' the idea has its predominant use in silencing the Other. It might be suggested that the intent is just the opposite. It is to provoke others to communicate that one diagnoses them as suffering from 'false consciousness'. It is certain beliefs (born out of certain interests) that have to be discredited. This might well be the guiding principle, but when put in practice, it is not difficult to understand why in discrediting those beliefs, it is people who get discredited. As a form of political engagement, 'consciousness-raising groups' might foster personal autonomy[7] but they do not help bridge gaps between people belonging to different 'communities of judgement'.[8]

The tentativeness that I have proposed would encourage an attitude of skilful persuasion while ruling out the use of force. It would, *practically,* enable one to make the distinction between 'presenting reasons to convince and blackmailing; refusing and being obstinate'.[9] But no clear distinction would be possible between 'consenting and being persuaded to do so'. The lesson to be drawn would be that nothing of great consequence must depend on the making of such a distinction.[10]

ACKNOWLEDGEMENT AND IDENTITY

Going back to our example, it may be suggested that C fails/refuses to acknowledge A, despite acknowledging all the relevant facts about A, because of one of the following reasons: (1) C does not grant that there may be any point of view other than her own; (2) C believes that the only point of view that there can be other than her own must be A's point of view, so that if she acknowledges that there may be another point of view she must necessarily accept that that point of view is A's point of view.

She believes that she must choose between her own and A's point of view. Reason (1) is directly opposed to the very basis of acknowledgement of others, so that if it is true of C that she does not grant that there can be a point of view other than her own, then there is no further need for an explanation of her failure/refusal to acknowledge A. It is a different story altogether if (2) is the case, i.e. if (2) prevents C from acknowledging A to be what she claims to be. The *sine qua non* for acknowledging the Other, as stated above, is that there may be a point of view other than one's own, and that that point of view may incidentally be the Other's point of view. C contravenes this condition by acting on the belief that she must choose between her own and A's point of view. She does not grant that if she is led to acknowledge another point of view owing to her acknowledgement of A, that point of view may not necessarily be A's point of view, but only incidentally might turn out to be A's point of view.

She does not grant that besides her own and A's challenging points of view there may be a host of *other undiscovered ones*. This prevents her from acknowledging A to be what she claims to be. Since she considers A's view of what it is to be a Sikh as the only other view that she can adopt if she is open about her own view, she cannot acknowledge A without in the same stroke giving up her own self-view of being a Sikh. The option of a radical switch from her own to A's point of view is not an option that she can take. To expect her to radically switch her point of view is, as noted earlier, begging the question of the need for acknowledgement.

The concept of acknowledgement or what constitutes an adequate attitude towards another person can be approached from two ends: (1) as an approximation to an ideal achievable by all persons; (2) as a limiting concept of a minimally required attitude that can pass for an acceptable attitude towards any person in a given context.

What I have said thus far about acknowledgement pertains to the sense of the concept in (2). As a limiting concept, acknowledgement is that which makes up for an insufficiently realized reciprocity and inexhaustible knowledge of others. Acknowledgement as an ideal, the sense of the concept in (1), is the acquisition of a habit, a disposition to conduct oneself in appropriate ways towards difference. As an ideal it requires all the preconditions that a liberal political culture promises but fails to deliver: adequate means of living a decent life – money, education, health, freedom and respect for all. It is clearly beyond the scope of this chapter to consider the prospects of 'acknowledgement' as an ideal in a liberal political culture.

Acknowledgement as a code of personal conduct in the face of ethical conflict is meant to supplement 'a public system of rights and duties'. It is an attempt to expand the moral point of view to include more than the concern for the dignity of persons as such. It is designed to address the concrete identities of others, not just to seek to transcend them, although a temporary transcendence might precede the acknowledgement of concrete others with whom we share only a little 'social space'.

In terms of Gibbard's 'communities of judgement' approach, acknowledgement can be described as a norm of accommodation among diverse communities of judgement. As he puts it,

> Life in a messy and dangerous world depends on being able to form broad communities of judgement on a restricted range of norms – norms that enable us to live together. To thrive, though, we need more intimate communities as well.
>
> (Gibbard 1989: 178)

Acknowledgement of someone with whom one does not share an intimate community is an attempt to include that someone in the broader community of judgement. It is a willingness to accept norms of accommodation with that person, a willingness to negotiate.

The final step that will take us closer to a fuller account of the concept of acknowledgement of persons involves making a distinction between the acknowledgement of someone as a person and the acknowledgement of the particular person that someone is.[11] In relation to oneself, acknowledgement of oneself would require as Dillon (1992) points out, 'acceptance and patience'. But the line between what to accept and what patiently to try to change in oneself, is one that I think can be drawn without insisting that 'having knowledge about and understanding of oneself is surely a necessary condition for self-respect', as Dillon (1992: 63) does. On the

256

contrary, *acknowledging oneself* as a person as such, as well as at the same time a particular person, is a necessary condition for the pursuit of knowledge, and understanding of oneself, to gain ground. An important evidence of acknowledgement of oneself is the confidence with which one does indeed draw the line between what to accept and what patiently to try to change in oneself. Dillon herself interestingly puts it as a mark of the self-respecting person that she is 'content in her quirks and idiosyncracies and does not pummel herself into likeness or conformity. But she also does not rebel against similarity and commonality. She respects the way she is like and unlike others' (Dillon 1992: 60).

To reassert: acknowledgement of another person is, at one level, recognition of the particular person; at another level, it is the recognition of another's personhood or status of being a person.[12] Keeping these two senses of acknowledgement of another person apart from each other, there is a need to examine their interrelation and the viability of this distinction for the purposes of understanding the concept of acknowledgement and the preconditions that must be met for acknowledgement to take place. To pursue this further is, however, outside the scope of this chapter.

In the above discussion I touched upon the place of consensus in ascription of identity. The examples of ethical conflict that are in part conflicts of identity can be multiplied. The conflict between a pro-lifer and a defender of safe abortion facilities is not the ultimate ethical conflict between the value of life itself and the quality of life. It is a conflict that can be better understood and perhaps better resolved as a conflict of identities. For a pro-lifer, being a mother is more important than being economically independent, for example, so she might choose to carry through an untimely pregnancy even at the risk of losing her job, or not getting one. Her mistake lies not in hierarchizing for herself the mother-identity, but in campaigning for conditions that will foist this identity on to other women who either do not want it or despite wanting cannot afford it.

My position on how a supporter of abortion should treat a pro-lifer might be criticized as being 'naive', a charge that Seyla Benhabib makes against Lyotard's 'neoliberal interest group pluralism' by using the very example of the abortion debate. She writes:

Lyotard cannot maintain that the current attempt of conservative, pro-life groups to establish a 'new reverence for life and creation', to deny the moral legitimacy of abortion, to even ask science to provide extra criteria as to when the fetus becomes a person, are 'narratives' in our culture that point to a happy polytheism of language games. The polytheism of language games either assumes that culture and society are harmonious wholes or that the struggles within them are plays only. But there are times when philosophy cannot afford to be a 'gay science', for reality itself becomes deadly serious. To deny that the play of language games may not turn into a matter of life and death and that the intellectual cannot remain the priest of many gods but must take a stance is cynical.

(Benhabib 1990: 123)

Contrary to the ultimatist, commitment-infused position of Benhabib, it is worth remembering Anne Seller's remark that 'unless we listen carefully to women opposed to abortion, the feminist movement will simply ignore (be ignorant) of them and cut them off' (Seller 1988: 176). The important difference between our respective approaches is that while Benhabib takes 'the moral legitimacy of abortion' as already proven for good, I consider it problematic. My support for free provision for abortion is a pragmatic support which I am willing to reconsider in my discussion with a pro-lifer provided that I can be convinced that for practical purposes in particular circumstances free abortion facility does more harm than good. Deontological considerations of the rights of the woman versus the rights of the child/foetus lead to a deadlock. Expressed other than in pragmatic terms, I find the abortion debate morally ambiguous. Therefore, rather than taking a stance towards the ultimate value or moral legitimacy of abortion I am concerned with the process of political debate that can further my goal of better facilities for those who need and want abortion while not offending or humiliating those who are against it.

People hierarchize different possibilities for self-development in different ways. The above considerations of the position of the abortionist versus the pro-lifer show that it is important to understand the implications of diverse ideals and goals of personal development before we start to accuse people of fundamental wrongheadedness or 'false consciousness'.

One way of addressing this diversity is to espouse an 'ethical pluralism'. As Ferguson writes,

> Only trial and error and the experience of juggling the various aspects of her self by trying out different private commitments can lead to what is most personally empowering to different women. The Aspect theory of the self, based as it is on the view that the self is an existential process whose integration may be different for different women, must assume an ethical pluralism on such matters of personal choice.
>
> (1989: 105)

The use of the phrases: 'trial and error' and 'juggling' conjures up the image of idle amusement and to that extent rightly invites the charge of miscontruing struggles as 'plays only'.[13]

The other way of dealing with ethical difference is to try and expand the broader community of judgement. More ambitious dealing with ethical difference would be an attempt to acquire a place in the 'social space' occupied by others. At both levels, the relationship in which the political agent stands to the Other is one between negotiators. And for this relationship to be fruitful the guiding norm has to be acknowledgement. In particular, the self-affirmed identities of people constructed within intimate groups of 'fellow searchers for truth and meaning in life' (Gibbard 1989: 178) need to be acknowledged. For, as Gibbard (1989: 179) puts it, 'People need intimate groups, not only widespread understandings'.

To be an effective negotiator, one would have to sense-from-the-inside, as it were, the judgements/positions likely to emerge from the other side. In acquiring this sensitivity, knowledge of others undoubtedly has a role to play. In one's own case, learning more about how one came to acquire the values one did would have an effect. It is questionable, however, whether that effect would necessarily be liberating.[14] When a growing child is persuaded to keep long hair not for the reason that her parents like it that way but because the tenth Guru of the Sikhs called upon the Sikhs to acquire such a form, she is being told a powerful causal story. A story that might induce her to hold more dearly to the 'value' of keeping long hair.

What can one do to weaken the hold of this causal story, if one needed to? (Clearly in the example above, there is a need to weaken the hold of C's story, because it does not make room for the acknowledgement of A's identity.) One way is to tell other more complex causal stories about why a certain value came to have the importance it has. Skinner (1991) advocates this tack. The other way is to tell stories of a different kind, ones that illustrate the limits of sense-making and the limits of control. If *this* were to happen what *would* you do? The attempt is to have an answer to that ultimate question[15] which might face anyone: of a choice to be human or inhuman. Put in another way one could say with Gibbard that 'in life, the chief quandary here is when to accept norms of accommodation and when to stand firmly against them' (1989: 182).

The force of circumstances, actual historical circumstances, might place me in situations where whatever I do is inhuman, and paradoxically, therefore, shot through with humanity. I end with a story which can be read in several ways: as a story about courage or cowardice, as a chronicle of hope in humanity or despair born out of inhumanity, as a saga of the unlimitedness of pain. . . . It is a true story, but . . . like all true stories that I can tell, I do not know the whole truth. A lot depends on how the story is understood and how we enter into its unfolding in the future or had perhaps already entered in its past. Not only the identities of the characters in the story at its current stage but also our own identities are bound up with it. It is in such actual circumstances that we are required to negotiate our identities, and acknowledge 'concrete' others.

A STORY

The plot takes place in a small village in the Indian Punjab where a battle for a separate Sikh state is being waged by a section of the population. Around 10 p.m. at night, the screams of a young man can be heard a kilometre away shouting, 'Bapu, open the gate or they will kill me'. Then a stream of abuse. '*** Come out you coward or we will kill the Singh's son.' More shouts imploring the father to open the gate and let the 'boys' take the Police Inspector hiding inside the house. More abuse from the 'boys' threatening the head of the house with dire consequences if the Inspector is not handed to them. Gunshots and then silence. The next morning the milkman from the village filled in details for everyone who had heard the agonizing screams, the gunshots, the silence of the night before in neighbouring villages. . . . The militants – the 'boys', as they are called in Punjab by the Sikh population – had kidnapped the son of the family who they had learnt were playing host to a 'wanted' Police Inspector, wanted because of his involvement with the arrests and tortures of 'boys' in the movement. The Inspector also happened to be a distant relative of the host. The 'boys' then demanded that the father should trade the life of his son for that of the Inspector. Inside the Inspector ordered them not to open the gate of the house and let the 'boys' in. The father did not open the gate, the 'boys' shot the son and set him on fire before leaving. The burnt body was found outside the gate after they left.

A COMMENT

A story such as the one above might tempt one to say with Benhabib that 'there might be times when the immanent norms and values of a culture are so reified, dead, or petrified that one can no longer speak in their name.'[16] And therefore, in such circumstances 'social exile' may be required for carrying on the task of social criticism. On such a view, trying to tell more complex stories to weaken the hold of values that need to be revised might be a futile task and in some circumstances dangerous as well. Social exile might enable one to gain the time and space to weave yet new stories. But hardly more than a few people can hope to escape into exile. What about those who stay back? Can they not make up stories from the materials at hand?

Fortunately, my story has a postscript that some may find instructive. It shows that resistance can be of many kinds. Seemingly insignificant attempts to quietly challenge the accepted view on such matters as keeping long hair, as well as 'vain' attempts to stand up firmly and refuse to succumb even in the face of death are equally the stuff out of which stories of resistance can be made. Both kinds of stories are needed to meet the challenge of powerful forces that erode moral community – a community where it must be possible to acknowledge the particular identities of people without sacrificing the need to acknowledge them as persons as such.

POSTSCRIPT TO THE STORY

While all the other members of the household stood petrified by the threats from without and within the walls of the house, the daughter of the family ran to open the gate. Her father urged her to consider the futility of trying to save her brother and 'persuaded' her to step back.

A few days later the 'boys' returned to leave a note at the gate of the house. In the note they expressed their apologies for having killed the innocent son of the family.

NOTES

The main portion of this paper was written while I was the Rhodes Junior Research Fellow in Philosophy at St Hilda's College, Oxford in 1990–1. I wish to thank the College and the Rhodes Trustees for their support. An earlier version of the paper was discussed at the annual conference of the Society for Women in Philosophy (SWIP) held at Leeds in September 1991, and at a more intimate SWIP meeting at Wolverhampton, for both of which I am very grateful. Shakuntala Banaji, Suzanne Bobzien, Rohini Hensman, Alan Montefiore, Joseph Raz, Pritam Singh and Bernard Williams have helped me to improve the paper by their critical and encouraging comments at different stages of its growth. Kathleen Lennon's editorial suggestions were very helpful. My mother, Sushila, and my daughter, Tanya, enabled me to work on the final draft, by creating the necessary time and space.

1 Restricting myself to Anglo-American philosophers, I am referring to Rorty (1989: esp. 23–4); Hekman (1990); Young (1987 and 1990). Also Di Stefano (1990) who, though not an enthusiast, is a sympathetic critic.
2 One of the strongest voices of protest and 'suspicion' has been Sabina Lovibond's. She writes: 'How can anyone ask me to say goodbye to "emancipatory metanarratives", when my own emancipation is still such a patchy, hit-and-miss affair?' (1989: 12). Similarly Nancy Hartsock asks:

> Why is it that just at the moment when so many of us who have been silenced begin to demand the right to name ourselves, to act as subjects rather than objects of history, that just then the concept of subjecthood becomes problematic?
>
> (1990: 163)

In their 'Introduction', Benhabib and Cornell also emphasize the importance of *renegotiation* of our psychosexual identities' (1987: 13). Although there is no offering of a consensus view on what it is we must renegotiate for, it is clear that a *constructive* purposive task is involved. On substantive proposals for 'constructive' change see Meyers (1989 and 1992). For further developments of the feminist/postmodernist debate see Benhabib (1991), Butler (1991), Fraser (1991) and Oliver (1991).
3 Williams (1991). This is a version of Bernard Williams's Inaugural Lecture as White's Professor of Moral Philosophy at the University of Oxford.

4 The reader may see Dhanda (1989) for my arguments supporting the normative nature of identity-ascription.

5 Although imaginary, these bits of conversation are modelled on 'an *actual* dialogue situation in which moral agents communicate with one another'. See Benhabib (1987: 92–5) for reasons why this is better than 'a *hypothetical* thought process, carried out singly by the moral agent or the moral philosopher' (93). While I agree that actual situations provide one with the requisite knowledge necessary for criticism to be relevant, I do not agree that more knowledge is therefore better than less in formulating a judgement. I hope to show this in my analysis of the example at hand.

6 J-F. Lyotard on the other hand, works on the basis of the principle that 'to speak is to fight, in the sense of playing' (1986: 10). The principle of 'negotiation' that is the fundamental element of my analysis is half-way between a 'fight' and 'uncoerced communication'.

7 Meyers (1989 and 1992) argues passionately for the need to foster personal autonomy and considers a consciousness-raising group as an example of 'autonomy-sensitive political engagement' (1992:130). Although her basic insight that what we need 'is a conception of the subject that allows for both commitment and innovation' (127) is appealing, the commitment and innovation are conceived in individualistic terms, and therefore her conception of subject does not adequately represent the person-in-the-group, such as the Sikh woman C in my example.

8 The phrase comes from the title of Gibbard (1989). My view of negotiation comes very close to his when he says that: 'Living together is often a matter of bargaining. . . . Bargaining involves normative discussion: working out, partly in community, what norms to accept as applying to a situation' (1989: 184).

9 Benhabib makes the demand for this distinction in her criticism of Lyotard's agonistics (1990: 115).

10 Compare with Rorty's comment on 'brainwashing, media hype and what Marxists call "false consciousness" '. He writes:

> There is, to be sure, no neat way to draw the line between persuasion and force, and therefore no neat way to draw a line between a cause of changed belief which was also a reason and one which was a 'mere' cause. But the distinction is no fuzzier than most.

(1989: 48)

11 Benhabib's remark: 'I would argue . . . for the validity of a moral theory that allows us to recognize the dignity of the generalized other through an acknowledgement of the moral identity of the concrete other' (1987: 92), is instructive in this regard. What needs working out is a response to the challenge posed by conflicts of acknowledgement in situations where the dignity of the person as such cannot be straightforwardly recognized *through* an acknowledgement of the 'concrete other'.

12 In a rather awkward phrase, Dillon (1992), adopting Stephen Darwall's terminology, refers to the phenomenon of taking appropriate account of someone's status as a person as 'recognition respect'. She then points out a 'kind of paradox' in the standard account of 'recognition respect', namely, 'if the particularities of our selves and lives are morally important, as many feminists claim, then recognition respect for ourselves requires disrespecting ourselves' (1992: 57).

13 Ferguson might defend herself by pointing out that along with her proposed ethical pluralism, she is also drawing generalizations for the political process of

empowerment of women in contemporary United States. A weakness in her account, however, is the lack of argument for 'collective networking' and 'prioritising friendships with other women that value personal autonomy' (Ferguson 1989: 105) as necessary steps for empowerment. These are introduced as necessary steps, but in the absence of argument do not seem to me to follow from her Aspect theory of the self.

14 Compare with Skinner (1991: 145), who writes that if a causal story of the triumph of one set of values over another, or one ideology over another could be told, the effect of learning more about it 'cannot but be to loosen the hold of our inherited values upon our emotional allegiances'.

15 Bernard Williams criticizes the interest in the 'ultimate case' when it is merely the interest in principle, in limiting cases, while most of our ethical differences are, according to him, less extreme. His criticism is not applicable to the ultimate question that I have raised, because this question is being faced, today, by countless people whose lives are being led in confrontation with extremities. It is not an answer in principle that is being searched for, but a response that helps one sail through difficult times without too many casualties.

16 Benhabib (1991: 146). Also in Benhabib (1992).

REFERENCES

Benhabib, Seyla (1987), 'The generalized and the concrete other: the Kohlberg-Gilligan controversy and feminist theory' in *Feminism as Critique*, ed. Seyla Benhabib and Drucilla Cornell, Cambridge: Polity Press, pp. 77–95.

Benhabib, Seyla (1990), 'Epistemologies of postmodernism: a rejoinder to Jean-François Lyotard' in *Feminism/Postmodernism* ed. Linda J. Nicholson, New York and London: Routledge, pp. 107–30.

Benhabib, Seyla (1991), 'Feminism and postmodernism: an uneasy alliance', *Praxis International*, vol. 11, no. 2, pp. 137–49.

Benhabib, Seyla (1992), *Situating the Self: Gender, Community and Postmodernism in Contemporary Ethics*, Cambridge: Polity Press.

Benhabib, Seyla and Cornell, Drucilla (eds) (1987), *Feminism as Critique: Essays on the Politics of Gender in Late Capitalist Societies*, Cambridge: Polity Press.

Butler, Judith (1991) 'Contingent foundations': feminism and the question of "postmodernism" ', *Praxis International*, vol, 11, no. 2, pp. 150–65.

Dhanda, Meena (1989), 'The first-person perspective, action and social change' in *Philosophy and Social Change*, ed. D. Goel, New Delhi: Ajanta Publications, pp. 247–58.

Dillon, Robin S. (1992), 'Toward a feminist conception of self-respect', *Hypatia*, vol. 7, no. 1, pp. 52–69.

Di Stefano, Christine (1990), 'Dilemmas of difference' in *Feminism/Postmodernism*, ed. Linda J. Nicholson, New York and London: Routledge, pp. 63–82.

Ferguson, Ann (1989), 'A feminist Aspect theory of the self' in *Women, Knowledge and Reality: Explorations in Feminist Philosophy*, ed. Ann Garry and Marilyn Pearsall, Boston: Unwin Hyman, pp. 93–107.

Fraser, Nancy (1991), 'False antithesis: a response to Seyla Benhabib and Judith Butler', *Praxis International*, vol. 11, no. 2, pp. 166–77.

Gibbard, Alan (1989), 'Communities of judgement', *Social Philosophy and Policy*, vol, 7, no. 1, pp. 175–89.

Griffiths, Morwenna and Whitford, Margaret (eds) (1988), *Feminist Perspectives in Philosophy*, London: Macmillan.

Hartsock, Nancy (1990), 'Foucault on power: a theory for women?' in *Feminism/*

Postmodernism, ed. Linda J. Nicholson, New York and London: Routledge, pp. 157–75.

Hekman, Susan (1990), *Gender and Knowledge: Elements of a Postmodern Feminism*, Cambridge: Polity Press.

Lovibond, Sabina (1989), 'Feminism and postmodernism', *New Left Review*, no. 178, pp. 5–28.

Lyotard, Jean-François (1986), *The Postmodern Condition: A Report on Knowledge*, trans. Geoff Bennington and Brian Massumi, Manchester: Manchester University Press.

Meyers, Diana T. (1989), *Self, Society and Personal Choice*, New York: Columbia University Press.

Meyers, Diana T. (1992), 'Personal autonomy and the deconstructed subject? A reply to Hekman', *Hypatia*, vol. 7, no. 1, pp. 124–32.

Nicholson, Linda J. (ed.) (1990), *Feminism/Postmodernism*, New York and London: Routledge.

Oliver, Kelly (1991), 'Fractal politics: how to use "the subject"', *Praxis International*, vol. 11, no. 2, pp. 178–94.

Rorty, Richard (1989), *Contingency, Irony and Solidarity*, Cambridge: Cambridge University Press.

Seller, Anne (1988), 'Realism versus relativism: towards a politically adequate epistemology' in *Feminist Perspectives in Philosophy*, ed. Morwenna Griffiths and Margaret Whitford, London: Macmillan, pp. 169–86.

Skinner, Quentin (1991), 'Who are "we"? Ambiguities of the modern self', *Inquiry*, vol. 34, no. 2, pp. 133–53.

Williams, Bernard (1991), 'Saint-Just's illusion – interpretation and the powers of philosophy', *London Review of Books*, vol. 13, no. 16 (29 August).

Young, Iris Marion (1987), 'Impartiality and the civic public' in *Feminism as Critique*, ed. Seyla Benhabib and Drucilla Cornell, Cambridge: Polity Press, pp. 56–76.

Young, Iris Marion (1990), 'The ideal of community and the politics of difference' in *Feminism/Postmodernism*, ed. Linda J. Nicholson, New York and London: Routledge, pp. 300–23.

17

FEMINISM, POSTMODERNISM AND DIFFERENCE

Susan Strickland

Feminist theorists have presented a critique of the key categories of Enlightenment thought, showing that what has been represented as 'human' or 'universal' has in fact been a reflection of the perspective of dominant white male westerners of the last few centuries; dependent on and exploitative of other genders, classes, races and cultures, whose own perspectives and experiences have been silenced and suppressed. In contrast to the misleading and unattainable ideal of transcendent reason and a view from nowhere, feminists have argued that all knowledge is situated and limited by its positioning; that it reflects our social experience, our understanding of our interests and our values; that objectivity seen in terms of political and personal disengagement and value-neutrality is neither possible nor desirable. Feminists have argued for the need for theorists to be aware of the historical, social and political context from which knowledge-claims are made, and against generalizing from limited experience into the lives of others.

However, there has been criticism of much feminist theory, from black, 'Third World', lesbian and other feminists, and women who don't identify with feminism, who feel that their knowledge and experience has been ignored, marginalized or silenced by a feminism that reflects the perspective of white, western, middle-class women. It has been claimed that feminist theory itself also indulges in false universalism and a lack of critical awareness of its own situatedness. Instead of 'Man' we are now presented with a generic 'Woman', a term, like the universal 'man' or 'human', that hides or denies differences in situation and experience, privilege and power – its content based not on actual commonalities between people, but on the experiences and interests of some who have the position and ability to impose these terms and define what they mean for themselves and others.

Alongside these critiques and partially in response to them, there has been within feminist theory a growing awareness and opposition to essentialism and universalism. Universalized assumptions about human or female nature, or about the common conditions of social life made by many earlier feminist writers, have been exposed and criticized. There is no longer an emphasis on monocausal explanations of the oppression of women, whether these be seen as lying in the spheres of biology, reproduction, child socialization, psychological inclinations or whatever, and there is a distrust of those that posit universal social factors like a nature–culture, or public–private split, or a common sexual division of labour to explain the position of women. Theories like these are seen as falsely generalizing and insufficiently attentive to historical and cultural diversity.

In the light of these criticisms some feminists have recently argued for a feminist postmodernism, or postmodern feminism, arguing variously that feminism should consciously become postmodern, rejecting its humanist/Enlightenment-based presumptions, or that we should somehow combine or integrate the strengths of feminist theory and postmodernism, which are described as complementary, capable of correcting each other's weaknesses.[1] One of the grounds upon which it is argued by feminists such as Linda Nicholson that feminism should become more postmodern, or should incorporate postmodern perspectives, is this concern with the problem of theorizing in the face of difference (see Nicholson 1990: 5; Fraser and Nicholson 1990). I use the term 'postmodern' (as I do 'feminist' and 'Enlightenment') in a very general and inclusive sense, in response, largely, to the very general way the term is used by many of those arguing for a postmodernist feminism – as a pointer to a certain way of theorizing. Whatever the differences between theorists termed by themselves and others as 'postmodern,' there are some common features, in contrast to traditional Enlightenment theory, especially Enlightenment humanism, which is taken as a negative point of reference. Postmodernism rejects humanist appeals to a universal subjectivity or human condition. It points out 'the partial and excluding quality of the supposedly inclusive "we" of much humanist discourse' (Soper 1990a: 11). Instead postmodernism offers a theoretical celebration of 'difference', partiality and multiplicity. It opposes the search for coherence and a desire for 'the right answer'. It suggests instead the continuation of 'conversations' – conversations having no given goal or end, and not aiming at a single representation of reality. Postmodern critique goes beyond the historicist recognition of the inevitable partiality and situatedness of human thought, to an insistence that justification and legitimation are internal to a practice, language game or tradition, with no wider standard to which they are answerable, no certain or external criteria against which to judge their adequacy.

Given that feminists are concerned with the problems of essentialism and universalism, about not making false generalizations from their own perspective, with marginalizing or excluding the perspective of others – it is understandable that postmodernist theory, with its wariness of generalizations that transcend the boundaries of culture and region, with its emphasis on partiality and multiplicity, with its apparent attention to difference, diversity and locale, is an attractive approach to take up or espouse. I want to argue, however, that this recommendation is mistaken – that despite certain similarities between the feminist and postmodernist critiques of Enlightenment thought, despite an apparently common opposition to many of its central categories and methods – feminism and postmodernism have come from very different perspectives, with different reasons, interests and objectives in mounting their critique of Enlightenment thought. The common aims are superficial only – they might use similar terms, but *why* they use them, what they *mean* by difference, location, situatedness, etc., are very different and not compatible. To take up a postmodernist conception of difference, far from assisting feminism to engage seriously with the challenge 'difference' offers and thus revise and transform its theories in the light of it, would be to do just the opposite; a postmodernist acknowledgement of 'difference' is in fact a way of evading it and the threat it poses to dominant ways of seeing the world.

When feminists pointed out that the purportedly universal categories of Enlightenment thought were not universal at all, but based on a false generalization from, and naturalization of, the experience of some men, they pointed out that their experience was very different to that described in these theories. However, they were not *simply* claiming difference; after all, they hardly had to do that – as women they had been defined and constructed as different all along, any inclusion of them in 'universal' categories being largely in name only and in the terms of ruling men. Nor were they simply arguing that their different experience and perspective should be acknowledged and heard, along with the dominant 'male' perspective; nor only that that perspective should be acknowledged as merely applicable to men (of a certain social position). Even if many feminists *began* by making these points, it soon became clear that dominant theories and categories were wrong not simply in universalizing beyond their scope, i.e., that they were partial in the sense of being limited, not universally applicable, but that they were also partial in the sense of being ideological, interested and distorted; in short to a greater or lesser extent false. The different perspective of women could not just be *added*; attempts to add women to liberal or Marxist theory, for instance, showed up gaps, inconsistencies and contradictions in those theories that exposed them as inadequate at the very least, and in need of radical revision and transformation. The assertion of feminist 'difference' was and is, basically a challenge and critique.

And that is how, I think, feminism should regard the claims of 'difference' between women. As I understand it, it is not simply that there are women who want to be recognized as 'different' from white middle-class western women, for when the latter do consider the experiences of others, it *is* often as different to their 'norm', in often stereotypical or racist ways (see for example Amos and Parmar 1984). Nor is the argument simply that different experiences should be heard and acknowledged in 'mainstream' feminist theory, for that says nothing about *how* different experiences are to be evaluated or explained; whether they will be taken seriously and centrally, or be explained away in terms that preserve the truth of the privileged theory, or treated as interesting but largely irrelevant asides (see for example Bhavnani and Coulson 1986). Women critical of, or excluded by, a white/western/middle-class/heterosexual or whatever perspective are not just claiming the space to speak for themselves; they have been speaking out but have not really been listened to. What they are offering is not just their 'difference' to acknowledge, but a challenge. It is not the case that all we have to do is declare our limitedness and situatedness and leave space for others to offer their own equally limited and situated perspectives – I have my (white western middle-class, etc.) view of the world and you have yours. This might be better than making sweeping and false generalizations, but it is not enough, for it basically leaves my perspective intact and unthreatened, though more limited in applicability than before. But if I am really to take others' experiences seriously, as I think black feminist critics and others intend, I have to ask what it means for my understanding of my *own* experience; how the two are related. I have to recognize not just that their experience is different, mediated by and structured by racism for instance, but that mine is too, in connected but different ways, and that my understanding of my own experiences may not be adequate or sufficient; I may indeed be wrong about them. I have to accept that others are offering their different experience at least partly in critique of my understanding of the world, and that I might need to change or revise my theories and understandings in the light of it. And it is this, I think, that a postmodernist acceptance of difference evades, or actually doesn't allow.

In order to respond to the challenge which taking difference seriously requires, it seems to me that we do have to utilize some larger-scale structural analyses of social and economic systems, and employ concepts and general categories that deal with gender, racial oppression and so on.[2] I don't think that use of such categories necessarily has to result in universalistic grand theory. While we should, for instance, respect and pay attention to cultural diversity, this does not mean abandoning all cross-cultural categories. Indeed, taking other cultures seriously often demands paying attention to how they are inserted in the world economic system, how they are related to other cultures, wider political forces, etc. While the local level should never be trivialized or ignored, it has to be seen within the wider context to be understood more adequately. I cannot see how you could understand the position and experiences of, for example, a small-scale coffee grower in Tanzania, or ourselves here (including our consuming of coffee) unless you could situate each within the wider political, social and historical context within which it is located. This is both because what happens at the individual or local level is the way it is because of structural and institutional forces operating at the wider societal or even global level and also because the operation of such structures is often not visible at the local or individual level, or if so only in a limited and distorted way (see Smith 1987a, 1990). One should pay attention to, and respect the 'local', but to do that requires 'going beyond' it, seeing it in relation and context.

The relations that the challenge of difference forces us to confront are not only differences of perspective or location, but also differences of power. As many of those who responded to Barrett and McIntosh's (1985) article 'Ethnocentrism and socialist-feminist theory' pointed out[3] – it is not specifically or only *ethnocentrism* that black feminists are accusing white feminists of, i.e., an (inevitable) perspectivity, which could and should however to some extent be ameliorated by 'extending the field of vision' (Ramazanoglu 1986), but racism, which is a relation of power and privilege. It is not *just* that we happen to be speaking from ethnically specific locations, for instance; for we could (in theory) be of different ethnicity and yet have no differences of power between us, but the charge is that there *are* these relations of power, and in pretending that we are all the same, *or* that we are all merely different, we evade these charges in 'politically reactionary ways' (Bhavnani and Coulson 1986). Concentrating on power means keeping in mind that it is a relation, that our different experiences and perspectives are connected and mutually implicated, part of the same processes that structure our lives in related but different ways depending on how we are situated along various axes of political and economic power.

As Elizabeth Spelman said in the context of feminism in general (Spelman 1988: 164), though I think it applies particularly well to postmodernism and its feminist appropriations – attempts to talk about difference can simply preserve the privilege they were supposed to challenge, as long as there are ways of appearing to talk about difference without really doing so. The postmodernist idea of difference seems to me very 'consumerist'. Someone once compared it to looking round an ethnological museum[4] – I think it is probably more like privileged, affluent westerners looking round a shop in an ethnological museum – where there are all these nice, colourful, aesthetic, ethnic things to buy and have; without any consideration of what they mean ethically or politically; how and why they got there; and especially who exploited whom in the process. Just all this diversity and no doubt. Or else it's a view of the world inspired by tourism[5] – we can be in the Seychelles one week, Tunisia the next, and seemingly never affect or be affected by either. As both Susan Bordo and Donna Haraway have pointed out, the 'View from Nowhere' has been replaced by the equally impossible view from everywhere – which is just as disembodied, just as disclaiming of one's own situatedness, one's own interests, one's own implicatedness in structures of domination and exploitation as the view from nowhere was (see Bordo 1990: 142–5; Haraway 1988). Marginalized groups are told they can celebrate their 'difference', but this difference won't be allowed to make a difference to those who are in power. We can have 'conversations' as though we were all equal in our colourful diversity, but we won't be allowed to challenge anyone, to say they are wrong, to point out the structural supports for their position, or how it relates to ours. We are told to doubt radically ourselves and our subjectivity, our conceptions of the world and our possibilities of understanding and transforming it. This allows those already powerful to maintain their privilege while deflecting the threat of criticism and opposition, dissolving challenges to the legitimacy of their position. By appealing to the partiality and perspectivity of all human thought, while neglecting or forbidding structural analyses of power and inequality, or concentration on connection and relation as well as difference, postmodernism hides the implications of its own situatedness behind a screen of multiple but essentially incomparable, unconnected differences.[6]

Obviously all knowledge is a product of certain specific circumstances – the product of a relation between a knower/knowers in certain particular social and political locations, and the 'world' as it appears to her/them, mediated by the concepts, codes, discourses at her/their disposal. Any knowledge-claims should thus be seen in relation to the context of their production and not in isolation, as though made 'from nowhere'. What I want to challenge however, is the idea that if we give up the myth of the Archimedean point, one neutral all-encompassing framework, or reality 'as it really is' unmediated by our perspectivity, we have to retreat into a scenario of a plurality of closed conceptual schemes or perspectives whose claims can only be understood or assessed from within. Faced with a different framework or perspective employing different concepts and discourses, we cannot, obviously, just employ our criteria and concepts as they are, or were, up until the encounter. As they stand they exclude the different schema and are not able to deal with it (in any satisfactory way). Nor can we just attempt to attach a different way of looking at things to our own so that it 'fits' nicely, without anything having to be altered. And neither can we step outside our own perspective to inhabit theirs, to know 'what it is like' from within, or step right outside any perspective to compare ours and theirs with 'Reality' and see which has 'got it right'. But the crucial phrase above was 'without anything having to be altered'. If we just want to preserve our perspective intact, without challenge or revision, then a picture of us all separated off into closed, static, self-centred 'circles' is perhaps attractive. But I would argue that, on the contrary, perspectives are open, changing and mutually informing and that we can understand, compare and judge over differences of perspective, from where we are situated, if we are prepared to risk or test our understandings in the process. Understanding can occur in encounter with others in response to the challenge their different experiences and understandings offer us, if we are prepared to question our own self-understandings in the light of theirs and revise them if need be. Understanding across difference involves a reflexive and dialectical interplay of perspectives.[7] Other perspectives inform me not only about them and their situation, but of me and mine; my now altered self-understanding allows new understanding of others which modifies my understandings further, and so on, in a continuous process of revision and expansion.

Such encounters are often characterized as 'dialogues', which does capture the to-and-fro nature I have in mind quite nicely. However, the term reminds me of 'conversation' which seems far too easy and dismissive of power inequalities. The process I have in mind is generally far more uncomfortable, a product of conflict and tension,[8] more like an argument where you go away angry and hurt and defensive of your own point of view, but can't forget theirs, which you keep mulling over and in the process, gradually altering your own point of view, so that at the next encounter, it has changed in interaction with theirs and so on. It is thus a slow and dialectical process but without closure or a final stability. My approach differs therefore from those who argue for consensus and does not necessarily depend on agreement.

To conclude, it seems to me that difference can only be taken seriously, in a way that matters, if one's motives and stance are definitely not postmodern in inspiration. A postmodernist feminism will do nothing to address the challenge black feminists and others have levelled against white, middle-class feminists; rather it will serve to evade its implications behind an apparent acknowledgement of difference – 'difference' serving here merely to imply diversity, rather than exposing privilege and challenging distortions. The challenge of 'difference' is not just that it opposes 'sameness' (as a postmodern conception would allow) but that it exposes relations that those in dominant positions would rather not acknowledge or have to deal with.

Marnia Lazreg argues that:

> The point is neither to subsume other women under one's own experience, nor to uphold a separate truth for them ... As it now stands, difference is seen as mere division. The danger of this undeveloped view lies in its verging on indifference.[9]

She warns that 'academic feminism cannot be allowed to hide behind a deconstructionist approach to legitimate its misapprehension of difference' nor 'be allowed to seek refuge in a Foucauldian[10] concept of power' when 'the actual instrumentality of power that some women (for example academic women) exercise over other women (such as third world women) is neglected' (Lazreg 1990: 338).

NOTES

1 See for example Nicholson (1990), Fraser and Nicholson (1990), Weedon (1987) and Hekman (1990b). Weedon argues specifically for a 'poststructuralist' feminism, but the area of theory she refers to is roughly the same as that of some who describe a 'postmodern' feminism.

2 See Lovibond (1989) for a similar point. Bordo (1990) argues for the necessity of the concept of gender. Fraser and Nicholson (1990: 34), in endorsing a postmodern approach, argue that it should not and need not forswear 'large historical narratives or analysis of macrostructures'. They say this after showing that Lyotard's conception of social criticism is inadequate as it *does* rule out large historical narrative and historically situated social theory 'which feminists rightly regard as indispensable'. I agree with this last point, but am more doubtful about the first.

3 See Ramazanoglu (1986), Kazi (1986) and Bhavnani and Coulson (1986).

4 Seyla Benhabib likens Lyotard's stance, that of an observer 'gazing in wonderment at the variety of discursive species' (Lyotard quoted in Benhabib 1990: 129) to that of the standpoint of the curator of an ethnological museum.

5 Elspeth Probyn (in Nicholson 1990) also describes an attitude toward difference suggested by the experience of tourism 'where diversity is experienced in its most superficial manifestations' (Fraser and Nicholson 1990: 14).

6 Harding (1990: 89) makes a distinction between difference as diversity and differences due to structures of domination, and argues that we need theories of knowledge that recognize this difference.

7 See Harding (1991) for a discussion of reflexivity. Hans Georg Gadamer (1975) provides, I think, a very promising account of understanding across differences of time and perspective.

8 Jennifer Ring (1991) argues for a minimalist dialectics (one 'agnostic' about 'origins and ends') which emphasizes tension, and which, rather than minimizing conflict, recognizes it as a 'central and unavoidable part of self-awareness and change' (33).

9 Lazreg also argues that without any basis for 'understanding the relationship between the varieties of modes of being different in the world [, d]ifference becomes essentialized'. See Lazreg (1990: 339).

10 See Hartsock (1990: esp. 165, 167); Smith (1990: 70) for criticisms of a Foucauldian conception of power – specifically that he writes from the perspective of a 'dominator', such that systematically unequal relations of power tend to vanish from his account, along with subjects or agents, so that power becomes reified and phenomena are described in the passive voice as though they just occurred by 'themselves' and not as the result of the actions of specific people in specific structural locations.

REFERENCES

Allen, Jeffner and Young, Iris Marion (eds) (1989), *The Thinking Muse: Feminism and Modern French Philosophy*, Bloomington: Indiana University Press.

Amos, Valerie and Parmar, Pratibha (1984), 'Challenging imperial feminism', *Feminist Review*, no. 17, pp. 3–19.

Barrett, Michèle (1987), 'The concept of difference', *Feminist Review*, no. 26, pp. 29–41.

Barrett, Michèle and McIntosh, Mary (1985), 'Ethnocentrism and socialist-feminist theory', *Feminist Review*, no. 20, pp. 23–47.

Benhabib, Seyla (1990), 'Epistemologies of postmodernism: a rejoinder to Jean-François Lyotard' in *Feminism/Postmodernism*, ed. Linda J. Nicholson, New York and London: Routledge, pp. 107–30.

Bernstein, Richard (1983), *Beyond Objectivism and Relativism*, Oxford: Blackwell.

Bhavnani, Kum-Kum and Coulson, Margaret (1986), 'Transforming socialist feminism: the challenge of racism', *Feminist Review*, no. 23, pp. 81–92.

Bordo, Susan (1990), 'Feminism, postmodernism and gender-scepticism' in *Feminism/Postmodernism*, ed. Linda J. Nicholson, New York and London: Routledge, pp. 133–56.

Childers, Mary and Hooks, Bell (1990), 'A conversation about race and class' in *Conflicts in Feminism*, ed. Marianne Hirsch and Evelyn Fox Keller, New York and London: Routledge, pp. 60–81.

Coole, Diana (forthcoming 1994), 'Master narratives and feminist subversions' in *The Politics of Modernity*, ed. Irving Velody and James Good, Cambridge: Cambridge University Press.

Di Stefano, Christine (1990), 'Dilemmas of difference: feminism, modernity and postmodernism' in *Feminism/Postmodernism*, ed. Linda J. Nicholson, New York and London: Routledge, p. 63–82.

Flax, Jane (1987), 'Postmodernism and gender relations in feminist theory', *Signs*, vol. 12, no. 4, pp. 621–43.

Flax, Jane (1988), 'Reply to Daryl McGowan Tress: "Comment on Flax's postmodernism and gender relations in feminist theory" ', *Signs*, vol. 14, no. 1, pp. 201–3.

Flax, Jane (1990), *Thinking Fragments: Psychoanalysis, Feminism and Postmodernism in the Contemporary West*, Berkeley: University of California Press.

Fraser, Nancy (1989), *Unruly Practices: Power, Discourse and Gender in Contemporary Social Theory*, Minneapolis: University of Minnesota Press.

Fraser, Nancy and Nicholson, Linda J. (1990), 'Social criticism without philosophy: an encounter between feminism and postmodernism' in *Feminism/Postmodernism*, ed. Linda J. Nicholson, New York and London: Routledge, p. 19–38.

Gadamer, Hans Georg (1975), *Truth and Method*, London: Sheed and Ward.

Haraway, Donna (1988), 'Situated knowledges: the science question in feminism and the privileges of partial perspective', *Feminist Studies*, vol. 14, no. 3, pp. 581–90.

Harding, Sandra (1986), 'The instability of the analytical categories of feminist theory', *Signs*, vol. 11, no. 4, pp. 645–64.

Harding, Sandra (1990), 'Feminism, science and the anti-Enlightenment critiques' in *Feminism/Postmodernism*, ed. Linda J. Nicholson, New York and London: Routledge, pp. 83–106.

Harding, Sandra (1991), *Whose Science? Whose Knowledge? Thinking from Women's Lives*, Milton Keynes: Open University Press.

Hartsock, Nancy (1990), 'Foucault on power: a theory for women?' in *Feminism/Postmodernism*, ed. Linda J. Nicholson, New York and London: Routledge, pp. 157–75.

Hawkesworth, Mary (1989), 'Knowers, knowing, known: feminist theory and claims of truth', *Signs*, vol. 14, no. 3, pp. 533–57.

Hawkesworth, Mary (1990), 'Reply to Hekman's comment on "Knowers, knowing, known: feminist theory and claims of truth" ', *Signs*, vol. 15, no. 2, pp. 420–3.

Hekman, Susan (1990a), 'Comment on Hawkesworth's "Knowers, knowing, known: feminist theory and claims of truth" ', *Signs*, vol. 15, no. 2, pp. 417–19.

Hekman, Susan (1990b), *Gender and Knowledge: Elements of a Postmodern Feminism*, Cambridge: Polity Press.

Hill Collins, Patricia (1990), *Black Feminist Thought: Knowledge, Consciousness and the Politics of Empowerment*, London: Unwin Hyman.

Hoy, David Cousins (1978), *The Critical Circle – Literature, History and Philosophical Hermeneutics*, Berkeley: University of California Press.

Kazi, Harmida (1986), 'The beginning of a debate long due: some observations on "ethnocentrism" and socialist-feminist theory', *Feminist Review*, no. 22, pp. 87–91.

Kintz, Linda (1989), 'In-different criticism: the deconstructive parole' in *The Thinking Muse: Feminism and Modern French Philosophy*, ed. Jeffner Allen and Iris Marion Young, Bloomington: Indiana University Press, pp. 113–35.

Lazreg, Marnia (1990), 'Feminism and difference: the perils of writing as a woman on women in Algeria' in *Conflicts in Feminism*, ed. Marianne Hirsch and Evelyn Fox Keller, New York and London: Routledge, pp. 326–48.

Lees, Sue (1986), 'Sex, race and culture: feminism and the limits of cultural pluralism', *Feminist Review*, no. 22, pp. 92–102.

Lovibond, Sabina (1989), 'Feminism and postmodernism' in *New Left Review*, no. 178, pp. 5–28.

Mangena, Oshadi (1991), 'Against fragmentation: the need for holism', *Journal of Gender Studies*, vol. 1, no. 1, pp. 3–12.

Narayan, Uma (1988), 'Working together across difference: some considerations on emotions and political practice', *Hypatia*, vol. 3, no. 2, pp. 31–47.

Nicholson, Linda J. (ed.) (1990), 'Introduction' in *Feminism/Postmodernism*, ed. Linda J. Nicholson, New York and London: Routledge, pp. 1–16.

Ramazanoglu, Caroline (1986), 'Ethnocentrism and socialist-feminist theory: a response to Barrett and McIntosh', *Feminist Review*, no. 22, pp. 83–6.

Ring, Jennifer (1991), *Modern Political Theory and Contemporary Feminism: A Dialectical Analysis*, Albany: SUNY Press.

Smith, Dorothy E. (1987a), *The Everyday World as Problematic – A Feminist Sociology*, Toronto: University of Toronto Press.

Smith, Dorothy E. (1987b), 'Women's perspective as a radical critique of sociology' in *Feminism and Methodology*, ed. Sandra Harding, Milton Keynes: Open University Press, pp. 84–96.

Smith, Dorothy E. (1990), *The Conceptual Practices of Power: A Feminist Sociology of Knowledge*, Toronto: University of Toronto Press.

Soper, Kate (1986), *Humanism and Anti-Humanism*, London: Hutchinson.

Soper, Kate (1990a), 'Feminism, humanism and postmodernism', *Radical Philosophy*, no. 55, pp. 11–17.

Soper, Kate (1990b), *Troubled Pleasures: Writings on Politics, Gender and Hedonism*, London: Verso.

Spelman, Elizabeth V. (1988), *Inessential Woman: Problems of Exclusion in Feminist Thought*, Boston: Beacon Press.

Weedon, Chris (1987), *Feminist Practice and Poststructuralist Theory*, Oxford: Blackwell.

Yeatman, Anna (1990), 'A feminist theory of social differentiation' in *Feminist/Postmodernism*, ed. Linda J. Nicholson, New York and London: Routledge, pp. 281–99.

18

AGAINST FRAGMENTATION
The need for holism
Oshadi Mangena

I

For a long time feminist science has levelled criticism against the male-defined concept of science. The latter made central the concept of objectivity as the criterion for the formulation and validation of knowledge. The feminist critique has been that objectivity as defined and applied in the male-defined scientific paradigm is one-sided, unrepresentative of the wholeness of human experience and fragmentative because it overlooks the fact of difference in human experience.

One point is that, whereas human experience is the ground for knowledge, human experience is different for different people because it is situational in at least two senses. The first sense involves the fact that human beings live in place and time; their experience is limited to place and time. Furthermore, in society there is a division of labour among individuals as well as groups. Therefore, individuals and groups occupy different positions and roles, some of which are based upon socially determined and established categories (Harding and Hintikka 1983; Mangena 1991). Related to the latter is the fact that men and women in society do not interact with nature in a similar manner. The situational character of human experience therefore implies that there may be similarities and differences as well as contradictions in the perceptions and experience of different human beings.

At the same time however, human experience is a whole in the sense that it pertains to the realm of Being (Existence) (Ramose 1986). This means that whether we are aware or know of other forms of experience or not, it does not follow that such experiences do not exist. Human experience is a whole also in the sense that that which is perceived is simultaneously experienced as a whole and raw (unmediated). However, there is a gap between the simultaneous and raw character of experience and its expression through language as the main medium of expression. This gap implies that in fact expression through language is only a *representation* of experience; it is not an expression of experience in its immediate and raw state, as it were. Further, language represents human experience in fragmented sequences. This is a human limitation which opens the way for all other limitations (Foucault 1970; Ramose 1983). An important point here is that inasmuch as that which is perceived is a whole, wholeness must take precedence over fragmentation as the goal of representation (Bohm 1971; Ramose 1983). The situational character of human experience has the potential to transcend situational limitations. In this connection, a holycyclic pattern of representation – understood here as paying attention to 'the relationship between the individual's outgoing movements and the incoming sensations' so as not to see objects 'as isolated entities' but with interrelatedness – is required (Ramose 1983: 233–41; Bohm 1971: 27–30).

II

Intellectual faculty, which is the property of all human beings, is the instrument by which humans formulate knowledge upon reflection on experience. Some authors refer to such natural knowledge as 'truth', in this way drawing a distinction between natural knowledge and scientific knowledge. Scientific knowledge is knowledge mediated by abstraction and representation (Acker *et al.* 1983 is an example here). Natural knowledge or truth is characteristic of all human situations. It means that, at the fundamental or primary level of things, the skilled scientific investigator is on an equal level with the investigated with regard to possession of natural knowledge. At the same time, both the investigator and the respondent may in their perception and reflection on daily experience be influenced also by accumulated indigenous mediated knowledge of their respective cultural backgrounds.

At the level of reflective knowledge, western scientific rationality is not the only rationality prevailing. Further, it is not necessarily superior to other forms of rationality developed in relation to the situational experiences of other peoples of the world. Because experience is space- and time-bound, rationality is also conditioned by this. It is precisely this that gives rise to various forms of rationality which issue in different translations and allocations of meaning to experience. Such differences hardly allow for claims of 'superior' or 'inferior' rationality, sometimes implied by suggestions that women (in the so-called Third World countries) have to be helped, that women have internalized oppression and exploitation and that women remain unaware and therefore require animators from the North.

This has consequences for the social scientific investigation of the behaviour of other people. At the level of the fundamental Subject–Object structure (or the researcher and respondent) we have in a fundamental sense 'equals' who each experience the other from the point of view of their own situational experience and accumulated indigenous knowledge. This is to say that at all times there is a real dichotomy at the fundamental level of the Subject–Object structure as the one and the other, each being the object of the experience of the other (Ramose 1983).

Despite such equality in difference between the investigator and the investigated concerning experience and knowledge, in the male-defined concept of science the investigator has the exclusive right to objectification of knowledge. His right is based on the principle that the investigator possesses scientific skill. The researched who does not possess such skill is said to be capable of colouring knowledge with subjective views, his own idiosyncrasies. Yet in reality, in the male-defined idea of science, as we have seen, 'objective knowledge' is defined and investigated by the subject who is simultaneously the subject and object of experience. As the former, the investigator inevitably reflects subjective idiosyncrasies in 'objective knowledge', thereby vitiating the claim to complete objectivity. Accordingly, objectivity is not completely obtainable; objectivity is always coloured by subjectivity. Knowledge obtained through objectivity as defined and applied in the male-defined scientific paradigm is therefore knowledge with tainted objectivity. Within this paradigm the respondent is made redundant in the objectification of knowledge. The very reduction and relegation of the respondent to redundancy implies that the resulting knowledge is *partial* knowledge formulated upon the experience of the investigator as seen by himself. It is this that we refer to as a fragmentative and reductive approach to human knowledge. On the part of the respondent in particular such knowledge presents abstract universality, an assumption that all human beings share a common universal experience. This is already a failed attempt to reduce everything to the level of the same. Thus Harding and Hintikka appositely argue that when such knowledge is used for social organization it fosters oppression on the part of those whose experiences and knowledge were subordinated in the process of analysis (Harding and Hintikka 1983).

It is important to note that we speak here of subordination rather than experience being 'left out of analysis' as we are usually told (for example Harding and Hintikka 1983). To say that female experience has been left out of analysis in mainstream male science is to overlook the interrelatedness of experience and to introduce fragmentation between male and female experience in society. This then opens the way for women also to be investigated through fragmentative approaches which, as if to turn the tables 'upside down', now formulate knowledge from the exclusive experiences of women as seen by women, an approach that feminist science as the quest for wholeness sought to correct.

It should be emphasized that once women said that their experiences were 'left out of analysis', that this causes oppression of women in society and that therefore it was necessary to bring female experience into the mainstream of analysis, they were by this recognizing the interrelatedness and interconnectedness of male and female experience in society and pleading or arguing for a holistic approach as a corrective. In particular women as well as indigenous peoples who were colonized by the Europeans have suffered oppression and exploitation under such fragmentation and reduction, which results in abstract universality (Harding and Hintikka 1983; Ramose 1986). The reality of women as well as that of indigenous people was subordinated to be incorporated into the reality of men and colonizers for their exploitation and oppression. It is clear that the corrective to the male idea of science is a holistic orientation to the construction of scientific knowledge. Along this path, *concrete universality* will emerge as the veritable substitute for abstract universality (the meaning of the term will emerge below). It was therefore correct that feminist science took issue with the fragmentative male idea of science.

III

Feminists argued for the redefinition of the male idea of objectivity as a main principle of science. In this connection, various suggestions deriving from different scientific standpoints were posited, all amounting to the deconstruction and reconstruction of the Subject–Object epistemology in which the respondent remains a passive participant at the level of objectification of knowledge. The common argument among such suggestions was the very sense that objectivity is not completely accessible because objectivity as 'something thrown over there' takes the subject to define it. Therefore, objectivity will always be coloured by some amount of subjectivity (Acker *et al.* 1973; Mies 1979; Harding 1986). Mies went further, to argue appositely that in fact the idea of objectivity as defined in male science is fragmentative because it presents the human mind functioning separately from the physical body and emotions. Thus the investigator is asked to suppress emotional feeling in order to be objective. According to Mies, knowledge obtained in that manner is *scientistic* rather than being *scientific* (Mies 1979). From this premise, injecting also a socio-psychological element, Mies argued that the definition of objectivity in the male idea of science was formulated upon the exclusive experiences of the powerful groups in society. It sets out to serve such groups to the subordination of the powerless. Women, as those among the oppressed groups in society, were to turn their instruments of science to the service of their own lot. Female social scientists would then use their skill to facilitate knowledge-formulation from the experiences of women as those 'below', the oppressed and exploited social group. In this context, according to Mies, the investigator adopts *partial identity* with the respondents. This is to say that the investigator is to see herself as part of the investigated group while exercising caution so that she can still maintain some amount of objectivity. At the level of objectification of knowledge, the investigator then stands in a relatively equal position and role with the investigated. She puts her own experiences of the situation of the researched into analysis together *with those* of the researched. She objectifies knowledge *together with* her respondents, her duty being merely to impart social knowledge to facilitate more awareness. The researcher and the researched must be able to find themselves in the end results. Knowledge obtained in this manner must serve both, Mies argues.

Acker was to carry this argument further, adding to it the idea of the *Subject–Subject approach* as a corrective to the male-defined *Subject–Object approach*. The Subject–Subject structure, according to Acker, requires the respondent to be treated as one who holds 'truth'. Such knowledge must be recognized by the researcher. For this reason, the respondent is elevated to the level of the researcher so that they can together objectify knowledge as relatively equal persons. The researcher and the researched then stand in a dialectical relationship to learn from each other. Again, the duty of the investigator here is to impart social theory in order to *deepen* awareness and to make explicit the implicit in the 'truth' that the investigated holds. This is to say that, according to Acker, the investigator tries by all means to formulate knowledge from the 'truth' that the respondent imparts rather than from the investigator's own perceptions, or from some set of abstract ideas which preceded the research. The investigator recognizes that the research is taking place in the situation of the respondent (Acker *et al.* 1993). In this way research shall not be oppressive and exploitative, according to Acker. The knowledge goes to facilitate the struggle waged by the disadvantaged. It may not be used to maintain the *status quo*.

Concurring with the above ideas, Harding suggests that in fact the Subject–Subject approach implies a holistic approach to knowledge in the sense that both subjects and objects of experience are together involved in the process of formulating human knowledge from their distinct but interrelated situational experiences. They will both benefit equally from such knowledge. Accordingly, knowledge can no more be policed (Harding 1986).

It was upon such ideas that feminists adopted Participatory Research Method for field-work. This was in an attempt to achieve a more humanly representative and less oppressive knowledge. However, especially at the level of practice, some residual fragmentation remains in feminist science. This is bound to affect the final product, theory.

IV

Although there is ontological and epistemological justification, for instance for Mies's idea of *conscious partiality*, it is none the less evident that the definition of the male as only part of the problem and the consequent *exclusion* of the male in the search for a solution undermines the feminist quest for liberative holistic scientific knowledge.

Experience has shown that under the feminist Subject–Subject approach and the exercise of conscious partiality, women are often investigated in isolation, that is to say, to the exclusion of males. Knowledge claimed from such patterns of enquiry is then used to facilitate antagonistic struggles with men most of whom have hardly developed enough consciousness to realize that women are in fact dialectically poor, oppressed and exploited in their interaction as well as in relations with men in social production. On the other hand, women themselves do not really acquire a true consciousness in terms of their *dialectical* relationship to men. For instance, in Africa class obviously forms a relationship with race and sex as categories in social organization. This means that men also undergo extreme exploitation and oppression internally and internationally. The exploitation and oppression of women is intertwined with that of men. Such relations must be seen in their interrelatedness. Some subtleties become explicit only when *the situation is exposed as a whole* by drawing everyone into the process of objectification, that is, men and women. Men are to be brought into the same process of participatory research to objectify their own situational experience in relation to women in society, so that the resulting theories will reflect *interrelated* situational experience objectified by both men and women. It is true that men and women are subjected to situational experience which is systematically different. But the reality of the underlying processes and their causal tendencies can be perceived and represented without distortion or inversion only when we consider the holistic nature of every process of interaction which we subject to investigation. It means that we cannot examine the experience of women in society without taking into account the fact of their interconnectedness with men.

African women, in particular, are often found speaking of themselves in terms which locate them in the context of families as integral parts rather than independent individuals. This is in contrast to western feminists, as Black correctly observes (Black and Baker 1981; see also Brunklaus 1990). It shows that African women do not themselves perceive gender relations in fragmentative terms, and this is a correct perception. African women will almost always search for an adequate holistic epistemology by which they can understand their true experience. It is now well-known that the Association of African Women for Research and Development (AAWORD) is already on this path. As those who come from the background of holism, African women are best placed in the feminist search for holism, in which men and women can be facilitated together to objectify their experience as an integrated wholeness. Research will itself benefit from this. Chaachii mentions that our suggestion here was an opinion also held in India by some women (Chaachii 1990).

We support Acker's suggestion that the investigator must try to formulate knowledge from *truth* constituted by both the investigated and the investigator. Once specific situations are attended to in this way, it will become clear that gender interrelates within people's experience to form very *specific wholes*. The universalization of the woman question cannot be based on a theory of women's nature (or human nature) founded on abstract universality. That is, forms of feminist thinking which explain female subjugation purely from the point of view of biology, or from the idea that all human societies transform biology into culture by effecting a common sex-gender system, cannot be accepted. Various human societies in the world did not historically understand nature and human life in a similar manner. The fact of difference is a characteristic of human beings proper. In such difference, we have a veritable manifestation of reality. A reality which is specific and whole. The specificity therefore matters; it is integral to the construction of the whole. Consequently gender oppression, for example, is very different in different situations. It is not the case that we all have a common experience as a consequence of our gender with differences of race, class and nationality simply added on. We are therefore aiming for an understanding of the whole here which remains true to such specificities. We are not aiming for a falsifying universalism.

There is one approach to such differences, however, which is consciously and deliberately opposed to the idea of holism as here defined and described. We have in mind in particular 'postmodernist feminism' which argues that the fact of difference in experience makes it impossible to bring together perspectives to form a coherent whole. Once male and female experience is different, for example, it is not possible to bring such experience together to form a whole picture. On the contrary, so the argument goes, we are to acknowledge that there is a multiplicity of different perspectives, conflicting and contradictory. The different experiences can never challenge or mutually inform each other. They simply coexist (Mangena 1991). In this, any understanding of a wholeness is ruled out.

In contrast the thesis I am defending insists that wholeness lies behind fragmentation, and insists that this be sustained both in the construction of social theory and in the translation of such a theory into practice. That is, we are required to represent reality as an integrated whole, albeit comprising distinct specificities. Accordingly the local or indigenous condition of women must be linked dialectically to the global condition of women. The South becomes dialectically poor, oppressed and exploited in its relation to the North. Similarly, the local condition of women must be seen in terms of interaction and dialectical relations with men. On that basis men will be seen not only as part of the problem but also as part of the solution to the fundamental, though less complex, question of authentic and integral human liberation. The scientific claims based on this approach would be universally valid in the sense that they would refer to a multiplicity of concrete experience, although in general terms. That is, we need to recognize that it is precisely the specifics which elucidate the general meaning of the universal elements and it is not for the specific form of existence to be relegated to the universal. The latter is abstract universality. Human experience is a potentially concrete universality and scientific claims to universality must take cognizance of this.

REFERENCES

Acker, J., Barry, K. and Essenveld, J. (1983), 'Objectivity and truth: problems in doing feminist research', *Women's Studies International Forum*, vol. 6, no. 4.

Black, N. and Baker, A. (1981), *Women and World Change*, London: Sage Publications.

Bohm, D. (1971), 'Fragmentation in science and society', in *The Social Impact of Modern Biology*, ed. W. Fuller, London: Routledge and Kegan Paul.

Brunklaus, Patricia (1990), ' "To stay well with the husband": Een feministisch-antropologisch onderzoek naar het verzet van plattelandsvrouwen in Zimbabwe tegen machtsongelijkheid in arbeid en huwelijk', Doctoral diss., Anthropological-Sociological Centre, University of Amsterdam.

Chaachii, A. (1990), 'Experiences with the South-Asian Workshop on Women and Development in Bangladesh in 1986', Seminar-Lecture given at the Institute of Development Research Amsterdam (INDRA), 22 October.

Foucault, M. (1970), *The Order of Things*, ed. R. D. Laing, London: Tavistock.

Gyekye, K. (1987), *The Akan Conceptual Scheme*, Cambridge: Cambridge University Press.

Harding, S. (1986), *The Science Question in Feminism*, Ithaca and London: Cornell University Press.

Harding, S. and Hintikka, M. B. (1983), *Discovering Reality: Feminist Perspectives on Epistemology, Metaphysics, Methodology, and Philosophy of Science*, Dordrecht: Reidel.

Lukács, G. (1980), *The Ontology of Social Being vol. III: Labour*, London: Merlin Press.

Mangena, O. (1986), 'Veranderende arbeidsverhoudingen in Zuid Afrika', *Antropologische Verkeningen*, special issue on 'Feministische Antropologie', vol. 5, no. 2 (June).

Mangena, O. (1991), 'Against fragmentation: the need for holism', *Journal for Gender Studies*, vol. 1, no. 1, pp. 3–12.

Mies, M. (1979), *Towards a Methodology of Women's Studies*, occasional paper, The Hague: Institute of Social Studies.

Ramose, M. B. (1983), 'The legalistic character of power in international relations: a philosophical essay on the ethics of defence in the nuclear age', unpublished Ph.D. dissertation, Faculty of Philosophy, Catholic University of Leuven.

Ramose, M. B. (1986), 'A history denied: African philosophy and social organization' in *The Self Evidence of Science* Series on Alternative Development Discussion paper no. 2, University of Amsterdam, Department of International Relations and International Law.

BIBLIOGRAPHY

Feminist philosophers working in epistemology have to work on (at least) three fronts: mainstream philosophy, feminist philosophy and the variety of feminist theories and constituencies. To take the smallest of these three areas: ten years ago, it would have been possible to produce a more or less comprehensive bibliography of work in feminist philosophy in English; today such a bibliography might be of book-length proportions. What we have tried to do in the brief bibliography below is to indicate the main theoretical reference points of the contributors to debates in feminist epistemology. We have also included feminist theory which has been of particular significance.

We have not included references to mainstream philosophy in the bibliography. However, there are several philosophers whose work has been particularly influential for feminists working in epistemology. In the Anglo-Saxon world, these are W. V. O. Quine (see *From a Logical Point of View* (1953) and *Ontological Relativity and Other Essays* (1969)), Richard Rorty (see *Philosophy and the Mirror of Nature* (1980)), and to a lesser extent Wittgenstein. Thomas Kuhn's *The Structure of Scientific Revolutions* (first published 1962) has also played a significant role, though he does not figure largely in the present collection. In the Continental tradition, all the thinkers associated with the critique of Enlightenment paradigms – Derrida, Lyotard, Lacan and Foucault in French, Adorno, Habermas and Gadamer in German – have been influential. The appropriation of Foucault has been particularly noticeable: his work on the interconnections between knowledge, truth and power had immediate resonances for feminism.

In addition, there is non-philosophical work which has had a direct impact on thinking about epistemology. There are so many strands here that it is difficult to disentangle them. It is essential to mention, however, the challenges that feminism itself has faced from groups who saw feminism in turn as hegemonic and dominant. We have included below references to some of the feminist literature on 'difference', but the challenge is much broader, and concerns the position of feminism in relation to other global and international issues such as postcolonialism. The relevance of epistemological issues to so many areas of thought means that the epistemologist, feminist or otherwise, can no longer 'stay at home'.

Addelson, Kathryn Pyne (1991), 'Making knowledge' in *Engendering Knowledge: Feminists in Academe*, ed. Ellen Messer Davidoff and Joan E. Hartmann, Knoxville, TE: University of Tennessee Press.

Alcoff, Linda (1988), 'Cultural feminism versus post-structuralism: the identity crisis in feminist theory', *Signs*, vol. 13, no. 3, pp. 405–36.

Alcoff, Linda (forthcoming), 'How is epistemology possible?' in *Theory, Power, and Human Emancipation: Dimensions of Radical Philosophy*, ed. Roger Gottlieb, Philadelphia: Temple University Press.

Alcoff, Linda and Potter, Elizabeth (eds) (1993), *Feminist Epistemologies*, London and New York: Routledge.

Antony, Louise M. and Witt, Charlotte (eds) (1993), *A Mind of One's Own: Feminist Essays on Reason and Objectivity*, Boulder, CO: Westview Press.

Barrett, Michèle (1987), 'The concept of difference', *Feminist Review*, no. 26, pp. 29–41.

Barrett, Michèle (1992), *The Politics of Truth: From Marx to Foucault*, Oxford/ Cambridge: Polity Press.

Barrett, Michèle and McIntosh, Mary (1985), 'Ethnocentrism and socialist-feminist theory', *Feminist Review*, no. 20, pp. 23–47.

Belenky, Mary Field, Clinchy, Blythe McGiven, Goldberger, Nancy Rule and Tarule, Jill Mattuck (eds) (1986), *Women's Ways of Knowing: The Development of Self, Voice and Mind*, New York: Basic Books.

Bhavnani, Kum-Kum and Coulson, Margaret (1986), 'Transforming socialist-feminism: the challenge of racism', *Feminist Review*, no. 23, pp. 81–92.

Bleier, Ruth (1984), *Science and Gender*, New York: Pergamon Press.

Bordo, Susan R. (1987), *The Flight to Objectivity: Essays on Cartesianism and Culture*, Albany, NY: SUNY Press.

Caine, Barbara, Grosz, E. A. and Delepervanche, Marie (eds) (1988), *Crossing Boundaries: Feminism and the Critique of Knowledges*, Sydney: Allen and Unwin.

Code, Lorraine (1981), 'Is the sex of the knower epistemologically significant?' *Metaphilosophy*, vol. 12, nos. 3–4 (July–October), pp. 267–76.

Code, Lorraine (1987), *Epistemic Responsibility*, Hanover, NH: University Press of New England.

Code, Lorraine (1988a), 'Credibility: a double standard' in *Feminist Perspectives: Philosophical Essays on Method and Morals*, ed. Lorraine Code, Sheila Mullett and Christine Overall, Toronto: Toronto University Press, pp. 64–88.

Code, Lorraine (1988b), 'Experience, knowledge and responsibility' in *Feminist Perspectives in Philosophy*, ed. Morwenna Griffiths and Margaret Whitford, London: Macmillan, pp. 187–204.

Code, Lorraine (1991), *What Can She Know? Feminist Theory and the Construction of Knowledge*, Ithaca and London: Cornell University Press.

Code, Lorraine, Mullett, Sheila and Overall, Christine (eds) (1988), *Feminist Perspectives: Philosophical Essays on Method and Morals*, Toronto: University of Toronto Press.

Collins, Patricia Hill (1990), *Black Feminist Thought: Knowledge, Consciousness and the Politics of Empowerment*, London: Unwin Hyman.

Corradi Fiumara, Gemma (1990), *The Other Side of Language: A Philosophy of Listening*, London: Routledge.

Corradi Fiumara, Gemma (1992), *The Symbolic Function: Psychoanalysis and the Philosophy of Language*, Oxford: Blackwell.

De Lauretis, Teresa (1984), *Alice Doesn't: Feminism, Semiotics, Cinema*, London: Macmillan.

De Lauretis, Teresa (1987), *Technologies of Gender: Essays on Theory: Film and Fiction*, Bloomington: Indiana University Press.

Duran, Jane (1991), *Toward a Feminist Epistemology*, Savage, MD: Rowman and Littlefield.

Feminist Review, no. 17 (1984), 'Many voices, one chant: black feminist perspectives'.

Flax, Jane (1989), 'Postmodernism and gender relations in feminist theory' in *Feminist Theory in Practice and Process*, ed. Micheline R. Malson, Jean F. O'Barr, Sarah Westphal-Wihl and Mary Wyer, Chicago and London: University of Chicago Press, pp. 51–73.

Flax, Jane (1990), *Thinking Fragments: Psychoanalysis, Feminism and Postmodernism in the Contemporary West*, Berkeley: University of California Press.

Fraser, Nancy (1989), *Unruly Practices: Power, Discourse and Gender in Contemporary Social Theory*, Cambridge: Polity Press.

Garry, Ann and Pearsall, Marilyn (eds) (1989), *Women, Knowledge and Reality: Explorations in Feminist Philosophy*, Boston: Unwin Hyman.

Gergen, Mary McCanney (ed.) (1988), *Feminist Thought and the Structure of Knowledge*, New York and London: New York University Press.

Grant, Judith (1987), 'I feel, therefore I am: a critique of female experience as the basis for a feminist epistemology', *Women and Politics*, vol. 7, no. 3, special issue on feminism and epistemology, pp. 99–114.

Griffiths, Morwenna and Whitford, Margaret (eds) (1988), *Feminist Perspectives in Philosophy*, London: Macmillan and Bloomington: Indiana University Press.

Grimshaw, Jean (1986), *Feminist Philosophers: Women's Perspectives on Philosophical Traditions*, Brighton: Wheatsheaf.

Gunew, Sneja (ed.) (1990a), *Feminist Knowledge: Critique and Construct*, London: Routledge.

Gunew, Sneja (ed.) (1990b), *A Reader in Feminist Knowledge*, London: Routledge.

Halberg, Margareta (1989), 'Feminist epistemology: an impossible project', *Radical Philosophy*, no. 53, pp. 3–7.

Haraway, Donna (1989), *Primate Visions: Gender, Race and Nature in the World of Modern Science*, New York: Routledge.

Haraway, Donna (1991), 'Situated knowledges: the science question in feminism and the privilege of partial perspective' in *Simians, Cyborgs and Women: The Reinvention of Nature*, London: Free Association, pp. 183–201.

Harding, Sandra (1980), 'The norms of inquiry and masculine experience' in *PSA 1980*, ed. Peter Asquith and Ronald Giere, East Lansing, MI: Philosophy of Science Association, pp. 305–24.

Harding, Sandra (1984), 'Is gender a variable in conceptions of rationality? A survey of issues' in *Beyond Domination: New Perspectives on Women and Philosophy*, ed. Carol C. Gould, Totowa, NJ: Rowman and Allanheld, pp. 43–63.

Harding, Sandra (1986), *The Science Question in Feminism*, Milton Keynes: Open University Press.

Harding, Sandra (1989), 'Feminist justificatory strategies' in *Women, Knowledge and Reality*, ed. Ann Garry and Marilyn Pearsall, Boston: Unwin Hyman, pp. 189–201.

Harding, Sandra (1991), *Whose Science? Whose Knowledge? Thinking from Women's Lives*, Milton Keynes: Open University Press.

Harding, Sandra (ed.) (1987), *Feminism and Methodology: Social Science Issues*, Milton Keynes: Open University Press.

Harding, Sandra and Hintikka, Merrill B. (eds) (1983), *Discovering Reality: Feminist Perspectives on Epistemology, Metaphysics, Methodology, and Philosophy of Science*, Dordrecht: Reidel.

Hartsock, Nancy (1983), 'The feminist standpoint: developing the ground for a specifically feminist historical materialism' in *Discovering Reality: Feminist Perspectives on Epistemology, Metaphysics, Methodology, and Philosophy of Science*, ed. Sandra Harding and Merrill B. Hintikka, Dordrecht: Reidel, pp. 283–310.

Harvey, Elizabeth D. and Okruhlik, Kathleen (eds) (1992), *Women and Reason*, Ann Arbor: University of Michigan Press.

Hawkesworth, Mary E. (1989), 'Knowers, knowing and known: feminist theory and claims of truth' in *Feminist Theory in Practice and Process*, ed. Micheline R. Malson, Jean F. O'Barr, Sarah Westphal-Wihl and Mary Wyer, Chicago and London: Chicago University Press, pp. 327–51.

Hekman, Susan (1987), 'The feminization of epistemology: gender and the social sciences', *Women and Politics*, vol. 7, no. 3, pp. 65–83.

Hekman, Susan (1990), *Gender and Knowledge: Elements of a Postmodern Feminism*, Boston: Northeastern University Press and Cambridge: Polity Press.

Hirsch, Marianne and Keller, Evelyn Fox (eds) (1990), *Conflicts in Feminism*, New York and London: Routledge.

Hirschmann, Nancy J. (1992), *Rethinking Obligation: A Feminist Method for Political Theory*, Ithaca and London: Cornell University Press (esp. chs 4 and 5).

Hubbard, Ruth (1988), 'Science, facts and feminism', *Hypatia*, vol. 3, no. 1, pp. 114–44.

Hubbard, Ruth (1990), *The Politics of Women's Biology*, New Brunswick and London: Rutgers University Press.

Irigaray, Luce (1989), 'Is the subject of science sexed?' in *Feminism and Science*, ed. Nancy Tuana, Bloomington: Indiana University Press, pp. 58–68.

Jaggar, Alison M. (1983), *Feminist Politics and Human Nature*, Brighton: Harvester.

Jaggar, Alison M. (1989), 'Love and knowledge: emotion in feminist epistemology' in *Gender/Body/Knowledge: Feminist Reconstructions of Being and Knowing*, ed. Alison M. Jaggar and Susan R. Bordo, New Brunswick and London: Rutgers University Press, pp. 145–71.

Jaggar, Alison M. and Bordo, Susan R. (eds) (1989), *Gender/Body/Knowledge: Feminist Reconstructions of Being and Knowing*, New Brunswick and London: Rutgers University Press.

Keller, Evelyn Fox (1985), *Reflections on Gender and Science*, New Haven: Yale University Press.

Lloyd, Genevieve (1984), *The Man of Reason: 'Male' and 'Female' in Western Philosophy*, London: Methuen.

Lloyd, Genevieve (1993), *Being in Time: Selves and Narrators in Philosophy and Literature*, New York and London: Routledge.

Longino, Helen (1981), 'Scientific objectivity and feminist theorizing', *Liberal Education*, vol. 67.

Longino, Helen (1988), 'Science, objectivity and feminist values', *Feminist Studies*, vol. 14, no. 3, pp. 92–109.

Longino, Helen (1989), 'Can there be a feminist science?' in *Feminism and Science*, ed. Nancy Tuana, Bloomington: Indiana University Press, pp. 45–57.

Longino, Helen (1990), *Science as Social Knowledge: Values and Objectivity in Scientific Inquiry*, Princeton: Princeton University Press.

Longino, Helen and Doell, Ruth (1983), 'Body, bias and behavior: a comparative analysis of reasoning in two areas of biological science', *Signs*, vol. 9, no. 2, pp. 206–27.

Longino, Helen and Hammonds, Evelynn (1990), 'Conflicts and tensions in the feminist study of gender and science' in *Conflicts in Feminism*, ed. Marianne Hirsch and Evelyn Fox Keller, New York and London: Routledge, pp. 164–83.

Lugones, María C. (1987), 'Playfulness, "world"-traveling, and loving perception', *Hypatia*, vol. 2, no. 2, pp. 3–19.

Lugones, María C. and Spelman, Elizabeth V. (1983), 'Have we got a theory for you! Feminist theory, cultural imperialism and the demand for "the woman's voice" ', *Women's Studies International Forum*, vol. 6, no. 6, pp. 573–81.

Malson, Micheline R., O'Barr, Jean F., Westphal-Wihl, Sarah and Wyer, Mary (eds) (1989), *Feminist Theory in Practice and Process*, Chicago and London: University of Chicago Press.

Milan Women's Bookstore Collective (1990), *Sexual Difference: A Theory of Social-Symbolic Practice*, Bloomington and Indianapolis: Indiana University Press.

Mohanty, Chandra Talpade (1988), 'Under western eyes: feminist scholarship and colonial discourses', *Feminist Review*, no. 30, pp. 61–89.

Mohanty, Chandra Talpade, Russo, Ann and Torres, Lourdes (eds) (1991), *Third World Women and the Politics of Feminism*, Bloomington and Indianapolis: Indiana University Press.

Narayan, Uma (1988), 'Working together across differences: some considerations on emotions and political practice', *Hypatia*, vol. 3, no. 2, pp. 31–48.

Narayan, Uma (1989), 'The project of feminist epistemology: perspectives from a non-western feminist' in *Gender/Body/Knowledge: Feminist Reconstructions of Being and Knowing*, ed. Alison M. Jaggar and Susan R. Bordo, New Brunswick and London: Rutgers University Press, pp. 256–69.

Nelson, Lynn Hankinson (1990), *Who Knows: From Quine to a Feminist Empiricism*, Philadelphia: Temple University Press.

Nicholson, Linda J. (ed.) (1990), *Feminism/Postmodernism*, New York and London: Routledge.

Ramazanoglu, Caroline (1989), *Feminism and the Contradictions of Oppression*, London: Routledge.

Rose, Hilary (1983), 'Hand, brain and heart: a feminist epistemology for the natural sciences', *Signs*, vol. 9, no. 1, pp. 73–90.

Rose, Hilary (1988), 'Beyond masculinist realities: a feminist epistemology for the sciences' in *Feminist Approaches to Science*, ed. Ruth Bleier, New York: Pergamon Press, pp. 57–77.

Scheman, Naomi (1993), *Engenderings: Constructions of Knowledge, Authority and Privilege*, New York: Routledge.

Seller, Anne (1988), 'Realism versus relativism: towards a politically adequate epistemology' in *Feminist Perspectives in Philosophy*, ed. Morwenna Griffiths and Margaret Whitford, London: Macmillan, pp. 169–86.

Smith, Dorothy (1987), *The Everyday World as Problematic: A Feminist Sociology*, Toronto: University of Toronto Press.

Smith, Dorothy (1990a), *The Conceptual Practices of Power: A Feminist Sociology of Knowledge*, Toronto: University of Toronto Press.

Smith, Dorothy (1990b), *Texts, Facts and Femininity: Exploring the Relations of Ruling*, London: Routledge.

Soper, Kate (1990), *Troubled Pleasures: Writings on Politics, Gender and Hedonism*, London: Verso.

Spelman, Elizabeth V. (1988), *Inessential Woman: Problems of Exclusion in Feminist Thought*, Boston: Beacon Press.

Spivak, Gayatri Chakravorty (1987), *In Other Worlds: Essays in Cultural Politics*, New York and London: Methuen.

Spivak, Gayatri Chakravorty (1988), 'Can the subaltern speak?' in *Marxism and the Interpretation of Culture*, ed. Cary Nelson and Lawrence Grossberg, Urbana and Chicago: University of Illinois Press, pp. 271–313.

Spivak, Gayatri Chakravorty (1989), 'Feminism and deconstruction, again: negotiating with unacknowledged masculinism' in *Between Feminism and Psychoanalysis*, ed. Teresa Brennan, New York and London: Routledge, pp. 206–23.

Spivak, Gayatri Chakravorty (1990), *The Post-Colonial Critic: Interviews, Strategies, Dialogues*, ed. Sarah Harasym, New York and London: Routledge.

Stanley, Liz (ed.) (1990), *Feminist Praxis: Research, Theory and Epistemology in Feminist Sociology*, London and New York: Routledge.

Stanley, Liz and Wise, Sue (1993), *Breaking Out Again: Feminist Ontology and Epistemology*, London: Routledge (first published as *Breaking Out*, in 1981).

Trinh T. Minh-ha (1989), *Woman, Native, Other: Writing Postcoloniality and Feminism*, Bloomington and Indianapolis: Indiana University Press.

Tuana, Nancy (ed.) (1989), *Feminism and Science*, Bloomington: Indiana University Press.

Whitford, Margaret (1991), *Luce Irigaray: Philosophy in the Feminine*, New York and London: Routledge.

Wylie, Alison, Okruhlik, Kathleen, Morton, Sandra and Thielen-Wilson, Leslie (1990), 'Philosophical feminism: a bibliographic guide to critiques of science' in *Resources for Feminist Research/ Documentation sur la Recherche Féministe*, vol. 19, no. 2, pp. 2–36.

NAME INDEX

SUBJECT INDEX

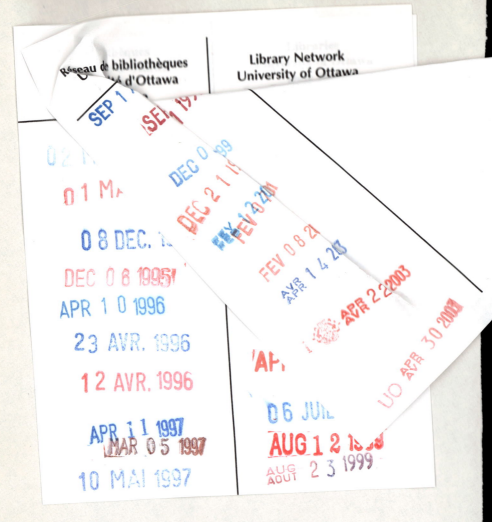